TALAVERA

Wellington's Early Peninsula Victories 1808–9

PETER EDWARDS

THE CROWOOD PRESS

First published in 2005 by
The Crowood Press Ltd
Ramsbury, Marlborough
Wiltshire SN8 2HR

www.crowood.com

British Library Cataloguing-in-Publication Data
A catalogue record for this book is available from the British Library.

ISBN 1 86126 767 3

Typeset by Jean Cussons Typesetting, Diss, Norfolk

Printed and bound in Great Britain by The Cromwell Press, Trowbridge

Contents

deployments. The four French assaults in front of Vimiero – charge of the
20th Light Dragoons – Solignac and Brennier assault the eastern ridge –
retreat of the French – casualties – Burrard forbids exploitation –
Kellerman's negotiation – concessions of the Convention of Cintra.
Overview: British and French doctrine and tactics – line, column, reverse
slopes, bayonet charges; British skirmishing questioned. Wellesley's
achievements – Junot's position.

Preface

'The young sleep sound; but the weather awakes
In veterans pains, from the past, that numb:
Old stabs of Ind, old Peninsula aches…'
                                    (Thomas Hardy, *The Dynasts*)

IN the Preface to his *Adventures*, William Grattan, late of the 88th Foot (Connaught Rangers), quotes Rousseau's belief that prefaces are seldom if ever read. His own, he said, was just to set out why he published at all. In my case, the aim is a simple act of remembrance. As one of those ever-scribbling Riflemen put it, supping sorrow with an uncharacteristically long spoon:

> Ere many years elapse, if the names of Vimiero, Talavera, Salamanca, Vittoria etc, etc, should be partially remembered, the actors in these scenes (with a very few exceptions) will be entirely forgotten. (Jonathan Leach, late Captain, 2/95th Rifles, *Rough Sketches*, 1831)

Well, that would be too sad, and must not be allowed. Therefore we shall saddle up, and do something about it, with another greencoat as our scout to point the way – Johnny Kincaid's *Random Shots* paints an affectionate picture of the typically knocked-up state of his brother officers at the close of the Peninsular War:

> When we returned to England… the officers commanding companies… Beckwith with a cork-leg… Pemberton and Manners with a shot each in the knee, making them as stiff as the other's tree one… Loftus Gray with a gash in the lip, and minus a portion of one heel, which made him march to the tune of dot and go one… Smith with a shot in the ankle… Eeles minus a thumb… Johnson, in addition to other shot holes, a stiff elbow, which deprived him of the power of disturbing his friends as a scratcher of Scotch reels upon the violin… Percival with a shot through his lungs… Hope with a grape-shot lacerated leg… George Simmons with his riddled body held together by a pair of stays… lest a burst of sigh should rend it asunder.

And Kincaid himself suffered a ball through his cap, grazing his skull so that *he fell as if a sledge hammer had hit him*. This description of limping young 95th veterans of 1814 was doubtless a common snapshot – in my own Northamptonshire Regiment, forty officers of the 1/48th started campaigning in 1809, but only fifteen remained officially unscathed in 1814. Seven were killed, seven severely and eleven slightly wounded, according to the casualty returns reported. It must be remembered, too, that either as a point of honour, or to avoid causing undue fear among loved ones at home, many severe wounds were reported as slight, and many slight ones were not recorded at all. With the further passage of time, wasting muscles, arthritic knees and melting memory do all diminish a man, except for the robust few. If over-marched, over-fought and generally harassed, soldiers rarely grow old gracefully. So as the years stretched out, following his concluding triumphs over Napoleon's soldiers in Spain, southern France and at Waterloo, more and more of the Duke of Wellington's old army were dying prematurely, from the occasional injuries and continuous fatigues suffered during the debilitating seven-year Peninsular campaign.

By 1828 – and therefore not before time – the War Office eventually roused itself sufficiently to send a circular letter to all serving and retired officers. It required them, on pain of losing their pensions, to complete a return giving a Statement of their Services, including details of their presence at any battles or sieges and on general campaigns, of any distinguished conduct, with awards granted, and of any wounds received in action. The returns dribbled in from regiments around the reddening globe throughout 1829 and 1830, and you can read them today in thick brown ledgers in the Public Record Office, at Kew in London. Here is one reply to the circular, from my regiment then in Madras (and still, I swear, smelling faintly of curry). It is beautifully penned in a clear, very firm copper-plate hand, by Captain Charles Jowett Vander Meulen, in the twenty-second of his uninterrupted thirty years of service with the 48th (Northamptonshire) Regiment of Foot:

> Born in St Albans, Hertfordshire, 3 January 1791. Aged 16 on first entry into the Army. Ensign, 48th, from 26 November 1807 to 10 August 1809. Lieutenant, 48th, from 10 August 1809 to 25 November 1823. Captain by purchase, 48th, from 25 November 1823 to the present.
>
> *Severely wounded* at Talavera with the 1st Battalion on 28 July 1809. *Severely wounded* at Albuera on 16 May 1811 and sent to England for recovery. *Severely wounded* at the battle of the Pyrenees on 28 July 1813. Received a year's pay for each wound, one as Ensign, one as Lieutenant, and the last as Captain in consequence of having the command of a company.
>
> Always with my regiment when employed abroad except when disabled by wounds received in action, and have received the approbation of my respective Commanding Officers viz Lieutenant-Colonel Donellan, Major Middlemore, Lieutenant-Colonel Sir James Wilson, Colonel Sir William Hutchinson, Colonel Erskine, Lieutenant-Colonel Taylor, and Lieutenant-Colonel Bell now in command of the Regiment.
>
> Present in the campaigns of 1809, 1810, 1811, part of 1812, 1813, and 1814 in the Peninsula and France under the command of his Grace the Duke of Wellington. Present with my Regiment at the battles of Talavera, Busaco, Albuera, Vittoria, Pyrenees, Nivelle, Orthes, and Toulouse – besides various

minor engagements and skirmishes with the Light Company, to which I was always appointed.

But in the column headed 'Awards' there is just the one word: 'None'. Well, that was par for the course in those days: three severe wounds, five long years on campaign, eight major battles, a teenage ensign at the battle of Talavera, and fourteen years a lieutenant thereafter – quite usual, he merely did his battered duty. No awards for that man, certainly – whatever next?

So in belated acknowledgement of the word 'None', and as some small apology for it, this work is dedicated to Captain Charles Vander Meulen and his Peninsula comrades in the Light Company, 1st Battalion, 48th (Northamptonshire) Regiment of Foot, that they never be forgotten. For while many of our village war memorials urge us to 'Remember these Men, Who Died for England', that concept expresses post-Victorian emotion towards a huge volunteer citizens' army, fighting to keep the Hun from our shores. England's villagers of a century earlier had not felt impelled to offer such expressions of gratitude towards a tiny and rather despised professional army operating a long way away. Indeed, even after Waterloo, Cromwell's army of the 1650s still cast a fading shadow as the perceived oppressor of liberty. When Britain fought Napoleon, the revered institution of choice remained the Royal Navy. You will find no conventional village crosses for the men who died in Portugal and Spain.

Fortunately, many subsequent writings have, of course, served much the same purpose: words on paper, rather than cut in stone. In that sense, remembrance has been fulsome enough, and our Peninsular Army has been well honoured. William Napier has thus been proved unnecessarily gloomy when he chose the final, biting sentence for his epic six-volume account: 'Thus the war terminated, and with it all remembrance of the veterans' services.'

Surprisingly, however, no book has ever been devoted to Wellington's first major Peninsula victory over the French, that which elevated him from a mere Knight of the Bath to Viscount Wellington of Talavera. It seems that the battle at Talavera remains the poor relative, overshadowed by more dramatic events at Busaco, Fuentes d'Onoro, Albuera, Cuidad Rodrigo, Badajoz, Salamanca, Vittoria and the masterly crossing of the Pyrenees, to say nothing of Waterloo. The Talavera campaign of 1809 has been too readily passed over by historians keen to plunge on to our hero's greater moments. Talavera, indeed, came close to being nearly as wretched a defeat on the battlefield as it was to prove strategically, and Wellington was forced on to the retreat within a week of his success there. Talavera was a whisker away from being that classic British military event – the Dunkirk Handicap – and perhaps it is little wonder that chroniclers have preferred to pass by on the other side. Yet a very great deal can be learnt from the story of the campaign – about Wellington the man, and about his embryonic army – without which a full understanding of their later triumphs cannot be achieved. The story of Talavera is the narration of what today would be called 'a learning curve'.

We necessarily begin at the beginning, with the battles of Rolica and Vimiero, from which so much energetic genius was to grow.

A Note on Military Designations

In this text British infantry units are referred to as either 'the 48th', or 'the 1/48th' (both meaning the 1st Battalion, 48th Regiment of Foot); or as the '2/97th' (meaning the 2nd Battalion, 97th Foot). The 43rd and 52nd Regiments, and in 1809 the 71st, were designated as Light Infantry; the distinction between these and the other regiments lay solely in their training, and the open-order tactical tasks which were sometimes given to such units. In all cases, these references to British infantry units are to a single battalion of ten companies, with an official establishment of aproximately 1,000 officers and men – though actual field strengths were often a good deal lower. The green-clad Rifle battalions (5/60th, 1/95th and 2/95th) are differentiated in the text; on the battlefield these units were routinely dispersed as skirmishers, sometimes in separate companies.

French infantry regiments are referred to as: 'the 86e Ligne' or '9e Léger' (meaning the 86th Regiment of the Line, or 9th Regiment of Light Infantry). As with the British, the distinction between the two types of regiment was purely tactical and often had little reality on the battlefield. The Line and Light regiment were both officially units of four battalions each of six companies (though in 1808 some were still in transition from the previous nine-company organization), with a full regimental establishment of just under 4,000 men. Again, field strengths might be much lower; but the reader should bear in mind that any mention of, for instance, a single British battalion confronting a whole French regiment is describing an encounter at very unequal odds. Two picked companies of each battalion, either British or French, were designated as the 'light' and 'grenadier' companies.

Regiments of British light cavalry – Light Dragoons and Hussars – normally had an active service establishment of four squadrons, each subdivided into two troops. Regimental establishment was 905 all ranks, but depending upon the fortunes of campaigning and – crucially – the supply of remounts, field strength could be greatly reduced. Like their British counterparts, French regiments – *Chasseurs, Dragons and Hussards* – had squadron establishments of about 120 officers and men, and might field four to six squadrons, each of two troops; but their actual strength in mounted men present might fluctuate widely.

1
Introduction

O NCE upon a time, nearly two centuries ago, various old men in London sent thousands of our rougher young men across the sea to Portugal and Spain, to kill Frenchmen. Killing Frenchmen had been regarded as a natural activity for English youth since the Middle Ages. One of the most memorable seasons had been the Hundred Years' War, which wrote the victories at Poitiers, Crécy and Agincourt into English national legend. As H.A.L. Fisher wrote in his magisterial *History of Europe*: 'A war with the French became part of the national background, and in the public mind of England almost assumed the aspect of an ordinance of fate.' In 1759, the great year of victories at Minden and Quebec, Sir Thomas Cave of the Leicester Militia told the Marquis of Granby that 'the spirit of the people to oppose the natural enemy of this kingdom is so great, that I had a roll of fifty volunteers offered me, every one a man of considerable property'. Four hundred years after the triumphs of the English and Welsh bowmen, this traditional hostility was still widely acknowledged: in 1809 Sergeant Lamb, 1/23rd (Royal Welsh Fusiliers), described the French as 'for many ages the professed and natural enemies of Britain'. And by that time – despite the opportunistic alliances sometimes offered by France to Scotland and Ireland – thousands of soldiers from the Celtic nations of Great Britain had also acquired this English habit of mind.

What briefing the infantryman of 1809 received from his officers, on why they were off to somewhere called Portugal to fight the French, we cannot tell. However, it is surely certain that some would have turned to their mates and said, 'Well, my grandfather fought them at Quebec in 1759 and won, and my father fought them in the Indies in 1773 and lost, and before I left home last year they both said it was up to me....' The explanation, if any was given, might conceivably have mentioned an army of French bullies sent to crush little Portugal for not shutting her ports to English ships, as ordered by the 'Corsican ogre' in Paris.

*   *   *

All Peninsular War stories are largely about the doings of the extraordinary Anglo-Irishman Arthur Wellesley – a soldier then in his late thirties, hugely experienced and confident in his profession, and poised like some magical reaper to deliver a prodigious cycle of military harvests. It will usefully set the general scene, therefore, to cover his early part in the story, since thereafter he becomes a more and more dominant character. Of course, the leading role – but played almost entirely in the wings – belongs to the Emperor of the French, an even more extraordinary man and dominant on an altogether wider stage. Of the same age as Wellesley, he had already been crowned as emperor (by his own hands) for three years. He had outman-oeuvred and captured an Austrian army with almost nonchalant ease at Ulm in October 1805, and had utterly defeated another Austrian and a Russian army at Austerlitz two months later. He had routed the Prussians at Jena-Auerstadt in October 1806, and in June 1807 he had crushed the Russians once again at Friedland, rending the Fourth Coalition of European powers into humiliating disorder. He had dictated his terms to the Tzar on a barge at Tilsit; Europe was at his feet, and his peace of mind and ambitions were troubled only by the damnable British, with their apparently invincible navy and their subversive gold.

By striking contrast, in March 1807 Sir Arthur Wellesley was a mere major-general in command of a small brigade of British infantry, based at Hastings in Sussex. He was also a Member of Parliament, and newly (though not happily) married; acquiring both his political and marital status had been largely matters of duty, as he saw it – his natural habitat was to be in command of troops in the field. In India four years earlier he had achieved a splendid victory at Assaye, against 40,000 French-trained troops; but as a so-called 'sepoy general' he had less influence than many in the home establishment. For the conqueror of the Mahrattas command of a single brigade imposed no great burden on his intellect nor adequately fed his ambition. Not that Arthur Wellesley was ambitious by the modern, self-seeking definition: his intention to climb the ladders of fame was rather fuelled by horror at the amateur abilities of so many British generals, lately demonstrated by the disaster at Buenos Aires, the reverses in Egypt and the failure of the Turkish expedition. Wellesley wrote in November 1807: 'We are very badly off for want of intelligent general officers.' He had a proper, dutiful belief that his own qualities, being of a higher order, should be deployed for the good of his country rather than being wasted.

When King George III sacked his 'Ministry of All the Talents' for having the presumption to propose that the ranks of officers of his army and navy should be opened up to Catholics and Dissenters alike, Arthur Wellesley – being of good family, with good connections – suddenly found himself appointed Chief Secretary for Ireland under the new administration headed by the old Duke of Portland. This Dublin post, being second only to that of the King's Lord Lieutenant, effectively put him in charge of Ireland's day-to-day government. Ireland, moving towards limited forms of self-government at a glacial pace during the late eighteenth century, had been deeply affected by the French Revolution's principles of Liberty, Equality and Fraternity. These had naturally resonated with the poor, and especially with the four million disenfranchized Irish Roman Catholics whose ambitions – despite recent concessions – were thwarted by legal limitations on many areas of their lives. In summer 1798 discontent with the Irish Protestant 'ascendancy' government, and conspiracies among both Protestants and Catholics, had led the Society of United Irishmen into open rebellion – spurred by promises, only meagrely and belatedly kept, of a supporting French landing. After the rising was put down with consider-able bloodshed, much of rural Ireland was a hostile country; 'the great bulk of the population was disaffected to British rule and looked to Napoleon, the great conqueror, for release from it' (Fortescue). Little wonder that a few years later a prudent Secretary of State for War and the Colonies should recommend an intelligent soldier for the post in Dublin. That minister was Lord Castlereagh, a man of Wellington's own age who shared his Irish background, and with whom he had already formed a good relationship. Wellesley accepted the appointment, with the proviso that he could give it up if military employment should arise.

Scarcely had Wellesley moved wife and baby son into the Chief Secretary's house in Phoenix Park, Dublin, before he started firing off reminders to London that he was not to be forgotten, militarily – he had caught rumours of an overseas expedition, destination unknown. It turned out to be Denmark, and Lord Castlereagh obligingly arranged Wellesley's appointment to command the reserve force of a strong brigade in the expedition that was fitting out, under Lord Cathcart, for Copenhagen. Its purpose was to 'acquire' the Danish fleet before Napoleon could do the same. This object was achieved, to French rage (because it was entirely unexpected), when the Copenhagen garrison surrendered on 8 September 1807. Wellesley's brigade fought the only battle of the campaign, at Kjöge, taking 1,500 prisoners, and he was appointed one of the three commissioners charged with negotiating the surrender.

By the end of that month Sir Arthur was reluctantly back in Dublin, having received the thanks of Parliament for his 'zeal, valour and exertions'. Only a fortnight later, however, he wrote rather piteously to George Canning at the Foreign Office: 'I shall be happy to aid the government in any manner they please, and am ready to set out for any part of the world at a moment's notice.' Clearly neither domestic bliss nor Ireland's many teasing problems were serving to absorb his available energy. He was, he said, 'a willing horse upon whose back every man thinks he has a right to put the saddle', yet the implied resentment was hardly false modesty in Wellesley's case – while the average general could scarcely fail to be flattered by Castlereagh's continuing patronage, Wellesley took it as his due. His professional comments were requested upon various of the Cabinet's military concerns: a possible expedition to Sweden; possible reactions to any French-Russian attack on India; on the military aspects of fostering revolution in Venezuela, and capturing the Spanish colonies in South America.

Notwithstanding his understandably negative response to the latter scenario, the newly-promoted Lieutenant-General Wellesley was tentatively appointed to command this enterprise, using 9,000 men assembling at Cork. But – happily for Wellesley, and for Britain – almost immediately there came news from Napoleon's sullen ally, Spain. There had been a general uprising in Madrid against the French occupiers; and in late May 1808 Sir Arthur took it upon himself to propose to Lord Castlereagh that the Cork force sail not to attack the Spanish as enemies in Venezuela, but to aid them as potential allies in Spain, for 'there was advantage to be derived from the temper of the spirit of the people of Spain'. The situation there was a 'crisis, in which a great effort might be made with advantage… the manner in which his [Napoleon's] armies are now spread in all parts of Europe… afford an opportunity which ought not to be passed by… any measures which distress the French in Spain would oblige them to delay for a season the execution of their other plans'.

On 4 June 1808 he wrote to warn the Duke of Richmond (as Lord Lieutenant, his effective superior in Dublin) that 'the government have lately been talking to me about taking the command of the corps destined for Spain, which is to be assembled at Cork, but nothing is settled yet'. Ten days later he was formally appointed to the Cork command, together with that of another 5,000 men at Gibraltar, 'to be employed upon a particular service', with further instructions to follow. These came on 30 June, when Lord Castlereagh wrote as Secretary of State for War to his colleague the Chief Secretary for Ireland: 'The occupation of Spain and Portugal by the troops of France, and the entire usurpation of their respective governments by that power, has determined His Majesty to direct a corps of his troops to be prepared for service, and to be employed under your orders, in counteracting the designs of the enemy, and in throwing off the yoke of France.' The aim of the expedition was to be 'the final and absolute evacuation of the Peninsula by the troops of France'. Sir Arthur Wellesley's force at that initial stage was to comprise some 13,500 men – just one tenth the size of the French army that we now know to have been in Spain at that time.

* * *

Britain's recent involvement in the Peninsula dated from the wars against Revolutionary France in the 1790s, although she had been loosely allied with Portugal for centuries, and British and Portuguese troops had fought together in several eighteenth-century campaigns. In 1798 a Portuguese naval squadron had operated damagingly against Napoleon's Egyptian expedition, and he had vowed revenge. He had encouraged Spain to threaten the Portuguese border, and a British expeditionary corps sent to aid the out-dated Portuguese army had been far too small to be effective. After Spain formally allied herself with France in 1804, Portugal's position was perilous. In 1807 the Treaty of Tilsit had effectively partitioned Europe between Napoleon and the now defeated Tzar of All the Russias. Russia could be left to deal with Sweden; the two emperors thus owned every continental European port, and every navy, except for the Danish and the Portuguese. The subjugation of these two small powers would therefore complete the isolation of Britain. The Danish and Portuguese battleships of the line (seventeen and ten respectively), when added to the French, Spanish, Dutch and Russian total of 129, would exceed the Royal Navy's 113, and their numerical advantage should theoretically make up for the Royal Navy's more practised sea-going skills. At Copenhagen, Britain had taken valuable advantage of Napoleon's delay between counting 'his' ships and actually cutting them out; but the Danish coast was soon patrolled by a Spanish corps, led there by the Marquis de la Romana at Napoleon's urging. The Portuguese ports were now the only loopholes in Napoleon's blockade against British ships – his leaky Continental System – and the Emperor was even more determined to close them.

In so doing he would be further serving his overweening strategic ambition, described by Sir Arthur Bryant as 'his dream of a drive across the Mediteranean towards the Orient – the source as he always believed of England's power'. To take control of the Mediterranean and thereby negate the power of the Royal Navy, Napoleon needed to achieve three things: at the eastern end of the Mediterranean, to threaten Britain's vital trade route to India by a joint Russian-Austrian-French descent on Turkey; in the centre, to invade Sicily; and above all, in the west, to cement his grip on Spain, overrun Portugal, capture Gibraltar and hold the ports of Morocco, and thereby to dominate the entrance to the Mediterranean. Thus the entire European coastline would deny Britain's fleets their resupply and her merchants their commerce, loosening British naval blockades and allowing the French and Spanish fleets to enter the fray.

The man sent by Napoleon to occupy Portugal was the 36-year old General Jean-Andoche Junot, later to be awarded a catch-penny dukedom named after Abrantes (a miserable town on the Tagus river). Junot was a brave and energetic officer, but within six years of being appointed to this command he was to die during an unsuccessful attempt to fly by leaping from a high casement in his father's house at Montbard, whither he had been forcibly retired due to mental derangement. This might well have begun with a head wound received at Lonato in Italy as Napoleon's ADC; and its progressive intensity could not have been eased in the interim by his experiences at Vimiero in 1808 (where he was defeated), at the siege of Saragossa in 1809 (where he was superseded), at Busaco in 1810 and Fuentes d'Onoro in 1811 (where his corps was left out of battle), in the 1812 Russian campaign (where he lost his reputation at Smolensk through dreadful indecision), and above all by being overlooked for promotion to Marshal of France, which he greatly resented. (Meanwhile, Junot's peace of mind was disturbed by chronic debts; his wife was one of the wittiest and most beautiful women in Paris, but also the most hopelessly extravagant.)

Selected by Napoleon as a positive, thrusting fighting man who, if not a great strategist, had the dual advantages of being immediately available and having previous knowledge of Portugal (as ambassador to Lisbon in 1805), Junot was promised a duchy and a marshal's baton if he succeeded. He got the former, but failure at Vimiero was to deny him the latter. Napier writes acidly of Junot that his

> ... natural capacity, though considerable, was neither enlarged by study nor strengthened by mental discipline. Of intemperate habits, indolent in business, prompt and brave in action, quick to give offence yet ready to forget an injury he was, at one moment a great man, the next below mediocrity, and at all times unsuited to the task of conciliation and governing a people like the Portuguese who, with passions as sudden and vehement as his own, retain a sense of injury or insult with incredible tenacity.

Yet Junot was about to march his small army along rudimentary roads (and worse) for a distance equivalent to that between John o'Groats and Land's End, and to capture Lisbon at the end of it.

In the autumn of 1807, after the British coup at Copenhagen, Junot had command of the innocently named Corps of Observation of the Gironde – some 25,000 men in twenty-two battalions of infantry and seven squadrons of cavalry (mostly dragoons), located around Bayonne just north of the Pyrenees. The battalions were still of the old 'large' variety, comprising nine companies each and totalling some 1,200 bayonets. Seventeen were veteran battalions, with only two of conscripts and three of foreign auxiliaries. Junot thus had a splendidly experienced force of six infantry brigades, organized in two divisions. Additionally he had three supporting Spanish corps: 6,000 men under General Taranco, and 9,000 men each under Generals Solano and Careffa, located respectively at Vigo, Badajoz and Cuidad Rodrigo.

On 18 October 1807 they crossed the Bidassoa river at Irun (also the scene of his future opponent's masterly crossing in the other direction six years later, almost to the day), and reached Salamanca by 12 November. Junot had traversed Navarre, Old Castile and half of Leon – some 300 steady miles – in just under four weeks. The second half of his journey, from Salamanca to Lisbon, then as now lay easiest on the route west through Cuidad Rodrigo to Celorico on the Viseu road, then south-west to Coimbra and south to Lisbon – another 300 miles. (This was the route Massena would take in 1810 when pursuing Wellington after Busaco.) As the traditional road into Portugal, established over centuries by those of evil intent, this route had blossomed with fortified towns, at Barba del Puerco, Fort Concepcion, Almeida, and at the aptly named Guarda. But when events in Madrid suddenly demanded that no time be lost, Napoleon changed his orders, switching Junot's route, with its base on Salamanca, to the slightly shorter one to the south via Alcantara and the Tagus. He could see the Spanish crown wobbling, and had every expectation that its disintegration was coming nicely to maturity.

Furthermore, Napoleon was becoming nervous of the growing possibility of a British presence: 'Continue your march,' he wrote to Junot on 31 October:

> I have reason to believe that Portugal has an understanding with England, to give time for the English troops to come from Copenhagen. You must be at Lisbon by 1 December, whether as friend or as enemy… Lisbon is everything… The march must not be delayed by a single day under pretext of want of supplies… 20,000 men can live anywhere, even in a desert… You must march straight to Lisbon, and when you arrive there, seize the fleet and arsenals… Your advance has been far too slow; ten days are precious; all the British troops of the Copenhagen expedition have returned to England.

Napoleon's concern over the westerly route via Coimbra was that the fortified towns could delay Junot if resolutely held. The general received his new orders on 19 November on arrival at Cuidad Rodrigo. However, the new southerly route demanded that the supplies gathered by the Spanish at Salamanca and Rodrigo be relocated to Alcantara, 150 miles away via a hill track that ran down alongside the Spanish border, crossing rugged, rocky terrain and now under the incessant downpours of the November rains. It took Junot's men most of five horrible days to claw their way up the endless muddy ridges and down the endless ravines, fording torrents, scavenging for food, struggling to tug the guns forward behind exhausted horses, the soldiers slipping away in the rain to seek shelter and food amongst the few scattered cottages. Halfway from Cuidad Rodrigo to Alcantara the track climbed up to the Pass of Perales, nearly 3,000 feet high and lost in the cold, drifting mists.

When Junot reached the old Roman bridge over the Tagus at Alcantara, it was with just six guns, half his horses, and with 5,000 of his soldiers missing – straggling back for miles in the stony wilderness. Seizing the food of the luckless Spanish battalions from General Caraffa's corps which were waiting to join his army, Junot pushed on towards Abrantes, eighty miles further down the Tagus. Unfortunately, Napoleon's choice of route had ignored the fact that there were no roads suitable for wheeled traffic within miles of the banks of the river (as, indeed, there still are not). Junot was forced up steep tracks north-west to Zibreira, and then across to Castello Branco, and down through the ravines and mists to Villa Velha. From there the unimproved track ran west through the foothills to the south of the Tagus, now much swollen by the rains. Only four Spanish horse artillery guns got through to Abrantes, the cavalry walking either to spare their mounts or because, simply, they no longer had mounts.

Abrantes was reached in four days, at twenty desperately tiring miles each day: by now his battalions were hopelessly strung out, taking three days to close up the stragglers – those who were not melting away from the column, still scavenging and malingering. On leaving Abrantes, Junot heard rumours of preparations by the Portuguese royal family to flee Lisbon together with 'all treasure and public funds'. Accordingly he pressed on with a composite force of four battalions, comprising the grenadier companies from such regiments as he had to hand together with the 70e Ligne. Junot entered the capital on 30 November – without artillery, without cavalry, with just 1,500 exhausted, famished soldiers with soaked powder in their useless muskets. His chief of staff, Thiebault, was later to write:

> Junot took possession of Lisbon and the entire kingdom without having in hand a single trooper, a single gun or a cartridge that would fire; with nothing, indeed, save 1,500 grenadiers remaining from the four battalions of his advance guard. Worn-out, unwashed, ghastly objects, these grenadiers no longer had even the strength to march to the beat of the drum... The rest of the army dropped in over the next two days in still worse condition; some of them fell dead at the gates of the city.

It was to be ten days before Junot's twenty-two battalions had finally closed up their stragglers, and longer still before his artillery got through, or his dragoons confiscated enough horses to make up their losses. There is little doubt that Junot was thus vulnerable on his march to Lisbon – especially from Abrantes onwards – to the mildest of organized resistance; but this never came. It says much for his contempt of the Portuguese leadership that he should press on as he did, and much also for the widespread reputation of the armies of France by 1807. Who were the Portuguese, for God's sake, to argue with regiments that had fought at Marengo, Austerlitz, Jena, Auerstadt, Eylau and Friedland?

Junot's march in itself confirmed the continuing ability of the Napoleonic elite to amaze and dominate. In six weeks he had taken his small army across 600 miles of Spain and Portugal, as the crow flies – say 800 on the ground. As anyone will know who has followed so-called tracks across Spain's rocky sierras, it is simply impossible to settle into a marching rhythm – that smooth, swinging gait which covers the ground with little effort and which allows a formed body of troops to keep the step and eat up the miles. There is absolutely nothing worse, for men in close column of threes, than having to contend individually with jutting stones, potholes, over-hanging branches, and a mixture of rock steps and muddy quagmires, all of which cause the man in the file in front to stumble and lose his rhythm. Such 'going' makes impossible that semi-sleep which a regular marching pace induces.

While the first half of Junot's progress had been relatively undemanding, once he received the new orders from Napoleon to change his route from Cuidad Rodrigo towards the south he inevitably outran his supplies. In pushing the pace across the bleak wilderness down to Alcantara, with its few and primitive tracks, it was equally inevitable that his battalions would become strung out and the stragglers more numerous. In Fortescue's words:

> So mercilessly had he hurried his wretched men forward over a rugged and miserable country, having, according to the French rule, made no provision for their subsistence, that he entered the Portuguese capital with barely one-tenth of his troops at his back; and these were no more than a mob of undis-ciplined stragglers, with little clothing, no shoes, no ammunition, and with arms ruined by ill-usage.

Junot had gambled that at the end of the last lap just a few bayonets in Lisbon, however weakly held, would suffice; and so it had proved, to Portugal's shame. It could all have gone badly wrong; only success turns foolish rashness into daring enterprise, yet if effort is admirable then surely Junot's men deserved their happy ending. Frustratingly, however, he had missed his prime prey by just one day. The Portuguese royal family took ship just hours before Junot's arrival, off to their huge possessions in Brazil. The Portuguese fleet of fifteen men-of-war together with twenty merchantmen, crowded with treasure, state papers, and no less than 15,000 officials, leading citizens and their families, passed slowly out of the Tagus. They were escorted away by a waiting British fleet under that same Admiral Sir Sydney Smith who, in the early summer of 1799, had held Acre against Napoleon, during the latter's campaign in Egypt and Syria. In November, ever mindful of the bigger picture, Napoleon had written: 'Junot will have succeeded indeed, if he becomes master of the Portuguese fleet.' Following the British seizure of the Danish fleet, his anger when told of the double loss of the Portuguese royal family and their fine ships of war may be imagined.

*   *   *

The invader's hand now began to rest heavily upon Portugal. Junot's Spanish generals belatedly arrived, Solano moving in to the southern half of the country early in December and Taranco's Galician corps reaching Oporto on the 13th. Other Spanish auxiliaries also crossed the border, until some 50,000 French and Spanish troops were on the ground. Opposition was entirely absent; from the beginning of the national crisis the Portuguese leadership had been deeply divided, with many influential voices arguing for submission to France. As his battalions staggered into Lisbon, and out again to their appointed garrisons, Junot must have marvelled at his supine reception. Yet the exodus to Brazil had creamed off the patriots among Lisbon's ruling class – those with most to lose – leaving few other than enthusiasts for a French alliance, and placemen who were content to co-operate with the new regime. Granted, a spontaneous riot briefly erupted in Lisbon on 13 December, when Junot ostentatiously replaced the Portuguese national flags on public buildings with the tricolour, thereby giving his cavalry a chance to try out their sabres and their remounts. Otherwise, the days passed quietly while Junot tightened his hold.

Lisbon's 1,200-strong police force rallied to him, under their French émigré chief the Comte de Novion, who became the keeper of all Lisbon society's inner secrets. The Portuguese Army was effectively disbanded at Christmas, with the militias following suit a fortnight later. Only men with between one and eight years' service were kept, reorganized into six new infantry and three cavalry regiments under the command of the Marquis de Alorna, who became a general in the French Army. Predictably, Junot marched him and his corps out of Portugal within two months, to southern France en route to an eventual exile in northern Germany; four years later the Portuguese regiments would largely perish on the retreat from Moscow, and few ever returned to their homeland.

Despite the apparent collapse of patriotic leadership from above, however, it was to be little more than six months before the merciless self-enrichment and violence of the occupiers fanned the slow-burning resentment of the Portuguese people into furious defiance. While ordinary French soldiers looted whatever took their eye, mistreating the peasants with the high-handedness that they had learned through years of victories, their generals acted as warlords in their district domains. As Napier put it:

> The arrogance of a conqueror, and the necessities of an army, which was to be subsisted and paid by an impoverished people, soon gave rise to all kinds of oppression; private abuses followed close upon the heels of public rapacity, and insolence left its sting to rankle in the wounds of the injured. The malignant humours broke out in quarrels and assassinations, and the severe punishments that ensued, many of them unjust and barbarous in the highest degree, created rage, not terror, for the nation had not tried its strength in battle, and would not believe that it was weak.

The French generals hastened to enforce Napoleon's decree that all property belonging to the 15,000 Brazilian escapees be confiscated; and they endeavoured to extract Napoleon's fine of 100 million French francs – though fruitlessly, since the refugees had sailed away with nearly half of Portugal's coinage. Heavy taxes, the ruination of the all-important wine exports to Britain and a general loss of overseas trade, the looting of the granaries and seizure of the fish catches, the shaming presence in the north of a Spanish occupation force (the traditional enemy) – all these factors deepened resentment, as the economy became more crippled and life immeasurably cheapened. The first military executions of bloody-minded civilians came in January 1808. The cruelty of the one-armed General Jean-Baptiste Loison – nicknamed 'Maneta' – founded such a black legend that even 200 years afterwards a Portuguese metaphor for facing a fearful ordeal is *Foi para o Maneta*, 'to be brought before Maneta'. By late spring of 1808 the Portuguese were more than ready to rise up and regain their national pride: the whole populace was ripe for general insurrection.

This tinderbox was about to receive a spark not from within, however, nor from British connivance, but blown across the mountains from the east.

*   *   *

The tangled political scene in Spain had been deftly exploited by Napoleon, to afford the excuse he needed to take power. The able and liberal King Carlos III had been succeeded by his near-imbecile son Carlos IV in 1788. By the early years of the new century the madhouse of a court was presided over by his scheming wife Queen Maria Luisa, their cowardly son Fernando and the queen's corrupt and ambitious favourite Manuel Godoy. Each intrigued against the others, while the deeply unpopular Godoy and his cronies looted the nation shamelessly.

In 1807–08 Napoleon manipulated each of them by planted rumours and false promises; Carlos, Fernando and Godoy each believed that the French regiments pouring through the Pyrenees would be placed at their disposal, as leverage against the others. By March 1808 there were at least 80,000 French troops in Spain, and 35,000 of them were in and around Madrid, commanded by Marshal Joachim Murat. Napoleon had ensured that the Spanish people believed Godoy to be responsible, and on 17 March a huge riot at Arranjuez swept the corrupt minister away. Carlos was forced to abdicate in favour of his son, who enjoyed a quite undeserved popularity among his people. Both Carlos IV and Fernando travelled to Bayonne to plead their separate causes to Napoleon, arousing considerable suspicion at home that they would make shameful concessions. Napoleon was plotting to put his brother Joseph Bonaparte on the throne of the Spanish Bourbons. This proved too much for the proud Spanish; they had seen the Portuguese trampled without resistance, and they were enraged by the prospect of suffering the same fate.

The final straw came on 2 May 1808, when it was learned that Fernando's infant younger brother Francisco had been preremptorily ordered by Napoleon to report to Bayonne. The Madrid mob rose against the French troops and massacred some 400 of the immediate garrison. Marshal Murat, as the Emperor's vice-regent, took swift and dreadful retribution, caught for ever in Goya's nightmarish painting of a summary execution entitled *The Second of May*. The French General Sarrazin, in his 1815 memoirs, quotes Murat's report as saying that 'grapeshot and the bayonet cleared the streets,' and estimate that: 'This conflict of 2 May cost the lives of more than ten thousand Spaniards, slaughtered when they were defenceless.' But the spark of rebellion proved too hot to be stamped out. Fanned with the oxygen of rumour, fear, frustration, anger and pride, it glowed brighter and burst into widening flames across the country.

First in the Asturias and Galicia in the far north-west, then in Andalusia in the south, Murcia and Valencia in the west, in Aragon and finally in Catalonia in the north-east, the people turned on the French and their Spanish collaborators in a spontaneous rash of uprisings led by local *juntas* (public safety committees) of landowners, priests, soldiers and ordinary citizens. By the end of May the pro-French governors of Badajoz, Cadiz, Corunna, Cartagena, Seville and Valencia had been dragged through the streets and butchered, while many others – such as the *corregidor* (chief magistrate) of Talavera – only narrowly escaped by flight. In all the great towns mob justice was meted out to those who denied the people or who supported the French; and, as always, fanatics jumped readily on to the bandwagon. A priest from Madrid, Canon Calvo, went to Valencia, raised a band of patriotic psychopaths, and started murdering the French civilian population; in the two days of 6 and 7 June Calvo's men killed 338 French residents.

It was on 6 June, in Bayonne, that King Fernando VII was forced to renounce his right of succession; and on 15 June, ostensibly at the request of carefully selected Spanish delegates, Joseph Bonaparte was proclaimed King of Spain. Despite the numbers of senior Spanish functionaries who lent him their support, back in Spain – in Fortescue's words – 'In a few weeks the French could hardly be said to hold a foot of Spanish soil outside the range of their cannon.' Leon and Estremadura – that great sweep of western Spain through which all communication between Madrid and Lisbon must run – sank into a spreading anarchy. Similarly, Madrid's link to France through Burgos and Vittoria to Bayonne necessarily used the valleys of Navarre, where insurrection ruled, and a mechanic was at the head of 1,000 armed peasants at Logrono. On the north coast the Bishop of Santander roused his flock and placed himself at their head. In Old Castile, only forty miles north of Madrid, 5,000 peasants and disbanded militiamen occupied the artillery depot at Segovia. Another 5,000 gathered at Torquemada, fifty miles west of Burgos.

At Cabezon, to the north of Valladolid and blocking the road between Madrid and Burgos, one of Spain's military liabilities – the elderly Captain-General of Estremadura, Don Gregorio Cuesta (a man we shall meet again in this story) – took up a suicidal position in front of the River Pisuerga on 12 June. He cleverly put the only bridge behind his 4,000 volunteers with their four miserable cannon, with nothing therefore standing between him and 9,000 French veterans under General Merle. Not surprisingly, Cuestas' men were slaughtered, for an almost laughable French loss of just twelve killed and thirty wounded. Merle went on to reoccupy Santander.

A month later, on 14 July, Cuesta again showed his comprehensive lack of tactical dexterity at the battle of Medina de Rio Seco, twenty-four miles north-west of Valladolid. This time, insisting on his right of seniority to command a combined Galician and Estremaduran force, he lost 3,000 of his and General Joachim Blake's 22,000 men and half their twenty guns. The 14,000 French under Marshal Bessières lost no guns, and just 400 soldiers. But astonishingly, a few days later on 19 July at Baylen, 200 miles to the south of Madrid, General Castanos' 34,000 Spaniards corralled General Dupont's 18,000 Frenchmen who had ventured into Andalusia, and forced their surrender after only brief resistance. They were mostly young second-line conscripts, led by a general in his first independent command; but the victory, while sensational – the first time an Imperial French army had surrendered – gave Spanish generals an inflated idea of their abilities, and thus a false sense of the skills needed to repeat the trick. As Wellington in later years said to Earl Stanhope, 'Baylen... was always in the head of the Spanish officers. They were always for attempting the same manoeuvre and surrounding the enemy, insomuch that at last I used to tell them before any engagement: "Now, this is not a battle of Baylen; don't attempt to make it a battle of Baylen".'

General Dupont is reported to have said condescendingly, when surrendering his sword to Castanos: 'You may be proud of this day, General; it is remarkable, because I have never lost a pitched battle until now – I, who have been in more than twenty, and gained them all.' To this Castanos replied, 'It is the more remarkable, because I was never in one before in my life.' Napoleon's reaction to the news of Baylen was incredulous rage: 'There has never been anything so stupid, so foolish, and so cowardly since the world began.' According to Marbot:

> His rage was fearful. Until then he had regarded the Spaniards as on a par in courage with the Italians, and supposed that their rising was merely a peasant revolt which would quickly be dispersed by a few French battalions. But his eagles had been humbled, and French troops had lost the prestige of unbroken victory. Deeply must he have regretted that he had allowed his army to be composed of recruits, instead of sending the veterans whom he had left in Germany.

*   *   *

The news of this French surrender, coming as it did shortly after the arrival in London of Spanish emissaries from the various juntas, did much to cement subsequent British support and an early decision to commit troops to the Peninsula.

The spreading Spanish flames had already run west into Portugal, firstly to the Spanish troops under Junot's command: around Oporto, the corps of 6,000 men originally commanded by General Taranco, but now by General Belesta, mutinied on 6 June, seized the French governor, raised the Portuguese flag and marched out across the border to join General Blake in Galicia – the Portuguese could fight their own war. Further south, General Solanos' corps quit Setubal for Cadiz, home and glory, although he himself was murdered by his own countrymen for cautiously refusing to attack the French warships in the harbour. In the centre, to the north of Lisbon itself, Junot acted immediately he heard of Belesta's withdrawal: the third Spanish corps under Caraffa was disarmed, some 6,000 of his 7,000 men being imprisoned on hulks moored on the Tagus, the remainder making good their escape.

Compared to the scope of the Spanish rebellion against the French occupiers, the Portuguese rising was, by neccessity, much more an affair of pitchforks and individual throat-cutting. Whereas Spain had retained its various army corps, its fortifications and arsenals, Junot had disbanded the Portuguese Army or sent them out of the country. So long as he controlled Lisbon, he kept locked up all the muskets and powder needed for any serious military opposition. Portugal, without help, was militarily incapable of throwing off the French yoke, and most of her natural leaders were far across the seas in Brazil.

The defection of Belesta and his Spanish garrison left the north of Portugal unguarded, however, and the mountainous provinces of Minho and Tras os Montes, lying to the north and east of Oporto, quickly found their manhood. Within a week the news had spread, and commanders had been appointed to lead the patriots now rallying to the colours: General Silveira on the Duoro, and the aged General Sepulveda up in the mountains around Braganza. Efforts commenced to re-form the old regular, militia and Ordenanza units disbanded by Junot the previous December and January. (The Ordenanza was an ancient system for calling up the male population as a temporary 'third line' of defence, in reserve for the regional regular and militia units.) The Portuguese flag flew once again over the square tower of Braganza castle. On 18 June 1808, after an earlier false start, the citizens of Oporto itself eventually took heart from the tales coming down from the hills, raised yet more flags, locked up those sympathetic to the French, and demanded a new and active junta of insurrection. Next day the Bishop of Oporto became its unlikely head – an authority figure who encouraged many local juntas in northern Portugal to unite and co-operate.

The stated purpose of the Supreme Junta in Oporto was to govern the country in the name of the absent Prince Regent, who was proclaimed to be the only legitimate ruler of the land. The local militia was reformed, but by men carrying pikes and billhooks, while the re-creation of the old regular regiments was limited entirely by the crippling want of muskets and powder. Oman names four line infantry, one light infantry and three cavalry regiments – some 5,000 men in all – which the Junta had re-embodied by the time the British landed on 1 August. In the first weeks of May and June, however, and before supplies could be landed by the Royal Navy, the Bishop of Oporto effectively had no army – just a lot of mouths to fill three times every day.

By 18 June the rebellion had also erupted down south, in the Algarve. A Colonel da Sousa led the insurrection in the port of Olhao, and Faro, the capital of the province, rose up two days later. The French governor was made prisoner, and as the whole coastal region took arms the small French occupying force under Colonel Maransin fell back northwards eighty miles to Beja.

Infuriated by a mere bishop's challenge, Junot ordered his divisional commander in Almeida, the hated General Loison, to take a column west from there to subdue the rebellion in Oporto. Two battalions of light infantry, six guns and fifty dragoons were deemed adequate – some 1,800 men. Halfway there, however, Loison was forced to withdraw from the hills around Teixeira, near Lamego, by a vastly more numerous if ragtag opposition led by General Silveira. The Portuguese leader had brought out some 3,000 men from Amarante to confront the French, but many thousands more lined the hills, billhooks in hand, rolling rocks down the plunging slopes and waiting to slice up the wounded and the stragglers. Loison eventually got back to Almeida and safety, but with 300 casualties and without half his guns.

It was 21 June when he turned back; and five days later in Lisbon, General Junot, realising at last the seriousness of his overall situation, called a council of war. This was to decide whether to leave Portugal and withdraw on Madrid, or to endeavour to retain Lisbon at the expense of abandoning the provinces of the north and the south. Junot could not do everything at once: he had only 25,000 French troops, of whom some 10,000 were in and around Lisbon, with a further 4,000 at the fortress of Almeida beyond the Coa on the Spanish border. In a perfect world he would have had robust garrisons in the other main border fortress of Elvas, in towns on the lines of communication such as Evora, Estremoz, Abrantes, Coimbra and Castelo Branco, together with the coastal forts of Peniche, Figueiras and Faro, with troops also available to take the battle up into the hills. Given their somewhat straitened circumstances, however, the council unsurprisingly resolved neither to risk Napoleon's fury by an evacuation that might well prove premature, nor to spread their strength too thinly; they would concentrate on holding Lisbon, with only a selection of outer fortresses.

By early July the regrouping of the various French brigades was well underway, although time and again the messengers carrying the orders were intercepted by the Portuguese and killed; General Foy's memoirs state that of twenty riders sent to General Loison up in Almeida, just one arrived. Battalion-sized garrisons were placed in a screen fifty miles to the north of Lisbon, at Peniche, Obidos and Santarem, with (curiously) a whole brigade twenty miles below the capital at Setubal on the coast. Abrantes on the Tagus, and the two border fortresses at Elvas and Almeida, were all garrisoned with strong battalions, and Junot now set about dominating his reduced territory as best he could.

On 5 July he sent General Margaron with a mobile brigade to Leira, where the resisting citizens were mercilessly suppressed, with 900 of them killed and the town sacked and burnt – a fate escaped by Thomar, fifteen miles to the east, only through the payment of a very large ransom. Five days later, over by the coast at Alcobaza, Margaron joined with General Kellerman to scatter what they estimated at 15,000 armed peasants. But Kellerman was then recalled by Junot as he set out for Coimbra, sixty miles to the north, on the next task of pacification: Lisbon was now awash with rumours of a British fleet and of a threatened landing.

Perhaps reminded by these rumours of a possibly necessary future move, Junot then struck east to re-clear his withdrawal route to Madrid via Badajoz and his garrison at Elvas. Fifteen miles south of the great road from Lisbon to Elvas lay Evora, the capital of Alemtejo province and the natural headquarters of the Portuguese rebellion in the south-east. On 29 July General Loison – that 'Maneta' who had already established a reputation for murderous cruelty to civilians, and for never leaving a village unruined behind him – took the town by storm, sacked it and put the inhabitants to the sword. Various sources put the death toll at Evora at anything between 2,000 and 8,000 with 4,000 prisoners, all for ninety French dead and twice that number wounded. There seems little doubt that the presumptious decision by the Portuguese commander General Leite (a former naval officer) to stand his 3,000 troops before the town walls in the face of 7,000 French of whom 1,200 were dragoons, with eight guns, was tantamount to suicide. So too was the subsequent decision by the town's elders to reject Loison's demand for surrender – he needed no further invitation to make a grisly example of Evora. He then marched on east, broke the blockade around Elvas, and was about to reconnoitre twenty miles further on to Badajoz when he received urgent recall orders from Junot. The British had landed on the coast in Mondego Bay, about halfway between Oporto and Lisbon.

The landings had taken place just below the fortress of Figuera da Foz, which had been captured (conveniently) a month earlier by a retired artillery sergeant, Bernardo Zagalo, and students from Coimbra University. Their remarkable victory was reinforced when the bishop's 5,000 ex-regular troops, under Bernardo Freire, moved down to the Mondego river. General Junot now had urgent need to concentrate his forces rapidly, and Loison lost no time in setting out once more on the 100-mile march for Lisbon. Fighting the British was a rare opportunity for any ambitious general. But the encouraging news of the arrival of a British force, coinciding with reports of Loison's terrible deeds at Evora, spread throughout Portugal and across the border into Spain, ensuring that he and his fellow French commanders would now have to operate in an environment more utterly hostile than anything in their previous experience.

In Italy, Austria and Prussia, once battle had been joined and the enemies' armies beaten, that was the end of it until the next battle. Now the French were in the midst of two nations in arms, whose *guerrilleros* were to give their name to an entirely new and merciless form of warfare. Extreme French reprisals against civilians instantly brought an answering barbarity down on French stragglers, wounded, prisoners and couriers. Men were nailed to trees, blinded, buried alive, sawn between two planks, slow-burnt, spitted, mutilated and flayed, and all such horrors were held to be justified acts of righteous vengeance. By the end of July 1808, even without a British army ashore, the French were coming to realize that they had ventured deeply into a landscape that not only hobbled the movement of troops by its extraordinary combination of physical obstacles, but was haunted by enemies more implacable than any they had ever known before.

2
Enter Sir Arthur:
June–August 1808

BY the end of May 1808 the Spanish provinces had all declared war on their occupiers. While there was some communication between neighbouring regions there was no national leadership, and these Davids sprang up around the feet of the French Goliath independently. This news had quickly filtered through to London, which had been alerted following the bloody events of *Dos Mayo* in Madrid. On 25 May, Lord Castlereagh promised that: 'The utmost exertion will be made to send out a reinforcement from hence, so as to enable His Majesty to afford the loyal party in Spain the assistance of 10,000 men.' The recipient of his letter, Lieutenant-General Sir Hew Dalrymple, governor and garrison commander in Gibraltar, was, however, to understand that London had not yet decided quite what these troops would actually do – 'His Majesty's ministers were too ill-informed to make constructive suggestions.' However, it was clear the British government had already rightly sensed its opportunity to stoke the small but growing Spanish fire. As we have seen, just over a week later, on 4 June, Castlereagh approached his Cabinet colleague Sir Arthur Wellesley with respect to the command of these 10,000 men, most of whom were gathering at Cork, and this approach was confirmed after ten days.

In the meantime there occurred one of those fortuitous events of which governments dream. It caught the public's imagination, providing a ground-swell of enthusiasm for this latest overseas venture. This is what Londoners read in their *Sun* evening paper on 8 June 1808:

> This morning about seven o'clock, two Spanish noblemen, viz Viscount Materosa, and Don Diego de la Vega, arrived at the Admiralty accompanied by Captain Hill of the *Humber*. These noblemen landed at Falmouth from the *Stag* privateer, to which vessel they had made their way in an open boat from Gijon, a seaport in the province of Asturias, and offered the captain five hundred guineas to convey them to England. The intelligence they bring is of the utmost importance respecting the disposition which prevails to resist the treacherous invasion of the French. It appears that, in consequence of the outrageous and barefaced conduct of the French tyrant, the whole province of Asturias had risen in arms, and 40,000 men had been embodied into an army. They had abundance of arms but ammunition was rather scarce. The same spirit prevailed in Galicia, where the population were rising en masse, and commissioners had sent there to organise a regular military force. So

general was the detestation of the French in these provinces that even the women were desirous of taking up arms in defence of their country. The inhabitants of St Andero [Santander] had manifested their determination not to submit to the French usurpation, in the most decisive manner, and had actually issued a formal declaration of war against the French. It was very generally supposed that the inhabitants of Catalonia and Biscay would follow the noble example which had been set them by Asturias and Galicia; indeed there appeared to be but one sentiment in the minds of the people of Spain with respect to the treacherous and atrocious conduct of the French.

The next day the *Morning Chronicle*, the leading opposition newspaper, wrote threateningly against the distractions of mere transatlantic adventures (which, as mentioned already, had indeed been considered):

> We trust that neither lukewarmness nor selfishness will be allowed to influence the conduct of the Government on this occasion. Spain is no longer our enemy when she ceases to act under the control of France… By assisting Spain against France we should be fighting our own battles… We must earnestly deprecate Ministers taking any of their own acts as models. Of plundering and marauding expeditions we have had quite enough; and the Spaniards in the old world will be but little disposed to thank us for that sympathy which would manifest itself by seizing upon their possessions in the new.

The *Courier*, also on 9 June, summed up the obvious deduction from the arrival of the Asturian deputies: 'There cannot be a doubt that a most favourable opportunity has occurred for this country to do something.' For the government, which had already decided to 'do something', it must have seemed that Christmas had come early with the Asturian delegates. As Napier wrote:

> The party in power saw with joy that the stamp of justice and high feeling would, for the first time, be affixed to their policy. The party out of power… could not consistently refuse their approbation to a struggle originating with, and carried on entirely by the Spanish multitude… the public mind was vehemently excited.

*   *   *

We may doubt whether many of the British soldiers earmarked for the job were equally excited, given their traditional phlegm; but it seems likely that their officers, at least, drank readily the time-honoured toast, 'Here's to a bloody war' (with the implication, 'and quick promotion'). Taking as a rough guide the contemporary officer-to-man ratio of 4:100, there might indeed have been some 1,280 glasses held high for that purpose, for that June there were no less than 32,000 troops immediately available worldwide, should they be chosen. The main body was gathering at Cork in southern Ireland: some 8,700 men in ten battalions – a division, by modern measurement – and all prime 1st Battalion regular troops (the 1st Battalion of each regiment received the pick of the available men for overseas service). All were well up to strength bar the 36th (Herefordshire) and 45th (Nottinghamshire), thanks to the reforms to the recruitment system brought in by Lord Castlereagh. According to Sir John Fortescue, these measures raised 45,000 new recruits for the regular Army in the course of 1807 and the first three months of 1808. These were not raw recruits but trained men, transferring from the home defence Militia, who were already certified competent in musketry drills. However, because this force at Cork had been put together for a possible expedition to South America, with a long sea passage, it lacked horses. The sole cavalry were an emaciated 20th Light Dragoons, who embarked just 381 all ranks and 224 horses – effectively only two squadrons.

In addition there were two infantry brigades, totalling some 4,800 men, located at Ramsgate and Harwich, already with their transports since they had previously been assembled for a cross-Channel raid on Boulogne – but again, with no cavalry component. Horseless too, floating off Gothenberg harbour in Sweden, were the 10,000 men of the eleven battalions under Sir John Moore, about to return home (3 July) after an abortive attempt to aid the mad King of Sweden. A fourth source of troops was Madeira, where Major-General Beresford had 3,000 men; and finally there were the five battalions – 5,100 men – with Major-General Brent Spencer who were bobbing around off Cadiz and Gibraltar.

Of this possible war-chest, in the first instance Lord Castlereagh gave Wellesley the ten Cork battalions and the five battalions with Spencer, some 13,000 men in total, with eighteen guns but light on horses. The Cork fleet sailed on 13 July, preceeded the previous day by Sir Arthur en route to Corunna, anxious for the latest intelligence. Two days later Castlereagh wrote after him to say that a decision had been taken to reinforce his Cork/Spencer grouping, firstly with the two brigades from Ramsgate and Harwich, and then as soon as possible with Sir John Moore's 10,000 already disembarking in home ports from Sweden. It was the arrival of the latter, coincident with receipt from General Spencer of a new, much higher estimate of French strength – at 20,000 men – which caused the Cabinet so quickly to earmark further battalions.

The bad news, however, was that with the combined expeditionary force now approaching a strength of 30,000 men, Castlereagh wrote that: 'His Majesty has been pleased to direct that Lieutenant-General Sir Hew Dalrymple shall have the chief command thereof, and that Lieutenant-General Sir Harry Burrard be second in command....' And as if that were not bad enough, later in the same despatch Wellesley read that Lieutenant-Generals Mackenzie Fraser, John Hope and Lord Paget, all senior to him, were appointed to command three of the divisions. Since Sir John Moore was also senior to Wellesley, this unwelcome letter was to place the latter potentially seventh in command.

The reason for this convoluted decision – which led weeks later to a predictable dog's breakfast of command mistakes – was quite simple: it was that Moore had to be kept from the command. Granted, Wellesley himself was not a universal first choice, since neither the Duke of York at Horse Guards nor his royal father were convinced that Wellesley's experience in India necessarily fitted him for war in Europe. But the Cabinet, and Foreign Minister Canning in particular, were equally determined that Moore should not command, whatever his talents as a general. Canning was too vain and egoistic a man to tolerate Moore – a Whig MP for six years and therefore 'the Whig general par excellence' – as commander in the Peninsula, after having experienced him as commander in Sweden and in the Mediterranean. On both occasions Moore had too publicly shown Canning's policies to be foolhardy and mistaken. Moore therefore returned from Sweden in bad odour where it mattered – politically. As Minister for War, Castlereagh was under pressure to come up with a solution. Dalrymple, who had not been near a battlefield since 1793 (when he commanded a Guards battalion in Flanders under the Duke of York), and Burrard, who was a Coldstreamer like the Duke of York and had previously been his ADC, were both acceptable to Horse Guards and the Palace; and in case anything should befall Dalrymple in the Peninsula, then Moore would still not succeed to the command, since Burrard was senior to him.

It would have suited the Cabinet best if Moore had conveniently chosen to resign; but, no doubt to ministerial chagrin, he calmly wrote that 'He was about to proceed on the duty to which he had been ordered, and should endeavour to acquit himself with the same zeal that he had always shown in his country's service.' As one would expect and hope, Wellesley also placed public interest before personal dignity when, hearing of his own relegation, he wrote back to Castlereagh: 'Whether I am to command this army or not, or am to quit it, I shall do my best to ensure its success... I shall not hurry the operations, or commence them one moment sooner than they ought to be commenced, in order that I may acquire the credit for the business.' It said much for the characters of both Moore and Wellesley that they should so react in the face of such mischievous political machinations.

There is little doubt that Castlereagh himself wanted Wellesley to command. That Wellesley was his favourite was clear from the temporary nature of Dalrymple's appointment, and from Castlereagh's strong hint when he wrote privately to Dalrymple on 15 July:

> Permit me to recommend to your particular confidence Lieutenant-General Sir Arthur Wellesley. His high reputation in the service as an officer would in itself dispose you, I am persuaded, to select him for any service that required great prudence and temper, combined with much military experience. The degree, however, to which he has been for a length of time past in the closest habits of communicating to His Majesty's Ministers... will, I am sure, point him out to you as an officer of whom it is desirable for you, on all accounts, to make the most prominent use which the rules of the service will permit.

It is said Dalrymple read this with much surprise and not much satisfaction, commenting correctly that 'something seemed to lurk under this most complicated arrangement'. Certainly, if Moore had resigned, then after a decent interval of operations against the French during which Wellesley would no doubt have demonstrated his qualities to a European audience and to Horse Guards, Dalrymple and Burrard could have been eased out of the scene. Wellesley was clearly a man with whom Castlereagh and the Cabinet could do business. He was one of them, after all; his family connections with the Tory party, and his friendship with its grandees – the Duke of Richmond, whom he served in Ireland, Lords Castlereagh and Liverpool – all brought him routinely into the corridors of power. He was surely England's second most respected general after Moore, if less loved (for Moore shared some of the same kind of following that Nelson had enjoyed). But Moore was a Whig, a know-all, a thorn in the flesh, and that was that.

*   *   *

Wellesley reached Corunna on 20 July after an eight-day passage. Immediately he plunged into that bemusing fog of exaggeration, boasting and misrepresentation that was later to bedevil his dealings with the Spanish, both civil and military. 'Very little reliance can be placed on the reports made to you by any Spanish general at the head of a body of troops. They generally exaggerate on one side or the other, and do not scruple of communicating supposed intelligence, in order to induce those to whom they communicate it to adopt a certain line of action,' he was to write in 1810, after two years of dealing with them. But on going ashore in July 1808 to confer with the Junta of Galicia, Sir Arthur's first impressions were clearly most positive; the next day he wrote to the Duke of Richmond:

> They manifested the greatest satisfaction upon our arrival, received us with the utmost civility and cordiality, illuminated the town at night, and the whole of the inhabitants attended us to our boat when we returned on board the frigate at night… The Spanish have defeated and destroyed several French detachments: viz one under Dupont to the southward, one under Lefebvre in Aragon, and two in Catalonia. They have taken the fort of Figueras, near Rosas in the Pyrenees, and have blockaded the French troops in Barcelona. But the great army of Galicia, consisting of 50,000 men, received a check on the 14th of this month from a French corps under Marshal Bessières. The French had not more than half that number, and lost about 7,000 men… The Spaniards lost two pieces of cannon, the French six; the Spanish army retreated about twenty miles towards this province.

He also wrote that same day to the Duke of Gordon:

> The whole of Spain, with the exception of Biscay and Navarre and the neighbourhood of Madrid, is in arms against the French… It is impossible to describe the sentiment which prevails throughout the country. I am informed that there is no such thing as a French party; and indeed, from what I have seen of the town, I should imagine that it could not be very safe for any man to declare himself in favour of the French… These accounts… are only private; but I credit them.

The Junta's description of the battle of Medina de Rio Seco was, of course, outra-geously misleading. The 'check' to the combined armies of Cuesta and Blake was a full-blown defeat, as we have seen, while the Junta's other claims put a shameless gloss on reality. The Spanish had not destroyed the French detachments listed, although Dupont's defeat (said to have happened on 22 June) was, curiously, indeed to take place the day before Wellesley's arrival in Corunna; the fort at Figueras had not been taken, and nor was Barcelona meaningfully blockaded.

Sir Arthur therefore came away from his conference with the Junta feeling reason-ably (if erroneously) content. As they met in the town, a British frigate had put into the harbour bringing £200,000 in gold, and Wellesley wrote to Castlereagh: 'The arrival of the British monies yesterday has entirely renewed their spirits, and neither in them nor in the inhabitants of this town do I see any sympton of alarm or doubt of their final success.' Since the Junta gratefully accepted his gold, but turned down his troops, Sir Arthur sailed forthwith for Portugal. The Spaniards had reported – correctly, for once – the progress of the rebellion in Oporto and the northern Portuguese provinces. They pressed him to take his army away to the south, plying him for this purpose with inaccurate estimates of Junot's forces, an incorrect state-ment of the numbers of Spanish and Portuguese armed and ready around Oporto, and a promise that they would send to that city a Spanish division (which never arrived). Sir Arthur had been comprehensively humbugged by the Junta.

*   *   *

In Oporto on 24 July, with his troop transports approaching the coast to rendezvous with Sir Charles Cotton's fleet off Lisbon, Wellesley met the bishop and his military men. From them he discovered that the patriot garrison of Oporto itself numbered just 1,500 men, and a further 5,000 had been sent four or five days' march away to the south, near Coimbra on the Mondego. This force under General Freire included about three squadrons of cavalry, and a thousand muskets donated by the Royal Navy. Freire also had a further 12,000 Portuguese peasants ineffectually armed with edged weapons and pikes. That was all that the Bishop of Oporto could offer, apart from a promise to produce 500 mules and 150 horses, and his recommendation that Wellesley disembark in Mondego Bay at Figuera da Foz. The fort there guarded a harbour of sorts at the mouth of the Mondego river, and was held by a small party of Cotton's Royal Marines. The admiral also named Figuera as his choice in a letter that Wellesley received in Oporto, in which Cotton suggested that they meet as soon as possible off Lisbon.

They did so two days later, when Cotton passed over a letter from Major-General Spencer written from Cadiz on 16 July. This contained the bad news that, at the time of Spencer's reconnaissance to the Tagus in June, he reckoned Junot had 20,000 men under arms, not the 15,000 estimated by the Spanish; and that of these nearly 13,000 were in Lisbon or nearby. Wellesley's own intelligence put Junot at 16,000 to 18,000 men in total; but both he and Spencer were well short of the truth – the French in fact had 26,000 troops in Portugal. So Wellesley's immediate decision to land his 9,000 in Mondego Bay was a confident act. He wrote to Spencer ordering him north, and himself set off that very day, 26 July, to meet his fleet of seventy ships and to prepare the landing.

Three items of news arrived in the choppy waters off the Mondego before the disembarkation began on 1 August, and all three were cheerful: firstly, Wellesley received intelligence of Loison's march, commenced a week earlier, to clear Junot's withdrawal route to Madrid via Badajoz and his garrison at Elvas. Loison had obligingly taken 7,000 of Junot's strength a useful 100 miles in the wrong direction, away from the Lisbon area. Secondly, on 30 July came Castlereagh's letter of the 15th telling him of the additional troops imminently on their way; and thirdly, the next day, came confirmation of the French disaster at Baylen. The latter meant Andalusia was effectively clear of the French, and therefore 'there can be nothing to detain General Spencer in that quarter', as Wellesley wrote to Admiral Cotton.

Thus, Sir Arthur's ten battalions then landing, and Spencer's five from Cadiz, could look forward to being joined by five from Ramsgate, three from Harwich and eleven from Sweden (God Save the Royal Navy, indeed), giving him over 30,000 men. Of this ultimate strength 13,000 were already to hand (Spencer began disembarking on 5 August), and Wellesley organized this immediate force into six brigades. If he was right in reckoning that Junot had 13,000 or 14,000 men around Lisbon, the majority tied down by garrison duties, then until Loison returned Junot was not a threat. But time was precious, and not just to get the men ashore in some sort of order, with mule transport and a working commissariat. Of an Army List led by two field marshals, seventy full generals and 130 lieutenant-generals, Wellesley was the fourth from the bottom, with six of his seniors even then on passage to supersede him. Not surprisingly, one finds him writing to the Duke of Richmond on the day after he received this news from Castlereagh: 'I hope I shall have beaten Junot before any of them arrive, and then they may do as they please with me.'

Supersession on the brink of a campaign had happened to him before, seven years earlier when he was a thirty-two year old colonel in India, when his brother the Governor-General had had to rescind a juicy command as rather too clearly an act of blatant nepotism. So Sir Arthur quickly set about the administrative arrangements necessary to make his force effective, before it should be taken from him. Not for the first time, nor the last, he now put his mind to the acquisition and carriage of meat, salt, flour, wine, spirits, water, biscuit, mail, forage, mules, horses, bullocks, carts, ammunition, shoes, tents, flints and much else. His professionalism, of an order rare indeed among his contemporary general officers, is reflected in his care over the minutiae of the landing:

> The haversacks and canteens now in the regimental stores are to be given out to the men. Tin camp kettles are to be issued from the Quartermaster-General's stores to the regiments... The men are to land, each with one pair of shoes, besides those on them, combs, razor, and a brush, which are to be packed up in their great coats. The knapsacks to be left in the transports, and the baggage of the officers, excepting such light articles as are necessary for them. A careful sergeant to be left in the headquarter ship of each regiment, and a careful private man in each of the other ships, in charge of the

baggage... The men will land with three days' bread and two days' meat cooked... Each soldier will have three good flints... Three days' oats to be landed with each of the horses.

Sir Arthur wrote to Castlereagh a week later: 'I have had the greatest difficulty in organising my commissariat for the march, and that department is very incompetent... The existence of the army depends upon it, and yet the people who manage it are incapable of managing anything out of a counting house.' His almost useless commissaries would soon find themselves on the receiving end of a bracing crash course of on-the-job training, and from the start Wellesley obviously believed that he had to do their most basic calculations for them:

> Besides the quantity of bread to be carried by the men themselves, a quantity, equal to three days' consumption for 10,000 men, must be carried, if possible on the backs of mules: viz two bags, or 224lb on each mule; this will require 130 mules... The medical department will require two carts to march with the army, carrying twenty-four bearers [stretchers] for wounded men, a case of utensils, and a medicine chest.

On 7 August, Wellesley met General Bernardino Freire, the commander of the 6,000-strong Portuguese force which the Bishop of Oporto had promised his ally. Five thousand British muskets and sets of pouch equipment were provided; but not content with this, Freire also tried to get his men taken on to both the British ration and pay strengths. Neither did he endear himself to Sir Arthur by trying to persuade him to march on Lisbon via Santarem, inland towards the Tagus. Wellesley rightly saw that his supply line would be vulnerable, Santarem being thirty miles from the sea. On the contrary, he needed to use the coast road, to facilitate naval resupply and a rendezvous with his reinforcements – the seven battalions from Ramsgate and Harwich were now approaching Portugal. They had been on passage for a fortnight, and Sir John Moore's eleven battalions were already a week out from Portsmouth. These troops were badly needed, for while Wellesley did not know it (he wrote to Burrard on 8 August assessing Junot's total strength at 18,000), his own 13,000 men were in fact currently outnumbered two to one. Worse, they had few guns and effectively no horse. The sooner he could link up with the new arrivals the better.

Freire seeming reluctant to march Wellesley's route to Lisbon, but as a compromise he undertook to provide the British with a token force of about 2,000 men – four battalions and three cavalry squadrons, albeit under strength – commanded by Lieutenant-Colonel Nicholas Trant, an Irish Catholic officer in the Portuguese service.

The road to Lisbon ran from Figuera da Foz through Lucar, Leiria, Alcobaza, Obidos, Rolica and Torres Vedras, with Vimiero on the coast just short of the latter town. It was an eight-day march, if no one stood in your way, and the first leg to Lucar proved especially hard; in the words of the anonymous 'Soldier of the 71st':

We marched for twelve miles, up to the knees in sand, which caused us to suffer much from thirst, for the marching made it rise and cover us. We lost four men of our regiment, who died of thirst. We buried them where they fell. At night we came to our camp ground in a wood, where we found plenty of water, to us more acceptable than any thing besides on earth.

There is further reference to the heat and deep sand by Rifleman Harris of the 2/95th Rifles, part of Fane's 6th or Light Brigade:

Being immediately pushed forward upcountry in advance of the main body, many of us, in this hot climate, very soon began to find out the misery of the frightful load we were condemmed to march and fight under, with a burning sun above our heads, and our feet sinking every step into the hot sand. The weight I myself toiled under was tremendous, and I often wonder at the strength I possessd at this period, which enabled me to endure it; for, indeed, I am convinced that many of our infantry sank and died under the weight of their knapsacks alone. For my own part, being a handicraft [craftsman – Harris was a cobbler], I marched under a weight sufficient to impede the free motions of a donkey; for besides my well-filled kit, there was the great coat rolled on its top, my blanket and camp kettle, my haversack, stuffed full of leather for repairing the men's shoes, together with a hammer and other tools (the lapstone I took the liberty of flinging to the devil), ship-biscuit and beef filled with water, my hatchet and rifle, and eighty rounds of ball cartridge, being the best thing I owned.

The second day's march of eighteen miles took the British to Leiria, and it was from there on 11 August that Wellesley gave his estimates of Junot's situation (to the Duke of Gordon). In particular he noted that 'of the disposable force about 4,000 are at Alcobaza, about sixteen miles from hence, under Generals Laborde and Thomières, and the remainder, under Generals Junot and Loison, are in the neighbourhood of Santarem.' While this assessment was incorrect as to the particulars, it was right as to the outline. Disregarding the Lisbon garrison and those elsewhere in Peniche, Almeida, Elvas and Setubal, Junot had just two mobile columns, about forty miles apart, with the nearest (at Alcobaza) being an easy day's march from Wellesley. Here was Wellesley's chance to use his superior numbers. Had he known that Loison was in fact a further two days' march beyond Santarem, with his troops hungry and exhausted, he would have been even more confident that he had a window of opportunity.

Junot had sent General Delaborde, with a mere two battalions, from Lisbon on 6 August, to be joined by General Thomières' three battalions from Peniche to form a blocking force, which was duly reported to Wellesley to be at Alcobaza. So Delaborde had some 5,000 men – say two brigades – and this included two strong squadrons of cavalry and five guns. Of course, Junot had also directed Loison and his 7,000 men to join Delaborde with all speed. He himself surprisingly remained in

Lisbon, a city by now such a hotbed of rumour and unrest that he feared for his continuing control of it.

Failing to find suitable defensive positions around Alcobaza on 9 and 10 August, General Delaborde pulled back twenty miles south, leaving a rearguard at Obidos on the 13th, and taking his column to form a block a few miles further down the Lisbon road, at nearby Rolica. Wellesley's vanguard bumped into the piquets of the rearguard near Obidos on the 15th, and here the first shots were hammered away in both directions, to signal the start of the war in the Peninsula. In one important regard this first encounter set an unfortunate precedent that was to recur regularly in the following years: when attacking the French the British troops, whether infantry or cavalry, tended not to know when it might be prudent to stop. This especially applied to the Rifles and to all cavalry: 'riflemen', 'horsemen' and 'dashing' are three words naturally and properly suited. It is appropriate, therefore, that 2nd Lieutenant John Cox, one of the 2/95th officers present at Obidos, wrote in his journal that:

> On approaching the place [Obidos] the enemy opened a fire of musketry from a windmill on rising ground adjoining the place, and a few shots came from the town; however, a rapid advance of the riflemen drew the French from all points of their posts, but being rather too elevated with this, our first collision with the foe, we *dashed* along the plain after them like young soldiers [Cox had just celebrated his 18th birthday!] but we were soon brought up by a body of French cavalry advancing from the main force. A retrograde movement was now imperative, in which we lost an officer and a few men.

The tactfully worded 'retrograde movement' was the more urgent because, in addition to the French cavalry, a battalion of infantry from Delaborde's main position now also came up. This affair at Obidos on 15 August was described the next day in Wellesley's despatch to Castlereagh from Caldas:

> I marched from Leyria on the 13th, and arrived at Alcobaza on the 14th, which place the enemy had abandoned in the preceeding night; and I arrived here yesterday. The enemy, about 4,000 in number, were posted about ten miles hence [sic], at Rolica; and they occupied Obidos, about three miles from hence, with their advanced posts. As the possession of this last village was important to our future operations, I determined to occupy it, and as soon as the British infantry arrived upon the ground I directed that it might be occupied by a detachment consisting of four companies of riflemen of the 60th and 95th Regiments. The enemy, consisting of a small piquet of infantry and a few cavalry, made a trifling resistance and retired; but they were followed by a detachment of our riflemen to the distance of three miles from Obidos. The riflemen were there attacked by a superior body of the enemy, who attempted to cut them off from the main body of the detachment to which they belonged, which had by now advanced to their support; larger bodies of the enemy appeared on both the flanks of the detachments, and it was with difficulty that Major-General Spencer, who had gone out to Obidos when he

heard that the riflemen had advanced in pursuit of the enemy, was enabled to effect their retreat to that village. They have since remained in possession of it, and the enemy have retired entirely from the neighbourhood.

In his accompanying not-for-publication despatch to Castlereagh, Wellesley privately commented that:

> The affair of the advanced posts of yesterday evening was unpleasant, because it was quite useless; and it was occasioned, contrary to orders, solely by the imprudence of the officer, and the dash and eagerness of the men: they behaved remarkably well, and did some execution with their rifles.

The advance guard consisted of four companies each of the 95th and the 5/60th, the whole commanded by Major Robert Travers. The vanguard of the advance guard comprised No. 4 Company 2/95th, commanded by Wellesley's brother-in-law Captain the Hon Hercules Pakenham, and three companies of the 5/60th, as well as an officers' party of the 20th Light Dragoons. The 'imprudent' officer was of course Major Travers, and he would certainly have kept out of eye contact with Sir Arthur next day. He had seen action in Holland, at Ferrol, in Egypt and Buenos Aires, and as an experienced field officer presumably would have been marching well up with his vanguard companies, to exercise control; but John Cox's choice of words above suggests that the men were simply out of hand and, further, his use of the word 'we' suggests that the junior officers joined in whole-heartedly.

Another primary source – if it can be so described, since while vivid and evocative, it was a disjointed narrative actually written up by someone else – is Rifleman Harris' *Recollections*. This renowned, lively but rambling work manages to sandwich the following piece on Obidos between two pieces on Rolica, and unfortunately merely touches on the final halting of the riflemen after the three-mile advance:

> It was on 15 August when we first came up with the French, and their skirmishers immediately commenced operations by raining a shower of balls upon us as we advanced, which we returned without delay. The first man that was hit was Lieutenant Bunbury; he fell pierced through the head with a musket ball, and died almost immediately. I thought I never heard such a tremendous noise as the firing made on this occasion, and the men on both sides of me, I could occasionally observe, were falling fast. Being overmatched, we retired to a rising ground, or hillock in our rear, and formed there all round its summit, standing three deep, the front rank kneeling. In this position we remained all night, expecting the whole host upon us every moment. At daybreak, however, we received instructions to fall back as quickly as possible upon the main body.

So no mention there of the three-mile dash, which one would have thought might stick in the memory; but confirmation of the night defensive position also mentioned by Captain Leach, commanding No. 3 Company 2/95th: 'Our companies, with some of the 60th, occupied during the night, as an advance post, an extensive knoll near the road by which the enemy had retired.'

While Leach, Harris and their friends in green chased the French piquets south, General Loison languished at Santarem, twenty miles to the east. He had rested there for two days, with his soldiers quite badly knocked up by the march from Elvas – 120 miles bare of food and water, under a brutal sun and stalked by vengeful peasants. The next day he marched west to Rio Major, half way to Obidos; but in those days the road then turned south towards Alcoentre, away from Obidos, Rolica and the fairly desperate General Delaborde.

Wellesley heard of this move late on 16 August, no doubt with much relief. Loison not only remained a good half day's march to the east, but the first third of such a march would have to be cross-country and therefore, given the condition of his troops, extremely arduous. (It is an interesting thought, however, that had a road or trail existed westwards the sixteen miles from Rio Major to the coast road around Obidos and Rolica, the opening engagement of the campaign would have been a numerically even match.) Also on 16 August, Junot at last set out from Lisbon; he left 7,000 troops in the capital under General Travot, taking with him just 2,000 infantry, six squadrons of cavalry and ten guns. He joined Loison at Alcoentre the next day.

So Sir Arthur was now finally in touch with French troops, on the continent of Europe. The sepoy general, unsuperseded as yet, found himself and his troops with an easy first test: his 13,000 against Delaborde's 4,300, the so-called classic 3:1 superiority required by any attacker anywhere, according to all the best military textbooks.

3
Rolica,
17 August 1808

ON 16 August, Sir Arthur Wellesley made his plan and issued his orders for the attack next day on Delaborde's small force at Rolica. Since his vanguard had penetrated deeply down the plain from Obidos the previous day, albeit temporarily, it is likely that he went forward at the first opportunity to examine the ground. There was a convenient rocky knoll a mile to the front.

He would at once have been struck by the enclosed plain running away southwards for three miles, with the road to Rolica and Lisbon undulating left of centre along the lower slopes of a ridge parallel to and east of the road. This north-south ridge, the high point of which was over 700ft, formed the left horizon. Nine gullies came off it, carved by the winter rains, and streams emerging from these cut the road, crossing half a mile to the west – to Wellesley's right – to join the main stream (presently dry), which the road to the south bridged just before it reached Rolica. That substantial village was at the eastern end of a low hill, half a mile wide and rising 100ft above the plain. A much more formidable east–west ridge five times that height loomed a mile behind the village, blocking the southern horizon. This menacing ridge was the far end of a circle of hills dominating the plain of Obidos/Rolica; a mile away on Wellesley's right another sweep of high ground completed the western rim, over which came the road from Peniche on the coast, twelve miles away.

Scattered southwards down the centre of the plain from Obidos, to the west of the road, were a line of six rocky outcrops separated by gullies, streams and various rough cart tracks criss-crossing the plain. Napier says that small French detachments held 'all the favourable points of defence in front, and on the hills on either side', so it is doubtful whether Sir Arthur's reconnaissance could have penetrated far. His glass, however, would have shown him Delaborde's troops on the low broad hill before the houses of Rolica; and we have the eyewitness testimony of Captain George Landmann, of the Engineers, that French troops could also be seen on the ridge beyond Rolica. Landmann had reconnoitered the approaches on that flank earlier in the day, as we should expect of any good sapper:

> I proceeded to the high Moorish tower at the southern angle of the town [Obidos] from the top of which I occupied myself in examining the position occupied by the enemy; and with the aid of my telescope (my famous three foot telescope, by Watson) I could distinctly see them moving about on the brow of the hills of Columbeira, beyond the town of Rolica.

Others have disputed Landmann's claim that the French position could be viewed from Obidos; but his supplementary claim that he conversed on the tower with Sir Arthur is too good not to repeat – even if it was published thirty-six years later, and is therefore in need of a pinch or three of salt:

> Whilst I was thus engaged, I suddenly heard the sound of the footsteps of several persons behind me, and also the rattling of steel scabbards, which indicated the presence of staff officers; then immediately I heard a voice asking hastily and in a tone of authority, for a glass, and at the same moment I was tapped on the shoulder and desired to make room, for the space was very small, and insufficient for two persons to rest their glasses, so as to observe the enemy at the same time. I now, as required, turned round, and Sir Arthur Wellesley was before me; upon which I presented my telescope to his Excellency.
>
> Sir Arthur took a very careful survey of the country, as far as it was possible from that spot, and particularly examined the position occupied by the enemy, after which I related to him my reconnaissance of the previous day, principally in regard of the hills to the Eastward, adding, that I fully believed from my own observation, and also from the information I had obtained, that the road I had there followed up to the two windmills, led to the rear of the enemy's position, round his right flank, and therefore offered a good opportunity for cutting off his retreat; whilst at the same time a movement by that route would intercept the expected juncture of General Loison with Laborde; the former being understood to be on his march from Thomar, or its vicinity, with 6,000 men, and the latter occupying the hills of Columbeira in our front.
>
> Sir Arthur Wellesley appeared to be satisfied with my commentary and not displeased at the liberty I had used in making the above suggestions; for he immediately ordered Major-General Ferguson and Brigadier-General Bowes, with their brigades, and the artillery of the Light Brigade, to march by the road I had spoken of to him; and then said to me: 'As you have reconnoitred that country, you will go with Ferguson'.

One may smile at Landmann's retrospective claim to be the part-architect of Wellesly's victorious tactics; but, taken together with his subsequent vexation (*see* below) when Sir Arthur cut short Ferguson's turning movement, the episode rings true.

On 16 August, Wellesley would know that Delaborde had piquetted the plain, and had chosen to stand at the far end, on the modest slope in front of Rolica and with necessarily exposed flanks; but with movement showing on the further, more formidable ridge, he would surely appreciate that Delaborde had depth to his tactics – unless what he, Wellesley, was being shown was a ruse. That Delaborde was merely making a show to force Wellesley to deploy, but never seriously intended to fight the ground (unless Loison came to his rescue) can be supported by an odd story quoted in Sir Herbert Maxwell's 1899 *Life of Wellington*:

During the night of 16 and 17 August Sir Arthur was roused from his sleep and informed that a stranger demanded an interview on business that would brook no delay. A monk was admitted. 'I am come', said he, 'to inform you that the French corps before you intends to retire before daylight, and if you want to catch your enemy you must be quick.'

'How do you know that?' asked Sir Arthur.

'Well', replied the monk, 'when General Junot's army first entered Portugal, he had his quarters in our convent of Alcobaça, and one of his staff shared my cell. We became very intimate, being both young men, and now the same officer is again lodged with me. Last evening he sat copying a despatch. I was curious to know what it was about. I stole behind him, clapped my hands over his eyes, and, in a feigned voice, challenged him to guess which of the brethren was his captor, for you must know that we and the younger officers are accustomed to play like schoolboys. He struggled to get free, but in vain, for I am a powerful fellow; then, while he was running over the names of the brethren, I quietly mastered the contents of his despatch, which were as I have informed you.'

Maxwell states in a footnote that: 'In the De Ros MS. the Duke of Wellington is reported as having said that the monk did not appear in person at his tent, but conveyed information by means of a peasant.'

The reader may believe what he will; but it is true that Delaborde was completely out-gunned and out-numbered, and would not seriously be looking to achieve miracles that day. The French general had only five battalions – two of the 70e Ligne, a battalion each of the 2e and 4e Léger and the 4e Suisse (Swiss mercenaries), plus two strong cavalry squadrons and five guns. The Swiss, moreover, were not an effective regiment, since six companies had been sent back to help garrison Peniche, and the four remaining, as we shall see, were only too ready to desert. Delaborde's reliable force was a mere four battalions, and Oman estimated his strength at a nominal 4,350 men.

Since Wellesley had fifteen British battalions and the equivalent of two more of Portuguese, Delaborde could realistically fight only a mild delaying action, if he were to fight at all. His fellow commander General Loison would seem to be his saviour, and on 16 August he was indeed en route with 5,000 exhausted men for Cercal, only five or six hours' march from Rolica; but tantalizingly, Delaborde had had no news of him for many days now, nor of Junot. In case Loison was just over the hill, marching to his rescue, his duty therefore was to buy time. But his brave delaying action at Rolica was based on hope and out-of-date orders; sadly for him, it was misplaced hope, since Loison was in fact now looking to join up with Junot, not march to the sound of Delaborde's five guns.

For Wellesley, of course, the reverse situation applied. He must deal with Delaborde with all speed, before Loison and Junot could come up. It is therefore curious that having effectively captured Obidos on the 15th, he made no move to cover the further three miles to Rolica until 7am on the 17th. This is especially puzzling since his after-battle despatch states that: 'There was some reason to believe that General Loison, who was at Rio Major yesterday, would join General Laborde in the course of the night.' His commissariat was presumably in an almighty muddle. It is a pity that Deputy Assistant Commissary-General August Schaumann did not join the army a fortnight earlier than he did, for then we should have the great joy of reading an account of those frenetic early days after landing in his splendid journal, *On the Road with Wellington.*

In planning his battle, Sir Arthur had a numerical superiority affording him the luxury of a double enveloping movement. In the terms that would soon become renowned from the Zulu armies of the invincible Shaka, he would send out 'horns' to left and right along the horseshoe heights in advance of his 'chest' on the valley floor, to cut in behind the French battalions and turn their flanks.

The left horn or eastern column, commanded by Major-General Ronald Ferguson, would be a powerful force comprising his own 2nd Brigade of the 1/36th (Herefordshire), 1/40th (2nd Somersets) and 1/71st (Glasgow Highlanders), plus the 4th Brigade under Brigadier Barnard Bowes and comprising the 1/6th (Warwicks) and 1/32nd (Cornwall) – a total of some 5,000 all ranks, together with a battery of guns. Ferguson's strength reflected his flank protection role against the approach of Loison, for which purpose his route was along the crest of the eastern ridge, aiming to come down behind Rolica.

The right horn or western column consisted of three battalions of Portuguese with fifty horse under Colonel Trant. His route lay through the hamlet of St Amias and along the inside of the horseshoe, again to get behind the French position.

Sir Arthur himself would lead the centre along the axis of the Rolica road: eight battalions in four brigades, plus some eleven rifle companies, 400 horse (half British, half Portuguese), the remaining battalion of Portuguese light troops, and 12 guns. On the right (west) of the line were Major-General Sir Rowland Hill's 1st Brigade comprising the 1/5th (Northumberland), 1/9th (Norfolk) and 1/38th (Staffordshire); in the centre were Brigadier Miles Nightingall's 3rd Brigade, of the 1/29th (Worcesters) and 1/82nd (Prince of Wales' Volunteers); and on the left (east) Brigadier Henry Fane's small but choice 6th Brigade had eleven companies of riflemen – four of the 2/95th and seven of the 5/60th. The reserve was to be Brigadier Catlin Craufurd's 5th Brigade, comprising the 1/45th (Nottinghamshire), 1/50th (West Kents) and 1/91st (Argyllshire Highlanders).

It will be noted that all the regiments present were represented by their 1st or senior battalion (bar the Rifles, who as ever were a law unto themselves). At this early stage in the Peninsular War no ordinary 2nd Battalions of Foot regiments had been sent to Portugal; according to Oman, a year later just over half of the twenty-six then comprising the Peninsular Field Army were 2nd Battalions. This bears upon the manpower available, since by definition 2nd Battalions had been designed usually to be home-based and to keep their 1st Battalions at full strength, themselves suffering the subsequent weakness. For example, in July 1809 the present author's own regiment, the 48th (Northamptonshire), had both battalions with Sir Arthur. The 1st landed 1,024 all ranks from Gibraltar, while the 2nd from Ireland – a much more productive recruiting ground – totalled a quarter less, at 753 men. So Wellesley's little Rolica army of thirteen battalions (less the Rifles), with the average 1st Battalion numbering some 900, was pretty much up to establishment – a happier state of affairs than was to be the case in later campaigns. On the other hand, not every battalion had recent combat experience; the 29th, for example, had last seen action nine years before.

It was well past dawn on 17 August, another warm, clear day which would grow swelteringly hot as the sun rose higher. The men had been up and doing since the 2am bugles, and were now more than ready to go. There was undoubtedly tension among the men, especially the majority who were facing action for the first time. The mood was confident nonetheless, because of their superior numbers. Several present remarked upon the special nature of the day, which clearly marked a new chapter for all of them: veterans, militia recruits, ploughboys, society's fops and flops, dandies and drunken gutter-sweepings alike. The specialness of the occasion lay not so much in their enemy, but the place of their meeting.

This time they were on the landmass of Europe – not in the Indies, nor India, nor Egypt, not Minorca or Malta or Martinique, Genoa, Naples, Calabria, nor Sicily; not far-away pinpricks, useful or not. Walk forward far enough from this battlefield, if they let you, and you could be in Paris. They were a tiny expeditionary force, but they had the sea (which they owned) and their ships behind them. In front, even fewer of the foe, but many more not far away. It was a historic moment, well caught by the 23-year-old Lieutenant Charles Leslie of the 29th, who wrote in his journal that a visitor to Obidos that morning

> … would not, perhaps, have noticed anything particular. He would have seen the arms piled, and the men occupied as they usually are on all occasions of a morning halt – some sitting on their knapsacks, others stretched on the grass, many with a morsel of cold meat on a ration biscuit for a plate in one hand, with a claspknife in the other, all doing justice to the contents of their haversacks, and not a few with their heads thrown back and canteens at their mouths, eagerly gulping down his Majesty's grog or the wine of the country, while others, whiffing their pipes, were jestingly promising their comrades better billets and softer beds for the next night, or repeating the valorous war-cry of the Portuguese.
>
> But to the person of reflecting mind there was more in this condensed formation than a casual halt required. A close observer would have noticed the silence and anxious looks of the several general officers of brigades, and the repeated departure and arrival of staff-officers and aides-de-camp, and he would have known that the enemy was not far distant, and that an important event was on the eve of taking place.

*   *   *

Sir Arthur, who was on a grey horse that day, waved his cocked hat at 7am, and his battalions stepped left foot forward to beat of drum, along the plain to Rolica. The bands struck up. Already on either flank the horns were well advanced. We have it from Landmann that the French down in the valley could not see the progress of Ferguson's force – that is not to say, however, that the three companies of the 70e Ligne positioned in the hills for that purpose were equally blind. Wellesley probably could not expect the particular joy of achieving an unseen turning movement that day; indeed, it is debatable whether he seriously expected Delaborde to stand and fight at all. The flanking hooks were worth a try – Loison was out there somewhere, after all; and should his frontal opponent prove inattentive, they might add a polish to victory.

More mundanely, Wellesley had the prime need to work his infantry through their first battle. He was a keen rider to hounds, and he knew that when hunting a new horse for the first time you take the early hedges with a steady hand, and pick the gaps. At Rolica he was not taking his untested command into the intricacies of an opposed river crossing, a night withdrawal, an encounter battle with cavalry, or any other advanced operation; even though he could not resist the two flanking horns, the decision would almost certainly come in the centre, after a straight-up-the-middle daylight approach.

Just after leaving Obidos, there was a triple fork in the road: paths to the left up to Ferguson's ridge, or straight ahead to Rolica, or off to the right down the slope towards St Amias under the western ridge of hills. Trant's Portuguese were already well forward along the latter, and at the fork General Hill turned right to follow, splitting into three columns of battalions, side by side. The 5th advanced on the right of the track, the 9th to its left, and the 38th stayed on it, with each battalion's Light Company trotting ahead to open into a skirmishing line.

Between Nos 4 and 5 Companies marched the regimental colour parties, each pair of Colours escorted by four sergeants. The bright distinguishing hues of the Regimental Colours were carried to the left of each pair – solid yellowish green for the 5th, plain yellow for the 38th and a much paler yellow for the 9th – each a huge 6½ × 6ft square flag of richly embroidered silk, with the Union Flag in the top quarter next to the spearhead on the 9ft pike, and the wreathed regimental designation in the centre. They made heavy burdens, both physically and psychologically, for the 16-year-old ensigns whose backs and right arms would soon be straining with the weight and their almost sacred responsibility. Alongside each boy, on the right, a fellow ensign carried the similarly huge King's Colour – the plain Union Flag, again bearing the regimental number. But with all respect to George III, all King's Colours looked the same once musket smoke blurred the vision – in the confusion of battle it was always the Regimental Colour that a man looked for, the same facing colour that he wore on his collar and cuffs. For the moment, however, the Colours would be carried furled and sloped, not flying; there was still too far to go.

Half a mile to Hill's left, Nightingall and Craufurd's brigades, and the guns, kept pace along the Rolica road, again in column of battalions, in the order 29th, 82nd, 45th, 91st and 50th: 4,500 red coats in a long column, three ranks wide – say a mile from front to back – with five bands playing.

Left again, on the lower slopes of the eastern side of the horseshoe, the riflemen of the 5/60th and beyond them the 2/95th were spreading out and moving independently, in pairs. Three companies of the 5/60th having been sent to join Ferguson, the remaining seven, together with Major Travers' four from the 2/95th, saw some 1,000 greencoats pushing forward.

Furthest left of all, and well in the lead, yet more redcoats belonging to Ferguson's 5,000 were moving on the reverse slope of the crest a mile and a half away. Ferguson took care to keep in the dead ground, as his sapper guide, Captain Landmann, confirms:

> We thus continued to advance about four miles by the road, which was suffi-
> ciently retired from the edge of the hills to conceal our line of march, no-one
> daring to go to the right of the crest of the range of hills we were on, lest the
> enemy should see us. On one occasion... I reconnoitred on foot to the
> distance of half a mile... and looked over into the valley, where I saw our main
> body considerably in the rear of us.

Some time before this, however, Sir Arthur felt the need to check on Ferguson's progress, perhaps because of the very fact that his left hook had long since disappeared from his sight. He would envisage the culmination of his approach march up the plain; without any sign of a flanking movement to stir the French, his centre would either have to halt and lie down under French cannon fire, or proceed unaided. He may also have begun to suspect that Ferguson had got lost, beyond the ridge; at all events, he sent an ADC flying off to Ferguson, as Captain Landmann recalls:

> Just as I had communicated my information [to Ferguson, that the main body
> were well in rear], I observed an Aide-de-camp with two epaulettes, the
> distinction worn by those attached to His Royal Highness the Duke of York
> only. This officer came up at a hand gallop, with a fine white sheepskin
> covering to his saddle, and extending much behind it, and ordered General
> Ferguson to descend from the heights, to join the main body in a frontal
> attack; adding, that he had ascertained the road we were following would not
> lead us to turn the right flank of the enemy, as had been misrepresented, but
> lead away to our left. I was never more vexed in my life, as I was on hearing
> Colonel Brown's order.

As the centre columns moved steadily forward, the French piquets on the rocky outcrops and in the plain were flushed southwards, without any argument and with an understandable keenness on their part, by the packs of light troops skirmishing ahead. Sergeant Hale of the 9th wrote: 'They had several skirmishing parties forward in the olive orchards, in order to check our advance; but the light companies of the different regiments soon scoured them out.' The advance was conducted slowly and precisely. When perhaps half a mile from the French position the British columns halted, deployed into line, primed and loaded their muskets, and continued the advance with shouldered arms. The surgeon of the 29th, Dr Guthrie, asked what was his place on such an occasion, and was told it was seven paces in rear of the Colours. Colonel Lake, commanding the 29th and riding about the same distance in front of the Colours, now turned round and called out to his ensigns, 'Gentlemen, display the Colours!' and they flew out into the wind. The watching French brigade commander General Foy, up on Rolica hill, was clearly impressed by the panorama unfolding before him: 'They came on slowly but in beautiful order, dressing at intervals to correct the gaps caused by the inequalities of the ground, and all converging on the hill of Rolica.'

Ferguson's five battalions on the French right also came down to link up with the main force; Landmann again:

> Down we all went, by a winding, steep, and almost impassable road for artillery, and so with much unnecessary fatigue joined the central column of attack, near the four windmills, on a sandy plain partly covered with pine and olive trees. The ground gently descended towards the hills occupied by the enemy, and within cannon-shot range of his field pieces.

From the same force, Major Ross-Lewin of the 32nd:

> We continued to advance in three columns. As we approached the enemy, the utmost order was preserved, and the columns were increased and diminished with as much regularity as if we were at a review. When within musket shot of the enemy, the line was formed, and we advanced over the uneven ground, doubling when an obstacle presented itself, and moving up when we had past it, with great exactness.

It really must have been quite a sight. Hill's brigade had the 5th as right of the line, with the 9th alongside, and the 38th dropped back in reserve in column of divisions – that is, in pairs of companies. The brigade's face of some 1,800 men, in two ranks, covered about 900yd of frontage. The line then continued eastwards with the 29th and 82nd from Nightingall's brigade, and then the 45th from Craufurd's brigade coming up on their left, on the road; Craufurd's 50th and 91st halted in reserve further back along the road, together with the battalion of Portuguese light troops. So five red battalions in line, perhaps a mile and a quarter across; five sets of Colours, four squadrons of cavalry and twelve guns, of which nine had by now unlimbered and opened fire at ineffectively long range. And across to their right, on the far slopes, the French would also see Ferguson's five further battalions dropping down to their right shoulders: in all, 10,000 redcoats on the march towards their centre and right – a brave and novel sight for the French.

Whether, as Jac Weller believes, Wellesley deliberately made a slow-moving spectacle in the centre, to concentrate French minds while his horns trapped them from behind, we do not know. But Delaborde was himself drawn up primarily for show, so it would have been a case of bluff and counter-bluff. With a second, serious defensive position a mile behind him, Delaborde was on Rolica hill only to force Wellesley to deploy and waste an hour or two. He had earlier warned his commanders to be prepared for a rapid withdrawal, and the moment for that was now imminent. He had sent three companies of the 70e Ligne and some cavalry into the hills to the east, to watch and report on Loison, and they also kept him posted on Ferguson's wide left hook.

With his *tirailleurs* becoming engaged with Wellesley's light troops in the centre, with Fane's riflemen and Ferguson descending on to the plain to his right, and on his left Trant's column now appearing at the nearby hamlet of Quinta Gruga, Delaborde gave the word, and extricated his four battalions 'with the utmost regularity and the greatest celerity' (as Wellesley would write in his Despatch). Firing grape and solid shot from his five guns, and screened by the 26e Chasseurs and his skirmishers, he moved his infantry rapidly back to the prepared positions on the formidable black ridge to their rear. Since Wellesley lacked 'a sufficient body of cavalry', and notwithstanding 'the rapid advance of the British infantry', the French completed this manoeuvre without serious interference.

Lieutenant Charles Leslie of the 29th would write of this first phase of the battle:

> The Army having broken up from the encampment at Caldes, at daylight on the morning of 17 August 1808, was assembled in contiguous columns on the plains of Obidos, where the final arrangements having been made for the attack, the army was put in motion soon after passing through Obidos. The columns struck off into different routes and reached the ordered points of attack. That under General Ferguson went to the left, and General Hill's to the right. The centre column proceeded on the main road. The third brigade, consisting of the 29th and 82nd regiments under General Nightingall, were in front, and the 29th the leading regiment.
>
> We continued to march direct for the enemy, whom we discovered apparently in three columns, posted on an elevated plain beyond the village of Mamed, having the commanding heights of Rolica at a short distance in their rear; we made a momentary halt; the men were ordered to prime and load; we moved forward through the village of Mamed; after crossing a bridge, formed line and advanced, expecting to engage every moment: when we arrived at the position where we first saw the French posted, we found they had retreated. Their right were filing to the rear, masked by a cloud of skirmishers, posted on some rising ground, covered with brushwood at the foot of the mountains, and warmly engaged with General Ferguson's riflemen. Their left had retired through the village of Columbeira, and occupied the heights of Rolica or Zamgubeira which ran to the rear of and commanded that village.
>
> Our artillery took up a position near a windmill on an eminence to the left of the village, which commanded the aforesaid rising ground, and opened a well directed fire on the enemy.

Wellesley now had to make a fresh plan, issue new orders, and re-deploy as necessary for an attack on the second position. As Oman says, 'half the morning had been wasted to no effect.' Delaborde, however, had achieved just the effect he sought – to delay. Sir Arthur wrote later in his Despatches:

During the action (of that day) a French officer, who was dying of his wounds, informed me that they had expected Loison to join them that day at 1 o'clock by their right, which was the reason for which they stood our attack... intelligence to the same purport was rec'd from other prisoners... I heard that Loison's corps was at that moment [dusk on the 17th] arriving at Bombarral, which was about five miles from the field of battle; I conclude that the juncture had been intended, and was prevented only by our early attack.

*   *   *

The ridge behind Rolica is continuous, blocking the southern end of the Obidos plain. A prominent central portion is flanked by two deep ravines, 1,400–1,500yd apart to east and west. The feature between these dominates the village of Columbeira to its left front; on its right the road from Rolica snakes up on to it, leading to the next village of Zambugeira and on towards Torres Vedras about six miles south. Looked at from the side, the slope of the ridge varies from 45 degrees to the near-vertical, and where the face is of rock two further ravines cut into the mass of the central ridge, providing lesser angles of approach but narrowing as one progresses. Thickets of bramble, brushwood, gorse and wild myrtle, with pine trees and loose scree, have to be waded through. It is a defender's dream. Visiting the position some months after the battle, General D'Urban remarked that the ridge 'was so difficult of ascent, and affords so much advantage to the defenders, that how they [the French] suffered a man to reach the summit must astonish every soldier who looks at the ground'. In truth, it was the kind of ground that later in the campaign might have attracted Sir Arthur himself. Fortescue, who visited the scene in 1903, wrote of it:

> The face of Delaborde's main position, though now uncovered saving by patches of scrub, was at that time thick with pines; but the bare rock protrudes in great sheets both on the sides and on the summit. The sides are so steep that a man could hardly ascend them without using his hands, were they not seamed by shallow gullies full of rough stones, where the water rushes down during the rains and washes away all vegetation. Upon the lowest slopes of these hills, where they melt into the plain, another curious feature is noticeable – a wall of grey rocks passing like the teeth of a shark along the whole length of the French position, and affording excellent cover for sharpshooters.

Verner's *History of the Rifle Brigade* describes the ridge as

> ... on heights one mile south of Rolica rising in steep and broken spurs, some 500ft above a stream flowing down a ravine which secured his left flank. The right flank was to some extent protected by another stream. The hills are exceedingly steep and broken, with masses of bare rock protruding from scrub, and high heath and fir-trees scattered over all.

Captain Wilkie of the 45th wrote that 'the hill was as steep as that at Malvern, and covered with loose pebbles, having only a few stunted shrubs here and there to give security to the footing'; while Sergeant Hale of the 9th said simply that 'We found great difficulty in some places in ascending... they continued pouring down musket fire on us very sharply.'

From the now vacated low hill at Rolica, at around noon Wellesley sent Ferguson and Trant back out to more flank marching. His two batteries of artillery again unlimbered on the near slope, by a windmill, and commenced firing on the French up on the crest of the ridge. He sent Hill, Nightingall and Craufurd forward to the slopes at the foot of the ridge, where they were then to halt, since his intention was not to proceed to climb the ridge until the French flanks had been turned. It is not clear if Fane's riflemen should similarly have halted, in the broken ground to the east of the road, but the action there was not in fact broken off. Not for the last time, one might observe the parallel between riflemen enthusiastically popping away at their opposite numbers, and foxhounds loathe to be lifted off a good scent.

Lieutenant John Cox, 2/95th, explains that 'the Riflemen on the left were considerably forward, having been sharply engaged *throughout* with large bodies of Voltigeurs who were posted in the steep hills, vineyards and enclosures from which they were successively driven.' The amount of legwork involved since 7am had been impressive, for Sir Arthur had given the 60th, and particularly the 95th higher out on their left, a formidable flanking movement. The distance covered by Fane's brigade (taking the route marked by Fortescue on Emery Walker's splendid map) was some seven miles as the crow flies, from the triple fork outside Obidos, up into the foothills, then south, then west to Rolica. Moreover, it involved climbing almost all the way for the first four miles, with the land height varying between 100 and 700ft. No wonder Captain Leach of the 95th wrote in a letter the following week that:

> You cannot conceive nor can anyone who was not present on that day the situation of ourselves and the 60th. We had to ascend first one mountain so covered with brushwood that our legs were ready to sink under us, the enemy on the top of it lying down in the heath keeping up a hot and constant fire in our face and the men dropping all round us. Before we could gain the summit the French had retreated to the next hill, when they again lay concealed and kept up a running galling fire on us as we ascended. Having beaten them off the second hill and taken possession of it the enemy retreated to a wood, there being a valley between us and it and recommenced a most tremendous fire, having received a reinforcement. The action now became very severe.

It seems likely that the valley was the one to the south-east of Rolica, and the wood (and the reinforcements) were the right flank of Delaborde's main defensive position. If so, Leach's 'most tremendous fire' in a 'very severe action' lends credence to one reason for Wellesley's plan going awry – for one of his regiments now jumped the gun.

His plan was that – from his right to left – the 5th, plus all the light companies from Hill's brigade, should attack up the westernmost ravine; the second ravine, directly south of Columbeira, was for the 29th (from Nightingall's brigade) supported by Hill's 9th; the other central ravine was for Nightingall's 82nd, and the left hand one and the adjacent road were for Nightingall's 45th and Fane's Rifle battalions. Crucially, however, none were to ascend until the flanking movements caused the French to stir backwards – that is, already back-pedalling and looking over their shoulders. Should the assault battalions reach the ravines before this, they were to fill in the time usefully by making noisy demonstrations. This all hangs together tactically, and is confirmed by one of the 29th's subalterns, Lieutenant Charles Leslie: 'We were merely in the first instance to have occupied the village of Columbeira and make a demonstration on the enemy's centre, whilst General Ferguson on the left and General Hill on the right, should attack and turn his flanks.'

Having explained his wishes, Sir Arthur ordered the battalions forward and, to save time, required them to shake out while on the march into the right order, that is by ravines. Since at the outset the 9th were marching to the right of the 29th, and were now to be in support of them, it followed that Lieutenant-Colonel Lake needed to get his 29th ahead of the 9th while en route to their ravine. During this cross-country march of rather more than a mile, the broken ground generally and the village of Columbeira in particular impeded progress. The village comprised about 180 houses, each (according to Landmann) with walled or fenced gardens and vineyards that obstructed easy access. So much so, indeed, that Lake ordered his left wing not to follow him and the right wing, but to detour round the east side of the village. The combined consequence of this, and his urge to get ahead, was that half the 29th became isolated out in front, and began to attract fire from the ridge above, as they moved laterally across to the foot of their allotted ravine.

We do not know how Sir Arthur intended to launch his assault battalions up the ridge, but he would never have left it to individual commanding officers to decide the moment. His start line was only about 1,300yd from west to east, a mile from his position on Rolica hill; from the latter he would also have been able to watch Ferguson's approach down the slopes from the east to get behind the French. When he judged the moment ripe, presumably he would have galloped an ADC forward to pass the order for attack to Hill, Nightingall and Fane – which would have taken a matter of three or four minutes.

Possibly because he assumed that the 'tremendous fire' encountered by the Rifles signified the start of the general assault, but more probably because of a hunger for glory, the commanding officer of the 29th set off immediately up his particular ravine – without halting to regroup from the march, without his left wing, and without having properly briefed his officers. Charles Leslie wrote that: 'We afterwards understood that it was not intended the 29th should have so soon attacked the strong pass, nor penetrated so far as we did... by some mistake, however, the order was misunderstood and our gallant Colonel pushed on.' So up the ravine trotted Lake with his right wing of five companies, complete with Colours. No other regiment moved forward at that stage; they would shortly be halting at the foot of their respective ravines, in accordance with Sir Arthur's orders.

Being the sole focus for the defenders at the top, not surprisingly Lake got into a terrible scrape. As we shall see, this sucked in a rescue attempt, which in turn forced Sir Arthur into signalling a premature general advance long before Ferguson and Trant had got behind the French flanks. He was not helped by Ferguson losing his way ('Our Brigade arrived rather late, and were scarcely engaged' – Captain Warre, ADC to Ferguson); or by Trant's Portuguese, who did not get into action at all. Thus Delaborde was not obliged to retire at that early stage, and could take the time to give the 29th a proper bloody nose. Once again, reading between the lines of Wellesley's Despatch, we may hear Sir Arthur regretting his army's tendency to over-step the mark: 'The 29th and 9th regiments… attacked with the *utmost impetuosity*, and reached the enemy before those whose attacks were to be made on the flanks.'

Captain George Landmann, Royal Engineers, had earlier watched the 29th approaching Columbeira:

> The 29th regiment was at this moment coming up with Lieut-Colonel the Honble G. Lake at their head, the band playing a country dance. Lake was mounted on a complete charger, nearly 17 hands high, with a famously long tail, and was dressed in an entire new suit, even his leathers, boots, hat, feather, epaulettes, sash etc being all new, and his hair powdered and queued, his cocked hat placed on his head square to the front.

Lake took the battalion half way up the ravine, where he stopped in an olive grove for the men to drop their packs. He bade his left wing (Nos 6, 7 and 8 Companies) to stay put, and led forward his grenadier company and his right wing of the first four battalion companies. They clambered in file up the gulley, and 'Though obliged at times to climb on hands and knees, nothing could restrain their impetuosity' (Captain Warre). One might suspect that the impetuosity was limited to the colonel, while the speed up the hill achieved by his grenadiers was in large part simply through the necessity of keeping up with him. Lake, we must recall, was ascending the slope on his long-legged charger, and while all horses will creep down a hill, few will willingly creep up one. The preferred momentum of a trot makes lighter work of a gradient, but would leave foot soldiers well behind. Also, we must not forget that the 29th had landed on terra firma only seven days earlier, after spending – like all General Spencer's troops – a full seven months cooped up on troopships, bobbing around between Cadiz and Gibraltar, with little time ashore. Lake's grenadiers were in no state to double up hills, packs or no packs; and they were alone, apart from the firefight between the Rifles and voltigeurs hundreds of yards away on their left.

During the first part of the climb French fire was light, being masked by the walls of the ravine. The further they climbed, the further the 29th entered the French position, as the gulley narrowed and snaked first to the right, then to the left, and the fire grew more effective. Soon Lake was 200yd behind the French front line, by now in single file and strung out along a narrow track in the bottom of a steep-sided, steeply climbing gorge. There are three eyewitness accounts of what happened next, but Ross-Lewin of the 32nd (who was across with Ferguson's column) gives the shortened, camp-fire version:

The 29th were obliged, by the nature of the ground, to climb a height in single files by a goat-path. On the summit, the 70th French were drawn up to receive them, and when Colonel Lake gained it, the summons to him to dismount and surrender, and his refusal, and his death, were the work of a minute. The grenadier company, and a splendid one it was, had followed their commanding officer closely; they were very much blown from the exertion of climbing the steep and from the heat of the weather, and all of them, with the exception of fifteen, were killed, wounded, or taken.

This is a fairly crude summary, as is that from the 'Soldier of the 71st', also with Ferguson: 'The 29th advanced up the hill, not perceiving an ambush of the enemy, which they had placed on each side of the road. As soon as the 29th was right between them they gave a volley which killed or wounded every man in the grenadier company except seven.'

Another account, from an anonymous officer of the 45th, on the immediate left of the 29th, was published in the *Star* newspaper on 1 November 1808:

In the action of 17 August we attacked the strongest part of the enemy, headed by the gallant General Spencer; but, from the 29th Regiment having advanced too quick, they having the road on our right, and we being obliged to climb a precipice, they suffered, as you have seen by the Gazette, very severely; whereas we that were exposed to the whole cannon of the French, while advancing, only lost one Ensign killed (R. Dawson, while carrying the King's Colour), one Lieutenant wounded (R. Burke) and nine rank and file. Captain Payne, who had been shot through the lungs at Buenos Ayres, re-opened the wound by the exertions of the climb and had to be sent back to England. The 29th completely saved us from being cut to pieces, for our Regiment was so entirely done up, that scarcely a man could stand when we got to the top of the precipice, some places of which only two men could get up at a time. You may recollect the rocks called Boor Hill near Ayr; the place we had to go up was something like it.

The French, since the business is over, have frequently inquired the name of the mad Regiment that climbed the rocks, and the still madder Officer that led them; they won't believe us when we aquaint them that the above was all our loss. They retired in astonishment when they saw the 29th and us formed in perfect order on the hill. We never fired a shot, and in consequence were not mentioned in orders; but all the army agree that we deserve to have been noticed in the strongest terms.

It was clearly a withering fire that swept the 29th's leading company. Sergeant-Major Richards stood over Colonel Lake when he was knocked off his horse, defending him, and himself later died of thirteen wounds from balls and bayonets. The first eyewitness account is that of an anonymous captain of the 29th; it appears in Francis Clarke's *The Life of the Most Noble Marquis of Wellington* (surely Sir Arthur's first biography, published in 1813). The captain commanded 'the right centre company, the fifth from the right', that is the last part of the right wing, but next to the Colours when in line:

> While climbing up through briars and brushwood [the French] plied us successively with grape and musketry. Each scrambled up the best way he could; and, on gaining the summit, I found several officers, and about sixty privates of the 29th, who were in front of me; only one of my Company reached the top with me, the rest following fast… Upon advancing, we were immediately attacked by a French platoon of ninety men, whom we repeatedly repulsed.

It would seem that Lake's penetration of their position had stirred up at least two companies of the French 70e Ligne on Delaborde's left (the 29th's regimental history specifies that one of the battalions on that part of the ridge was the 1/70e.) Since they would know – they had had three days to look around their position – that only mountain goats could assail them frontally, they would be thoroughly alert to the dangers of infiltration up the easier pitches. After all, for seasoned troops on the defensive a ravine would closely resemble a breach sloping up through the broken walls of any besieged town, and Lake's men were lucky not to find *chevaux-de-frise* of sharpened timber fixed across the end of their climb.

When the 70e Ligne piled in, the 29th's right wing was simply overwhelmed. The anonymous captain continues:

> [The platoon of ninety Frenchmen] were joined by another of the same number, who charged us with the bayonet, with whom we sustained the unequal conflict; but our little band being now considerably advanced in front [meaning that those following up the ravine were prudently hanging back] and reduced to twenty-five, Major Way, Captain Ford and myself, and our brave companions, were under the painful necessity of surrendering [they were, after all, outnumbered perhaps 8:1]. Even this, however, did not satisfy the sanguinary enemy, who seemed bent on bayoneting us all. After many narrow escapes, General Brennier at last came up, and with difficulty put an end to the carnage, and to the distressing scene around the dead and dying.

Sergeant Hale of the 9th, whose battalion worked their way up the ridge partly to the right of the 29th, reckoned that about three companies' worth of the 29th were out of action (it was later established that the 29th's casualties totalled some 197 all ranks, or about two companies): 'The 29th Regiment being about a quarter mile [sic] on our left, and having some little better road than our regiment, they ascended the heights a few minutes before us; upon which, the enemy immediately attacked them with a much superior force, and caused them to fall back with the loss of their Colours and about three hundred men.' Sergeant Hale's reference to more than one path leading up the ravine is echoed by Napier: 'It was intended that those battalions [9th and 29th] should take the right hand path of two leading up the same hollow, and thus have come in on Laborde's flank in conjunction with Trant's column; but as the left path led more directly to the enemy, the 29th followed it, the 9th being close behind.'

It was at this stage that Rifleman Harris and Major-General Sir Rowland Hill, commander of the 1st Brigade (of which the 9th was a part) enter the story – according to Harris. Quite what any riflemen were doing so far to the right, a good 500 yards from the road the 95th were climbing, we do not know. However, this is what Harris says he saw:

> I remember remarking Lord Hill... the 29th regiment received so terrible a fire, that I saw the right wing almost annihilated, and the colonel lay sprawling amongst the rest. We had ourselves caught it pretty handsomely; for there was no cover for us, and we were rather too near. The living skirmishers were lying besides heaps of their dead; but still we held our own till the battalion regiments came up... the 29th, however, had got their fairing [i.e. a present] here at this time; and the shock of that fire seemed to stagger the whole line, and make them recoil. At the moment a little confusion appeared in the ranks, I thought. Lord Hill was near at hand and saw it, and I observed him come galloping up. He put himself at the head of the regiment, and restored them to order in a moment.

Harris implies that General Hill then took the 29th's left wing, plus the remnants of the right, up the ravine, for he continues: 'Pouring a regular and sharp fire upon the enemy, he galled them in return; and, remaining with the 29th til he brought them to the charge, quickly sent the foe to the right-about. It seemed to me that few men could have conducted the business with more coolness and quietude of manner, under such a storm of balls as he was exposed to. Indeed, I have never forgotten him from that day.' No one else mentions Hill in this particular role, and it should be noted that of course the 29th belonged not to Hill's, but to Nightingall's 3rd Brigade. With Colonel Lake dead it was certainly in order for firm leadership to be exerted when the right wing came down the ravine rather quicker than they went up; but it was a role for Nightingall, not Hill. Yet back up that ravine the rest of the 29th did go, at pretty much the same time as the 9th reached the summit to their right. Sergeant Hale again:

> As soon as we made our appearance on the top of the heights, it was a great relief to them [the 29th]; and the first thing our Colonel thought most proper to do, was to show them [the French] the bayonet, which we immediately did; much to their shame and disgrace, we drove them off the heights in a few minutes; at the same time, the remains of the 29th regiment gave them another grand charge, by which they retook their Colours and some prisoners.

But of all the descriptions of the 29th's fortunes that day, the following lengthy but compelling account sounds the most authoritative. Lieutenant Charles Leslie was one of only three officers in the 29th's right wing not to be killed, wounded or taken:

The 82nd regiment being ordered to another point of attack, the 29th broke up into open columns, and advanced by column of sections through the village of Columbeira, led by the gallant Colonel Lake. They were now much galled by the enemy's sharpshooters from the heights, particularly from a high pinnacle commanding the village, and by a cannonade of round-shot on the left. It being observed that the regiment was so much exposed, the left wing was ordered not to follow the right through the village, but to move round it to the left, and hence it did not reach the entrance of the pass until a considerable time after the right wing. The Light Company of the 29th was also detached with those of the 5th and 82nd regiments to make a demonstration on a pass further to our right. On leaving the village, the right wing turned to the left through some vineyards and advanced along the foot of the heights, in order to gain the pass, exposed to a flank fire the whole way, from which we suffered considerably.

We now entered the pass, which was extremely steep, narrow and craggy, being the dried-up bed of a mountain torrent, so that at some places only two or three men could get up at a time. The enemy kept up a tremendous fire at point blank upon us to which not a shot was returned; but we kept eagerly pushing on as fast as circumstances would admit. About half-way up there was a small olive grove, in which we halted to form, and the men were ordered to take off their haversacks, great-coats etc which was done under a continual shower of bullets. The pass turned again very difficult, we could only advance by files, but no disorder took place, the men showing a laudible anxiety to push forward. The further we advanced the more the ravine receded into the centre of the enemy, and numbers were now falling from the continued fire on all sides.

Colonel Lake's horse was shot about this time, upon which Major Way dismounted, and gave up his horse to the Colonel [this Black Jack was in fact Lake's own second horse.] After clearing the narrow defile, we entered upon some open ground thinly wooded, under shelter of which the officers lost no time in forming the men; the whole then pushed forward, and at last gained the wished-for heights; but we were now obliged, under a heavy fire, to take ground to the right, previous to forming into line, in order to give room for the rear to form as they came up, there not being at this time above three or four companies in line, and these much reduced by casualties. When the enemy, who appeared to have been lying down behind a broken earthen fence, which ran rather in an oblique direction along our front, suddenly rose up and opened their fire, which their officers seemed endeavouring to restrain, and apparently urging them on to the charge, as we observed them knocking down the men's firelocks with their swords. But they did not advance.

Colonel Lake called out 'Don't fire, men; don't fire; wait a little, we shall soon charge' [meaning when more companies should come up], adding 'The bayonet is the true weapon for a British soldier', which were his dying words, for as he moved towards the left to superintend the line being prolonged, he was marked and killed by a skirmisher, and his horse galloped into the French lines. [Black Jack became the property of General Delaborde.]

The right [in consequence of Lake's death] not receiving any orders to advance, opened their fire, and a desperate engagement ensued. Some of the enemy in front of the extreme right, either as a ruse, or in earnest, called out that they were poor Swiss, and did not want to fight the English; some were actually shaking hands, and a parley ensued; during which the enemy's troops, who had been posted on the side of the ravine, finding we had forced it, and that they were likely to be cut off, began to retire, and coming in the rear of our right, dashed through, carrying with them one Major, who was dismounted, as before stated, five officers and about twenty-five privates.

Owing to this accident, and the enemy continuing a tremendous fire from all sides, being left without support or a superior officer to command, and our numbers decreasing very fast, Brevet Major Egerton, seeing the impossiblility of making an effectual resistance, ordered us to fall back upon our left wing, which was still in the rear; we accordingly retired and got under cover of the wood.

On observing this the enemy set up a shout, and then, but not till then, advanced upon us, as if with a view to charge; some individuals on both sides got mixed, and had personal encounters with the bayonet; they however did not venture to press us, nor to follow us into the woody ground, where we formed on the left wing, which had now come up; being also joined by the 9th regiment [which was sent to support the 29th, when it was found that they were so seriously engaged]. The whole now rapidly pushed forward and cleared the front of the enemy, who after an ineffectual resistance were driven from their position.

The 29th were then halted, and on mustering the regiment, there were found one Lieut-Colonel and one Lieutenant killed; two Captains severely wounded; one Major and seven officers and 25 men prisoners, and 177 rank and file lying on the field killed and wounded, making a total of 214, excluding of several officers who were hit but not returned as wounded. The whole of those taken prisoner belonged to the three or four right companies, and not any from the left wing. There were but three officers remaining in the right wing, of whom I was one.

... so close had been the hand to hand fighting, that Private Millbank, servant of Captain Davie of the company to which I belonged, was found lying opposite a Frenchman, both killed by bayonet wounds.

The third eyewitness was the unfortunate 30-year-old Major Gegory Way, deprived by Colonel Lake of his borrowed Black Jack, and now taken prisoner (not for the first time). He would write to his father from a prison ship on 26 August:

My Dearest Father,
As some uncertain & perhaps incorrect accounts of the action of the 17th inst may have reached you I seize the first opportunity that has offered to set you

all at ease with regard to myself – & tho' again in captivity, I am thank God! Alive and well, my usual good fortune attended me in the Day of Battle, which for the time we were engaged, was as hot as it could well be – my brave and ever to be lamented Commander Lt Col Lake fell by my side at the head of a few remaining Grenadiers – I was dismounted having given Col Lake my Horse, he having had his own shot under him, and himself wounded in the neck – a second shot from a Rifle entered his right side, and came out thro' the left – the Blade of my sword was shot off, leaving only the hilt in my hand – out of about 70 men principally Grenadiers, who attained the summit of a height where the enemy were strongly posted, only 20 remained at which time the French in considerable force, charged us – and myself and two more officers may thank the French General of Brigade Breunier for our lives – who rescued us from the Bayonets of fury of the Soldiers – At the moment we were captured I had the point of one entering my Sash at the time the French General averted the Blow – The 29th after 9 years of inaction highly distinguished themselves – tho' Victory was on our side we have suffered considerably. I learn that out of the 400 who fell on that day 204 belonged to the 29th, and thirteen officers were killed & wounded – immediately on being captured we were marched off rapidly on the high road to Lisbon – 26 miles that Day, and 34 the next – on foot the whole way… Eight officers were taken with me and we hope that the 29th will be mentioned in Despatches as nothing could exceed their gallantry under great disadvantage of ground etc – we had an almost inaccessible Precipice to mount and at the top of which the French were posted – my saddle on the Horse's Tail, instead of his Back – A French officer, whom I have since seen, informed me he aimed at me with his Rifle and afterwards killed the gallant Col Lake…

The 70e Ligne stuck it out obstinately, trying to push the 29th and 9th off the heights. Sergeant Hale again: 'The enemy fell back a little distance, and then turned and attacked us again; but was received most gallantly, and soon repulsed. They afterwards made several attacks upon our regiment and the 29th, before any other regiment came up to our assistance.' Sir Arthur wrote in his Despatch that: 'the enemy here made three most gallant attacks upon the 29th and 9th Regiments… [who] for a considerable length of time… alone were advanced to this position'.

For there was necessarily quite a gap in this unco-ordinated action along the ridge – it can scarcely be called an attack, for it now became a series of attacks. Sir Arthur, giving up hopes of his 'horns' ever materializing, ordered a general advance. The 5th, 82nd, 45th and the riflemen clambered up as best they could, with the French waiting at the top for a worthwhile group of gasping, knee-quivering skirmishers to gather before making a charge and tumbling them back down again. Delaborde was particularly obdurate on his right, keen to hang on there as long as possible in case Loison should be marching to join him. On the French left the 5th found their task relatively easy, according to their Sergeant Morley:

... we saw the enemy, by their fires, posted to great advantage... we found a difficulty at first in getting within range. The hills on which the enemy was posted were high, and too perpendicular, to attempt a direct ascent. Our staff officers, however, discovered certain chasms or openings, made, it would seem, by the rain, up which we were led. As soon as we began our ascent, Colonel McKenzie who was riding on a noble grey, dismounted, turned the animal adrift, and sword in hand, conducted us onwards until we gained the summit of the first hill; the enemy playing upon us all the time. Having gained the crest, we rushed on them in a charge; whoever opposed us fell by the ball or bayonet. We then proceeded towards another hill, where the enemy had formed again; but as one route lay through vineyards, we were annoyed by a destructive fire. Our Colonel, whom no impediment could intimidate, said, 'Charge' we did so, but I could go no further, having received a wound in my leg.

On the eastern flank, where the going was even more broken up by gullies and scrub, it was close range stuff for the eleven companies of riflemen. Both Captain Leach and Rifleman Harris relate similar incidents of comrades hit in either head or hand while drinking out of canteens – good shooting with a musket; and Harris' choice of words – 'sharp contest... caught it severely... the Frenchmen's balls were flying very wickedly... the Frenchmen's bullets fell pretty thickly around... we lost many men' – indicate a pretty close range, of only fifty yards or so (since the French did not have the advantage of rifled barrels). In such fighting the Baker rifle's splendid 300yd range was of no advantage; indeed, in so far as it was slower to reload than the smooth-bore muskets used by the *voltigeurs*, the British were actually handicapped in close country. A flavour of the attack on the British left is given by Harris:

All was action with us Rifles just at this moment; and the barrel of my piece was so hot from continued firing that I could hardly bear to touch it, and was obliged to grasp the stock beneath the iron, as I continued to blaze away... at length, after a sharp contest, we forced them to give ground and, following them up, drove them from their position on the heights, and hung upon their skirts till they made another stand, and then the game began again.

The Rifles, indeed, fought well this day, and we lost many men. They seemed in high spirits, and delighted at having driven the enemy before them. Joseph Cochan was by my side loading and firing very industriously about this period of the day. Thirsting with heat and action, he lifted his canteen to his mouth; 'Here's to you, old boy', he said, as he took a pull at its contents. As he did so, a bullet went through the canteen, and perforating his brain, killed him in a moment. Another man fell close to him almost immediately, struck by a ball in the thigh.

Indeed we caught it severely just here, and the old iron was also playing its part amongst our poor fellows very merrily. I saw a man named Symmonds struck full in the face by a round shot, and he came to the ground a headless trunk. Meanwhile, many large balls bounded along the ground amongst us so deliberately that we could occasionally evade them without difficulty. I could relate many more of the casualties I witnessed on this day, but the above will suffice.

At some point in the late afternoon – Leach says about 5 or 6pm – three things happened which, taken together, caused General Delaborde to order an immediate withdrawal. Firstly, and at long last, General Ferguson's five battalions began to appear away to his right, and disconcertingly towards his rear; secondly, the 95th Rifles broke through on that part of the ridge he had most wished to cling to – the eastern end nearest to Loison's hoped-for approach; and thirdly, British cavalry appeared on his vacated ridge as he pulled back from it.

Ferguson was now clearly unstoppable, and unless Loison arrived without delay behind him, all was up. But the 95th's penetration presented a much more proximate threat: that Wellesley himself could flank Delaborde, by leap-frogging his reserve brigade through the 95th. If they got down the road to Zambugeira on his right before he could extricate his four battalions from the ridge to his left, the consequences might be severe. We can only surmise this scenario from an episode related by Rifleman Harris, whose description of its location is predictably imprecise. However, it is clear that the event took place at the limit of the 95th's tactical progress, at the point they had reached when the battle ended and the French did indeed withdraw:

> There were two small buildings in our front; and the French, having managed to get into them, annoyed us much from that quarter. A small rise in the ground close before these houses also favoured them; and our men were being handled very severely in consequence. They became angry, and wouldn't stand it any longer. One of the skirmishers, jumping up, rushed forward, crying, 'Over, boys! Over! Over' when instantly the whole line responded to the cry, 'Over! Over! Over!' They ran along the grass like wildfire, and dashed at the rise, fixing their sword-bayonets as they ran. The French light bobs could not stand the sight, but turned about, and fled; and, getting possession of their ground, we were soon inside the buildings. After the battle was over, I stepped across to the other house I have mentioned in order to see what was going on there, for the one I remained in was now pretty well filled with the wounded (both French and English), who had managed to get there for a little shelter. Two or three surgeons, also, had arrived at this house, and were busily engaged in giving their assistance to the wounded, now also lying here as thickly as in the building I had left; but what struck me most forcibly was, that from the circumstance of some wine-butts having been left in the apartment, and their having in the engagement been perforated by bullets, and otherwise broken, the red wine had escaped most plentifully, and ran down upon the earthen floor, where the wounded were lying, so that many of them were soaked in the wine with which their blood was mingled.

We do not know where these two houses were, but they were surely adjacent to the road, now captured, to Zambugeira. Since they were where Harris' company finished up 'after the battle was over', they had to be on the high ground beyond the ridge up which the 95th had so valiantly struggled.

In the event, Sir Arthur did not call forward his reserve brigade to exploit the capture of the road; but we have it on the authority of Sergeant Norbert Landsheit, 20th Light Dragoons, that he called forward his horse. Up the road they clattered, no doubt loosening sabres in their scabbards and taking a pull at their horses' heads, if not at their flasks:

> We had watched the progress of the battle for some time, without sustaining any injury, except from a single shell, which, bursting over our column, sent a fragment through the backbone of a troop-horse, and killed him on the spot – when a cry arose, 'The cavalry to the front!' and we pushed up a sort of hollowed road towards the top of a ridge before us. Though driven from their first position, the enemy, it appeared, had rallied, and showing a line both of horse and foot, were preparing to renew the fight. Now, our cavalry were altogether incapable of coping with that of the French; and the fact became abundantly manifest, so soon as our leading files gained the brow of the hill – for the slope of a rising ground opposite was covered with them in such numbers, as to render any attempt to charge, on our part, utterly ridiculous. Accordingly, we were directed to form up, file by file, as each emerged from the road – not in two ranks, as is usually done both on parade and in action – but in rank entire. Moreover, we were so placed, that the French officers could not possibly tell what was behind us; and thus [we] made a show which appeared to startle them; for they soon began to change their dispositions, the infantry moving off first, the cavalry following, upon which we likewise broke again into column of threes, and rode slowly after them. But we had no desire to overtake them. They therefore pursued their march unmolested, except by a few discharges of cannon; and we, after seeing them fairly under weigh, halted on the field of battle.

It is not clear whether Delaborde knew that Sir Arthur had just two squadrons of the 20th Light Dragoons (and the equivalent of two Portuguese squadrons – some 400 sabres in all) in the centre column. However, with (according to Oman) only 263 horsemen of his own in the 26e Chasseurs, Delaborde was still outnumbered in cavalry. It is surely curious that Sergeant Landsheit was so adamantly fearful of Delaborde's horse – one would think the French had 1,000 sabres mounted that day. And it is curious, too, that Wellesley himself seemed to share the sergeant's apprehension, and did not let loose the two British dragoon squadrons – though he can be excused for not counting on the Portuguese. If he had not had it in mind to do so, why bring the cavalry forward at all? Still, this was not the only instance on that day of Sir Arthur favouring prudence; and he was never a great admirer of British cavalry.

We may now close the tale of Rolica, with the French leap-frogging pairs of battalions backwards down the half-mile spur beyond the ridge, to the village of Zambugeira. No doubt they kept half an eye on Ferguson's progress to their right, and the other half on the 20th Light Dragoons. Their 26e Chasseurs made mock charges to keep Wellesley's light troops at bay, although in one of these they lost their colonel. Beyond the village the spur narrows, with a defile. Although the French were not being unduly harried by the British (*see* Landsheit above), something of a traffic jam built up in the defile, with consequent panic and the abandonment of three guns and some prisoners.

Delaborde was joined a couple of miles down the Torres Vedras road by the three companies of the 70e Ligne who had spent the day in the eastern hills. Together they pressed on southwards all of twenty miles to Montechique, half way to Lisbon and deep in the broken, exhausting country that would later become host to the Lines of Torres Vedras. There Delaborde heard that his worn-out troops would now have to turn around and backtrack ten miles: Junot, and Loison at last, had marched in from the east behind him, and were at Torres Vedras. He joined them the next day, 20 August, and no doubt gave a positive report on this first encounter with the *Rosbiffs*. He had held the British on the Obidos plain for 48 hours and given them a bloody nose, gaining time for Junot and Loison to close up; and now here they were, three French generals together, concentrating a respectable force of some 11,000 infantry, 2,000 cavalry and twenty-three guns. He had fought a sound defensive battle on what amounted to a reverse slope, thus off-setting his inferiority in guns, fighting off repeated attempts at frontal assault, and twice extricating his battalions with sweet timing. For a man outnumbered four to one, Napoleon would surely approve the efforts that day of General of Division Henri-Francois Delaborde.

While Delaborde's retreat might conventionally imply a defeat, any fighting withdrawal in fair order which delays the enemy to good purpose, at the expense of modest own casualties, is rather a victory. So did Sir Arthur in fact lose the battle at Rolica?

* * *

That would be going too far the other way. He certainly achieved his aim of seeing off one of the two existing French columns he found on landing, before the second could join and before a third could materialize; and had he wished to press forward he had opened up another ten miles of the route to Lisbon, his geographical and political objective – Lisbon would then have been distant just one short march.

Given an enemy whose commander cannot afford to fight but can only seek to delay, any realistic prospect of doing him serious damage requires a swift envelopment. Some have therefore argued that Wellesley should have sent his flanking 'horns' on a night march, to get into a blocking position behind Delaborde before a quick dawn assault up the plain. After all, we know Wellesley received the news that Loison had turned south from Rio Major (away from Rolica) late on 16 August. If that were trustworthy intelligence, Ferguson need not have been given a dual role next morning, but simply sent hell-for-leather round behind Delaborde's right flank.

However, we must recall the events of eight years earlier in India, near Seringapatam, when in April 1799 the 29-year-old Lieutenant-Colonel Wellesley of the 33rd experienced all the confused horrors of an out-of-control night attack, put in without due reconnaissance. After this trauma he stated categorically that: 'I have come to a determination, when in my power, never to suffer an attack to be made by night upon an enemy who is prepared and strongly posted, and whose posts have not been reconnoitred by daylight.'

There speaks a prudent man – which is not the same as a cautious one, for caution had not hitherto characterized Wellesley's fighting career. In India he had invariably been outnumbered while frequently also unsure of his enemy's strengths and deployment. Yet time and again he would aim directly for his enemy's throat, promptly, decisively and without hesitation – his own version of Nelson's dictum, 'Never mind manoeuvring, go straight at 'em.' His conduct at Malavelly, Damal, Manauli, Arrakhera, Ahmednager, Assaye, Arguan and Gawilgarh between March 1799 and December 1803 was not that of a cautious commander. Yet at Rolica, up against a force that he believed to be less than half his own strength, he manoeuvered the morning away and then, when Delaborde finally started to fall back, refrained from committing either his reserve infantry brigade or his cavalry. (And this with six generals senior to him on the high seas to supersede him, and due any day.)

It is yet possible that Wellesley simply viewed Rolica as a necessary first opportunity to 'bed in' the small British army, for whoever was to command it. We should remind ourselves that only seventeen days earlier he had assured Castlereagh that 'I shall not hurry the operations, or commence them one moment sooner than they ought to be commenced, in order that I may acquire the credit for the business.' He would certainly be conscious of the army's general lack of physical stamina, of the untried command chain, of the inexperience of the soldiers, the commissariat and his own staff; and in this context a steady day's work on the plain at Obidos would be ideal. Sir Arthur could readily view 17 August as no more than a useful field day, assuming that he believed the intelligence reputedly passed to him by the nameless monk on the 16th, that Delaborde did not intend to fight. However, the overly gallant Colonel Lake turned the day into something more than a field-day, with 479 casualties of whom 190 were of Lake's battalion, and 72 of the 9th – that is, 269 or half Wellesley's losses were suffered in that one ravine behind Columbeira.

We close this chapter on the evening of 17 August with the words of an exhausted Lieutenant Charles Leslie of the 29th:

> The baggage did not come up until late in the evening. My servant had been severely wounded by a ball through his arm, so I had no one to do anything for me, and no means of cooking. I was fain to content myself with a morsel of cold beef and a ration biscuit which I found in my haversack, wrapped myself in my cloak, and lay down on the open heath, and slept soundly until before daybreak, when we stood to our arms (about two o'clock). The number of officers' servants who were hit in this action was very remarkable, there being no less than fifteen amongst the killed and wounded.

Without Lake's gallant but over-impetuous keenness, Wellesley would probably have done his business more cheaply, and poor Leslie would not have missed his cooked supper. But the great lesson of Rolica was that his largely inexperienced soldiers had gone up that ridge, faced fierce resistance at the top with true determination, and had eventually seen the backs of the French. They had given themselves stature, and thus confidence for the next time.

4
Vimiero,
21 August 1808

IN case Generals Junot and Loison joined up and decided to counter-attack, the well-exercised British battalions passed the hot, sticky night of 17 August – accoutred, cartridge boxes refilled and new flints fitted – on the starlit heights beyond Rolica. But dawn came quietly, and, having breakfasted and shaved, the troops were put to burying their dead and scouring the wooded hills for any wounded not collected the evening before – those, that is, not murdered, stripped and plundered by those few roving camp followers, peasants and malingers-on-the-make who hereafter were to dishonour every peninsula field of battle.

At 9am came news of reinforcements arrived from England, off Peniche twelve miles away. Since that place was still in French hands, Sir Arthur ordered their disembarkation at Maceira Bay, a further fifteen miles down the coast, near a village called Vimiero. He would march south-west immediately to cover the landings, the French reportedly having drawn off to the south-east. He despatched those orders with the greatest satisfaction: he would now have in hand another six battalions, and two more rifle companies – some 4,000 men in total, under Brigadiers Anstruther and Acland. He was all set to pursue Junot and advance to Lisbon, only two or three days' march away, and that with a choice of roads. There was the direct main route south through Torres Vedras (where the French lay) and Montechique, while to the west of it curled the longer coastal approach via Mafra. He would march that day (the 18th) towards Vimiero and his reinforcements, get them ashore on the 19th and 20th, and crack on for Lisbon the next day. While en route to Vimiero he could ponder how best to make his next move.

The general position that Sir Arthur mulled over in his saddle was thus: his 13,000 men plus eighteen guns would reach Lourinhao that afternoon; Brigadier Acland, 2,500 men and the supply ships were en route from Peniche to Maceira Bay, half a march from Lourinhao, with Brigadier Anstruther and another 1,500 men following a day behind; Junot and Loison with 6,500 and ten guns were at Torres Vedras, twelve miles from Wellesley; Delaborde with his 3,500 men and three guns was further down the Lisbon road at Montechique, twenty-five miles from Wellesley; and the 3,000 men with the ten guns Junot had extracted from the Lisbon garrison were en route to Torres Vedras from Villa Franca, way off to the east. The Lisbon garrison was now down to about 6,500 men, and the six companies of the 4e Suisse in Peniche were effectively bottled in, since Wellesley held the country to their east.

Thus the French total when concentrated was 13,000 men and twenty-three guns. Since 2,000 of these were cavalry he had a great superiority in that arm, for Sir Arthur still had only the 240 troopers of the skeletal 20th Light Dragoons. With eighteen guns the British were also uncomfortably adrift in that other vital department. But Wellesley's 17,000 infantry in twenty-one battalions (counting his newly arriving reinforcements) outnumbered Junot's 10,500 in fifteen battalions by about 3:2, and this edge was of course the important one, and more than he felt he needed. He wrote that day to Castlereagh: 'As soon as Anstruther is landed I shall be able to give you a good account of the French army; but I am afraid that I shall not gain a complete victory: that is, I shall not entirely destroy them, for want of cavalry.'

The wider picture, which Sir Arthur knew was looming over the horizon, was his supersession in command by Sir Hew Dalrymple or Sir Harry Burrard, whoever got there first; and the arrival of Sir John Moore's substantial reinforcement of 14,000 men and 1,500 horse. The former would incline any man to press on while he may; the latter would be a comforting thought while he did so, in case the French should overnight grow 10ft tall. In fact, Sir Harry was but two days' sail away, and Wellesley's time effectively had run out. Moore's vast 181-ship armada was tacking back and forth 300 miles to the north off Oporto, having been told by Burrard (oddly) to await further orders, but Moore sensibly chose to ignore this instruction when such orders failed to arrive. He pushed on to reach the Mondego late on 20 August, only two days behind Sir Harry. Finally, if the hovering Burrard was insufficient to quell Sir Arthur's offensive spirit, Sir Hew Dalrymple himself had now left Gibraltar for his new command and was just a day's sail below the Tagus. The shadow of imminent supersession deepened over Wellesley by the day.

On 19 August he reached the beaches near Vimiero, and that evening the 2/9th, 2/43rd, 2/52nd and 2/97th Foot – with an average strength of just over 600 each – came ashore under Brigadier Anstruther; Acland's 2nd, 1/20th and two rifle companies of the 1/95th landed on the evening of the next day. By lunchtime on the 20th Sir Arthur, wasting not a minute, had already ordered that the march to Lisbon would commence at 4.30am on the 21st, with 'half a pint of wine per man, and one day's meat for tomorrow, to be issued at four this evening to all the troops excepting Brigadier-General Anstruther's brigade, which will receive one pint of wine per man' (a decent welcome to the newcomers, indeed). The march was not to be against Junot's strong position behind Torres Vedras, but around him, along the coast road and then to Mafra, 25 miles from Lisbon.

This move being Junot's main fear now that he had concentrated his forces at Torres Vedras, the French general resolved to pre-empt the British coastal hook by bringing Wellesley to battle first, in his present location to the north and preferably with his back to the sea. It is believed that the arrival of Anstruther's and Acland's reinforcements had not been reported to Junot, notwithstanding that his cavalry had been venturing right on to the disembarkation beaches. (Napier states that they even carried off some of the women from the rear of the English camp.') It may have been, of course, that Junot did receive such reports but discounted them, as generals commonly do when an item of new intelligence tends to upset a plan already laid and going forward. Or it may more simply have been that Junot reckoned any two Frenchmen were more than a match for three Englishmen (or rather, two Englishmen and one Irishman, since it is thought that around a quarter of Wellesley's men were from Ireland).

So, with his reserve from Lisbon joining him on the morning of the 20th, after resting during the daylight hours Junot marched under cover of darkness to close the ten miles to Vimiero. It was a bold decision, if he knew that his fifteen battalions and four cavalry regiments faced twenty-one enemy battalions, and says much for the opinion that French generals had acquired of themselves while somewhat sheltered over the years by Napoleon's genius (and, invariably, by his presence).

Having now brought Sir Arthur and his opposite number within battle distance of one another for the second time in four days, we need to pause in the narrative of events to consider, at a tangent as it were, the approach of Sir Harry Burrard and his state of mind – so far as that is possible. It was to be Sir Harry who let Junot off Wellesley's hook, and prevented Sir Arthur from landing a far heavier catch. Burrard thus has much to answer for – yet perhaps even more so do the soldiers' political masters back in London.

*   *   *

Two days earlier, when he reached Mondego Bay, Burrard had received three letters from Wellesley, all of them at least a week old. Apart from two gun batteries that lacked their horses, Wellesley and his army had left the bay ten days since. In his evidence to the Cintra inquiry, Burrard would state that 'Some rumours had reached Captain Malcolm that day [the naval commander who had handed over Wellesley's letters] that an engagement had taken place, and as the intelligence ought to have reached him regularly [that is, not simply as rumours], he [Malcolm] seemed uneasy.'

Burrard might well have been put out that Wellesley was not at Mondego Bay, courteously awaiting both himself and his reinforcements. His sense of unease at the rumours of battle, and the absence of the army he had been sent to command pending the arrival of Dalrymple, would not have been quietened when he opened Wellesley's letters. For while taking in Sir Arthur's gloomy if realistic opinion that 'no reliance could be placed on the resources of the country', Burrard then had to grapple with the eye-popping recommendation that Sir John Moore 'should march upon Santarem on the Tagus [a mere 100 miles away], and there take up a position to stop the enemy should he attempt that route'. A quick look at his maps would have convinced Sir Harry not to leave any such orders for Sir John (neither did he deign to leave any others, either), but to put back to sea immediately, to sail south find Wellesley, and discover just what the blazes this young sepoy general was about. For in his letter Wellsley had put the French strength at 16,000-18,000 men compared to his own 13,500 – yet here he was, calmly proposing to dispatch Moore's 14,000 reinforcement on a seven-day march inland. Clearly, the obvious thing to do was to join forces and thus outnumber the French. As for Santarem, Burrard was to tell the Cintra inquiry that he doubted if

Sir John's division [was] sufficiently strong to check the French army… [If] the intention of its chief had been to force his way to Almeida… the danger of pushing a corps to Santarem, much inferior to what the enemy could have brought against it, would have made me decline that operation… The division on the coast would have also been inferior, though in a lesser degree, and that want of cooperation might have been equally felt by both. On all these considerations I rather put this operation out of my mind at that time.

So Burrard fretted his way south on 18 August towards Maceira Bay. Unfortunately for his peace of mind, the next day off Sao Martinho do Porto, adjacent to Alcobaza, his ship met up with a despatch boat

with two English soldiers and a marine, who were returning from St Martins to the Burlings; from them we learned that a sharp action had taken place on the 17th, at or near Obidos, and that a great many men were killed on both sides, that we had suffered much, but that the enemy had retreated. The man gave me so many proofs of having been present at what he said he had seen, that I could have no doubt, and I therefore became extremely anxious that some part, or all, of Sir John Moore's corps should land at Mondego, and either support Sir Arthur Wellesley if his division should be obliged to fall back, or to assist it to advance if a superior force had stopped it… It was evident, from the intelligence of these men [two private soldiers and a marine!] that Peniche was not in our possession, and I knew of no certainty, or even probability of a landing elsewhere to the south of it.

Poor Sir Harry was by now an increasingly unhappy general. Visions would be growing in his mind of a marginal victory won at great cost by rash young Wellesley, now up against a more numerous enemy and either held or – much worse – retiring. Quickly Sir Harry scribbled a few lines to Moore, with copies of Wellesley's letters, and sent a staff officer at all best speed in the despatch boat:

I began to be apprehensive that, should he [Wellesley] meet with a superior force, he will have nothing to fall back upon; and as I find he means to go directly on to the attack of Junot at Lisbon, there is no time to be lost… I think you cannot do better than to land with all expedition, procuring as many mules and bullock carts as you can, and proceeding to Leira.

Yet the distance from Mondego Bay to Obidos is eighty miles, and if Wellesley was really pushing forward 'to attack Junot at Lisbon' – another fifty miles on – then how on earth could Moore get into any sort of early position where he could join forces? Putting Moore ashore up at Mondego Bay made sense only if a beaten Wellesley were retiring; it was otherwise a disastrous course of action, and speaks much for Burrard's ever-growing concerns and cautions.

The next day his simmering doubts came to the boil. Arriving in Maceira Bay in the afternoon of 20 August, and threading his way through the mass of transports, supply ships and escorts riding calmly at anchor, his enormous relief at joining at last his temporary command, and any pleasure at that prospect, were shattered when Sir Arthur himself climbed aboard with his briefing and his plans. According to Burrard's evidence to the Cintra inquiry, Sir Arthur

> told me most fully what the difficulties were I should have to encounter; he mentioned his want of cavalry, and the inefficiency of the artillery horse, and that the enemy were strong in the former; that their cavalry had already come very near them, and had kept them close to their encampments, and it was unsafe to stray out of them; that it would not be possible to go so far into the country, at a distance from the victuallers [i.e. ships], for from them we must depend on our bread.

This gloomy briefing (if such it really was, and not just portrayed as such to the inquiry) clearly put Burrard in the the worst possible frame of mind for Wellesley's next bombshell: that notwithstanding these difficulties, he had just issued orders to the army to march south early the next morning. Sir Harry promptly demurred from undertaking any such apparently doubtful operation, there being 'considerations... sufficiently weighty to authorize me to wait for the reinforcements which were at hand [that is, Moore]'. Burrard would not be shaken from this determination by Wellesley's subsequent arguments for the push to Mafra. Wellesley also brought up the reasons for Moore's corps to take up a blocking position at Santarem, concluding – to Burrard's obvious horror – that he 'considered this position [Santarem] so little dangerous, and at the same time so advantageous, that if the brigades of Brigadier-Generals Acland and Anstruther had been equipped to act independently of any other body of troops, [he] should have ordered those brigades to occupy it' – that is, Wellesley was calmly prepared to cut his own strength back to 13,500 in the face of Junot's 16,000–18,000.

Faced with what he regarded as astonishing irresponsibility, Sir Harry decided that he must act before Sir Arthur came up with something even more outrageous. He again forbade the next day's move, and in Wellesley's presence wrote new orders to Moore, who was now to re-embark himself and his disembarked troops immediately and sail for Maceira Bay, 'as I am desirous that you should join me yourself as soon as you can... circumstances seeming to render it expedient that the force here should be reinforced by the addition of the troops under your orders.' This letter he gave to Sir Arthur, requesting that it be sent quickly to Sir John – a little matter of a hundred miles up the coast.

Croker quotes Wellesley thus: '[Burrard] desired me to suspend all operations and said he would do nothing until he had collected all the force... a decision with which I was not pleased any more than I was with the manner in which it was made.' He was still furious nine hours later, after a broken sleep and in disappointed frustration, after news of Junot's night advance (*see* below) seemed false; he wrote to Castlereagh:

My Dear Lord, Sir Harry Burrard will probably acquaint your Lordship with the reasons which have induced him to call Sir John Moore's corps to the assistance of our army, which consists of 20,000 men, including the Portuguese army… and is opposed, I am convinced, by not more than 12,000 or 14,000 Frenchmen, and to halt them here until Sir John's corps shall join. You will readily believe, however, that this determination is not in conformity with my opinion, and I only wish Sir Harry had landed and seen things with his own eyes.

After Wellesley had gone ashore at around 9pm, Burrard wrote a second letter to Moore, which went immediately by frigate, and which carried the clear and urgent message that the army at Maceira was in a critical position. Having duly spread his alarm and despondency, Burrard went to bed aboard ship, while Wellesley sent round to his brigades the counter-order that 'the army will halt tomorrow. The men to sleep accoutred tonight, in readiness to turn out, and to be under arms at three o'clock in the morning.'

While Sir Harry's final and most critical application of the brakes upon Sir Arthur was yet to come, sympathy for his position at this stage is quite in order. Here was a man who had arrived on the eve of battle, entirely ignorant of the local situation, as second-in-command but without his commander, and therefore as nominal commander-in-chief stranded temporarily in a most invidious limbo. He would get no acclaim for any victory, but any disaster – in his view a much more likely outcome – would certainly fall on his shoulders. The man on the ground was plainly overconfident and disdainful of his enemy; he had already demonstrated his imprudence, yet planned to continue it, with the lightest of hearts. And all this a long way from home, with the ultimate guarantor of safety – His Majesty's ships – necessarily dependent upon wind and tide. In this context, we should take into account that ten years previously, near Ostend, Sir Harry had been forced to surrender with over 1,000 men because a gale stopped his re-embarkation after a raid, and also that the following year he was very nearly forced to repeat the experience during the Helder expedition under the Duke of York. In his present situation, therefore, caution was quite understandable.

Burrard was also, as it happened, quite right to believe that the French were stronger than Wellesley allowed, if wrong in his deduction therefrom – i.e. the imperative to keep clear of them until Moore joined up. It is also the case, as Fortescue reminds us, that this 'steady old Guardsman of no exceptional military talent' was an admirer of Moore. He was certainly ready and willing to be superseded in due course by Sir John, and it may well be that when he climbed into his cot on HMS *Brazon* that night before the battle of Vimiero, he was heartily wishing he were somewhere else. On the other hand, when he woke next morning to hear incoming French cannon fire just over Vimiero hill, he must have taken some satisfaction at the sepoy general's embarrassment ('now, tell me, Nimmuk Wallah – didn't you say they were at Torres Vedras, ten miles away?'…)

*   *   *

For the French were indeed coming for the British, before they got any stronger. Junot's night approach march to Vimiero was reported to Sir Arthur around midnight on 20 August, so within three hours of leaving Burrard his low spirits would have soared, and one imagines he made no great effort to send a boat to rouse Sir Harry. Could it be possible that Junot was proposing to hurl his army at the British, presumably at first light? Could the Frenchman be so stupid? 'In the dead of night a fellow came in – a German sergeant or quarter-master – in a great fright – so that his hair seemed actually to stand on end – who told us that the enemy was advancing rapidly, and would soon be on us.' That German was Sergeant Norbert Landsheit of the 20th Light Dragoons, whose memoirs (while denying that he was in any sort of fright, still less with upstanding hair), provide us with an evocative insight into the workings of a small cavalry patrol that night:

> The patrol, consisting of twelve men and a corporal, besides myself, mounted and took the road as soon as I had received my instructions. These were, to move very slowly to the front, keeping every eye and ear on the alert, til we should reach the Red Chapel – not to engage an enemy's patrol, should we fall in with one – to hasten back to the piquet on the first appearance of danger – and on no account to trust ourselves beyond the limits which General Fane had marked out. Thus instructed, I ordered the men to march; and, as far as silence and an acute observation could go, we obeyed the officer's directions to the letter. Nor, indeed, would it have been easy, on such a night, and when so occupied, to indulge in idle or ribald conversation. The moon shone full and bright, millions of stars were abroad, and the silence was so profound, that the very ripple of the stream could be heard as it wound its tortuous way along the base of the hill down the slope of which we were riding... The world seemed asleep; and we reached the Red Chapel, fully assured that no enemy was or could be within many miles of us. At the Red Chapel we halted, quitted our horses and, holding the bridles over our arms, applied ourselves to the contents of our haversacks and canteens... My men again mounted, and taking every possible precaution, by sending forward a corporal and a file of troopers to feel the way, we pushed on. At the meeting of the roads the advanced file had pulled up, and once more we were all together; when I directed two men to pass to the right, two to the left, and, with the main body under my command, I kept the centre. We were to meet in the square or open space round which the village was built, and to communicate each to the other the results of our investigations.
>
> Everything was done with the most perfect regularity. My party, having the shortest distance to travel, was the first to reach the village square, though the detachments were not long after us; and we found, on comparing notes, that the same tranquility had prevailed here which had prevailed else-where. Now then, what should we do? I recollected the innkeeper, and thinking it not impossible that he might have acquired more information since General Fane had examined him, I rode to his house, and asked whether all was quiet?

'I am glad you have come,' replied the padrone, 'for I have some important news to tell you. My young man came home from Lisbon an hour ago, and passed the whole of the French army on its march; and so close are they by this time, that I expect them in the village in less than half an hour.' I questioned him very closely as to the degree of dependence that might be placed on his report, and he assured me there could be no mistake in it; adding, his advice that I would return to the English camp without delay, and put the General on his guard. I did not think that it would be prudent to neglect the recommendation, so I stated to my comrades how matters stood, and we evacuated the village.

It is not our policy, however, to return to the camp with a vague rumour. We were inclined to believe the innkeeper, certainly, yet we wished to have his tale confirmed; so I halted the patrol as soon as we regained the Red Chapel, and determined to wait the event. I knew that the advance of the enemy, if it did occur, would be made known to us clearly enough by the clatter of their horses' hoofs when crossing the wooden bridge, by which alone they would enter the village; and being now within my prescribed limits, and having a good half-mile start of all pursuers, the thought of danger never crossed my mind. Accordingly, having placed a couple of vedettes somewhat lower on the slope, in such a situation that they could not be surprised, I directed the remainder to alight, and to keep their ears open. For a while all was still. Not a breeze stirred the branches; not a bird or beast uttered a cry; indeed, the only sound distinguishable was the running water, which came upon us most musically. But by and by 'a change came over the spirit of our dream'. Wheels began to rumble; there was a dead heavy noise, like the tread of many feet over a soft soil; and then, the wooden bridge rang again with the iron hoofs of horses. Immediately the vedettes fell back, according to my orders, to report what they had heard, and to learn from us that we had heard it also; and then, after waiting a sufficient time, to leave no doubt upon our minds as to the formidable extent of the column that was moving, we vaulted into our saddles, and returned at a brisk trot towards the piquet.

There was much challenging, of course, as we drew towards the vedettes, and demanding and giving the countersign; for we rode briskly; and whether we came as friend or foes, our people knew that there must be something in the wind.

Sergeant Landsheit reported at once to Brigadier Fane, commanding the outposts, who of course sent him straight to repeat his story to Sir Arthur:

I rode to the house where the general dwelt, and being admitted, I found him, with a large staff, all seated on a long table in the hall, back to back, swinging their legs to and fro, like men on whose minds not a shadow of anxiety rested. The general himself... closely examined me, and told me I had done my duty well. He then desired me go below and get something to eat and drink from his servant, which I did, though not till I heard him give his orders, in a calm, clear and cheerful voice. They were in substance these: 'Now, gentlemen, go to your stations; but let there be no noise made – no sounding of bugles or beating of drums. Get your men quietly under arms, and desire all the outposts to be on the alert.'

It may be, however, that Sir Arthur already knew, hours earlier, of Junot's intentions. Captain Landmann, the senior engineer, tells us that all commanding officers had already been briefed on the expected French attack at 8pm at headquarters. Landmann not being able to attend, he says that:

> Sir Arthur had desired Robe [the artillery commander] to acquaint me that tomorrow we should be attacked and therefore I must make any arrangements I might think necessary to meet that event; and he particularly enjoined that the strictest secrecy must be observed. The secret was properly kept from the army in general... at between seven and eight o'clock [in the morning], some distant firing of small arms announced that the advanced piquets were engaged, and that the information Sir Arthur had received on the preceeding day was correct.

Perhaps, as before Rolica, a friendly monk had tipped Wellesley off. However, this recollection of Landmann's does not tie in with other sources stating that Sir Arthur was with Sir Harry Burrard until 9pm the previous evening; we should also note that Landmann's *Recollections* were published nearly half a century after the battle.

In any case, our gallant German dragoon certainly put confident words into his general's mouth that night, and we may be sure they reflect the spirit of whatever Sir Arthur actually said. In the mind of any ordinary commander there must have lurked a private uncertainty. His present dispositions had not been made to fight a defensive battle, but were no more than a temporary overnight camp site to cover the landing of his reinforcements, prior to launching his own approach march at dawn. Junot had beaten him to it; he had been humbugged, as he would say. Junot was about to erupt out of the darkness from the south with fifteen battalions totalling 10,000 foot and 2,000 horse, while Wellesley's first line comprised just seven battalions totalling 4,700 men. Much worse, behind this tripwire but in front of the remainder of his army, Sir Arthur – when planning to march out the next morning – had positioned a thousand bullocks, 400 to 500 mules, 400 bullock carts, his commissariat stores, food, fodder, ammunition, baggage, his artillery park, his cavalry lines and his headquarters. The only escape route for all this impedimenta back to the beachhead lay through a narrow gorge immediately in rear, between two formidable ridges, while behind his main line was the sea itself. If Junot could only get into this soft centre – if he could just slip his twenty squadrons of sabre-wielding cavalry in there – the word impedimenta would demonstrate its real meaning, and the British would be plunged into the greatest difficulties.

Sir Arthur's administrative dispositions of the previous evening now not only fell short of a model Staff College solution, they were looking foolhardy. He had clearly banked on getting away to the south early on the morning of 21 August (in which case the train could indeed laager anywhere); but the sudden appearance of Burrard and his veto on the march turned Wellesley's decision to put the tail of his planned column in front of his main position into an uncomfortable nonsense.

Since it could well take Sir John Moore ten days to a fortnight to concentrate and march down from Mondego (if that is where he had reached when Sir Harry's urgent call got through), then the next morning – faced with such a lengthy stay at Vimiero, and if Junot had not appeared immediately – any ordinary general would certainly have set about constructing a proper defensive position, removing his train from where they were cluttering up the potential battlefield and repositioning them back towards Porto Novo. But after leaving Sir Harry's ship so late in the evening Wellesley had had no time to effect changes that night; and Junot was thus presented with a juicy target for the morning.

Sir Arthur had positioned his train in an area measuring roughly a half-mile by a quarter, conveniently next to the bridge and the five roads meeting at Vimiero. Captain Landmann had been told to reconnoitre and recommend a suitable location for the artillery park and so forth, and what he describes as a 'fine level meadow... [with] the Maceira stream serpentining thro' this flat space' was readily accepted. Charles Leslie of the 29th described the area as

> a flat low space between [the village] and the foot of the heights, on which were placed the parks of artillery, commissariat stores, bullock-carts, oxen etc. The whole had an imposing and picturesque effect, particularly at night, when illuminated with the glare of the camp fires on the heights, and those of the artillery and stores, surrounded by groups of soldiers and peasants, drivers, and others, in the low grounds, and the advance guard beyond the town.

Half a mile to the south-east lay the forward slopes of a rising ground, which had the village on the northern side. On these slopes Wellesley had placed Fane and Anstruther's seven battalions, with six guns. Fortescue, who walked the ground in 1903, says that the battalions 'were drawn up with their artillery on the flat summit of the hill, upon open ground, with a belt of scrub about 150 yards to their front.' There was a fold in the ground on the right (Anstruther's) side, enough to shelter and hide from their front a battalion in line. Hedges, vineyards and small woods ran away to the south-east, and to the east up the long valley taking the Lourinhao road. The rising ground has become known as Vimiero Hill, but in truth it is merely the nearest of five such modest features to the south and east of the village.

Behind Vimiero sat a huge ridge five miles long, broken in two by the deep gorge of the River Maceira immediately north of the village. The ridge on the eastern side towered over the road to Lourinhao, a three mile spur merging eventually into the hill system to the north. A hamlet called Ventosa lay half way along this eastern ridge, 500ft above Vimiero and a mile and a half north-east from it, on a flattish plateau where the ridge broadens. A north-south track connects Ventosa with a similar hamlet called Toledo, down on the Lourinhao road, the line of which parallels a sharp-sided dry ravine cut by the winter rains.

The ridge on the western side of the Vimiero gorge is a formidable defensive position, 300ft high and with a virtually unclimbable southern face at the seaward end, while the northern is a rocky precipice rising sheer from the River Maceira. Both western and eastern ridges have rough tracks running down from the spines, into the central gorge above Vimiero. Sir Arthur had parked thirteen battalions on the western ridge, where there was water, and one battalion on the eastern ridge, where there was none. Trant's Portuguese battalions were at the village of Maceira, just in rear of the gorge. It is plain, therefore, that both the British bridgehead and the baggage train were wide open from the north, via the hill road from Mariquiteira to Maceira, and from the eastern ridge itself via Ventosa. Only a French attack on Vimiero village up from the south, along the axis of the Torres Vedras road in the valley of the Maceira river, could be resisted with confidence by Wellesley's troops as presently deployed. All other approaches would demand that he thinned out the largely irrelevant western ridge, and redeploy accordingly.

Interestingly – since it shows that Wellesley was no ordinary general – as dawn came and went without the French, and the early morning hours passed, Wellesley made no effort to shift his train away from the front, and nor did he redeploy troops to the nearly empty eastern ridge. The only troop movements that he made were to hurry Acland's brigade, who had only finally come up at 6am, to the western ridge, to thicken the defensive line. Since the most likely French approach from the south would be directly up the Maceira river road, Wellesley was quite right to sit tight and await events. In such a dry landscape, events would come well-heralded by clouds of dust. With thirteen battalions within one mile of the nearly defenceless eastern ridge, he needed only an hour's warning of French intentions to make his adjustments, and we may be sure that the nearest battalions would be on very short notice to move. As for his train behind the village, doubtless he could picture the scene would probably ensue if he gave an order to move it back. The combination of a single road down a gorge, 1,000 Portuguese muleteers, 2,000 animals, and hundreds of carts, moving along a road that crossed his vital access tracks from west to east ridges, would make no sense at that early stage in the proceedings. Even so, many generals would have taken that risk, out of a lack of confidence in their ability to manoeuvre in the face of their enemy. Sir Arthur did not suffer any such lack.

Neither did General Jean-Andoche Junot, who halted his men just before first light, four miles from Vimiero near the village of Villa Facaia, where the wooden bridge had echoed to Sergeant Landsheit's dragoons the night before. The French ate breakfast, rested their feet, took off their faded blue coats and strapped them across their knapsacks, donning instead the long white linen 'frocks' (soon to turn khaki in the dust) which were so much better suited to the coming furnace of a day. Junot had reorganized his force into two divisions, under Delaborde and Loison, each of two brigades, under Brigadiers Brennier, Thomières, Solignac and Charlot respectively. It should be noted that Junot kept Brennier's and Solignac's brigades at twice the size of those of Thomières and Charlot. In addition, General of Division Francois Kellerman commanded the reserve, of four weakish battalions formed of the grenadier companies drawn from every battalion in Portugal. Grenadiers being chosen men – an honourable selection – we should regard Kellerman's command as the elite formation; however, since Brennier's four battalions were those that had held the ridge at Rolica, they too could claim to know something about fighting British troops.

Finally, apart from the twenty-three guns, we note Junot's 2,200 sabres in one chasseur and three dragoon regiments, commanded by General Margaron. The going around Vimiero was not exactly ideal cavalry country, but that would not matter if they got in amongst those 1,000 muleteers and their charges behind the hill.

There are conflicting views on whether, while his men ate and rested, Junot made a reconnaissance of Wellesley's positions. He was known in the army as 'the Hurricane', and described by his own chief-of-staff General Thiebault as 'headstrong and fiery... blindly courageous... the only thing he understood was shock action', so any reconnaissance he undertook was likely to be perfunctory. At the very least the size of the western ridge, once seen, would confirm any right-thinking general in the view that it should be left quite alone. The sea being where it was, most would prefer a bludgeon straight at Vimiero in the middle, and a right hook to block the retreat – all finished by mid-morning, and another predictable success for the invincible French army (news of Baylen not yet having reached Junot). So Charlot's and Thomières' small brigades, totalling just four battalions, would be sent to take Vimiero, with Solignac's three in the second line, and Kellerman's four in reserve ready to exploit wherever the British first gave way, as they surely would. Meanwhile Brennier's big brigade, plus the 3e Dragons and six guns, would get astride the Ventosa–Lourinhao road up on the eastern ridge. This was an entirely sound if obvious plan, and if Junot came to it after scant reconnaissance then it was all the more luckily inspired: unless Wellesley took counter-measures Junot would be bringing eleven battalions against Anstruther and Fane's six-and-a half on Vimiero Hill.

A couple of hours after he had written his rather bitter letter to Castlereagh about 'Betty' Burrard's veto on offensive action, Sir Arthur's delighted attention was drawn to a moving dust cloud away to the south-east. It was another hour before the khaki-coated French beneath it could be seen, according to Wellesley's Despatch, 'as large bodies of cavalry on our left, upon the heights on the road to Lourinhao; and it was soon obvious that the attack would be made upon our advance guard and the left of our position.' By then the progress of the dust clearly indicated that the French advance was well to the east of the British, along the Torres Vedras-Lourinhao road – that is, not directly north to Vimiero. Unless this was a ruse, Wellesley's thirteen battalions on the western ridge were becoming quite redundant, and the eastern ridge was quite bare. After a prudent pause orders were sent to ten of the thirteen battalions to move ridges as soon as may be, leaving just 'Daddy' Hill's 1st Brigade on the heights west of the gorge; and he was relocated much closer, a few hundred yards above and to the west of the area of the baggage train, south of the Maceira gorge and to the west of the village. William Warre, a captain in the 23rd Dragoons and ADC to General Ferguson, wrote of this a month later:

> About eight I was woken by a sergeant, who told me that our piquets of the 40th [sic] on the left were driven in and the enemy advancing. I ran to tell

Genl Ferguson, and we were soon on horseback and on the hill on the left, from whence we had a full view of the French Army, on its march to attack us in two strong columns. The strongest and principal attack was on our centre, and the other against the hill, and left of our position, which was separated from the centre by a deep valley covered with vineyards, occupied by our light troops, and to the top of which Genl Ferguson ordered his Brigade to advance to await their attack.

Sir A. Wellesley arrived soon after, as I had been sent to tell him of the attack, and perceiving the intention of the enemy, ordered Genl Bowes' and Genl Acland's brigades to support Genl Ferguson's; he made his dispositions in the most cool and masterly style, as from our commanding situation we could see all the movements of the French and of our own army.

(It is curious that Warre has his beloved brigade commander initiating the movement of troops from west to east ridges, with the commander-in-chief arriving after the event apparently just to confirm it and to finish off the redeployment. We may reasonably question this version of events…)

A similar bird's-eye view from the new position of Nightingall's brigade was described by Lieutenant Charles Leslie of the battered 29th:

Our brigade, consisting of the 29th and 82nd Regiments, under General Nightingall, were ordered to support the force under General Ferguson, who was posted on the heights to the left of the town, and towards which the enemy's column was pointing. Our men were directed to leave their knapsacks in the camp under charge of the quarter guard. On reaching the foot of the heights the road was found to be so steep and heavy that two companies of the 29th Regiment were ordered to assist in dragging the guns up in addition to the artillery horses. After gaining the ascent, the 29th, being the leading regiment, moved along the edge of the heights, which sloped abruptly to the valley below. From this point we had a grand view of the country to our right below. We could distinctly observe every movement made either by our own right wing, which was posted partly in the town and along a rising ground to a wood on the extreme right, or those made by the enemy, then forming preparatory to their grand attack, while the light troops and riflemen were warmly engaged.

Opinions vary as to whether Junot saw this west-to-east movement of some 9,000 redcoats. The descent of the western ridge would have been mostly in view, but not the climb up beyond Vimiero and behind the crest of the eastern ridge – though presumably there was a tell-tale dust cloud. In any case, Junot now had second thoughts about the security of Brennier's large brigade, well on their way north to turn that same eastern ridge. His natural but misguided reaction to Wellesley's redeployment, which called into question the strength of Brennier's right hook, was to redeploy himself: and he sent away Solignac's large brigade, to climb the eastern ridge towards Ventosa in support of Brennier's left.

Thus Junot gave up his intended second wave of attack against Vimiero village; and, since Brennier was well out into the hills by this time, Solignac's march in pursuit now meant that the French army was already divided into three parts. These were very muddled parts, too: for the direct advance against Vimiero, Junot had retained a small brigade from each of his two divisions, separating off Brennier's stronger brigade from Delaborde's division and now Solignac's from Loison's, so that neither general had his division intact under his hand, or complete command of his own regiments. Much the better solution (as Junot's chief-of-staff would later write) would have been to send not Solignac to join Brennier, but Delaborde himself with his second brigade, that of Thomières, leaving Loison and his complete division to capture Vimiero village.

In the event, as we shall see, Junot seemed to make no attempt to co-ordinate the movements of the two brigades out in the hills, either in their own approach marches to a blocking position, or in relation to his own central thrust against Vimiero. His lack of thorough reconnaissance meant that neither he nor his brigadiers appreciated the steepness of the Toledo valley along the southern edge of the eastern ridge, which therefore required a much wider turning movement. And Junot's thrust at Vimiero, now of just four battalions and seventeen guns, was never going to break Anstruther and Fane's six-and-a half with twelve guns, still less get near the baggage train. In effect, although he did not know it, Junot had just engineered two quite separate battles.

Before a shot was fired, Junot's decisions were causing raised eyebrows. Thiebault, then his chief staff officer, was later to write the following extraordinary criticism of his commander: 'Some thought that during the outdoor breakfast of which we had just been partaking, at which the General had drunk various wines and liqueurs, he had taken too much or, at any rate, too much considering the heat of the day, if not in actual quantity. Others maintained that the sight of the enemy or the smell of the powder excited him until he lost the use of his faculties.' Strong feelings, strongly expressed, even for an egalitarian army – and presumably written with some of the hindsight that Junot's eventual insanity would reasonably permit. Yet while there is often only a thin line between madness and boldness, and it would be good to judge him bold rather than mad, the whole of Junot's plan and its execution reeked of contempt for the British. The looseness of his arrangements, however, was about to extract an instructive price.

*   *   *

Sir Arthur was up on the eastern ridge, placing his brigades and keeping an eye on the progress of Brennier's dust – followed by Solignac's – when he saw Junot's approach develop towards Vimiero. Two French columns, a quarter-mile apart, were moving across his front from left to right, on either side of the road from Carrasqueira. Horsemen skirted along the flanks and forward, as best they could over the broken ground, with field guns in the centre. *Tirailleurs* began to run out ahead of the columns as shields, and would soon be in business. Each column comprised two battalions, one behind the other, some thirty men wide and forty-two ranks in depth – great masses of men, dirty white and dust-covered, keeping step to the beat of the drums. Thomières' brigade (led by Delaborde himself) was on the right – the 1st and 2nd Battalions of the 86e Ligne, plus two companies of the 4e Suisse; in the left column, Loison led Charlot's 3/32e and 3/82e Ligne – a total of some 4,000 infantry with seven guns. Behind the two assault columns came more horse, Junot and his staff, and then his reserve of the four grenadier battalions, led by General Kellerman and commanded in pairs by Colonels Maransin and St Clair. The thudding rhythm of the drums echoed two miles to the eastern ridge, where British spectators watched this splendid spectacle.

Wellesley had placed the two brigades on Vimiero Hill under the command of Brigadier Anstruther. Three battalions lined the reverse slopes of the crest: Fane's 1/50th (West Kents) on the left behind a minor hillock, with Anstruther's 2/97th (Queen's Own Germans) on its right, in a fold in the ground which hid it from the front, and the 2/52nd (Oxfordshire) angled slightly in echelon. Anstruther's other two battalions were in open column behind the crest, the 2/9th (Norfolk) behind the left flank of the 2/97th, and the 2/43rd (Monmouthshire) behind their right flank. Batteries of 9-pounder and 6-pounder guns – twelve pieces – were distributed in fours in the centre and on the flanks.

Apart from the 50th, Fane's brigade comprised three companies of the 5/60th Rifles, four of the 2/95th Rifles under the popular Major Travers, and one of the 1/95th (the other seven had been allocated one each to the other brigades, in Sir Arthur's pre-battle reorganization to improve the marksmanship of the skirmishing lines). Of these eight rifle companies, most had been sent forward to the bottom of Vimiero Hill to act as a thick tripwire spreading right across the front of both brigades. The 5/60th were in front of Fane's 50th and the 95th in front of Anstruther's 2/97th and 2/52nd, with a thin piquet line half a mile forward in the brushwood, vines, and broken woodlands on the far slopes, where the ground rose up to the Carrasqueira feature.

A light infantryman could ask for little better than the nature of the ground in front of Vimiero Hill – open fields mixed with thickets, vineyards, hedges and trees. It is classic skirmishing country, which would have been appreciated not only by Fane's riflemen below the hill, but also by Anstruther's 2/43rd and 2/52nd at the top; these units were specialist light infantry, who had been trained by Sir John Moore himself at Shorncliffe (with the 95th Rifles) only four years previously. Indeed, we may note that the landing of Acland's and Anstruther's battalions concluded an historic concentration of trained light troops, destined now to march together and fight the French for the next six years: the 1st and 2nd Battalions, 95th (Rifles), the rifle-armed 5/60th (Royal Americans), the 2/43rd (Monmouthshire) Light Infantry and 2/52nd (Oxfordshire) Light Infantry. The two companies of the 1/95th commanded by Captains Cameron and Ramage came 200 strong from Harwich, under the renowned Lieutenant-Colonel Beckwith, and after the battle of Vimiero they effectively joined the 2nd Battalion.

It was certainly hot work for the men in green. Brigadier Robert Anstruther wrote in his journal that: 'The enemy came rapidly along the road, directly in front of the

50th, and when within nine hundred yards deployed to their left, so as to put their front parallel to ours.' The captain of Harris' company in the 2/95th, Jonathan Leach, wrote in a letter penned four days after the battle :'On the night of the 20th I was on an out-piquet with a Field Officer (Major Hill, 50th) and one hundred men. Nothing occurred during the night but about seven in the morning the enemy began to appear on some hills to our front'. Later, in his *Sketches*, Leach would add: 'and shortly… several immense columns made their appearance towards the right and centre… The piquets being only a handful of men by way of a look-out to prevent surprise, were ordered to check the French columns by a running fire as much as possible, and to retreat firing.' Indeed, so quickly did the French come on that a number of riflemen in the piquets were taken prisoner. Captain Patterson, of the Light Company of the 50th:

> About 8 o'clock… the piquets, commanded by Captain Thos Snowe of the 60th… strengthened by the 4th battalion company of that regiment, under Captain Coote… a sharp discharge of small arms was kept up by a cloud of French riflemen [sic], who gathering round under cover of the vines and corn-fields, gave their fire with a degree of activity that certainly did them credit… They [60th] kept their ground under a galling and destructive fire, from an enemy whom they were unable to answer or even see…

Captain Leach again:

> About 8 or 9 o'clock a cloud of light troops, supported by a heavy column of infantry, entered the wood, and assailing the piquets with great impetuosity, obliged us to fall back. We remained in the wood until several men were killed and the shots flew like hail when the Field Officer of the piquets ordered us to retreat precipitately as our Artillery dare not fire a shot at the French columns (which were pressing hastily on) til we fell back.

Captain Patterson:

> The piquets extending right and left immediately fell back, under a shower of bullets, from the enemy's light troops, who continued forcing on in spite of all opposition.

Rifleman Harris:

> I myself was so soon hotly engaged, loading and firing away, enveloped in the smoke I created, and the cloud which hung about me from the continued fire of my comrades, that I could see nothing for a few minutes but the red flash of my piece amongst the white vapour clinging to my very clothes… the French, in great numbers, came steadily down upon us, and we pelted away upon them like a shower of leaden hail.

Captain Leach:

> We retreated down a vineyard and up another hill before we could gain the British line, the whole time exposed to the fire of a battalion of infantry.

Captain Patterson:

> We gave them in return the full benefit of our small shot, as we occasionally drew up, covered by vine hedges and olive trees, that lay within our path; and in this manner, alternatively firing and retreating, so as to keep the foe aloof, we gained our situation in the line.

In his letter, Leach wrote: 'When we reached the lines, the Artillery opened with most wonderful effect... I gathered the few of my scattered piquet who I could get together, and found our companies with the 50th Regt in the thickest of it, and here there was nothing else (I can describe it no better) than a hail-shower of bullets.'

Brigadier Anstruther was acutely aware that his twelve guns could not engage the approaching columns until the rifle companies were out of the way. Lieutenant-Colonel William Robe, Sir Arthur's artillery commander, was just as keen to open fire, not least because he wished to try Major Shrapnel's new spherical case-shot. Consequently, Anstruther sent out the Light Company of the 2/97th and three companies of the 2/52nd, to cover and thereby hasten the retreat of the riflemen. The movement forward of these four companies caught the horrified eye of Sir Arthur, up on the eastern ridge, who for a moment must have feared for Anstruther's sanity. He told Lieutenant-Colonel Henry Torrens, his military secretary,

> to ride as fast as I could to General Anstruther and General Fane, and to convey to them his orders that they should not move from the position which they occupied... without further orders from Sir Arthur. On my arrival at that position, I found that General Fane had advanced a little way in front, and was engaged with some French light troops. I followed him and delivered those orders, and he consequently retired; this was about half past nine in the morning.

Presumably Anstruther reassured Torrens that his movement was only temporary, although he did later in his journal say that 'the three companies 52nd... made a gallant stand, but were at length driven in to the position, and the enemy advanced to the edge of the copse, one hundred and fifty yards from us.' Fane's riflemen, having extricated themselves around the right flank of the 2/97th, were in the process of re-forming in their companies when Thomières' column of the 1/86e and 2/86e Ligne, led by General Delaborde himself, set off up the hill for the 1/50th (West Kents), which at that stage was not visible as a line. Landmann was sitting his horse near the reserve guns, and tells us that:

The 50th were in line, on the right of the reserve guns, and just sufficiently retired from the crest of the hill to be out of sight of the enemy; and instead of advancing in line, or by divisions or corps, to fire on the enemy, each man advanced singly when he had loaded, so as to see into the valley, and fired, on having taken his aim; he then fell back into his place to reload. By this management the enemy concluded that the guns were supported by a small number of Light Infantry only.

Jonathan Leach of the 2/95 recalled that: 'Heavy masses of infantry, preceeded by a swarm of light troops, were advancing with great resolution, and with loud cries of "Vive l'Empereur! En Avant!" etc against the hill on which our brigade was posted… they continued to press forward with great determination.'

The surgeon Adam Neale was watching from his position on the eastern ridge, and wrote in his letter home:

> The valley, village and the extent of its beautiful and romantic environs, were stretched beneath my eye as on a plan. The atmosphere was serene, the sun blazed forth from a blue and silvery sky, streaked with fleecy clouds, and I could distinctly perceive every motion of the contending armies. The French were at this moment advancing, with several columns from the eastward, under cover of some pine woods… on these columns a tremendous fire was kept up by the artillery belonging to the centre, which was placed in front of two white windmills on the height. The fire was returned by the guns of the enemy with great spirit; but it was evident that our artillery was much better served, and that the carnage caused by the lately invented Shrapnell shells was prodigious… making considerable gaps in the enemy's columns.

Captain Patterson again:

> The 50th regiment, commanded by Colonel George Walker, stood as firm as a rock, while a strong division under General Delaborde continued to advance, at a rapid step, from the deep woods in our front, covered by a legion of tirailleurs, who quickened their pace as they neared our line. Walker now ordered his men to prepare for close attack, and he watched with an eagle eye the favourable moment for pouncing on the enemy.

This is how Colonel Walker himself took up the story, in a memorandum written (for some reason in the third person) four years later:

> A massive column of the enemy in close order, supported by seven pieces of cannon, made a rapid advance towards the hill, and although much shaken by the fire of the artillery, after a short pause behind a hedge to recover, it again continued to advance; till Lieut-Colonel Robe RA, no longer able to use the guns, considered them lost. Up to this time the 50th had remained at ordered arms, but it was impossible on the ground on which it stood to contend

against so superior a force and Colonel Walker, having observed that the enemy's column inclined to the left, proposed to Brigadier-General Fane to attempt to turn its flank by a wheel of the right wing.

Fortescue tells us that the French edged to their right because three companies of the 1/50th's left wing happened to have been 'thrown out rather wide on its left flank, and that these by their fire attracted the French'. Presumably the other companies were still behind the crest, over the top of which they had been popping up to take their individual shots. Brigadier Fane gave his nod, and Walker continues:

> Permission for this having been obtained, this wing was immediately thrown into echelon of half companies of about four paces to the left. The rapidity, however, of the enemy's advance, and their having already opened a confused though very hot fire from the flank of their column – though only two companies of the wing were yet formed – these were so nearly in contact with and bearing upon the angle of the column that Colonel Walker, thinking no time was to be lost, ordered an immediate volley and charge.
>
> The result exceeded his most sanguine expectations. The angle was instantly broken, and the drivers of the three guns advanced in front, alarmed at the fire in their rear, cutting the traces of their horses, and rushing back with them, created great confusion which, by the time the three outer companies could arrive to take part in the charge, became general. Then this immense mass, so threatening in its appearance a few minutes before, became in an instant an ungovernable mob, carrying off its officers and flying like a flock of sheep, almost without resistance.

A different but recognizable description comes from Captain Landmann, positioned on the left of the 1/50th:

> Near the 50th Regiment and reserve guns… a large column of attack at a short distance to the left of our direct front. The column was in close order, and appeared to consist of about 5,000 grenadiers [sic], and was advancing upon the reserve guns in double quick time, covered by a swarm of Voltigeurs, and the latter running up in the most daring manner to within about twenty yards of the guns.

As Ross-Lewin of the 32nd wrote later, 'Had this corps (the 50th) given way, our commissariat and military chest would have been in danger.' Landmann continues:

> During the whole progress of this column, the artillery kept up a most destructive fire, each of the guns being loaded with a round shot, and over that a canister; and I could most distinctly perceive at every discharge that a complete lane was cut through the column from front to rear by the round shot, whilst the canister was committing dreadful carnage on the foremost ranks.

At this period, Lieut-Colonel Robe, commanding the Artillery, and near whom I happened to be, turning to me and observed, 'You're a lucky fellow to be mounted, for by God! If something be not very quickly done, the enemy will, in a few minutes, have our guns, and we shall be bayonetted'. 'Then,' said I, 'order up your horse, and be ready for the worst'. 'No, no!' exclaimed the gallant Robe with scorn, 'I'll neither leave my guns nor my gunners – I'll share the fate of my brave boys, be it what it may.' The words here recorded are verbatim those used by Robe in expressing his entire devotion to the service.

The enemy's column was now advancing in a most gallant style, the drums by the side beating the short taps, marking the double-quick time of the pas-de-charge. I could distinctly hear the officers in the ranks exhorting their men to preservere in the attack, by the constant expressions of 'en-avant – en-avant – en-avant, mes amis', and I could distinguish the animated looks and gestures of the mounted officers, who, with raised swords, waving forwards, strongly manifested their impatience at the slowness of their advance, and to which they also loudly added every expression of sentiments, which they thought best calculated to urge their men to be firm in their attack and irresistible in their charge.

In this way, the enemy having very quickly approached the guns to within about sixty or seventy yards, they halted, and endeavoured to deploy and form their line, under cover of the Voltigeurs. I was then by the side of Anstruther, to whom I said, 'Sir, something must be done, or the position will be carried,' when the General replied, 'You are quite right;' and, without a moment's delay, he called out to the 43rd and 50th Regiments, as he raised his hat as one about to cheer. 'Remember, my lads, the glorious 21 March in Egypt; this day must be another glorious 21st.' I have no doubt that this appeal had its effect.

Walker immediately advanced his gallant 50th to the crest of the hill, where he gave the words, 'Ready, present! And let every man fire when he has taken his aim.' This order was most strictly observed, and produced a commencement of destruction and carnage which the enemy had not anticipated. Then Walker called out, raising his drawn sword and waving it high over his head, 'Three cheers and charge, my fine fellows!' and away went this gallant regiment, huzzaing all the time of their charge down the hill, before the French had recovered from their astonishment at discovering that the guns were not unprotected by infantry, as I afterwards was informed they had up to that instant fully believed.

This rush forward was awfully grand; the enemy remained firm and almost motionless, until our men were within ten to twenty yards from them; then discharged a confused and ill-directed fire from some of the front ranks, for the line had not yet been formed to its full extent, and the rear were already breaking up and partially running off. The whole now turned around and started off, every man throwing away his arms and accoutrements as also his knapsack, cap, and, in short, everything that could have obstructed his utmost speed; and thus a gallant column, which but a very few minutes before this moment had numbered 5,000, at least, was repulsed, scattered and completely thrown out of action.

The dispersing of this column presented a most interesting and curious sight; the whole of them being dressed in white linen great-coats, gave them, while in confusion and running for their lives, exactly the appearance of an immense flock of sheep scampering away from the much-dreaded shepherd's dog.

It is thought that Delaborde's and Thomières' attack on Fane took place a few minutes before Loison's and Charlot's on Anstruther, and thus claims its place in the history books as the archetypical British defence against the French. Time and again over the years to come, the same features recur: the heavy skirmish line, the use of reverse slopes to shelter and thus to achieve surprise, the numerical musket advantage of line over column (1,000 men in line can bring to bear 1,000 muskets – in column, only 200), the lapping by the line around a column's sides, the rolling volleys, the cheer and the quick charge. Also demonstrated – by Thomières – was an early example of the impossibility of deploying from column to line if left too late.

Landmann's powerful description of this confrontation with a French column is very believable, because it confirms other sources, especially on the point that the British charge was deemed necessary the minute the French showed an attempt to deploy into line – and how, having been caught in good time, the French then sensibly ran. Neither is Landmann alone among observers in commenting on the pace of the French assault – not just in quick time, but double quick time, which is tantamount to modern jogging – with the drums to the side, not the front of the mass, and the company officers with their men inside the column's ranks. We can picture, too, the 50th coming forward to the hill's crest, the volley, the cheers, the charge and the chase.

Brigadier Charlot on the left was now to experience much the same, during his attack against the main hill. He too had deployed into column when some half a mile from the 2/97th, pushing the skirmishing riflemen back, and reaching the pine trees a 150yd short of Vimiero Hill. As his 32e and 82e Ligne cleared the wood, Robe's guns briefly cut into them. Anstruther wrote that he

> ... ordered the 97th, who were concealed behind a dip in the ground, to rise and fire; after firing two or three rounds they began to advance from the position, and finding it impossible to stop them without great risk, I ordered the 52nd to support them on their right, and if possible to turn the left of the enemy. This they did very dexterously; while the 97th made a vigorous attack in front. The enemy soon gave way, and was pursued to the skirts of the wood beyond, beyond which his superiority made it imprudent to advance. I rallied the 97th, and leaving strong piquets in the wood, brought them back to the position: the 9th remained in reserve but was very little engaged.

But the 2/9th's Sergeant Hale was at least a spectator, and made the interesting comment that: 'As it is not the English fashion to play ball long, if there is a possibility of giving a charge, so likewise, at this time we soon presented them the point of the bayonet, and gave them a charge that was not acceptable; for they soon turned about, and made off as well as they could.' This English liking for the bayonet is something we shall examine later.

So three volleys – say one minute – after the 2/97th stood up and came forward into full view, 700 strong, more than 2,000 lead musket balls had shrieked down the slope at the French column's frontage of thirty men – say a target twenty-five yards wide. Once the 2/52nd came alongside the 2/97th, standing there a second longer was simply not an option for the French. The greater part of 2,000 men turned their backs and ran. Delaborde was wounded, so too Charlot; the colonel of the 82e Ligne was killed, and all seven guns deployed were abandoned and lost.

During this attack by the four battalions, Junot sat his horse back up the road amongst his reserve of four further battalions; now he ordered Kellerman to send forward the two battalions under Colonel St Clair, with four more guns. Their attack was to follow the same route on which Delaborde had led Thomières' brigade, whose shaken fugitives were re-forming in the woods, and who were to be taken along in support. Also at about this point, Junot tried to put a force of cavalry round to his left, towards Anstruther's right rear. Landmann saw it from a windmill on the right flank,

> ... where a Drum Major and all his little fry were gathered and crowded together behind the mill, in hope of protecting themselves from shots. I could not behold these poor little fellows, pale, and with looks manifesting extreme anxiety, without experiencing many painful feelings... I soon perceived the head of a column of cavalry, winding round the end of a hill, as if endeavouring to turn our right flank, and so cut in between the first and second lines; the latter was on a range of high ground, commanded by General Hill. Just at this time a few nine pounders, loaded with spherical cases [shrapnel shells], fired by Captain Eliott from the right of the second line and about 2,000 yards distant from the cavalry, were so perfectly directed, and the fuzes cut with so much accuracy, that the cavalry turned away and effected a hasty retreat.

Colonel St Clair and the grenadiers set off down the road in the narrower column of platoons – half the width of the earlier attempts – and immediately took casualties from Robe's new shrapnel shells bursting overhead. The French guns, which were wheeled forward by hand and by rope, were limited in their response by the presence of their own *tirailleurs*. The column was about to run into a brick wall in the form of the 2/97th, 2/9th and 1/50th – 2,000 muskets. Against such an obstacle a brigade in column of platoons – about sixteen files wide, and therefore able to bring to bear all of thirty-two muskets – was scarcely a sensible proposition, and the French did not have the time to deploy into line.

Somewhat unnecessarily, the 2/97th and 1/50th had wheeled to wrap around the French left and right flanks, and opened volley fire. St Clair's grenadier battalions got half way up the hill before being stopped in their tracks, the first five ranks or so cut down in straight lines; the British advanced, firing further volleys; the artillery horses went down, so too both colonels of artillery; the gunners fled, and so did the grenadiers. The four guns were taken, and the broken ranks fell back both east-wards and northwards across the road, down into the deep hollow beneath the eastern heights – anywhere to get into dead ground, away from the bone-smashing lead balls.

Now General Kellerman's last two grenadier battalions, under Colonel Maransin, were to be given their chance of glory, *pour en finir,* as Junot mysteriously said to Thiebault. Kellerman understandably decided not to test the 1/50th, 2/9th and 2/97th's lethal combination for a third time, but led his force into the protected hollow beyond but parallel to the road, striking instead from behind Fane's left flank for the northern edge of the village – and the Portuguese muleteers, with their agitated charges, beyond it. The way was quite clear of British troops, with just a few hundred yards to cover. But across the valley at the base of the eastern ridge, from Acland's brigade higher up, there appeared Captain Alexander Cameron with two companies of the 1/95th, and the two light companies of Acland's 2nd and 20th. Two hundred rifles and 200 muskets began to play on the grenadiers from their right as they grimly sought the shelter of the buildings. But Brigadier Anstruther, seeing the danger to his rear and to the train, on his own initiative sent the 2/43rd doubling down the hill behind the 2/97th and into the village. Two companies manned the nearest houses, and opened up on Kellerman's approaching column. Now under the fire of the better part of 1,100 light troops, the French grenadiers were desperate to get into the village and the cover of its narrow streets and walled gardens. Lieutenant Leslie, with the 29th up on the eastern ridge, saw it all:

> While watching with intense interest the progress of the enemy's attack on our centre, we observed a party of the 43rd Light Infantry stealing out of the village and moving behind a wall to gain the right flank of the enemy's lines, on which they opened a fire at the moment when the enemy came in contact with our troops in position. The French had been allowed to come close, then our gallant fellows, suddenly springing up, rapidly poured on them two or three volleys with great precision, and rushing on, charged with the bayonet. We soon had the satisfaction of seeing the enemy broken and retreating in the utmost haste and disorder, closely pursued by our small force of cavalry.

Leach of the 2/95th wrote: 'The 2/43rd being let loose at them, a desperate conflict ensued in and near the road which leads into the village. The 43rd highly distin-guished itself, and repulsed the enemy; but there were many broken heads on each side.' Vimiero became the scene of confused street fights by small groups, mostly around the cemetery; savage, hand-to-hand or very short range work with musket and bayonet, until the French lost their final impetus and fell back, through the still-galling fire from across the valley. A measure of the determination of Kellerman's grenadiers, and the intensity of close-quarter battle, is that in a short space the 2/43rd had lost 40 killed and 79 wounded – nearly a fifth of their strength.

So Junot's fourth attack had also failed. The slopes of Vimiero, and the road running away up the rising country to the east were a mass of several thousand retreating Frenchmen – Kellerman's grenadiers were going, and so too the survivors of Thomières' and Charlot's earlier attempts. Landmann was an observant witness, as usual:

> The ground between us was variously scattered over with killed, wounded, arms, drums, caps, knapsacks, canteens, dead horses and ammunition wagons, and some cannon; but the track, which the aforementioned column of attack had followed, was conspicuously marked to a great distance, by the number of killed and wounded, who had fallen by our Artillery, in its progress towards us, and which regularly increased in numbers as the column had approached; at the extreme point of its advance, where an attempt had been made to deploy to form a line, the dead and dying were in some places absolutely lying in heaps three or four men in height.

Fane gave the 1/50th and his riflemen the order to pursue, and we have Captain Patterson's description:

> As far as the eye could reach over the well-planted valley, and across the open country lying beyond the forest, the fugitives were running in wild disorder, their white sheep-skin knapsacks discernable among woods far distant. There were, however many resolute fellows who, in retiring, took cover behind the hedgerows, saluting us with parting volleys, which did considerable execution amongst our advancing troops. At length, even this remnant of the vanquished foe, dispersed and broken in piece-meal, betook themselves to flight in every quarter of the field. The ground was thickly strewed with muskets, side arms, bayonets, accoutrements, and well-filled knapsacks, all of which had been hastily flung away as dangerous encumbrances. Several of the packs contained various articles of plunder, including plate in many shapes and forms, which they had robbed from the unfortunate Portuguese... While we were pursuing our opponents, the 20th Light Dragoons, led on by Colonel Taylor, galloped furiously past us, in order to put a finishing stroke to the business.

For Fane had also ordered out Wellesley's cavalry, such as it was, and Sergeant Landsheit describes what then took place:

> Colonel Taylor, who commanded us, repeatedly asked leave to charge, but on each occasion was held back, by the assurance that the proper moment was not yet come; till at last General Fane rode up and exclaimed, 'Now, Twentieth! Now we want you. At them, my lads, and let them see what you

are made of.' Then came the word, 'threes about and forward', and with the rapidity of thought we swept round the elbow of the hill, and the battle lay before us. As we emerged up this slope, we were directed to form in half squadrons, the 20th in the centre, the Portuguese cavalry on the flanks... 'Now, Twentieth! Now!' shouted Sir Arthur, while his staff clapped their hands and gave us a cheer.

The Portuguese likewise pushed forward, but through the dust which entirely enveloped us, the enemy threw in a fire, which seemed to have the effect of paralyzing altogether our handsome allies. Right and left they pulled up, as if by word of command, and we never saw more of them till the battle was over. But we went very differently to work. In an instant we were in the very heart of the French cavalry, (who were covering the retreat) cutting and hacking, and upsetting men and horses in the most extraordinary manner possible, till they broke and fled in every direction, and then we fell upon the infantry. It was here that our gallant Colonel met his fate.　We were entirely ignorant of the fall of our commanding officer, and had the case been otherwise, we were too eager in following up the advantages which we had gained, to regard it at the moment. Though scattered, as always happens, by the shock of a charge, we still kept laying about us, till our white leather breeches, our hands, arms, and swords, were all besmeared with blood. Moreover, as the enemy gave way we continued to advance, amid a cloud of dust so thick, that to see beyond the distance of those immediately about yourself, was impossible. Thus it was until we reached a low fence, through which several gaps had been made by the French to facilitate the movements of their cavalry; and we instantly leapt it. The operation cost some valuable lives, for about twenty or thirty of the French grenadiers had laid themselves on their bellies beneath it, and now received us as well as they could upon their bayonets. Several of our men and horses were stabbed, but of the enemy not a soul survived to speak of his exploit – we literally slew them all – and then, while in pursuit of the horse, rushed into an enclosure, where to a man we well nigh perished. For the fold in which we were caught was fenced round to a great height, and had but a single aperture – the door of which, the enemy, who hastened to take advantage of our blunder, immediately closed. Then was our situation trying enough, for we could neither escape nor resist; while looking over the wall we beheld that the French had halted, and were returning in something like order to the front.

While we were thus situated, vainly looking for an aperture through which to make a bolt, one of our men, the same Corporal Marshall, of whom I have elsewhere spoken, was maintaining a most unequal combat outside the close, with four French dragoons that beset him together. An active and powerful man himself, he was particularly fortunate in the charger which he bestrode – a noble stallion which did his part in the melee, not less effectively than his master. The animal bit, kicked, lashed out with his fore-feet, and wheeled about and about like a piece of machinery, screaming all the time; while the rider, now catching a blow, now parrying a thrust, seemed invulnerable. At last he clove one of the enemy to the teeth, and with a back stroke took another across the face, and sent him forth from his saddle. The other two hung back, and made signs to some of their comrades, but these had no time to help them, for a hearty British cheer sounded above the battle, and the 50th Regiment advanced in line with fixed bayonets. The consequence was, an immediate flight by the enemy, who had calculated on making every man of the 20th prisoners; and our release from a situation, of all others the most annoying to men who, like ourselves, had no taste for laying down their arms. Moreover, to that charge, supported as it was by the simultaneous advance of other portions of the line, the enemy did not venture to show a front. They were beaten on all sides, and retreated in great disorder, leaving the field covered with their dead.

It was about 10.30 or 11am when the survivors of the 20th Light Dragoons returned their knocked-up horses, drooping and lather-necked, to their lines behind Vimiero Hill. There is some doubt as to their casualties, Fortescue and Weller favouring half their strength, Oman a quarter – specifying twenty-one killed, twenty-four wounded and eleven prisoners. The precise numbers put out of action are irrelevant to the obvious point: for the first time but definitely not the last in the Peninsula, British cavalry had gone on too far, and suffered for it. They were lucky not to lose more. Many commanders would not have ventured their only horse when so outnumbered – Colonel Taylor paraded just two British squadrons, while Junot had the equivalent of fourteen.

Sources put Wellesley on the eastern ridge during Junot's attacks on the 1/50th and 2/97th, with his brigadiers necessarily moving their battalions on their own initiative – the lapping of the 2/52nd, the sideways doubling of the 2/43rd, Acland's role in stemming the final grenadier assault on the village – and if Sergeant Landsheit says it was Brigadier Fane who ordered the light dragoons forward, maybe we should believe him. (The fact that he also said Wellesley did the same, on Vimiero Hill only seconds later, may perhaps be ignored.) Captain Landmann confidently states that: 'Up to this time [the end of the fighting around Vimiero Hill] I had not seen, nor could I obtain any information of Sir Arthur. I was now accidentally informed he had been during the whole of the morning at or about the extreme left with Major-General Ferguson.'

As to the uncontrolled charge by the 20th, the present author finds it curious – as one who has often hurtled across miles of country with up to 200 well-horsed followers of the Duke of Beaufort's Hounds, with passion ignited if lacking a sabre in the hand – that whenever the Field Master, well-identified in the Duke's green livery, raises his hand, we all reluctantly grind to a halt. Some tearaways do this by turning a circle, many by a mere gentle pressure in the saddle, most by a more primitive tugging on the bit, a few with curses; but all quickly re-form in the several lines, and none pass the Field Master. The same mass of horsemen travelling equally fast against Frenchmen, however, were apparently in a different world – and that notwithstanding the vicious bits then in military use, the like of which are never seen today. Because troop horses were a permanent herd, not an ad hoc herd formed temporarily three or four times a week, individual troopers presumably had less say over where they went and at what speed. Thus enormous pressure was put on the lead horse – the military equivalent of the Field Master – and in the case of the 20th Light Dragoons, we hear from Landsheit that the gallant (soon-to-be-late) Colonel Taylor 'rode that day a horse, which was so hot that not all his exertions would suffice to control it, and he was carried headlong upon the bayonets of the French infantry, a corporal of whom shot him through the heart.'

When the fighting around the village ceased, Captain Ross-Lewin of the 32nd

> ... walked over a part of the ground where the action had been most severe. Upon entering the churchyard of the village of Vimiero, my attention was arrested by very unpleasant objects – one, a very large wooden dish filled with hands that had just been amputated – another, a heap of legs placed opposite. On one side of the entrance of the church lay a French surgeon, who had received a six-pound shot in the body. The men, who had undergone amputation, were ranged round the interior of the building. In the morning they had rushed to the combat, full of ardour and enthusiasm, and now they were stretched pale, bloody, and mangled on the cold flags, some writhing in agony, others fainting with loss of blood. A great number of the 43rd lay dead in the vineyards, which a part of that regiment had occupied; they had landed only the day before, and they looked so clean, and had their appointments in such bright and shining order, that at first view, they seemed to be men resting after a recent parade, rather than corpses of the fallen in a fiercely-contested engagement. This corps, which suffered so severely, had passed us in the morning in beautiful order, with their band playing merrily before them... marching to the sound of national quicksteps, all life and spirits.

*   *   *

So Junot's eight battalions at Vimiero Hill had all been tried against seven of Wellesley's, and found wanting, in the space of a couple of hours. Now, on the eastern ridge, his other seven battalions were to try their luck, against seven British.

As we have seen, Sir Arthur had moved the brigades of Ferguson, Nightingall, Bowes, Craufurd and Acland from west to east at around 8am that morning. We have also seen how the latter's light troops had played a devastating part in the dismissal of the grenadiers' last fling. Sir Arthur's choice of Acland's location thus proved inspired, and his other placings were entirely workmanlike.

Facing north-east astride the Vimiero-Lourinhao track going up the ridge to Ventosa, he put a first line of (from right to left) Nightingall's 82nd (Prince of Wales Volunteers); then the 36th (Herefordshire), 40th (Somerset) and 71st (Glasgow Highlanders) of Ferguson's brigade. Behind them in a second line (again from right to left) were Nightingall's 29th (Worcestershire); and the 6th (Warwickshire) and 32nd (Cornwall) of Bowes' brigade. These seven battalions totalled 5,800 men; and half a mile behind them, just 15 minutes' march away, were Craufurd's 45th (Nottinghamshire) and 91st (Highlanders) – another 1,800 men. This force wa halfway between the first line and Acland's command on the slopes above Vimiero; the whole linked together as one manageable layout. Presumably Acland faced north-east, on the assumption that the valley from Vimiero to Toledo and beyond, forming a steep southern edge to the eastern ridge and in some places inaccessible to guns, was a much less likely approach than down the road from Ventosa. The progress of Brennier's dust cloud, going ever further north, would confirm this view.

But he was wrong. For while Brennier took one look at the Toledo valley and, reckoning it was impracticable for his three guns, went on a much wider sweep to the north (where he got snarled up in the ravines), Solignac – Junot's afterthought – turned earlier and found the track from Toledo to Ventosa. Up he went, guns and all. His progress, and that of Brennier, was visible to the watchers on the eastern ridge, who had been avidly charting the attacks on Vimiero Hill – which was two miles away, if that, and 300ft lower, so they had a good view. At some early point, seeing that the first threat would materialize from the Toledo valley rather than the ridge line beyond Ventosa, Sir Arthur moved Ferguson's first line from astride the ridge facing north-east, to line the top of the Toledo valley, facing now to the south-east, and unseen just back from the crest. Leslie of the 29th wrote 'Our men were ordered to lie flat down on the ground.' The Ventosa–Vimiero road was behind them. So of 3,300 muskets in the first line, only about 700 were deployed out in front, visible to Solignac: the skirmishers.

According to Wellesley's military secretary, Lieutenant-Colonel Torrens: 'The right [Solignac's] column of the French arrived at the point of attack on our left in about ten minutes or a quarter of an hour after his left column was defeated by our centre.' Solignac's force comprised three battalions in parallel, 300yd apart, with a thick swarm of *tirailleurs* out ahead, climbing the rough slopes on either side of the track up to Ventosa. His guns were in the intervals. Only the British skirmishers – seven companies – were visible on the forward slopes throughout the approach and climb, but this was a large enough number for the French to mistakenly take them for the entire British force. Solignac was not to know what awaited him, since he had not witnessed his fellow commanders' destruction in front of Vimiero, nor, four days earlier, had he seen the redcoats at Rolica. So up he went, still in column, pushing back the British light troops – straight into four battalions lying down in line. Standing up so that the hill was suddenly rimmed with a red edge, these came forward to a range of a hundred yards, and fired one volley. The French immediately tried to deploy from column into line, and apparently succeeded – Charles Vane wrote 'nor did they make the slightest pause, till they beheld the 36th, the 40th, and the 71st regiments in close array before them. Their line was likewise formed in a moment.' But the 3,000 balls of that first British volley knocked down the *tirailleurs* and many in the French front ranks. The long British line lapped around them, and fired again; then, having reloaded, the redcoats silently marched forward down the slope. The anonymous T.S., the 'Soldier of the 71st', wrote:

> We marched out two miles to meet the enemy, formed line and lay under cover of a hill for about an hour, until they came to us. We gave them one volley and three cheers – three distinct cheers. Then all was as still as death.

They came upon us, crying and shouting, to the very point of our bayonets. Our awful silence and determined advance they could not stand. They put about and fled... In our first charge I felt my mind wander; a breathless sensation came over me. The silence was appalling. I looked along the line. It was enough to assure me. The steady determined scowl of my companions assured my heart and gave me determination. How unlike the noisy advance of the French!

Again, from Ferguson's ADC William Warre:

As soon as they were within reach, Genl Ferguson ordered his Brigade to charge them, which was done with all the intrepidity and courage of British soldiers, and the enemy retired before us, keeping up a sharp fire. A part of them rallied, but Genl Ferguson hurraed the 36th, a very weak [600-strong] tho' fine Regt to charge, which was done in great style three successive times, till, when they were very much thinned, and in some disorder from the rapid advance, I was sent back to hasten the support which was far behind, the gallant little Regt forming to rally again under cover of a hedge of American aloes, tho' much pressed.

Inevitably, there is no clear eyewitness account of how long the French stood, nor how close they got, nor precisely how the British line went for them; but it would seem that the first few ranks of Solignac's 3/12e Léger, 3/15e Léger and 3/58e Ligne – each in its battalion column, thirty men wide – would have seen their preceeding *tirailleurs* and drummers knocked into the grass on the first volley, the red crest then disappearing into a long line of white smoke; and after a thought-provoking pause of fifteen seconds, those first few ranks would themselves have fallen to the next volley to come blazing out of it. The next hundred or so Frenchmen, as they climbed the steep slop, stumbling now over corpses and wounded, would be only too conscious that the British had reloaded for a third volley: their turn next... But the muskets were being raised to the high port, bayonets fixed, and the British line was choosing to shorten the range to them, advancing down the slope. Jac Weller, who is usually right about musket work, says that in the space of two minutes the British fired ten volleys, by rolling platoon fire. This is largely confirmed by an anonymous officer of the 36th's Grenadier Company, who wrote in his diary:

Took possession of a hill on the left of the village. From our position we could see the enemy's columns sweeping along in all directions. Our camp was soon attacked on all sides. While the right was warmly engaged we saw, with confidence in the result, several columns advancing to the attack of our position. Our artillery now began a well-directed fire, our Rifles (5/60th) and our skirmishers (our Light Company) to pop, but these were soon driven in by the rapid advance of the French, the left of their line extending beyond our right. The Grenadiers with the 1st and 2nd Companies are detached to preserve the wing, awaiting their approach with the greatest steadiness notwithstanding a galling fire which was kept up during their advance. When the enemy came within 80 yards our detachment began to throw in volleys amongst them – 8 rounds were expended by the time they had gained 40 yards. We now, 'una voce', gave three cheers and charged. They retreated precipitately.

So the French columns were utterly stopped, mangled and looking to run. The sheer length of the British line, and particularly the way it was bending around their flanks, presented them with a stark and immediate choice: either they stayed to be trapped and taken, those that survived, or they got out quickly – *Sauve qui peut.* They took the latter option.

General Ferguson put the 36th and the 40th at the retreating French, leading them himself, while leaving the 71st and the 82nd with the captured guns. Bowes' brigade had earlier been sent towards Vimiero, as a precaution when Kellerman's grenadiers closed on the village, but the 29th also remained near the captured guns. A gap opened up on the ridge, as the French went away along the spine to the north-east, taking the injured General Solignac with them, harried by further volleys from the 36th and the 40th – and all the time being forced further away from Junot in the valley to the south.

As the 71st and the 82nd relaxed around the three French guns, they suddenly heard, with some curiosity, the jingle of curb chains and the thud of many hooves; and then, to their horror, over the skyline appeared the brass helmets of scores of French dragoons – too many to count, as they crested the ridge. Drumbeats echoed from the village of Ventosa. General Brennier's brigade – those four battalions who had held the ridge at Rolica – at long last had completed their wide hook and arrived on the field. Leslie of the 29th wrote: 'While resting, we suddenly observed a column of the enemy, which, it seems, had remained concealed in a village on the opposite heights, make a dash down as if they meant to attack us, while a body of cavalry at the same time appeared on our right flank, threatening to turn and attack us in that flank.'

What might the scene have been, had Brennier been ten minutes earlier? If Junot could have put these four new battalions across the ridge from the north, as Solignac's three tested from the south, Sir Arthur would have had a nice situation to resolve. Seven against seven – or seven against five, if Bowes' two had marched away by then – with the British the meat in a French sandwich, caught between two fires. For it is clear that Solignac's attack had taken British minds from his fellow brigadier, whose earlier dust clouds would have ceased to flag his progress once he left the dry tracks and struck off into the dead ground of the valley between Ventosa and Mariquiteira. It would have taken just a couple of horsemen, to be detailed to keep watch on Brennier; but the precaution was omitted.

The French came up fast, retaking Solignac's guns, the dragoons circling to the east of the 71st and 82nd, pushing the redcoats back. In the process of hurriedly re-forming, the 29th put themselves into four ranks in the face of the two squadrons, then bravely marched out on their own (some say led by Sir Arthur himself) to flank Brennier's battalion columns and confront them from the west. The 71st and 82nd poured fire in from the east, and, as Leslie reports, 'our artillery opened a well-directed fire upon them... They made an attempt to rally in the village [Ventosa] again, but our guns made it too hot for them, so they continued their flight right over the hill, and disappeared from our view. The cavalry, which had threatened us, on observing the discomfiture of their infantry, rapidly retired.' William Warre saw some of this: 'I just returned in time to join the 71st, who were charging six pieces of the enemy's cannon that were retiring, and the fire at this time from the enemy was really tremendous. The enemy attempted to rally and advanced with drums beating, but the 71st charged them so manfully that they retired in confusion, and the retreat became general... The action was over before 2pm.'

So – amazingly, given their superior numbers, their cavalry and the element of surprise – the French did not perservere. Perhaps Bowes' brigade was seen to be returning at the double; perhaps Brennier could see Solignac retreating away to his left; perhaps, in the boiling midday heat with the sun near its zenith, after that long march across country, there was just no heart left in the French. Perhaps these battalions recalled the ridge at Rolica, and even recognized the 29th's facings? Whatever their reasons, away they went, covered by their dragoons, south-west across the Ventosa ridge, actually behind Ferguson's 36th and 40th, who were in the process of bottling up the remnants of Solignac's battalions in a steep-sided valley near Perenza. The 71st, 82nd and 29th would be looking to their numerous wounded, and thanking their lucky stars. Ross-Lewin of the 32nd recounts a happy remark made at this point, which deservedly passed from lip to lip: 'The 71st were opposed to the French 70th, and after the action a soldier of the first-mentioned corps, looking at the buttons of some men of the other that lay dead near him, uttered the bon-mot "I well knew we were one too many for them."'

Out of the 272 casualties Wellesley's force had suffered on the eastern ridge – only 7 per cent of the battalions involved – the 71st and 82nd accounted for 173 of them. Generally, we must recall that the brigades of Hill, Bowes, Craufurd and most of Acland's had been spectators throughout the morning's work. The total British casualties of 704 – apart from 122 riflemen and 44 dragoons – came almost entirely from the nine line battalions actively engaged on the two hill features. The 2/43rd took slightly more (118) in the street fighting in Vimiero than the 71st near Ventosa (112). But the 538 line battalion casualties represented only 8 per cent of the strength of those battalions – a light butcher's bill by later standards. So whereas Wellesley now had eight unused battalions champing at their bits, and his entire command structure intact (apart from the 20th Light Dragoons' colonel), all Junot's fifteen French battalions had been engaged, with significant losses and above all with their leadership decimated. Various estimates have put French casualties in the order of 1,400-1,500 killed and wounded, 300–400 prisoners or missing, that is around 2,000 men *hors de combat*, and thirteen to fifteen guns taken out of twenty-three. These losses represented some 20 per cent of his infantry. In addition, one of his two divisional commanders (Delaborde), his adjutant-general (General Pillet), three of his four brigade commanders (Brennier, Charlot and Solignac), and two of his artillery colonels (Foy and Prost) were wounded, with Brennier a prisoner; two battalion commanders had been killed and a third wounded. Fifteen French battalions and 2,000 horse had failed against, effectively, nine British and 240 horse.

The immediate victory was Sir Arthur's. All he had to do now was to fire up his eight fresh battalions and march south, the French having retreated to the north-east. That would put him between Junot and Lisbon; what then could the Frenchman do, adrift from his land base and with no sea support? The Portuguese would surely rise up and see to his garrison: he would then have an exceedingly long march to Madrid, en route to his Emperor's retribution.

*   *   *

The first task was to put Solignac's brigade in the bag. However, the battle being over and Sir Harry Burrard now in command, Wellesley needed permission. Burrard had come ashore earlier, about 10am, when the French grenadiers were getting their bloody nose in Vimiero village. At that stage he was happy to remain a spectator, and to let Sir Arthur continue his battle, since 'I have reason to be perfectly satisfied with his disposition, and the means he proposed to repulse them.' After the strained meeting of the previous evening, Sir Arthur must have been relieved that Sir Harry was content to let him get on with things. But he was wrong if he presumed a continuance of that freedom, as he now cantered swiftly along the eastern ridge to Burrard with the news of the complete French retreat on that side. According to Torrens, he said: 'Sir Harry, now is your time to advance, the enemy are completely beaten, and we shall be in Lisbon in three days. We have a large body of troops which have not been in action. Let us move from the right on the road to Torres Vedras, and I will follow them with the left.'

But Burrard would have none of it. The artillery horses were exhausted, the cavalry destroyed, the commissariat in turmoil after being shot over and at ('It was with much difficulty that my ADC got thro' them'), and only half the transport was available for an advance (fifty carts had disappeared in the panic, while 120 were needed to shift the wounded). The British wings being three miles apart made a general advance hazardous; the French might have an intact reserve, there was what Napier called 'a line of fresh French troops on the ridge behind that occupied by the French Army', they certainly had numerous horse, there was an R in the month, and so on. Sir Harry would await the arrival of Sir John Moore's 14,000 before making any further move.

Faced with this extraordinary lassitude – even timidity – Sir Arthur pressed his arguments for immediate action, both tactical and administrative, including (according to Torrens) pointing out that 'the troops were perfectly ready to advance, having provisions already cooked in their haversacks, according to the orders of the day before... there was plenty of ammunition, that the mules with the reserve of musket ammunition were in rear of the brigades, that we had an abundance of stores and plenty of provisions.' Sir Harry replied that he saw 'no reason for altering my former resolution of not advancing and... I added that the same reasoning which before had determined me to wait for the reinforcements had still its full force in my judgement and opinion.' Doubtless grinding his teeth with barely-contained rage, Sir Arthur would then have held his breath when Captain Mellish, ADC to General Ferguson, galloped up with his general's compliments, and might he have permission please to make just one further short advance, for 'a column of broken troops 1,500 to 2,000 strong had in their confusion got into a hollow, and could be cut off from their main body by a movement in advance of his brigade.'

No, said 'Betty' Burrard, and tell your general to return to his original position – we are already too spread out. Captain Landmann says he witnessed Sir Arthur's reaction:

> On perceiving that Sir Harry Burrard had determined on not following up our advantages, Sir Arthur reined in his horse four or five yards, dropped the bridle on his horse's neck, pulled down his cocked hat to the bridge of his nose, and having folded his arms, he drooped his head, and remained during some minutes in that position, evidently regretting that he could not follow his own opinion.

Another source, quoted by Michael Glover, says that 'Sir Arthur turned his horse's head, and with a cold contemptuous bitterness, said aloud to his aide-de-camp, "You may think about dinner, for there is nothing more for soldiers to do this day."' Both anecdotes may well be entirely accurate.

For there was indeed nothing more to do that day, nor the next day, nor for a while thereafter. The French got back to Torres Vedras, Burrard was in turn superseded by Sir Hew Dalrymple, and Junot proposed an armistice preparatory to trying to negotiate a way out of the desperate situation in which he now found himself. His council of war on the evening of the battle – Loison, Kellerman, the twice-wounded Delaborde, Thiebault, plus the chief engineer and the commissary – saw no future in a further battle there and then, nor one in front of a rebellious Lisbon; nor in a penitential retreat far into Spain (King Joseph had by now evacuated Madrid). They would have to haggle for the best terms they could get from the British, who held the whip hand. Kellerman was sent to Vimiero under a white flag, with two troops of dragoons as escort.

To Kellerman's barely concealed amazement, 'Dowager' Dalrymple (who had now landed) immediately accepted the French opening proposition: Junot's army would simply be allowed to go home, to French ports. Astonishingly, they could take with them all their warlike stores – guns, ammunition, horses, wagons, the military chest; and even the contents of their knapsacks – all the looted riches of Portugal, including melted-down church plate, the royal family's personal cambric sheets, two state carriages belonging bizarrely to the Duke of Sussex, and a Bible from the Royal Library sent home by Junot himself and which his wife subsequently sold for 85,000 francs. And the most incredible concession of all was that they would be carried home on a fleet of ships supplied by King George.

Official news of this Convention of Cintra finally arrived in London from Dalrymple on 15 September, where the stunned reaction soon engulfed Burrard, Dalrymple, Wellesley and Moore. We shall examine this when we return to the historical narrative in the next chapter; but this is an appropriate point at which to review Vimiero, and try to separate out the main features of this first major confrontation with the French. There is no doubt that Sir Arthur himself, back in

England, must have done the same; for on his return to the Peninsula in April 1809, for the Douro and Talavera campaigns, he was to refashion his army, drawing lessons from their brief experiences at Rolica and Vimiero to lay the foundation of what would emerge as the invincible Peninsular Field Army.

In August 1808 he had fought with what he was given, at short notice: six weeks in the case of the ten Cork battalions, just two weeks for Spencer's five from Andalusia, and twenty-four hours or less for the six battalions – nearly a third of his strength – from Ramsgate and Harwich. Of these later arrivals, Anstruther's brigade of the 2/9th, 2/43rd, 2/52nd and 2/97th fought a skilful series of defensive actions on Vimiero Hill, using doctrine and techniques that they brought with them rather than any inculcated by Wellesley. To examine this existing doctrine will help us understand Wellesley's subsequent additions, which began to blossom at Talavera.

*   *   *

If we agree that most officers were commissioned ensign at the age of sixteen, then in 1808 those who joined their regiments around the turn of the century would still have been lieutenants in their early twenties, and looking for promotion to command a company. These were the fighting officers. The establishment in 1801 of the Royal Military College at High Wycombe (and the Junior Department the following year, for boys as young as thirteen) certainly began to produce trained ensigns; but knowledge for aspiring leaders still came largely from existing 'perceived wisdom', and very much from unofficial sources, both books and pamphlets, some of which were set out as domestic instructions by individual commanding officers. One thinks of *A Practical Guide for the Light Infantry Officer*, Baron Gross' *Duties of an Officer in the Field*, Count Turpin's *Art of War*, Williamson's *Elements of Military Arrangement*, or James' *Military Dictionary*, while the Adjutant-General's *Rules & Regulations for Field Exercise* were also required reading, as certainly were Dundas' *Rules*.

More recent generations of young officers have read pamphlets on courage by William Slim, or on leadership by Montgomery – avidly, on their authors' reputation. So, around 1800, did the keen, newly-joined subaltern read Wolfe's popular *Instructions to Young Officers*, which had run to various editions, the main part having been first printed back in 1755 simply as Instructions for the 20th Regiment. The future victor at Quebec wrote how one must seek for a firepower advantage, and then for the early, quiet use of the bayonet. He recommended that flank platoons either fire obliquely at a smaller enemy, or wheel inwards to work their way round a larger, with the centre companies loading two or three balls for a volley at twenty yards, followed by a charge with the bayonet. The only shout was to be upon the order 'Charge!', otherwise complete silence was required. The aim was to avoid lengthy, indeterminate firefights; in effect, said Wolfe, a volley, a cheer and a charge generally did the business.

Clearly, the demand for reprints of Wolfe's wisdom at the turn of the century grew out of heightened awareness of the coming conflict with the French. Napoleon's campaigns in Italy, Egypt and Syria were being closely followed. This interest also accounted for the appearance of a periodical called the *British Military Library*, among the British and foreign military experts who contributed articles was the anonymous author of a piece excitingly entitled 'On the Defence of Heights'. This article urged that those battalion companies not directly assaulted by the enemy's column should 'fall on its flanks, and endeavour to throw it into confusion'. Light troops were to be deployed well forward, pursuit was not to be prolonged, and indecisive firefights leading to equal casualties on both sides must be avoided; firing should be deliberately aimed, and followed by an early bayonet charge.

So Vimiero demonstrated that attention had been paid both to the immortal Wolfe and to this anonymous author: they would have felt quite at home on Vimiero Hill that day in 1808. They would have recognized much of their creed in the failure of the six separate French assaults. And while one of Sir Arthur's personal contributions to the tactics of his day was said to be the lying of his line down on reverse slopes, both to protect his own troops and to surprise the enemy, there were others who had come to the same conclusion – for example, at Corunna, Colonel Sterling of the 42nd (Black Watch), who had not been at Vimiero. According to the anonymous 'Private of the 42nd':

> The French Army did not advance very rapidly, on account of the badness of the ground. Our Colonel gave orders for us to lie on the ground, at the back of the height our position was on; and whenever the French were within a few yards of us, we were to start up and fire our muskets, and then give them the bayonet... All the word of command that was given was, 'Forty-second, Charge!'. In one moment every man was up with a cheer, and the sound of his musket, and every shot did execution. They were so close upon us that we gave them the bayonet the instant we fired.

There had to be some reason why the French – intelligent, experienced, albeit arrogant in their expectations of success – should not only manoeuvre forward in column, but apparently also, according to Sir Charles Oman, assault in column. But Sir Charles must surely be wrong to imply that the French were unaware of the obviously stupid mathematics of pitting the muskets of just the first three ranks of a battalion column (the lead company of say 100 men) against the 900 or so of a British battalion in line. Just because the shock action of charging forward en masse had broken many continental conscript armies, without need to deploy into line to deliver fire, this surely cannot have blinded French commanders to the risk they ran if and when an enemy line held firm.

Yet time and again – at Vimiero, as throughout the Peninsula campaigns – British lines devastated French formations commonly described as 'still in column', as Oman's mathematical view decreed that they must. A clue is given by the word 'still'. If we examine representative eyewitness descriptions of the actions with which we are now familiar, we can see that there was more to it than Oman assumed. Of course the few references are vague, and made in passing: one of the drawbacks of all memoirs is that they often left unsaid anything which the author assumed the reader would know about. Nonetheless, the relevance of the following examples is plain enough. Of the assault by the 1/86e and 2/86e Ligne on the 1/50th Foot, Landmann noted that when 'within about 60 or 70 yards' of Robe's guns, 'they halted, and endeavoured to deploy and form their line.' And of the 1/50th's charge down upon the 86e, that the French response was but 'a confused and ill-directed fire from some of the front ranks, for the line had not yet been formed to its full extent.' Of the assault by Colonel St Clair's grenadiers, Kellerman reported that 'they did not even have time to complete their deployment'; or as Landmann observed, 'at the extreme point of its advance, where an attempt had been made to deploy to form a line, the dead and dying were in some places absolutely lying in heaps three or four men high.' General Foy tells us 'the grenadier regiment pushed on until it came within 100 yards of the flat summit. At the moment of its forming for the attack, the column was assailed by the converging fire of six British regiments... the regiment could not form line of battle.' And of Solignac's assault on Ferguson from the Toledo valley, Charles Vane wrote: 'nor did they make the slightest pause, till they beheld the 36th, the 40th and the 71st regiments in close array before them. Their line was likewise formed in a moment.'

These matter-of-fact references to French columns deploying into line all involve a time element – or a lack of time. What caught out the French commanders? Well, in three of the six assaults Wellesley's brigadiers had their men back behind the visible crest. Up the French went, pushing back the skirmishers, quite ready to deploy into line, but not needlessly or prematurely. As they climbed, no doubt they thought that the British position was yet at some distance. Then suddenly the red British line stands up from the long grass, by definition now within musket range, the redcoats disappearing behind white smoke as the first volley is hammered away – in effect, an ambush. So Sir Arthur's liking for the reverse slope, both to protect his troops from direct fire and for the surprise factor, lured the French columns further than was prudent before deploying into a line formation to improve their firepower.

But what of the many assaults where the British line was perfectly visible throughout? There one may suspect that the practical difficulties of deploying into line, and taking the logical next step of commencing volley fire, might be sufficiently unattractive, that the moment was put off, and put off again. Unfiring columns have impetus, they are one cohesive mass and can be centrally controlled; the formation of a line, on the other hand, sees that control fragment to sub-units. Maintaining direction becomes much harder as the inequalities of the ground distort any uniform pace. Once troops start firing, commanders start to lose control of the forward momentum: individuals in the first line will inevitably reload at different stages. Will some halt to do so, or can all men reload their muskets on the march? (The present author cannot, for one.) Will you fire – wildly – on the march, or stop to aim? What of the muskets in the second line? And all the time the officers and men want to close the gap to the enemy line, to cover the ground and get off it before the next lead blizzard howls down towards them. It takes almost inhuman control to halt a firing line which is itself under fire.

So why not just charge with the bayonet – surely easier when drawn up in the original column? It seems that the French officers may have faced real life's usual dilemma – choice between a range of options that each presented difficulties. They had grown used to finding on other fields that a column often sufficed to break their enemy. Where that happy outcome was denied, they had grown equally used to finding time to form a line, and break their enemy with fire. At Vimiero, however, their enemy showed themselves adept at pouncing first – with their bayonets. For all Sir Charles Oman's preference for his decisive balance of firepower, most of the assaults at Vimiero were seen off with cold steel, as our eyewitnesses consistently attest.

The *first* attack on the 1/50th by Thomières' 86e Ligne was countered when Colonel Walker 'ordered an immediate volley and charge' by the 'only two companies of the wing' yet formed, which 'created great confusion which, by the time the three outer companies could arrive to take part in the charge, became general.' Landmann heard Walker call out, 'raising his drawn sword and waving it high over his head, "Three cheers and charge, my fine fellows!" and away went this gallant regiment, huzzaing all the time of their charge down the hill.'

The *second* attack by Charlot's 32e and 82e Ligne was countered when the 2/97th, 'after firing two or three rounds began to advance from their position [and] made a vigorous attack in front – the enemy soon gave way' – this is the moment when Sergeant Hale commented that 'it is not the English fashion to play at ball long, if there is a possibility of giving a charge.'

The *third* attack by St Clair's grenadiers was defeated by volley fire alone, from the 2/97th, the 2/9th and the 1/50th; while the *fourth* attack into Vimiero village was countered by musket and rifle fire from the flanks; by the 2/43rd's bayonets in the village itself – one of those rare instances of bayonet fighting, as opposed to bayonet charges; and when 'our gallant fellows… suddenly springing up, rapidly poured on them two or three volleys with great precision, and rushing on, charged with the bayonet' (Leslie).

The *fifth* attack, by Solignac on Ferguson, was countered when the latter 'ordered his Brigade to charge them, which was done with all the intrepidity and courage of British soldiers, and the enemy retired before us' (Warre); and when the French rallied, the 36th were 'hurraed to charge, which was done in great style three successive times.' Leslie says that the 29th 'marched steadily on, ready to charge. But on our continuing to push on, they rapidly retreated before we could close with them, and abandoned all their guns.'

Finally, in the *sixth* attack, by Brennier, which initially recaptured Solignac's guns, Warre saw 'the 71st… charging six pieces of the enemy's cannon… The enemy advanced with drums beating, but the 71st charged them so manfully that they retired in confusion.'

So in five of the six distinct attacks by the French, eyewitnesses attribute British success to the bayonet charge (that single word 'charge' is repeated over and over again) – not to decimating musket fire, however mathematically overpowering; nor to the artillery, the cavalry, or the preliminary depredations by the light troops. This charge with the bayonet, over a short distance and immediately following just one or two unanswerable volleys, emerges as the main feature of the fighting at Vimiero. Sir Arthur's positioning of his battalions out of sight of the approaching French, whereever possible, contributed in three of the six fights; and French reluctance (again, on three documented occasions) to deploy into line in the face of their highly manoeuvrable enemy, saw them caught flat-footed, with only one way to go.

On a less triumphant note, one is not so happy, on reading the eyewitness accounts, about the British skirmishing at Vimiero. Some commentators seem convinced of its excellence: Michael Glover says that the British riflemen 'established a superiority over the opposing tirailleurs which they were to maintain for the next six years... they did great execution.' Jac Weller writes that: 'The tirailleurs required the help of their columns to force back the riflemen.' Julian Paget refers to 'the skilful tactics of the British skirmishers.'

It is nevertheless repeatedly implied by our eyewitnesses that at no point did Delaborde or Charlot seem particularly incommoded in the skirmishing phase. They did not stop: they 'pressed hastily on' (Leach); 'came rapidly along the road' (Anstruther); 'came steadily down upon us' (Harris); 'they moved with great rapidity and admirable regularity, pushing on in the most gallant and daring manner' (Leslie); they 'were advancing with great resolution' (Leach), 'at a rapid step' (Patterson); 'our riflemen and skirmishers... were soon driven in by the rapid advance of the French' ('Subaltern of the 36th'); the French 'made a rapid advance towards the hill' (Walker).

There is no evidence here of the British light troops causing problems, only of the French speed of advance. Yet a heavy price was exchanged in casualties, just as at Rolica: the average loss in each rifle company was ten killed and ten wounded. Rifleman Harris' remark, 'when once engaged, we never went further from the enemy than we could possibly help,' hints that – again, as at Rolica – the Rifles were not getting the full potential from their specialist long range weapon. The Baker rifle supposedly had an effective range five times that of the French tirailleurs' smooth-bore musket: so why fight so close? Is it possible that the Rifles' marksmanship in August 1808 was not as sharp as it became later? Or might the answer conceivably lie in some peculiarity in the amounts of made-up cartridge and of loose powder and ball they had been issued?

In concluding these comments, by way of summary, it seems fair to say that Sir Arthur Wellesley in fact had remarkably little to do with his victory at Vimiero, after placing his battalions and his artillery. He was certainly swift (but not premature) in re-adjusting his formations on Junot's two-pronged approach, and his techniques of lying his men down and use of reverse slopes posed the French columns a novel challenge, to which they failed to rise. Yet the use of reverse slopes was not exactly – in today's slang – 'rocket science'; and anyway, four of the six brigade attacks unfolded (apparently) in his absence on the eastern ridge. After the deployment of his army the battle was won for him by his brigadiers' leadership, his soldiers' manoeuvring and volley fire, and especially by their readiness to get stuck in with the bayonet – or more accurately, to threaten to get stuck in, for little actual bayonet fighting took place, and on each occasion the French turned tail without crossing blades.

So while the genius of Sir Arthur which emerged as the Peninsula campaign continued is not in doubt, and will demand our amazement and applause, at this early stage it is only right to acknowledge the competence generally exhibited by lower commanders. That came from an existing, standardized approach within the

British infantry battalions which was largely intelligent, which worked, and which Wellesley himself rightly took for granted.

As for Junot, once he had split his force into three there was no way he could win unless the separate thrusts could be co-ordinated; Sir Arthur had arranged his position so that he had the advantage of interior lines for reinforcement, one flank to another, and of more than adequate reserve troops. Junot's one hope, and Wellesley's one Achilles Heel, was to get his 2,200 sabres into the baggage train, vulnerably parked just behind Vimiero village. His probable lack of any proper reconnaissance, however, may well have left him quite ignorant of this opportunity. 'Time spent in reconnaissance is seldom wasted' is an old saw; so too is 'Pride cometh before a fall'. One suspects that Junot had become over-familiar with the gods of victory, believing them all to be Frenchmen.

5
Moore and Corunna:
October 1808–January 1809

THE armistice procured so easily by General Kellerman on 22 August had progressed to the status of a Convention by the 31st, when it was ratified by Dalrymple and Junot at Cintra. On 17 September it was published in London, to be greeted immediately and inevitably by outraged indignation from all quarters. 'Scandalously disgraceful... calamitous... shameful... dishonourable... ignominious... unprecedented... sickening' were some of the terms used by the press. The next day, appropriately enough, the French army actually embarked on the British ships, and sailed happily away for La Rochelle with their plunder.

Three days after that Sir Arthur himself sailed for England: he had earlier written to his brother William, 'These people [Dalrymple and Burrard] are really more stupid and incapable than any I have ever met with; and if things go on in this disgraceful manner I must quit them.' He reached Plymouth on 4 October, at the height of the furore surrounding the Convention. According to Captain Ross-Lewin of the 32nd, who took passage with Wellesley's staff, 'the inhabitants of Devonshire were so incensed by the Convention of Cintra that they seem to have forgotten Rolica and Vimiero, and consequently received Sir Arthur with every mark of disapprobation; indeed, hissings and booings greeted him at every town and village of that county, through which he had to pass on the way to the metropolis.' Being the man who signed the initial armistice, Wellesley seemed the obvious target.

In London he learned that Dalrymple and Burrard had been recalled, handing command of the Peninsular Field Army to Sir John Moore, and that there was to be a board of inquiry into the Convention. This concluded in mid-January 1809, with Sir Hew and Sir Harry quietly cast into that military wilderness where further command is forever blocked. Sir Arthur, however, was cleared of any blame for failing to exploit his victory at Vimiero:

> Considering the extraordinary circumstances under which two Commanding Generals arrived from the ocean and joined the army (the one during, and the other immediately after a battle, and those successively superseding each other, and both the original Commander within the space of twenty-four hours), it is not surprising that the army was not carried forward until the second day after the action, from the necessity of the Generals being acquainted with the actual state of things, and of their army, and proceeded accordingly.

A week later, on 27 January 1809, the House of Commons passed a vote of thanks to the Victor of Vimiero, which was repeated in the Lords. Wellesley, who had prudently taken cover in his Dublin office, now found himself no longer the lead story in the headlines. One word replaced him – Corunna; for a few days after the Cintra inquiry ended, there arrived the deeply depressing news of the army's retreat to that port, the death of Moore, and the loss of some 6,000 of his 35,000 men (at that stage the true figure could not be known, of course, nor that many would straggle their way to Lisbon), together with huge quantities of stores, monies, guns and all the horses, in a desperate fighting withdrawal across the icy Galician mountains. The appearance of the filthy surviving skeletons, as they stumbled along the roads from the harbours of southern England sick, verminous, tattered, shoeless and dirty-bandaged, stunned onlookers and gave the country another subject for their shamed indignation.

It is not our purpose here to cover the painful saga of Corunna very fully; yet Moore's frustrating contacts with Napoleon's troops – for the Emperor himself had taken the field in Spain – are all part of the Peninsular Army's development, and therefore grist to our particular mill. Clearly, we must listen to Moore's infantry, horse and commissariat, for their stories take our understanding several steps further, and set the stage for the return of Wellesley to the Peninsula in April 1809, and his blitzkrieg campaign against Marshal Jean-de-Dieu Soult, the Duke of Dalmatia.

*   *   *

Two days after Sir Arthur Wellesley landed at Plymouth on 4 October 1808, Sir John Moore received his appointment from Castlereagh, and also his orders. He was to co-operate with the various Spanish armies deployed up on the Ebro, beyond which the French had surprisingly retired following the shocking defeat of General Dupont at Baylen back in August. All of Spain except the north-east provinces was thus clear of the French, Madrid was a free city once more and Romana's Spanish division had been shipped home from the Baltic by the Royal Navy to join the patriots. With the remaining French strength reckoned at 50,000 men, it was surely a practical proposition for Moore – who was about to be reinforced by General Baird's 14,000 en route to Corunna, making him 40,000 strong – to join with 100,000 Spaniards and so clear northern Spain.

In mid-October, Moore marched into Spain, reaching Salamanca on 13 November; Baird was to march down from Corunna to rendezvous with him. In the meantime, unknown to Moore, Napoleon had left Paris to take personal command of no fewer than a quarter of a million troops from all over Europe that he had ordered to assemble on the Franco-Spanish border. 'It took many weeks for the veteran divisions from Glogau and Erfurt, from Bayreuth and Berlin, to traverse the whole breadth of the French Empire and reach the Pyrenees' (Oman); but the Emperor arrived at Bayonne on 3 November, a few days after 100,000 men of three corps from Germany, with the entire Imperial Guard and several divisions of cavalry still to follow. (Some 27,000 of the newly assembled army would be Junot's veterans, shipped home courtesy of Sir Hew Dalrymple.)

Already, on 29 October, General Lefebvre had pushed Joachim Blake's army back from Zornosa; it would be defeated again at Espinosa on 10 November, by Marshal Victor, and on the same day Marshal Soult routed the Conde de Belvedere's army at Gamonal. On the 11th Napoleon himself reached Burgos after forcing the pass at Somosierra. On the 22nd, Marshal Lannes defeated Castanos at Tudela. The news of the destruction of the Spanish armies with which he was supposed to co-operate did not reach Moore until the end of November; sending orders to Baird to join up with him at Burgos, he chose to strike north-east at Napoleon's lines of communication, to relieve the threat to Madrid and to buy time for the Spanish to complete a promised reorganization. He saw his duty as supporting the national movement, whatever the obvious dangers to his own troops. He left Salamanca for Valladolid on 11 December, but had not been long on the march when he learned that Madrid had already fallen to Napoleon on 4 December.

Moore reached Rueda on 15 December, just a day's march from Valladolid and thus within a whisker of cutting Napoleon's route home from Madrid to Bayonne. Suitably galvanized, the Emperor crossed the 5,000ft Guadarrama mountains north of Madrid on 19 December, leading his veterans on foot through deep snow; while Napoleon drove north-west, Soult also moved against Moore, southwards from Saldana. The next day Moore and Baird at last met up at Mayorga; and on the 21st, General Lord Paget's hussar brigade beat their opposite numbers in a small but encouraging battle at Sahagun – almost Moore's last throw before turning to run into the hills. The principal eyewitnesses were Captain Alexander Gordon of the 15th Hussars, and Trooper James Tale; Gordon's account is so rich in detail and atmosphere that it is worth quoting at length:

20 December 1808

The officers commanding troops and squadrons were summoned to Colonel Grant's quarters at ten o'clock in the evening, when he acquainted us that Lord Paget had directed the regiment to be formed in readiness to march on a particular service precisely at midnight, and that we should probably be engaged with the enemy before daylight. The Colonel ordered the troops to be assembled as silently as possible at eleven o'clock, and cautioned us to keep the Spaniards in ignorance of the intended march, that they might not have it in their power to give information to the enemy. The regiment was formed at the hour appointed, but owing to the irregular manner in which we had been obliged to take up our quarters, and the bugles not being allowed to sound, several men were left behind whom the non-commissioned officers had not informed of the order to turn out. Lieutenant Buckley, who had joined us in the evening with a number of men and horses that had been left in Galicia, remained in the village to follow with the baggage and ineffectives in the morning.

21st – Whilst we were drawn up at the alarm-post, waiting for the arrival of Lord Paget, a fire broke out in the vilage, occasioned, probably, by the carelessness of some of our dragoons. The glare of the flames partially illuminated the ground where we stood, and contrasted finely with the dark mass of our column; while the melancholy sound of the church bell, which was struck to rouse the sleeping inhabitants, broke the silence of the night, and, combined with the object and probable consequences of our expedition, made the whole scene peculiarly awful and interesting.

Captain Thornhill, of the Seventh, who attended Lord Paget, with ten or twelve orderlies of his regiment, rode beside me during part of the night, and told me the object of our movement was to surprise a body of cavalry and artillery posted in a convent at Sahagun, a large town on the Cea, five leagues from Melgar de Abaxo. I afterwards learned that General Slade was directed to attack the convent with the Tenth and Horse Artillery, whilst the Fifteenth was to make a circuit and form on the opposite side of the town, in order to intercept their retreat. This plan, however, was rendered abortive by the bad state of the roads and the dilatory proceedings of the Brigadier [Slade], who on this occasion is reported to have made a long speech to the troops, which he concluded with the energetic peroration of 'Blood and slaughter – march!'

Our march was disagreeable, and even dangerous, owing to the slippery state of the roads; there was seldom an interval of many minutes without two or three horses falling, but fortunately few of their riders were hurt by these falls. The snow was drifted in many places to a considerable depth, and the frost was extremely keen. We left Melgar in the midst of a heavy fall of snow, and when that ceased I observed several vivid flashes of lightning.

We passed through two small towns or villages; in one of these, about two leagues from Sahagun, is a noble castle, which appeared to great advantage 'by the pale moonlight.' Near this place our advanced guard came upon the enemy's piquet, which they immediately charged; the Frenchmen ran away, and in the pursuit both parties fell into a deep ditch filled with snow. Two of the enemy were killed, and six or eight made prisoners; the remainder escaped and gave the alarm to the troops at Sahagun. Just at this period, when despatch was particualrly required, our progress was very much impeded by two long narrow bridges, without parapets, and covered with ice, which we were obliged to cross in single file.

On our arrival at Sahagun we made a detour, to avoid passing through the streets, and discovered the enemy formed in a close column of squadrons near the road to Carrion de los Condes; but, owing to the darkness of the morning and a thin mist, we could neither distinguish the number nor the description of the force opposed to us, further than to ascertain it consisted of cavalry.

Lord Paget immediately ordered us to form open column of divisions and trot, as the French, upon our coming in sight, made a flank movement, apparently with the intention of getting away; but the rapidity of our advance soon convinced them of the futility of such an attempt. They therefore halted, deployed from column of squadrons, and formed a close column of regiments, which, as it is their custom to tell off in three ranks, made their formation six ranks deep. During the time the two corps were moving in a parallel direction, the enemy's flankers, who came within twenty or thirty yards of our column, repeatedly challenged, 'Qui vive?' but did not fire, although they received no answer. As soon as the enemy's order of battle was formed, they cheered in a very gallant manner, and immediately began firing. The Fifteenth then halted, wheeled into line, huzzaed, and advanced.

Trooper Tale recollected the moment of contact:

As the grey morn dawned upon us, we seemed to emerge from our narrow path into more open ground. The silence hitherto maintained was now interrupted by hummings, buzzing, whispering, and indistinct sounds of human voices. Then followed the words of command – 'Form divisions! Wheel into line!' A dark living mass was in front, not to be plainly distinguished by the eye; onward we rushed. There followed a plunge – a crash – hacking and hewing, and the devil to pay.

Captain Gordon continues:

The interval betwixt us was perhaps 400 yards, but it was so quickly passed that they had only time to fire a few shots before we came upon them, shouting 'Emsdorff and victory!' The shock was terrible; horses and men were overthrown, and a shriek of terror, intermixed with oaths, groans, and prayers for mercy, issued from the whole extent of their front. Our men, although surprised at the depth of the ranks, pressed forward until they had cut their way quite through the column. In many places the bodies of the fallen formed a complete mound of men and horses, but very few of our people were hurt. Colonel Grant, who led the right centre squadron, and the Adjutant who attended him, were amongst the foremost who penetrated the enemy's mass; they were both wounded – the former slightly on the forehead, the latter severely in the face. It is probable neither of them would have been hurt if our fur caps had been hooped with iron like those of the French Chasseurs, instead of being stiffened with pasteboard.

It was allowed, by everyone who witnessed the advance of the Fifteenth, that more correct movements, both in column and in line, were never performed at a review; every interval was accurately kept, and the dressing admirably preserved, notwithstanding the disadvantages under which we laboured. The attack was made just before daybreak, when our hands were so benumbed with the intense cold that we could scarcely feel the reins or hold our swords. The ground was laid out in vineyards intersected by deep ditches and covered with snow. Our horses, which had suffered from confinement on shipboard, change of forage, and the fatigues of incessant marches in inclement weather, were not in their usual condition; and, as the commanding officer had neglected to halt the regiment during the march for the purpose of tightening their girths, they had become so slack that when we began to gallop several of the blankets slipped from under the saddles. The

French were well posted, having a ditch in their front, which they expected to check the impetus of our charge; in this, however, they were deceived. Lord Paget misjudged the distance or halted the Fifteenth too soon, by which means our right was considerably outflanked, and we outflanked theirs by a squadron's length. It was said afterwards that he intended the left squadron should have remained in reserve to support the charge, but no explicit order to that effect reached us. After the horses had begun to gallop, indeed, the word of command, 'Left squadron to support!' was passed from the centre, but so indistinctly that Major Leitch did not feel authorized to act upon it, and at that moment we were so near the enemy that it would have been difficult to restrain either the men or the horses.

My post being on the left of the line, I found nothing opposed to my troop, and therefore ordered, 'Left shoulders forward!' with the intention of taking the French column in flank; but when we reached the ground they had occupied, we found them broken and flying in all directions, and so intermixed with our hussars that, in the uncertain twilight of a misty morning, it was difficult to distinguish friend from foe. Notwithstanding this there was a smart firing of pistols, and our lads were making good use of their sabres. Upon reaching the spot where the French column had stood, I observed an officer withdrawn from the mêlée. I followed, and, having overtaken him, was in the act of making a cut at him which must have cleft the skull, when I thought I distinguished the features of Lieutenant Hancox; and, as I then remembered that he wore a black fur cap and a cloak which, in the dim light of the morning, looked like blue, I was confirmed in the idea that he belonged to our regiment.

Under this impression, although his conduct in quitting the field at such a period struck me as very extraordinary, I sloped my sword, and merely exclaiming: 'What, Hancox is it you? I took you for a Frenchman!' turned my horse and galloped back to the scene of action. The shock I felt from the idea that I had been on the point of destroying a brother officer instead of an enemy deprived me of all inclination to use my sword except in defence of my own life; and the hostility I had cherished against the French only a few minutes before was converted into pity for them. When I met with Hancox after the action, I found that he wore an oilskin cover on his cap, and was not the person I had followed, who, I conclude, was an officer of the *grenadiers à cheval* or *compagnie d'élite*, which is attached to each regiment of dragoons in the French service, and doubtless was much astonished at my sudden appearance and abrupt departure. For my own part, I shall always consider it a most fortunate circumstance that I was thus deceived, since I have escaped the feeling of remorse to which I should have been exposed had I taken that man's life.

Many mistakes of the same kind must have occurred in the confusion after the charge. One of our men told me that I had a narrow escape myself, for during the mêlée he had his sword raised to cut me down, but luckily recognized his officer in time to withhold the stroke.

At this time I witnessed an occurrence which afforded a good deal of amusement to those who were near the place. Hearing the report of a pistol close behind me, I looked round and saw one of the Fifteenth fall. I concluded the man was killed, but was quickly undeceived by a burst of laughter from his comrades, who exclaimed that the awkward fellow had shot his own horse, and many good jokes passed at his expense.

The mêlée lasted about ten minutes, the enemy always endeavouring to gain the Carrion road. The appearance of their heavy dragoons was extremely martial and imposing; they wore brass helmets of the ancient Roman form, and the long black horsehair streaming from their crests had a very fine effect.

Having rode together nearly a mile, pell-mell, cutting and slashing each other, it appeared to me indispensable that order should be re-established, as the men were quite wild and the horses almost blown; therefore, seeing no superior officer near, I pressed through the throng until I overtook and halted those who were farthest advanced in pursuit. As soon as I had accomplished this object, the bugles sounded the 'rally'. Whilst we were re-forming our squadrons, the enemy also rallied and continued their flight by different routes. Our left and centre squadrons were detached in pursuit of the *chasseurs à cheval*, who took the road to Carrion; the other two squadrons followed the dragoons, who retired in the direction of Saldana.

Lord Paget accompanied the left centre squadron, and allowed the body he pursued to escape by sending an officer, with a white handkerchief as a sign of truce, to propose to them to surrender. The French took advantage of the delay this occasioned, and gained so great a start as to render further pursuit hopeless. The left squadron was more successful, and made about seventy prisoners, amongst whom were a Lieutenant-Colonel and three other officers; but we could not prevent the escape of the main body, which, although more than double our number, never attempted to face us. Soon after our left squadron was put in motion in pursuit of the *chasseurs à cheval*, Baron Tripp came up to us and said that Lord Paget had sent him to desire the commanding officer to ride forward with a flag of truce and propose to them to surrender. Major Leitch made no answer, but, as if he had misunderstood the order, immediately gave the word of command to 'Gallop!' upon which the squadron rushed on, leaving the Aide-de-Camp petrified with astonishment. It was entirely owing to Major Leitch's judicious conduct, in declining to act upon the flag of truce system, that his squadron was enabled to secure so many prisoners.

Whilst we were engaged in the pursuit of this division, my mare fell with me leaping a very wide ditch, and floundered in a snow-wreath on the farther side; my foot hung in the stirrup, and, being encumbered with my cloak, it was some time before I could extricate myself. The mare in the meantime ran away, leaving me in no very enviable situation.

Whilst I was pursuing the squadron on foot… I was greatly shocked at witnessing an act of wanton cruelty which it was not in my power to prevent. A man of Griffith's troop rode up to a French dragoon who was lying wounded on the ground, and at his approach raised himself with difficulty to beg for mercy, stripping off his cross-belts at the same time to show that he surrendered. I hallooed to the fellow to spare him, but before I could reach the spot the villain had split the Frenchman's skull with a blow of his sabre, and galloped away. It was fortunate for him that he got out of my reach, for, in the indignation that I felt at his conduct, I should certainly have treated him in the same manner. I heard afterwards that the excuse he offered for this dastardly conduct, when twitted by his comrades, was that he did not like 'to let the day pass without cutting down a Frenchman, and could not suffer such a favourable opportunity to slip!' It was also reported that several of the French who were wounded and had received quarter, fired at our men as soon as their backs were turned, and of course paid the forfeit of this treachery with their lives.

After running three or four hundred yards, I met some men of my troop leading captured French horses, from which I selected one to replace my lost charger. Several straggling Frenchmen passed close beside me, whilst I was on foot, without offering me the slightest molestation; they probably took me for one of their own people, or were too intent on providing for their own safety to think of any other object. The animal I selected was a bad goer and very ill-broke; it had belonged to a quartermaster or subaltern officer, and was hand-somely caparisoned, but the saddle was far from comfortable, and the stirrups so long that I could scarcely reach them with the point of my toe. This horse was such a headstrong beast that he was near placing me in an awkard predica-ment. In the act of leading the men I had collected against the squadron of Chasseurs which had escaped from Lord Paget, I leaped over a ditch which lay between the two bodies; and when the attack was countermanded, I suppose my steed recognized his old companions, as the enemy was then passing at the distance of little more than a hundred yards, and I had the greatest difficulty in forcing him to recross the ditch, and for some time expected to be carried into the midst of the French squadron in spite of all my exertions to the contrary.

When I was remounted, I saw that the squadron was so far advanced I had no chance of overtaking it. I therefore employed myself in collecting the pris-oners we had taken, whom I sent to the rear under an escort. They seemed very much terrified, having, as I understood, been taught to expect no quarter would be given them; and when I assured them they had no cause for appre-hension of that sort, they kissed my hands, embraced my knees, and committed all manner of extravagancies. Many of these men were Germans and remarkably fine-looking fellows.

I had now collected about thirty hussars – including those who had been sent back with the prisoners, and whose horses had been unable to keep up with the rest – when the Tenth appeared on an eminence near the scene of the action, and were supposed to belong to the enemy. As soon as I noticed this fresh body of cavalry, I looked anxiously round the plain in hopes of discov-ering a rallying point; but the regiment was so completely scattered in pursuit that I could not perceive a single squadron formed on the field, and our situation appeared so desperate that I considered the only thing that remained for us to do was to sell our lives as dearly as possible. I therefore determined to lead my small division against the body of Chasseurs which had escaped from Lord Paget; but I had scarcely given the word to advance, when his lordship, who as well as every other officer had been deceived by the appearance of the Tenth in a quarter where they were not expected, ordered the 'rally' to be sounded, and Colonel Grant, who had just arrived on the spot and approved of my design, said the signal must be immediately obeyed. I was thus reluctantly obliged to abandon the meditated attack, which, fronm our relative positions, would in all probability have been attended with complete success, as we had an opportunity of charging on the enemy's flank.

I was happy to exchange the French horse for my own mare, which was brought to me soon after the regiment had reassembled, having been found in the custody of some men of the Tenth, but I was not so fortunate as to recover the valise with my baggage, which was strapped to the saddle at the time I lost her.

We learned from the prisoners that their force consisted of the 8th Regiment of Dragoons and a provisional regiment of *chasseurs à cheval,* commanded by the General of Brigade, Debelle, whose horses and baggage fell into our hands. It appeared by the returns found in his portfolio that the French had about eight hundred men mounted in the field, whilst we only mustered betwixt three and four hundred, as, independent of various small detachments, above a hundred men and horses were left at Melgar de Abaxo. Although but few of the enemy were killed on the spot, a great proportion of the prisoners were severely wounded, chiefly by the sabre; their total loss exceeded 300 men, for a number of their wounded who, after escaping from the field had been left on the road from inability to proceed, were secured and brought to headquarters by our infantry, who afterwards occupied the villages where they had taken shelter.

Colonel Dud'huit and twelve officers of the 8th Dragoons were taken. This regiment, which was in the front, bore the brunt of the attack, and suffered most severely. Colonel Dugens, three officers and about a hundred of the Chasseurs were made prisoners. We understood that the Eighth was a favourite corps; it had served in all the late campaigns, and gained great credit at Marengo, Austerlitz, Jena, Eylau, and Friedland; several of the officers wore the Cross of the Legion of Honour; and several of the sergeants and privates bore honorary badges. The clothing and appointments, both of men and horses, were strong and serviceable; and the brass helmets, in the point of utility and martial appearance, might be substituted with advantage in our Service for the cocked hat of the heavy dragoon. At first they took us for Spaniards, and expected an easy victory. It is but doing them justice to remark that they received our charge with the most determined firmness, but after their ranks were once broken they made no effort to retrieve the day, but appeared panic-struck, and only intent on making their escape.

Colonel Tascher, nephew to the Empress Josephine, commanded the Chasseurs, but we could not ascertain whether he was present in the action. The French were better mounted than we had been led to expect from the report of some of our officers who had been on service with the regiment in the campaigns of 1794 and 1799. None of their horses were under fourteen hands and a half, and several were taken into our brigade to replace such as had become unfit for service. They were in pretty good condition, but most of their backs were galled; this was not surprising, as they had only arrived at Sahagun a few days before, having made almost daily marches since the beginning of October, when they left Hanover; and the French dragoons had taken very little care of their horses.

There was not a single man of the Fifteenth killed in the field; we had about thirty wounded, five or six severely, two of whom died the next day; most of the others were so slightly hurt that they returned to their duty within a week. I expected the French would have displayed more skill in the use of the sabre than our men, but the fact proved quite the reverse, for notwithstanding their swords were considerably longer, they had no chance with us. Our hussars obtained a good deal of plunder, as the prisoners were well supplied with many trinkets and ingots of silver, the produce of plate stolen from the churches and houses of the Spaniards, and melted to render it more portable. Many of their valises contained fans and parasols – rather extraordinary articles of equipment for a winter campaign... We also got possession of the papers belonging to the staff of the brigade, and the seals of the 8th Regiment, besides a great number of private letters which were scattered about the fields of the captors without any regard to the tender nature of the contents.

Although the success of the action was rendered incomplete, owing to the very extraordinary conduct of General Slade and some mistakes of Lord Paget, it nevertheless impressed such an idea of the superiority of our cavalry on the mind of the enemy as induced them to avoid as much as possible coming in contact with us. Indeed, I can only attribute the want of enterprise displayed by them on many subsequent occasions, when, owing to their immense superiority in point of numbers and the inefficient state of our horses, they had favourable opportunities of destroying the regiment, to the lessons they had received at Sahagun, Rueda, Valencia, etc.

In fact the French horse at Sahagun totalled some 600 sabres, and their loss that morning was perhaps 300 killed, wounded and taken, including both colonels. The 15th Hussars lost just two killed and twenty-three wounded; since it is thought that they started only 400 strong, it was certainly a handsome victory, and news of it would have spread quickly on both sides. Cavalry being, by nature, competitive creatures, it is no surprise that within a few days, at Villada, a troop of the 18th Light Dragoons charged a French squadron of 150 men, killing twelve and capturing twenty; while near Mayorga, the 10th Hussars charged up-hill and broke a French light cavalry regiment, taking 100 prisoners. Later, in a beautifully timed ambush at

Benavente on 29 December, Paget with 450 sabres from the 10th Hussars swooped upon 600 men in four squadrons of the Chasseurs of the Imperial Guard, and broke them against a piquet line of about 200 men from the 7th and 18th Hussars and the 3rd Light Dragoons of the King's German Legion. The French commander, General Lefebvre-Desnouettes, was among the seventy-three captured; fifty-five others were killed and wounded; and to make victory even sweeter, Napoleon himself watched the whole affair from high ground on the far bank of the Esla river.

Taken together, these convincing if small scale cavalry victories at the start of the retreat to Corunna established a sense of moral superiority that was never to desert the British mounted arm. There is but a thin line between confidence and rashness, however; and these successes may be part of the reason for the later difficulties that cavalry commanders were to experience, time and again, in reining back their charging squadrons. While Paget's particular regiments were to languish in Britain for four years after their return from Corunna, their successors in the Peninsula clearly inherited the belief that they were expected to be unstoppable, and did their level best not to disappoint either the British or the French armies in this respect.

*   *   *

Two days after Sahagun, on 23 December, Moore finally learned of the full extent of his danger from the converging French armies. With his own lines back to Portugal now in turn directly threatened, he could only run for the coast. He escaped from the immediate trap, but Soult and Napoleon joined forces on 27 December and settled down to pursue Moore's retreat westwards, in appalling winter conditions. Once Sir John's troops entered the mountains Paget's troopers naturally saw no further actions of a fluid nature; but they were worked until they dropped as a vital part of the rearguard, constantly patrolling, piquetting, skirmishing and acting as sheepdogs for the stragglers on foot. Many a man's life must have been saved, at least temporarily, when the rearguard's trumpets cut into his exhausted stupor and moved him on again.

Unlike the cavalry, the British infantry were cheated of the one thing that would have lifted their morale as they retreated – a good fight. Fifteen of Sir John's thirty-five battalions had fought at Vimiero, and so were confident of the outcome of any such clash. Denied one, it is small surprise that under the wretched conditions of the retreat they grew increasingly surly, ill-disciplined and (whenever opportunity offered) drunk. An endless series of small rearguard fights were not enough to lift morale; the anonymous 'Soldier of the 71st' says it all:

> … our sufferings were so great that many of our troops lost all their natural activity and spirits, and became savage in their dispositions. The idea of running away from an enemy we had beat with so much ease at Vimiero, without even firing a shot, as too galling to their feelings. Each spoke to his fellow, even in common conversation, with bitterness, rage flashing from their eyes, even on the most trifling occasions of disagreement.

The 30-year-old German commissary, August Schaumann, agreed:

> The disorder, lack of discipline and subordination... was brought about...
> through the dejection and sense of ignominy caused by a continuous retreat
> and the inability to measure oneself with the enemy.

The sufferings of the retreat were indeed severe, as described below in extracts from
Schaumann's vibrant memoir of this episode in his Peninsula service. To summarize,
the men marched 200 miles in three weeks, in terrible winter weather, over seemingly endless 3,000ft ridges, from their different starting points beyond Astorga; and
at the end of their ordeal they fought a battle while waiting desperately for their
transport fleet to sail in. The first extract from Schaumann describes the departure
from Astorga:

> On the morning of 31 December, I was despatched on all sorts of errands. I
> was to harass the Junta about provisions and forage for the cavalry; I was to do
> the same at the slaughter-houses outside the town, where it demanded an
> enormous amount of art to secure anything; and, finally, I was to go to the
> town to spy out the stores of corn. Chaos reigned everywhere. The majority of
> the inhabitants had flown, and all the shops had either sold out to the army
> passing through or else had been plundered. There was not a particle of bread
> or chocolate to be had anywhere. At the Junta they snorted at me angrily.
> 'What do you English think?' they cried. 'You are retreating, and yet we are
> expected to supply you with provisions! To-morrow the French will arrive,
> and we shall have to scrape something together for them unless we want to be
> hanged.'...
>
> It had been misty the whole day, and our rearguard had found it difficult
> to observe the approach and position of the enemy. The night was dark,
> stormy and wet. The remaining inhabitants of the town, alarmed by
> the retreating army, and even more so by the rapid approach of the
> French, ran about the streets in desperation, bemoaning their lot. Marauders
> rushed noisily out of the houses and store-cellars, which they had entered
> by force, while the streets were thronged with baggage, wagons, horses,
> bullock carts, cattle, soldiers, and moaning natives. Now and again the
> light of a torch of straw and resin would pass quickly by, or a fire, fed
> with the fragments of a broken ammunition wagon would suddenly shed
> its harsh light upon the scene of disorder and misery, only to leave it
> in darkness again a moment later. Meanwhile, the chatter of the muskets
> in the distance, and the monotonous staccato calls of the bugles, mustering
> the scattered rearguard together, mingled with the cries of the women pray-
> ing to the Virgin and the uproar created by the cursing of the military
> close at hand; and the whole town presented such a ghastly spectacle,
> that in the end, feeling feeble and exhausted, I left Lord Paget's dinner
> to its fate, and went in search of my quarters. But peace had departed
> from Astorga!

Eleven o'clock had just struck, when suddenly one of the hussars in my billet, springing up as if electrified, cried, 'Get up, get up! The trumpets are blowing!' and ran out into the kitchen, followed by us all. But before I could even bridle my horse these centaurs were already galloping out of the yard. All you could hear in the streets was the ominous clatter of horses' hoofs, the cries of command, and the sound of general flight. In a great hurry I wanted to bridle my horse, which, by the bye, had re-mained saddled the whole night, but forgetting to tighten his girth, which I had loosened to let him feed more easily, I fell, saddle and all, on to the floor at his feet. Fortunately the beast stood stock still. I was obliged patiently to un-fasten the valise, one of the straps of which was broken, so it hung askew, and to loosen all the other straps, and put the saddle on afresh. It was pitch dark in the yard. Never shall I forget the despair which I felt at this accident. From sheer rage I did nothing but swear disgustedly or weep like a child. Moreover, I was in such a hurry that I did not know what to do first, and thus lost much time. At last I succeeded, and forthwith scampered out of the house.

But the hussars had vanished, the streets were dark and deserted, and I did not even know out of which gate the troops had gone. My position was desperate. At last through the darkness I caught sight of a few English servants in white overalls who were riding spare horses; and joining them we rode out of the town where we kept to the left of a broad highway. We had not gone far before we encountered a number of men of the 18th Hussars, who told us that if we had not had the good fortune to meet them we should have taken a bee-line to the French army!...

... It was pitch dark, and the road taken by the army ran to the right across the mountains. We passed a filthy little village, and reached a highway, where a regiment of hussars were posted with a battery of horse artillery. The gunners had unlimbered and seemed to be awaiting the enemy. Together with various detachments of troops, I rode forward the whole night, and in the mountains we came upon glaciers or roads which were so deep in snow and ice that the horses could not stand, and we were obliged to dismount. I passed by a number of glowing bivouac fires which, flaring up now and then, illuminated the wild, desolate, wintry scene, the expressive stillness of which was gruesomely broken by the retreating army. The sausage I had had for supper made me feel dreadfuly thirsty; and my horse, too, badly wanted a drink. But there was no water; everything was frozen hard. Both of us therefore ate the snow. I slept while walking, for the road was too steep and slippery to ride, and it was too cold to sit in the saddle. At last the day broke and we found ourselves in the mountains that join Galicia and Asturias to Leon. The road was incredibly bad, and we sank knee-deep in mud and snow. ...

;chaumann's eye and vivid pen leave us a classic account of the age-old nightmare of winter flight before the enemy:

The road we followed showed all the traces of the horrors and destruction that war leaves in its path. Starving inhabitants of the country fled in front and past us with faces distorted by fear, despair and vindictiveness; and the weaker among them, the aged, the children and the women, laden with their belongings, and perishing from fear, and from the rain, the storms, the snow and the hunger to which they had been exposed night and day, sank in the mire at our feet imploring in vain for help, which we could not give even our own men. But the road was not only strewn with human corpses; horses, mules and draft-bullocks suffered the same fate. They collapsed beneath their load, and in order that their misery might end and they might not fall into the enemy's hands, they were shot and their corpses left as obstacles in our wake.

All the way from Salamanca snow and sleet fell day and night; the roads offered no foothold, the swollen waters of the streams flooded the valleys and plains, and turned them into swamps or bogs through which the whole army waded up to the knees. The transport wagons stuck, the soldiers' boots were torn from their feet, and there was no fire to warm the men who were crippled with the wet and the cold, nor any fortifying nourishment either.

In the end Villafranca was literally plundered, and the drunkenness that prevailed among the troops led to the most shameful incidents. Down by the river the artillery destroyed all their stores, and lighting big fires burnt all their ammunition wagons, which they broke up for the purpose. They also threw all their ammunition into the river. Several hundred horses, which could go no further, were led to the same spot and shot. Day and night we could hear the sound of pistol fire. Everything was destroyed. Discipline was at an end, and the officers were no longer heeded. ...

The French pursuit pressed close on the tail of the column, and repeated rearguard actions were fought to hold them back:

On the afternoon of 4 January, some sharp firing, intermingled with gunshots [i.e. artillery] was heard just outside the gate of the town. Many of the rearguard marched in, and told us as they went by that things were very warm out there. 'But we popped them off, whenever they showed their ugly faces, like mice in the sun,' said one of them. A sapper officer then galloped through the streets shouting that by six o'clock everybody was to be over the bridge as it was then to be blown up. Now the uproar began! Women, children, the sick, and baggage wagons, all tried to get across at once. The troops making their way across by force, slowly marched away regiment by regiment, while other troops, fresh from the battle outside, arrived in the town. ...

... The fire of the skirmishers became so fierce at the entrance to Villafranca, where I happened to be standing, that the bullets rattled on the surrounding roofs. The rearguard poured in in masses. One or two sapper officers ran hither and thither, urging everyone to proceed to the bridge, for the gate of the town was not going to be held after the bridge had been blown up. Now all who still happened to be in the town made haste to escape. ...

Night soon fell, and we marched slowly forward in the darkness. A loud report in the direction of Villafranca announced that the bridge had been blown up, and at the same moment the horizon was illuminated as if the town were in flames. At the entrance of a certain defile, we all marched higgledy-piggledy or rather pushed each other forward through the darkness in one compact mass. Never shall I forget the heartrending cries of some wounded men, when their cart broke down, and they were deposited in a shed on the road and left behind. These poor devils implored us fervently not to leave them to the mercy of the French advance guard; but the whole procession marched on unfeelingly. Some of the senior and more experienced officers were completely astonished at the speed with which General Moore made the army retreat, and were of the opinion that if it were continued at one stretch as far as Corunna, two-thirds of our troops would be left lying on the roadside. Others defended the General, and declared that they had heard that a French army was on its way across Leon with the view of cutting us off near Lugo, in which case the utmost speed was imperative. In the end it was the latter who proved to have been right.

Again, we are reminded that this was not the panic flight of a beaten army, but the sullen withdrawal of one that resented not being allowed to fight:

> … Many of the soldiers, worn out with hunger and fatigue, had fallen out of the ranks during this rapid march, and had flung themselves in despair in the midst of the mud and filth on the side of the road. Insubordination was noticeable everywhere. The men regarded the retreat as an indignity, and many bitter remarks were made, all of which usually ended with the following prayer: 'Give us something to eat; let us just take a little rest, then lead us against the enemy, and we shall beat him!' As for any order on the march, or regular halts – such things were not even thought of! He who could go no further, stood still; he who still had something to eat, that ate he in secret, and then continued marching onwards; the misery of the whole thing was appalling – huge mountains, intense cold, no houses, no shelter or cover of any kind, no inhabitants, no bread. Every minute a horse would collapse beneath its rider, and be shot dead. The road was strewn with dead horses, bloodstained snow, broken carts, scrapped ammunition, boxes, cases, spiked guns, dead mules, donkeys and dogs, starved and frozen soldiers, women and children – in short, the sight of it all was terrible and heartrending to behold. In addition, the road frequently followed a zigzag course along the very edge of a precipice. We often reached small villages completely deserted by their inhabitants, and anybody who at night succeeded, by dint of many appeals to the soldiers, in being given a tiny bit of space either in a stable or a sty, in which to lie down and rest, together with a small fragment of bread, considered himself lucky. …
>
> … Everybody was so drunk with lack of sleep that again and again one of the throng would stop, and in spite of all appeals and warnings, drop down

and fall asleep and freeze, and never wake again. Many wounded and sick men, whom we had brought all the way with us, met their end now. ...

One of Schaumann's best known passages reminds us of the entirely relative value of money during life-and-death ordeals:

Beasts of draught and beasts of burden gradually sank in ever greater numbers beneath their load and died of hunger, after they had devoured the snow in the hope of slaking their thirst. I saw one bullock cart, belonging to the Paymaster-General's department, loaded with six barrels full of Spanish dollars, standing on the side of the road... The bullocks were lying on the ground under their yokes, utterly exhausted. A soldier with bayonet fixed stood guard over the treasure, and with a desperate air implored every officer that passed by to relieve him of his duty. But of course no one dared to do so! If only those dollars had been bread! Now, however, nobody paid any heed; the most confirmed thief passed by unmoved. ... Among the disasters that befell us while ascending this dreadful mountain, was the fact that we found ourselves compelled to rid our wagons of the load of Spanish dollars which constituted our war treasure. Most of the mules and bullocks that were drawing it had fallen down dead, and we had no fodder for those that still remained. The speed with which the French were pursuing us, moreover, left us no time in which to take any measures to save this money. A hussar regiment had, indeed, been furnsihed with bags, in order that they might carry some of it on their saddles; but as the men could not endure the load, they put as much of it as they could in their pockets and flung the rest away. As, therefore, it was impossible to conceal the stuff, the barrels containing it were rolled over the side of the precipice, where they smashed to pieces, and hurled their bright silver contents ringing into the abyss. And there, when the snow melted, many a poor shepherd or peasant must have found his fortune. For much the same reasons we had been obliged, when two miles beyond Villafranca, to abandon seventy or eighty wagonloads of arms and equipment intended for the Spanish army, which was either plundered by the body of a hundred Spanish patriots escorting and protecting them, or, what is more likely, taken by the French advanced guard.

By the time Moore's army reached the last leg of its march before descending to the coast they had almost exhausted their powers of endurance:

The road now became more terrible than ever. It was so stormy that we could hardly stand against the wind and snow, and it was horribly cold. A division which had been unable to continue on its way had evidently bivouacked here on the previous night, and had left melancholy traces of its sojourn. To the right, at the summit of the peak, we saw by the wayside, under the shelter of a ledge of rock, an overturned cart with the mules lying dead beside it. Under the cart lay a soldier's wife with two babies in her arms, evidently twins, which could not have been more than a day or two old. She and a man, who was probably a canteen attendant, lay frozen to death, but the children were still alive. I halted for a moment to contemplate the wretched group. A blanket was thrown over the bodies, and I had the pleasure of witnessing the rescue of the infants, who were handed over to a woman who came along in a bullock cart, to whom a few officers offered a substantial reward for taking care of them. It was a most harrowing spectacle. The enemy did not need to inquire the way we had gone; our remains marked out his route. From the eminence on which I stood I saw our army winding its way along the serpentine road, and the motionless blotches of red, left and right, upon the white snow, indicated the bodies of those whom hunger and cold had accounted for. …

… From the officers we heard that the march from Quitterez had proved a greater trial than all former marches for the troops. Officers and men of all regiments came along in groups, or alone, jaded, exhausted, starving and numb. Their feet were swollen, frostbitten, and bleeding, from walking over roads consisting chiefly of granite, quartz, or deep mud. A soldier's wife, probably the last to have got so far, also collapsed and died just outside Betanzos. …

… A sad affair took place at the bridge over the Minho. A party of about 500 stragglers and exhausted men came up who wanted to cross it, and found it already blown up. Just at that moment the French advanced and the Polish Lancers of the Imperial Guard suddenly appeared, and raising a loud cry and brandishing their lances, prepared to charge. But our stragglers from all regiments were not dismayed, and electing a sergeant as their commanding officer, formed a square, and with a cheer opened fire on the lancers. This kept the enemy at a respectful distance for some while, and it was only when several other French regiments appeared that they were compelled to capitulate and allow themselves to be taken prisoners.

*   *   *

The horrors of the retreat turned to grim relief when the redcoats finally and necessarily turned to confront their pursuers on the hills above Corunna harbour. Despite their condition, this was what the men had wanted for all those weary miles: a chance to hit back, and show their mettle. In a footnote to his description of the battle of Corunna, Sir Charles Oman states firmly that 'every student of the Pensinsular War should read Charles Napier's vivid and thrilling account of the storm of Elvina' – which was reprinted in 1857 by another great historian, Charles' younger brother William. Major Charles Napier commanded the 1/50th (West Kents), the battalion which had fought so splendidly under Colonel Walker on Vimiero Hill. His highly personal account of the fighting on 16 January 1809 around the pivotal village of Elvina, on the British right flank, merits all due admiration and sympathy:

I stood in front of my left wing, on a knoll, from whence the greater part of the field could be seen, and my piquets were fifty yards below, disputing the ground with the French skirmishers: but a heavy French column, which had descended the mountain at a run, was coming up behind with great rapidity, and shouting 'En avant, tue, tue, en avant, tue!'... their cannon [fire] at the same time, plunging from above, ploughed the ground and tore our ranks... I walked to the right of my regiment, where the French fire from the village of Elvina was now very sharp, and our piquets were being driven in by the attacking columns... Sir John Moore now returned, and I asked him to let me throw our grenadiers, who were losing men fast, into the enclosures in front. 'No,' he said, 'they will fire on our own piquets in the village.' 'Sir, our piquets, and those of the 4th Regiment also, were driven from thence.' 'Were they, then you are right, send out your grenadiers'; and away he galloped.

Turning around I saw Captain Clunes, and said to him 'Clunes, take your grenadiers and open the ball!'... Lord William Bentinck [Napier's brigade commander] now came up on his quiet mule, and though the fire was heavy began talking to me as if we were going to breakfast; his manner was his ordinary one, with perhaps an increase of good humour and placidity... Lord William and his mule, which seemed to care as little for the fire as his rider, sheltered me from shot, which I liked well enough; but having heard officers and men jeer at Colonel Walker for thus sheltering himself behind General Fane's horse at Vimiero, I went to the exposed side: yet it gave me the most uncomfortable feeling I experienced that day. Lord William borrowed my spy-glass, a very fine one... I never saw it again.

The fire falling on the 50th was such that the men were becoming uneasy. In the absence of the expected order to advance, and so as to occupy the men, Napier repeatedly ordered and shouldered their arms, as if on a drill parade, and caused the Colours to be lowered since 'they were a mark for the enemy's great guns'. The 42nd (Black Watch) on his left flank had been sent forward to the charge; although Napier as still without orders, he decided to support them:

I advanced without orders... at that moment the 42nd checked a short distance from a wall and commenced firing, and though a loud cry arose of 'Forward! Forward!' no man passed the wall. This check seemed to prove that my advance was right, and we passed the 42nd. Then I said to my men, 'Do you see your enemy's eyes plain enough to hit them?' Many voices shouted 'By Jasus we do!' 'Then blaze away!' and such a rolling fire broke out as I have hardly ever heard since.

After passing the 42nd we came to the wall, which was breast high and my line checked, but several officers leaped over, calling on the men to follow. At first about a hundred did at a low point, no more and therefore leaping back, I took a halberd [a sergeant's half-pike] and holding it horizontally pushed men over the low part... We then got to marshy ground close to the village, where the fire from the houses was terrible, the howitzers from the hills also pelting us. Still I led the men forward, followed closely by Ensigns Moore and Stewart with the Colours until both fell, and the Colours were caught up by

Sgt Magee and another Sergeant. My sword belt was shot off, scabbard and all.

... at this place stood the church, and towards the enemy a rocky mound, behind which, and on it, were the grenadiers... [the line] had been broken in carrying the village of Elvina, and as a lane went straight towards the enemy, I ran forward calling out to follow: about thirty privates (and three officers) did so, but the fire was then terrible, many shells bursting among us, and the crack of these things deafened me, making my ears ring. Half way up the lane I fell, without knowing why, but was much hurt, though at the moment unconscious of it, a soldier cried out 'The major is killed.' 'Not yet! Come on!'

We reached the end of this murderous lane, but a dozen of those who entered it with me fell 'ere we got through it... beyond the lane... a breast-work of loose stones... about a dozen of us lodged ourselves behind this, and then it appeared to me that by a rush forward we could carry the battery above; it was evident we must go on or go back, we could not last long where we were. Three or four men were killed at my side, for the breastwork was but slender protection, and two were killed by the fire of our men from the village behind.

Having sent back for reinforcements to attack the battery, but receiving none, and having tried to make contact with the 42nd, Napier returned to the church after various nightmare adventures. Here he was himself hit in the calf. He found that:

Where two other lanes met at the corner of the church, there were three privates of the 50th and one of the 42nd, an Irishman, who said we were cut off, and indeed Frenchmen were then coming up both lanes... the party from the position of the 42nd appeared the least numerous, they were not thirty yards from us, and forgetting my poor leg... I said to the four soldiers 'Follow me, and we'll cut through them'; then with a shout I rushed forard.

The Frenchmen had halted, but now ran on to us, and just as my spring and shout was made the wounded leg failed and I felt a stab in the back; it gave me no pain, but felt cold and threw me on my face. Turning to rise I saw the man who had stabbed me making a second thrust: whereupon letting go my sabre I caught his bayonet by the socket, turned the thrust, and raising myself by the exertion grasped his firelock with both hands, thus in mortal struggle regaining my feet. His companions had now come up and I heard the dying cries of the four men with me, who were all bayonetted instantly. We had been attacked from behind by men not before seen, as we stood with our backs to a doorway, out of which must have rushed several men, for we were all stabbed in an instant, before the two parties coming up the road reached us. ...

... being the strongest, I forced him between myself and his comrades... they struck me with their muskets clubbed and bruised me much... a tall dark man came up, seized the end of the musket with his left hand, whirled his brass-hilted sabre round and struck me a powerful blow on the head, which was bare, for my cocked hat had fallen off... it fell exactly on the top, cutting into the bone but not through it... fire sparkled from my eyes, I fell on my knees, blinded.

There is something remarkably modern about much of this account of the action around Elvina, between the two British battalions and the eight French battalions of the 31er Léger and 47e Ligne: it could almost be street fighting in Stalingrad. There are few references to conventional lines and columns, but rather to the difficulty of getting men to leave their momentary shelter among the stone-walled alleys, and the confusion of knowing who was where. The lack of visibility comes across strongly; twice Napier observed that the French smoke had not advanced, yet the British smoke had fallen back – a desperately vague way of tracking the swaying fortunes of battle. Napier's problem was, of course, that Elvina's buildings, lanes and gardens separated his battalion's line into parties who could not see each other to co-ordinate their efforts, and ruined any hope of conventional control. Any chance he had of exploiting further was lost when, unknown to him, his brigade commander recalled the 1/50th from the village, shortly after which it and he were both taken by the next French counter-attack.

*   *   *

Those who have persevered through these lengthy stories by Captain Gordon, Commissary Schaumann and Major Napier will, it is hoped, now see more clearly some aspects of Sir John Moore's Corunna campaign in the winter of 1808–09. As to the battle of Corunna itself, in declining to explain in any detail the part played by Elvina and the 1/50th in the larger picture, our motive is not to belittle the action in any way, but rather to move the story on to the return of Sir Arthur Wellesley to the Peninsula. A few comments are, however, inevitable.

Firstly, the French lost about 1,500 of the 16,000 men they fielded that day – say 10 per cent; and the British half that number, from a force of similar size. And the next day the British did get away in their ships, albeit only after burying Sir John Moore (for whom a great affection existed – he was not only one of the most intelligent, but also the most humane of commanders). The Corunna campaign can no more be called a victory than can that of Dunkirk; but under the circumstances, it was enough.

Secondly, it introduced a limited number of French infantrymen and their generals to British muskets and bayonets, and thus spread some measure of apprehension about future encounters. Soldiers always talk about the skills of their enemies (and sometimes, perhaps, pay undue regard to them). But while one may trace in 1809 a slow but insidious growth in fear of the Brown Bess, its 17-inch bayonet, and the men in red coats who wielded them, the benefit of this 'learning curve' was to be available to only a very limited number of the troops who would face them again at Talavera. Of the thirty-nine French battalions present at Corunna, only five had fought at Vimiero; and, looking ahead, of the sixty-two due to face Wellesley at Talavera, only three had fought him a year before at Vimiero, and none at all had been at Corunna.

*   *   *

The retreat to Corunna, notwithstanding the losses, the pain and the aftermath, was still a major failure for Napoleon. Moore's 35,000 men – of whom about 5,000 perished or disappeared – dragged 125,000 Frenchmen way up into north-west Spain when they should have been consolidating their newly-won thrusts into the heart of that country. Napoleon's failure to catch Moore quickly, and his subsequent return to Paris to manage greater matters, left his brother Joseph at centre stage in his place. This was undoubtedly a most fortunate development for the allies, since the inability of either King Joseph or his nominal chief of staff, Marshal Jourdan, to command his brother's generals and to co-ordinate their efforts doomed Napoleon's design of hunting the British out of the Peninsula. That required a strategy with various joined-up parts; and there was nothing joined-up about French command and control in the Peninsula in 1809 (or indeed at any later stage before the closing campaign in the Pyrenees). Conversely, the command discord created by Moore's effrontery at Christmas 1808 opened the door for Wellesley's astonishing opportunity, in May 1809, to deal separate blows first at Soult, then at Victor and King Joseph.

6
Crossing the Duoro,
12 May 1809

THE three winter months following Corunna saw the French push down into Spain again, constantly harried by bands of peasants and irregular troops. Even had communications been reliable, it is unlikely that Napoleon's brother Joseph and his chief of staff Marshal Jourdan would have been able to exercise much actual control over the distant and mutually jealous regional commanders. In London, on the other hand, the Cabinet took two early and crucial decisions: firstly, to appoint Wellesley to command in the Peninsula; and secondly – assuming their government agreed – to turn thousands of Portuguese peasants effectively into British auxiliaries, equipped, trained and partly commanded by British officers. Whilst the former decision may have been the easier, the latter was the most inspired, for over the coming four years of campaigning the emergence of really excellent and reliable Portuguese battalions proved a continuing boon to their brigadiers – and enormously so to Wellesley. The concept had already been proven in the form of the King's German Legion, a first class corps of foot, horse and guns formed from refugee Hanoverian soldiers and officers; while in India, of course, for many years John Company had routinely fielded formidably large armies built around a tiny core of redcoats. General Beresford – an officer who spoke the language and felt a genuine admiration for Portuguese potential – arrived in Portugal in March 1809; given the local rank of Marshal and overall command of the army, he began with his staff a whirlwind programme of reforms, which would be accepted eagerly by all but the most conservative elements.

The Cabinet's keenness to claw back some sort of public relations advantage after the catastrophic Convention of Cintra, followed so quickly by Corunna, was partly provoked by the earlier secret assurances from Austria of her willingness to contribute towards renewed opposition to Napoleon's designs. The Austrians promised 400,000 men, in exchange for a £2 million lump sum and a £400,000 monthly subsidy thereafter. While Whitehall doubtless hoped to cook Napoleon's goose before too many monthly payments had clocked up, it was felt that the allied cause generally would be aided if the French could be further embroiled in Spain. There was also the small matter of the French troops just 150 miles away from the Suffolk coast, in the Netherlands. A reinforcement for the expeditionary force already in Portugal was therefore to be assembled, and Horse Guards simultaneously dusted off the maps of Walcheren.

It all came together quite quickly: in February 1809 the Portuguese agreed to the British paying, supplying, training and leading their army; in early March Castlereagh asked Wellesley to put forward a case for defending Portugal; and when he had done so, rewarded him with appointment to the command, on 28 March. Sir Arthur's memorandum had stipulated 30,000 regular Portuguese backed by a militia of 40,000, together with 20,000 British. He got reinforcements earmarked in England to take him up to about 26,000, of whom 3,300 were cavalry; and with that he would have to do the business, since just about every other soldier was being committed to the expedition to Walcheren, to say nothing of an enormous transport fleet.

Sir Arthur sailed for Portugal in the middle of April. Among the 5,000 infantry in seven battalions also on the high seas was the 2/48th (Northamptonshire), like the other six a 2nd Battalion comprised largely of youngsters, and not many of them. These units averaged some 700 all ranks, or a third below establishment, having been severely milked the previous year to keep their 1st Battalions in full trim. The 1/48th, for example, which was to sail from Gibraltar a month later to join Wellesley, embarked over 1,000 all ranks.

Wellesley, characteristically, left as little as possible to luck. His ability to plan ahead was perfectly demonstrated within thirty-six hours of stepping on to Portuguese soil after his eight-day passage from Portsmouth on the frigate HMS *Surveillantes*. He wrote these precise, nearly nonchalant words to Secretary of State Castlereagh from Lisbon on 24 April, just two days after landing:

> I should prefer an attack on Victor in concert with Cuesta, if Soult were not in possession of a fertile province of this kingdom, and of the favourite town of Oporto, of which it is most desirable to deprive him. But any operation upon Victor, connected with Cuesta's movements, would require time to concert, which may as well be employed in dislodging Soult from the north of Portugal, before bringing the British army to the eastern frontier.

One has to admire 'which may as well…'.

There will be much mention in following pages of the names Soult, Victor and Cuesta, together with those of other leaders, and of a deal of unfamiliar places in both Portugal and Spain. The map overleaf is a snapshot of who was where at the time of Wellesley's landing in Lisbon towards the end of April 1809, and as he reviewed the situation.

The first good news was that rumours received before sailing from England were false: Soult's 2nd Corps was not on the move south from Oporto to Lisbon; Victor's 1st Corps was neither 35,000 strong nor moving west to Badajoz and Abrantes also en route to Lisbon, nor had he been reinforced by Sebastiani's 4th Corps. Instead, Soult's 20,000 men, having reached and captured Oporto in the face of Spanish irregular opposition, were dispersed and vulnerable, lightly engaged with Silveira's 12,000 patchily armed Portuguese levies. Behind Soult, but way off in the hills of Galicia, Ney's 17,000-strong 6th Corps was trying to cope with both insurrection and the Spanish army of General Romana. Down south, Victor had just 23,000 men; and having beaten old Cuesta at Medellin, far from invading Portugal, they now lay peaceably sixty miles to the east at Merida on the River Guadiana. Behind Victor's 1st Corps, further up the Guadiana, lay Sebastiani's 22,000-strong 4th Corps, but they remained separate. Both were flanked, threatened and therefore pre-occupied by the reorganizing Spanish armies of Cuesta and Venegas (35,000 and 30,000 men respectively) further south. Best of all was the news that Victor had called General Lapisse's reinforced division of 7,000 men to march down and join him, leaving the Cuidad Rodrigo/Salamanca area. As Fortescue comments, 'the effect of this movement was to isolate Soult completely'; a huge gap lay relatively open between Soult and Victor – 200 miles wide, nearly from the Galician foothills down deep into Estremadura.

With insurrections and Spanish armies distracting both French commanders in the west, and no love lost between them, neither one could or would rush to aid the other; therefore both might be defeated individually, if not exactly with ease then at least in comparative safety. Finally, soon after reaching Lisbon, Wellesley had been much heartened to learn from the French traitor Captain Argenton that Marshal Soult 'was entirely ignorant of the situation of Victor and all the other French corps in Spain'. It is an astonishing measure of King Joseph's ineptitude and Marshal Jourdan's impotence that neither Soult nor Victor, both instructed by the Emperor to go for Lisbon, had demonstrated any sense of urgency or of interest in co-ordinating that joint endeavour.

Thus we begin to see the basis for Wellesley's confident strategy, as expressed to Lord Castlereagh. The initiative lay with him. While it would be another year before Beresford's reforms brought complete Portuguese brigades into the field army, some 16,000 men were already undergoing 'on the job training' from cadres of British officers and NCOs, and could make a contribution in support of his 26,000 British troops. He could take either Soult or Victor, so long as the other did not intervene;

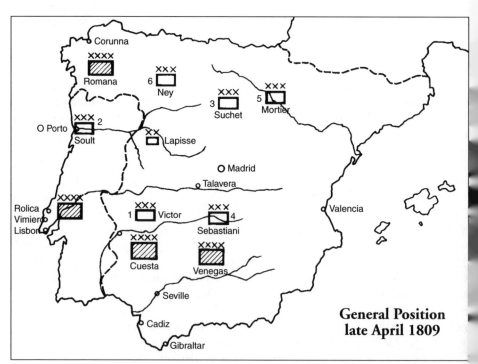

**General Position
late April 1809**

and it was Soult who lost the toss. Leaving General Mackenzie with 4,500 British and 7,500 Portuguese to guard his rear, he sent Beresford with 1,800 British and 4,200 Portuguese to effect a turning movement far inland of Soult, meeting up with the Portuguese general Silveira at Lamego, south of the Duoro and fifty miles east of Oporto. At the end of the first week in May he himself marched north from Coimbra with 16,000 British and 2,400 Portuguese troops and 24 guns. We may let the 1935 edition of the 48th (Northamptonshire) Regiment's regimental history commence the story:

On 5 May 1809 (four days after Wellesley's 40th birthday) the troops were reviewed at Coimbra ('The regiments having formed a line reaching above two miles, wheeled into column, marched past, and filed to their quarters' – Captain Hawker, 14th Light Dragoons) and reorganised into brigades, some of the best of the Portuguese battalions being included in the British brigades. The 2/48th were, however, in an all-British brigade under General Hill along with the 1/3rd and the 2/66th.

While the main body of Soult's army was still north of the Duoro, Mermet's division had been thrown across the river, with Franceschi's cavalry pushed out as a covering screen towards the River Vouga, which runs into the sea at Aviero. On 6 May Wellesley commenced his advance on Oporto. There were two roads from Coimbra, one inland by which he moved his main body, and the other along the coast through Aviero and Ovar by which he sent the brigades of General Hill (including the 2/48th) and Cameron.

At Aviero the River Vouga flows through a great lagoon before finally reaching the sea, the town of Ovar being at the north end of the lagoon. Wellesley had made arrangements to collect at Aviero all the fishing boats available, and by this means to transfer Hill's troops to Ovar and so take Franceschi in the rear. Hill's own brigade was transported first, there to remain concealed at Ovar while the ships returned for Cameron's troops, but by the time they arrived the French had discovered the danger threatening them and had withdrawn. It will be seen that, though in itself unsuccessful, this manoeuvre had considerable effect in future operations. The French south of the Duoro now fell back steadily, and on the night of 11 May their rearguard had crossed the river, the bridge of boats had been destroyed, and all boats removed to the north side of the river.

One brief snapshot of the approach march is contained in the journal of Captain Peter Hawker, a troop commander in the 14th Light Dragoons:

10 May – At five we came in sight of the enemy's videttes; formed a line; and were joined by a strong squadron of Portuguese cavalry… but finding ourselves opposed to a strong column of cavalry, we retired to a short distance. Being reinforced with two three pounders from General Stuart's brigade, which immediately opened their fire with some execution; and animated by the appearance of our infantry; we again advanced. A partial charge was made by the 16th, so as to occasion a loss to the enemy of seven men killed and a great many wounded. Of this regiment but few were wounded, and only one was taken prisoner – we at length succeeded in driving the enemy out of the field. Their retreat was to Olivera, which they soon abandoned, so as almost immediately to leave it in our possession. The number of French cavalry here amounted to about four thousand: they were supported by small detachments of infantry.

11 May – At eight in the morning we began our march; and, after advancing about two leagues, came up with the infantry, whom we found sharply engaged, driving the enemy out of a wood. A squadron of the 16th, and another of the 20th, made a charge, with the loss of several men... We then advanced along the road to Oporto, which was strewn with dead men and horses, and spoils of every description. Among other objects of horror, we observed the bodies of six Portuguese hanging... three of the above were suspended from a single tree... in consequence of the murder of Soult's aide-de-camp; and that four of the sufferers were priests, who had refused to deliver up the criminals.

The two squadrons mentioned above by Hawker had been specifically put under command of Wellesley's Adjutant-General, Charles Stewart, who later wrote: 'It occurred to me that a good opportunity was furnished of making a successful charge with a few troops of cavalry. Sir Arthur Wellesley instantly acceded to my proposal and two squadrons being entrusted to me, we galloped forward in sections along the road and overthrew, by repeated attacks, everything which stood in our way. The prisoners numbered upwards of a hundred men.'

The operations of 10 and 11 May described by Hawker were entirely satisfactory to Wellesley, with the added bonus that the Portuguese 'behaved remarkably well' – a judgement he was at pains to ensure was passed on to the Portuguese Regency via Ambassador Villiers. For himself, he had manoeuvred the French rearguard out of quite good defensive positions, in what he lightheartedly called a 'field day'. His spirits were high. The 48th's regimental history continues:

> Soult's troops, amounting to some 20,000 men, were now in what appeared to be an almost impregnable position on the north bank of the Duoro. Soult's one fear of attack was that the boats which had moved Hill's brigade to Ovar would be brought round to the Duoro and the same manoeuvre repeated of landing the troops in his rear. He therefore concentrated his attention on the mouth of the river, and left the river bank at the town of Oporto almost unguarded. Above the town the river is fully 500 yards across, but from the Convent of Serra it narrows and deepens, flowing between lofty cliffs past the city.

For the British infantry brigades the march on Oporto had been a grim experience. Sergeant John Cooper, 2/7th (Royal Fusiliers), recalled that 'The last (fourth) day's march under a scorching sun and clouds of dust was really horrible. The road was narrow, and little or no water all the way. We had heavy knapsacks, sore feet, and after marching between 20 and 30 miles, for a finish *we ran*, to get into action, about

4 miles to a town opposite Oporto called Villa Nova, but the enemy were beaten before we arrived.'

*   *   *

Some time after 8am on 12 May, Sir Arthur, together with his staff and a few local worthies who knew the ground, climbed the hill on which lay the Serra Convent on the south bank of the Duoro in the suburb of Villa Nova. This built-up area was opposite Oporto town, to which it had always been connected – prior to the exertions of Soult's engineers the night before – by a bridge laid on boats. The river was as wide here as the Thames at Westminster.

The Serra hill was high (150ft) and long enough to provide plenty of dead ground in its rear, so Wellesley's brigades had quietly closed up adjacent to the river. They were below and behind him now, resting, as he opened his 3ft telescope in the Convent garden. Across to his left, about 400yd away, Sir Arthur had a good view of the quaysides on the far bank, running away beyond where the bridge had been. He could see the blue coats of Soult's piquets at the corners of the narrow streets that ran down to the quays; but opposite and to his right it was a different story. For half a mile a rocky bank edged the water, and above it the town petered out, with just a few houses and gardens, and the road to Vallongo and Amarante curling away north-eastwards through a mixture of open ground and olive groves. Two high stone walls came down to the river and around the Bishop's Seminary, a partially built two storey structure, standing quite isolated, and reached from the riverbank by a narrow zigzagging flight of steps; an iron gate in the far wall gave access to a lane that led to the Vallongo road. Napier tells us that the area enclosed within the walls was sufficient to contain at least two battalions in order of battle'. There was no visible French presence.

Down below him, Sir Arthur saw four boats – wine barges, with high curving ends – being brought back one at a time from the north bank. The scratch crew charmingly comprised the Prior of Amarante, a barber, Colonel John Waters (one of Wellesley's roving reconnaissance officers) and four 'volunteer' peasants. The barges had been discovered hidden on the far bank by the barber, who owned a skiff, who told Waters, who met the prior, who in turn organized the musclepower. Captain George FitzClarence, ADC to Brigadier Charles Stewart: 'This patriotic priest, on learning of the desire of the British, joined with Colonel Waters in inducing peasants, after some persuading, to accompany the Colonel across, who brought back our boats.' Waters told Sir Arthur that each barge could carry thirty men – and that the Seminary building was quite deserted... Wellesley had also just heard that three or four miles up-river to the east, a large ferryboat which had been scuttled by the French was already being baled out and put to rights by the villagers of Avintes. There was a good road right to it.

Since the open ground on the approaches to the Seminary was within artillery range from the eastern slopes of the Convent gardens, Sir Arthur's daring plan must have come together in his mind with great clarity: a crossing four miles up-river, which could catch any French withdrawal from the town, and a bridgehead here into the Seminary, which his guns could isolate until the force there became viable.

The first thing was to get the guns and ammunition – preferably unseen – into the Convent garden. Then the flanking force must be started on its way; and then the big risk must taken – using the barges to slip an advance party across to the Seminary without being seen. For even as the plan emerged, it needed but one alert Frenchman to wonder what a succession of boats, supposedly all locked up, were doing being paddled slowly, one by one, across to the south bank.

Three batteries moved up into the gardens: eighteen 3- and 6-pounder guns, and a couple of howitzers. Major-General John Murray took the 1st and 2nd Battalions of his KGL Brigade, two guns and two squadrons of the 14th Light Dragoons to cross by the ferry at Avintes; then, with a nonchalant 'Well, let the men cross', Wellesley had the 1/3rd (Buffs) from Hill's brigade close on the water and embark.

There was more to the capture of the Seminary than the usual authorities state. All seem agreed that (Oman) 'a subaltern and twenty-five men rushed up into the empty enclosure of the Seminary, and closed the big iron gate opening into the Vallongo road'; or (Fortescue) 'an officer and twenty-five men hastened to occupy the Seminary and to close the iron gate on the northern side'; or (Weller) 'a Lieutenant and his platoon of the Buffs (3rd Foot) ferried over on the first barge, ran up the hill to the Seminary, closed and secured the iron gate in front, and began fortifying the place.' It would seem from this that none of Hill's brigade ventured outside the Seminary walls from start to finish. Yet the 17-year-old Ensign Thomas Bunbury of the 3rd, in his 1861 *Reminiscences*, tells us that:

> The Light Company, and that under command of Brevet-Major Wellington to which I belonged, were ordered to the banks of the river, opposite the Seminario, where we crossed in two boats that had been brought to our side of the river for that purpose. I passed with the men in the second boat, and the Light Company was pushed forward as an advanced piquet under Captain Cameron, no enemy as yet having appeared. A lady in the Seminary gave me some wine and cake, which quite restored me for the coming fight [he had woken that morning 'with a dreadful bowel complaint']. I had scarcely time to ruminate, before I heard the firing of musketry close to the house and being the only officer in the court-yard which led to the road from which the firing was heard, I sallied out to support the Light Company with such men as I could collect; these were nearly the whole of my Company. We had not proceeded far before we met the Light Company retreating before a superior force, and Cameron, its Captain, ordered me back, when the whole re-entered the Seminary. I was posted at the iron gateway to the court-yard, with orders to let in any of our men, but to exclude their pursuers; these however entered the gardens, and endeavoured, as I afterwards learned, to get between us and the river, so as to prevent the passage of more troops coming to our assistance. The affair was rather serious in the orange grove and garden, but five or six youngsters of different corps I met in the court-yard, and as many soldiers... all sallied out at the gateway, up the paved road by which we had before retreated, and never looking behind us, proceeded to attack the different small parties of French who were coming up to reinforce their companions in their attempt upon the Seminario. The advancing French made a great noise when

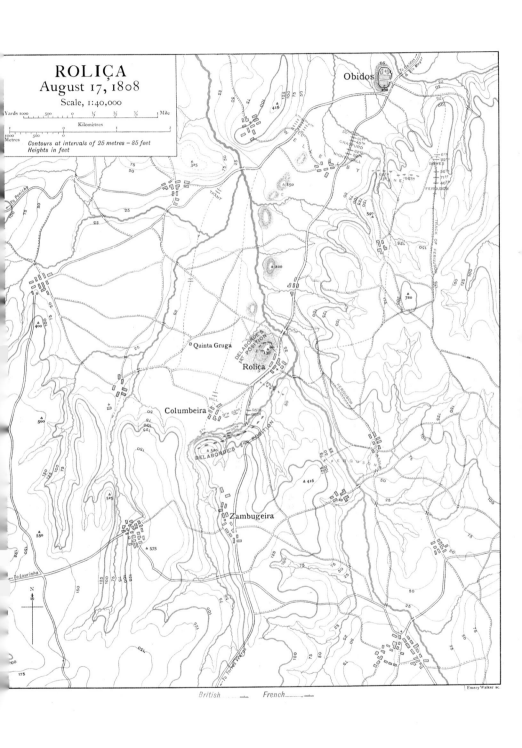

ROLIÇA
August 17, 1808
Scale, 1:40,000

Yards 1000   500   0   ¼   ½   ¾   1 Mile

Kilomètres

1000 Metres   500   0

Contours at intervals of 25 metres = 85 feet
Heights in feet

Obidos

Quinta Gruga

Roliça

Columbeira

Zambugeira

DELABORDE'S 1ST POSITION

DELABORDE'S 2ND POSITION

To Peniche

To Lourinha

N

British ——— French ———

Emery Walker sc.

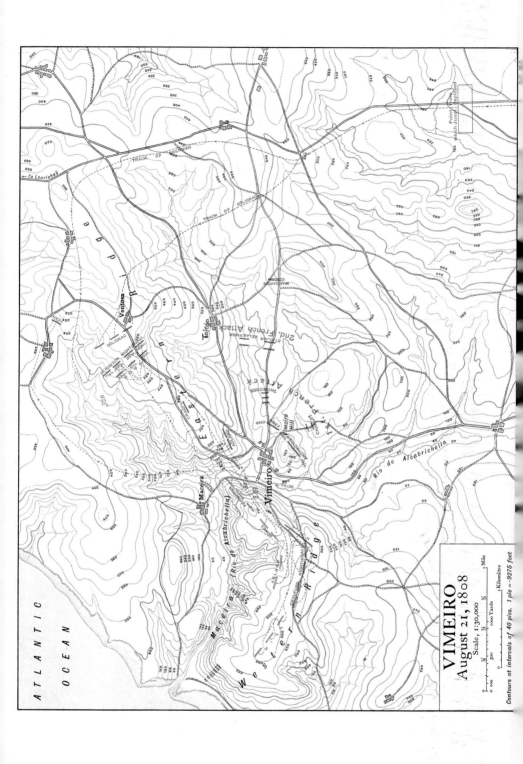

VIMEIRO
August 21, 1808

Scale, 1:30,000

Contours at intervals of 40 pies. 1 pie = .9275 feet

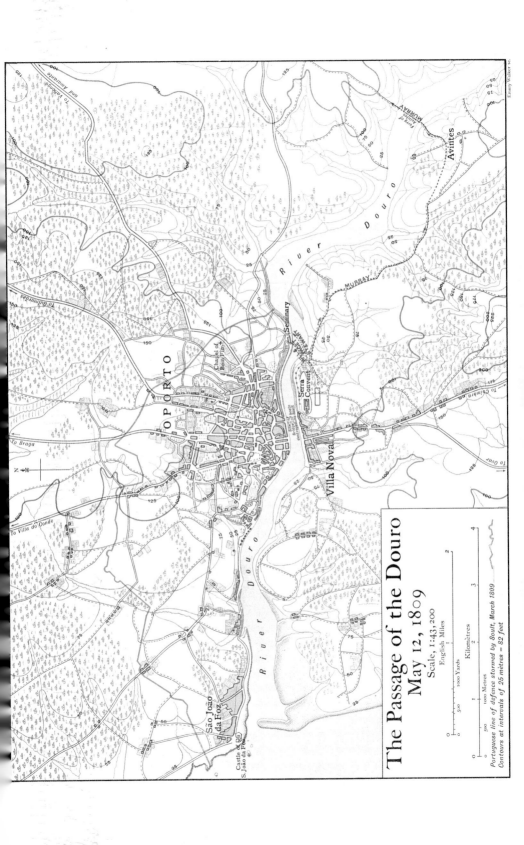

The Passage of the Douro
May 12, 1809

Scale, 1:43,200

English Miles

1000 Yards

Kilomètres

1000 Mètres

1000 Metres

Portuguese line of defence stormed by Soult, March 1809
Contours at intervals of 25 mètres = 82 feet

Emery Walker sc.

OPORTO

Chapel of Bom Fim

Seminary

Serra Convent

Villa Nova

MURRAY

MURRAY

Avintes

River Douro

River Douro

São João da Foz

Castle of S. João da Foz

To Villa do Conde

To Braga

To Guimarães

To Valongo and Amarante

To Coimbra

To Ovar

N

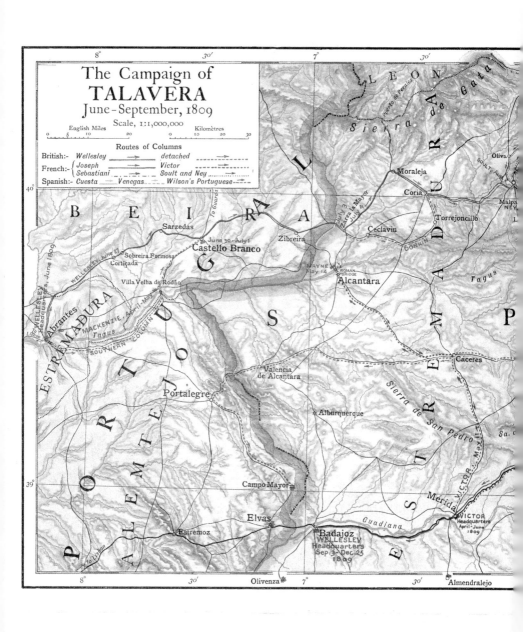

The Campaign of
TALAVERA
June–September, 1809

Scale, 1:1,000,000

English Miles
Kilomètres

Routes of Columns

British:- *Wellesley* ——→ *detached* – – –→
French:- { *Joseph* ——— *Victor* – – – – –
{ *Sebastiani* – – –→ *Soult and Ney* ....→
Spanish:- *Cuesta* ——— *Venegas* – · – · *Wilson's Portuguese* – ·→

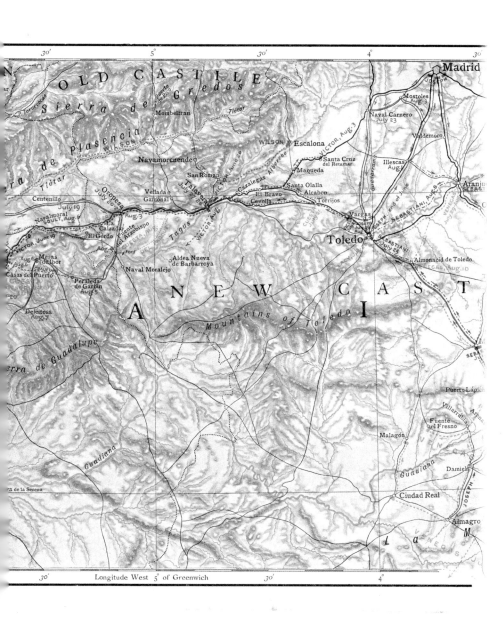

Madrid

OLD CASTILE
Sierra de Gredos
Sierra de Plasencia

Mombeltran
Tiétar
Puerto del Pico
Navamorcuende
WILSON
Escalona
VICTOR, Aug. 3
Santa Cruz
del Retamar
Maqueda
Mostoles
AUG. 3
Naval Carnero
July 23
Valdemoro
Illescas
Aug.
Aranjue
San Roman
Santa Olalla
Cazalegas Alberche
El Bravo
Cevolla
Alcabon
Torrijos
Vellada
Gamonal
Talavera
July 26
VICTOR Aug. 3
Centenillo
July 19
Oropesa
July 20
Guadarrama
SEBASTIANI, AUG. 5
VEDESCA, AUG. 3
SEBASTIANI end of June
Aug. 6
Navalmoral
SOULT, Aug. 8
Calzada
El Puente
del Arzobispo
Vargas
Aug. 8
Tagus
VICTOR Aug. 3
Cyuga
Toledo
SEBASTIANI
July 25
Almonacid de Toledo
El Gordo
Aug. 4
Ford
Aldea Nueva
de Barbarroya
Naval Moralejo
Mesas
del Ibor
Aug. 6
Casas del Puerto
Peraleda
de Garbin
Aug. 5
A N E W   C A S T
I
Deleitosa
Aug. 7
Sierra de Guadalupe
Mountains of Toledo
Puerto Lápice
Villarrubia
Arenas
Fuente
del Fresno
Malagón
Guadiana
Sierra de la Serena
Guadiana
Damiel
Ciudad Real
JOSEPH
Almagro
M

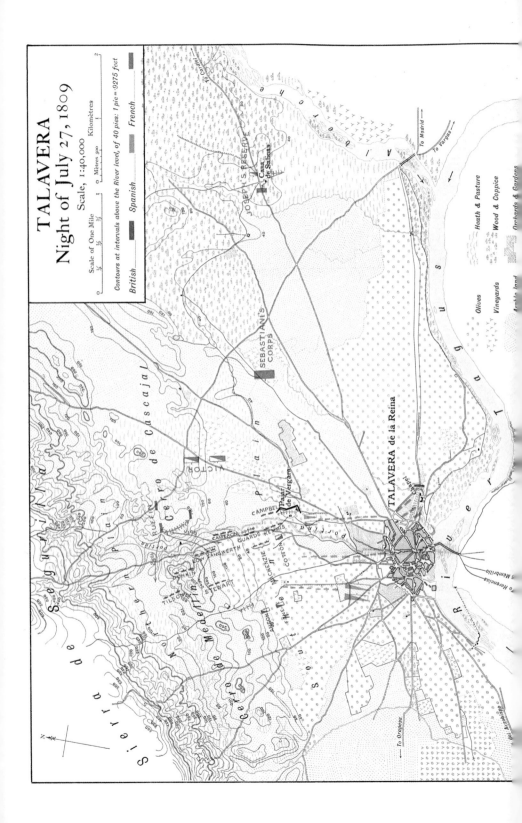

TALAVERA
Night of July 27, 1809
Scale, 1:40,000

Scale of One Mile

Contours at intervals above the River level, of 40 pies: 1 pie = .9275 feet

British   Spanish   French

Kilomètres

Mètres 900

Heath & Pasture

Wood & Coppice

Orchards & Gardens

Olives

Vineyards

Arable land

To Madrid

To Vargas

JOSEPH'S RESERVE

Casa de Salinas

SEBASTIANI'S CORPS

VICTOR

Cerro de Cascajal

Plain

Ruffin

Cerro de Medellin

Northern Plain

Sierra de Seguril_a

TILSON

LOW

LANGWERTH

STEWART

CAMERON

GUARDS KEMMIS

MACKENZIE

COTTON

Hill

Southern

Palajo de Vergara

CAMPBELL

Portina

TALAVERA de la Reina

River

To Oropesa

To Herencias

To Membrillo

To Arzobisho

N

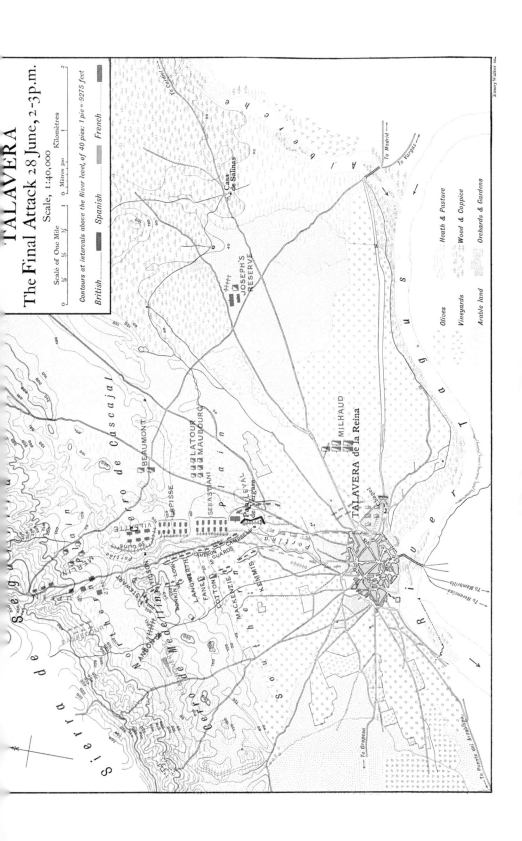

TALAVERA
The Final Attack 28 June, 2-3 p.m.

Scale, 1:40,000

Scale of One Mile

0   ¼   ½   ¾   1

Kilomètres

0   Mètres 500   1   2

Contours at intervals above the River level, of 40 pies: 1 pie = .9275 feet

British   Spanish   French

Heath & Pasture

Olives

Vineyards

Wood & Coppice

Arable land

Orchards & Gardens

Emery Walker sc.

Corporal, the 48th Regiment, at Talavera, by Alex Barker

marching – every small party having a drummer thumping away with all his might, and against these poor devils of drummers our fire was principally directed. We shot several.

Bunbury's account then describes his spirited defence of a walled cottage and garden against sixty Frenchmen, being bundled out on their second assault, which was preceeded by a direct hit from a howitzer shell; a withdrawal to a crossroads where he met a French column; and the use of loopholes in dry-stone walls, together with putting the men's caps on the top to draw fire and empty the enemy's muskets. He ends: 'Our opponents were now in full retreat and I made for the first regiment I could discover on the British side. This proved to be the 29th Foot. The head of the column was on the point of charging the rear of the French.'

So, making all due allowance for Bunbury's memory at the age of 70, it was clearly Major Wellington's battalion company who first garrisoned the Seminary, with the iron gate not closed and barred – since Captain Cameron's Light Company was outside all the time, until gone 11.30am, when the French 17e Léger's attack developed. The Buffs' commanding officer, Lieutenant-Colonel Muter, presumably gave Cameron his outlying role, and would have trusted his judgement to fall back inside the gates once French pressure became too great – the usual end to all skirmishing or piquetting. So neither Muter, nor particularly his company commander Major Wellington, would have approved of young Bunbury promptly rushing out again with a dozen various soldiers, to set up strongpoints in the cottages. Indeed, Bunbury's account makes it plain that the boy never fought from within the Seminary at all, staying outside on his adventures until he joined up with the 29th, which would be about three hours later. (Might this explain why Bunbury exchanged out of the 3rd into the 91st just three months later, and into the Portuguese service two months after that?)

The second party of the Buffs to cross the river created stepped firing positions on the 9ft foot Seminary wall and behind the strong parapet of the flat roof; the third wave taking over General Edward Paget to command, the better part of four companies were now in position. The Buffs' crossing had not gone unnoticed, however. They had been spotted quite early – some say immediately – and the news had been passed to General of Brigade Foy; that officer immediately sent his ADC to wake Soult (who had been up all night writing letters) in his headquarters to the west of the town. 'Push the English into the river' was his fairly obvious response, with or without the swearwords; but Foy took over half an hour to gather his 17e Léger, and it was 11.30am before its three battalions were launched against the northern and western walls of the Seminary. (It would be now that Ensign Bunbury was enjoying his restorative cake in the Seminary courtyard.)

Foy had also got some artillery down to the river bank to engage the crossing site, under the interested gaze of Sir Arthur's gunners from across the river. Much technical gunnery talk would have followed concerning the range, and what allowance to make in cutting the fuzes for a shell's parabolic fall of 150 feet in 500 yards. Immediately under the eyes of his commander-in-chief and all the staff, doubtless Captain Lane double-checked his sums: in the event, the first shrapnel shell from his battery's howitzer burst precisely over the heads of the first French gun team to unlimber, and all were killed or wounded – horses and all – by the lethal blast of musket balls. Further efforts were similarly discouraged. The other seventeen British guns then opened up on the 17e Léger, sweeping the open approaches to the Seminary. The French edged to their left, to get the Seminary building between their line of advance and the deadly guns; but after half an hour it was clear that the firing positions at the Seminary walls, windows and roof were too strongly held.

The 2/48th and 2/66th were also crossing the river by now; but, undaunted, a further three French battalions took up the challenge. These were our old friends the 70e Ligne from Rolica ridge, and led by their commander of that day, General Delaborde. His attempt on the Seminary was much more determined and persistant, and was described as 'the *serious* attack' by the 36-year-old Major-General Rowland Hill, who had taken command in the Seminary when General Paget was wounded. But before 3pm it was over: thanks to the guns, the Seminary held, with the Buffs suffering fifty casualties, the 2/48th seventeen and the 2/66th just ten. Brigadier Foy later put the French losses at 177 men.

In a final throw, Soult ordered up the troops of Reynaud's brigade from their guard duties on the quays. Not surprisingly, the Portuguese promptly freed all the unguarded boats and took them across to the British. The remainder of Sir Arthur's force began to cross – Stewart's brigade led by the 1/29th, then the Guards. The 29th climbed the streets up through the town, and came in on the flank of the final French assault on the Seminary. Soult had already ordered the retreat, and Generals Delaborde and Foy were desperately trying to extricate their battalions and organize a covering rearguard. This was precisely the opportunity Wellesley had foreseen when he sent General Murray off to cross the river with his Germans at Avintes, and then to close on the town. Only one of Murray's two squadrons of the 14th Light Dragoons was well over the river, however, when Wellesley's Adjutant-General, Brigadier-General Charles Stewart, arrived on the scene. Despairing of Murray's apparent lack of urgency to hit the retreating French columns on the Vallongo road, he took command of the squadron and pressed the pursuit. Stewart later wrote: 'They were pursued by the dragoons from General Murray's corps, under my orders, with the gallant Colonel Hervey of the 14th who unfortunately lost his arm in this skirmish. The slaughter was very great, for a panic had evidently fallen upon them; and as we followed them a considerable way, repeated opportunities were furnished of charging to advantage.'

We have two other eyewitness accounts. Firstly, Ensign Bunbury of the 1/3rd:

> The 29th… was on the point of charging the rear of the French who, through the heavy sand, were endeavouring to get away from them. At this critical moment a staff officer rode up to the head of the 29th and ordered the men to halt. The officer commanding the regiment seemed unwilling to obey, but the staff officer placing his horse across the road, said 'Sir, I order you to halt, to let the cavalry pass to the front'… By this time (the cavalry having passed) the enemy had reached a deep cut through a sand hill, on the road leading to Guimaraes, and a number of them, perceiving our cavalry in pursuit, scrambled up the sides of the road, and remained there to cover the retreat of their column. The whole space was lined with sharpshooters, and the loss inflicted

upon our brave fellows, who could not get at them, was dreadful. Amongst the wounded was Colonel Hervey, who lost an arm. I think it very doubtful whether our cavalry ever reached the rear of the French column in this charge. Had they tried to head the enemy by pushing parties round the flanks of the French… the result might have been different.

Bunbury's final statement of the obvious is rather confirmed by the account of Captain Peter Hawker, who charged with the second troop:

We hastened forward as fast as was possible from the nature of the ground; and, after surmounting many impediments among the stone walls, got into the main road, on reaching the outskirts of the town – our infantry here extended along the road. We then, forming up in threes, passed all our lines at a full gallop; whilst they greeted us with one continued huzza. After this, going almost at speed, enveloped in a cloud of dust, for nearly two miles, we cleared our infantry, and that of the French appeared. A strong body was drawn up in close column, with bayonets ready to receive us in front. On each flank of the road was a stone wall, bordered outwardly by trees; with other walls, projecting in various directions; so as to give every advantage to the operations of infantry, and to screen those by whom we were annoyed. On our left, in particular, numbers were posted in a line, with their pieces rested on the wall which flanked the road, ready to give us a running fire as we passed. This could not but be effectual, as our left men by threes were nearly close to the muzzles of the muskets, and barely out of the reach of a coup de sabre. In a few seconds, the ground was covered with men and horses: notwithstanding these obstacles, we penetrated the battalion opposed to us; the men of which, relying on their bayonets, did not give way until we were nearly close upon it, when they fled in great confusion. For some time this contest was kept up, hand to hand; and, for the time it lasted, was severe.

After many efforts, we succeeded in cutting off three hundred, most of whom were secured as prisoners: but our own loss was very considerable. Our squadron consisted of scarcely forty file; and the brunt of the action, of course, fell the heaviest on the troop in front: of the fifty-two men composing it, ten were killed, eleven severely wounded (besides others slightly), and six taken prisoners: of the four officers engaged, three were on the wounded list. For my own part, my horse being shot under me, the moment after a ball had grazed my upper lip, I had to scramble my way on foot, amidst the killed and wounded – among whom the enemy, from the side walls, were continually firing – and thus effected my escape from this agreeable situation. On the approach of our infantry, the French brigade was compelled to retire. Our few remaining men… brought with them the prisoners in triumph.

… On the merits of our charge, the comment of the French General (Foy) ought not to be omitted: he sent for our men (who had been his prisoners, and afterwards escaped), and declared to them that, in his opinion, 'we must have all been drunk or mad; as the brigade we had attacked was nearly two thousand strong.'

While General Delaborde was unhorsed and briefly captured, and Foy took a sabre cut to the shoulder, their rearguard ambush – avoidable, had the British cavalry so chosen – cost the 14th's squadron thirty-five of its strength of 110 men killed, wounded or taken before the approaching British infantry put the rearguard to flight, leaving behind some 300 prisoners. This unfortunate clash is partly memorable for the lethargy shown by Major-General Murray, but also conversely for the seizing of an over-active role by one of Wellesley's chief staff officers. A squadron of 110 men scarcely required such august leadership, and one sympathizes with the squadron's officers, while suspecting they were not averse to a charge. It is hard to disagree with the comment from Lieutenant Leslie of the 29th, who watched it: 'It may be true that General Murray did not attack the flying enemy as he might have done in the flank, but the attack made by General Stewart and Major Hervey, which was no doubt a dashing affair on their part, did more credit to their gallantry and courage than to their judgement.' All cavalrymen would, of course, take that as a compliment. (Hervey, incidentally, also took a pension of £300 a year for his lost right arm – quite a handsome sum.)

The French marched in disarray ten miles east from Oporto, until darkness fell, and spent the night at Baltar on the Amarante road just the other side of Vallongo. Wellesley's headquarters 'being established in the house which Soult had occupied', says Charles Stewart, 'we found every preparation for a comfortable dinner in progress; for the French Marshal quitted the place so lately as two in the afternoon, long after his sumptuous meal had been ordered. It will be readily imagined that we were not backward in doing ample justice to it.' Having finished Soult's dinner, Wellesley studied the reports of the action. He had lost just twenty-three killed, ninety-eight wounded and two men missing – a remarkably light bill; whereas the French attacks on the Seminary had cost them about 300 killed and wounded, and another 300 taken prisoner. In addition, Soult's hospital held a further 1,500 abandoned sick. The British had taken six of his field guns and – a real treasure – no less than fifty-two Portuguese guns discovered in Oporto arsenal, in pieces but recoverable. The French manpower loss was the equivalent of four battalions.

So Wellesley had, in a morning's work, bundled out Soult's fourteen battalions (not counting Mermet's division, which was already leaving) and four cavalry regiments, simply by inserting three battalions into the Seminary. Had Murray pressed the Alvines flanking movement the French loss would certainly have been greater. Sir Arthur's decision to cross his troops a company at a time, in broad daylight and in just four ponderous boats, made no conventional military sense, being outrageously audacious; but it made entire sense given his eye for ground, which spotted that the approaches to the Seminary could be dominated by artillery from the Convent hill. It was a decision few other generals would have made, given a large ferryboat an hour's march away, which itself threatened the enemy's likely withdrawal route. It certainly demonstrated to the French commanders (and to his own troops) that here was a general who had better be shown some respect. It was another marker for the future; and Wellesley's audacity and skill was in sharp contrast to French carelessness on the river line. Once again, as at Vimiero, they had shown their own continuing contempt for their enemy, and had suffered for it.

7

The Generals' Game:
April–June 1809

MARSHAL Soult's sleep was disturbed with bad news for the second night in succession when, at 1.30am on 13 May, a messenger rode in at last from the missing General Loison. Soult had heard nothing from him for six days, having prudently sent him to open up a withdrawal route to the east towards Spain. Loison was to hold at all costs the bridge over the Tamega at Amarante, since the river was still mostly impassable from earlier flooding, and all the bridges except that at Amarante were useless. The messenger therefore brought a sort of nightmare to Soult's wakening brain; the marshal now heard that the bridge had been abandoned and Loison had commenced a retreat north-west towards Guimaraes and Braga, pursued – incredibly – by the Portuguese general Silveira and about 4,000 men (but, importantly, with Beresford's 6,000 right behind them.)

Silveira had earlier been bumped out of Amarante by the superior Loison, and had withdrawn down to but not beyond the Duoro. Stiffened by Beresford's arrival on 10 May, Silveira, to his credit, held Loison's next push, and in the face of Beresford's visibly massing reinforcements the latter drew back to Amarante, and its all-important bridge over the Tamega, on the 11th. Unbelievably, however, Loison now decided to retreat from Amarante late on 12 May, at the very time when Soult was himself retreating towards that vital river crossing. Napier comments acidly: 'Although at the head of six thousand men, cavalry, infantry, and artillery, that night and without another shot being fired, he abandoned the only passage by which, so far as he knew, the rest of the army could escape from its perilous situation with honour. It was not General Loison's fault if England did not triumph a second time for the capture of a French marshal.'

One can only imagine Soult's feelings on receiving Loison's message. He was a greedy and ambitious plunderer, who was alleged (by his rivals, admittedly) to have dreamt of the throne of Portugal; but he was also the soldier who had risen from second-lieutenant to divisional general in just seven years, and whom Napoleon, after Austerlitz, had called the finest tactician in Europe. Now he found himself prevented from crossing the one possible bridge, by Beresford and what Soult no doubt considered a mere rabble, with Wellesley closing fast from behind; unable to turn to face Wellesley, with Beresford then close behind him; unable to go south, where the impassable Duoro lay – the only course he was able to pursue was an escape northwards, through the mountains.

There was no road, naturally. A guide was found, but the mule tracks he described would allow no wheeled vehicles, and Soult immediately ordered his guns destroyed, the baggage wagons burnt and the powder wagons exploded; his men would carry only food and ammunition, while the redundant artillery and wagon horses were loaded with the reserve musket cartridges. Much baggage, plate, general plunder and the military chest were therefore abandoned beside the River Souza, their starting point at the foot of the Sierra de Santa Catalina. At daybreak on 13 May, as the hurried retreat began, the heavens opened and rain fell in torrents, and it did not stop for the next three days. The French infantry, with muskets reversed, toiled in exhausting single files all that day, climbing north across the ridge and down into the valley of the Ave, reaching the village of Pombeiro as the light failed. There they passed a horribly wet night some few miles short of Guimaraes, having put fifteen tortuous miles between themselves and the Oporto–Amarante road.

Back in Oporto, as the French set out in the rain, the British continued the lengthy business of ferrying across the river their guns, wagons, baggage, horses and men. Having marched eighty miles in four days, those who could rest were glad to do so. They had no provisions up with them yet, and precious little sustenance was found in Oporto (except for unimaginable quantities of port wine, which was rigorously guarded – in theory). So far as Wellesley knew, Loison held the Amarante bridge and Beresford was twenty miles beyond, around Villa Real. He had sent Murray and the KGL Brigade on towards Amarante to feel for Soult, and from Murray's headquarters in the afternoon of 13 May there came a report that heavy explosions and much smoke were evident around Penafiel; at 5pm came further definite news, from a deserter, that Soult's columns were northbound into the mountains towards Guimaraes. Wellesley sent Murray to check the position at Amarante and, later, to chase Soult's rearguard.

While the Germans were following in his bloodied footsteps, Soult joined Loison at Guimaraes on 14 May. Some sixth sense told him to continue his retreat not up the good road north-west to Braga, but by further mule tracks north across the mountains to Lanhozo, then north-east towards Salamondo and the valley of the Cavado. It thus became Loison's turn to sacrifice his guns, ammunition train, baggage, plunder and wagons; and the French columns spent their second night in the mountains, making it to Lanhozo by nightfall. The rains continued. This same day, 14 May, saw Wellesley march twenty-two of the thirty miles to Braga, and early next morning his advanced guard cavalry were actually seen by the dragoons Soult had sent west precisely to confirm whether Braga was clear. Soult continued north-east, reaching Salamondo; and on that evening of the 15th, Murray's KGL joined Wellesley, having crossed the mountains from Guimaraes. Beresford on his own initiative had progressed to within a day's march of Chaves, sending Silveira's division across country to block the Braga–Chaves road at Salamondo. We are fortunate to have an eyewitness account of Beresford's march in an unpublished letter dated 23 June, to his father from Lord Gough, then a major in the 2/87th (Prince of Wales' Irish):

> We left this scene of misery (Oporto) on 15 May, having the evening before received orders to proceed to Chaves by forced marches. Within a league of the town we had to ford the Tamega, a small river in dry weather. It was the

turn of 87th, unfortunately, to be the rear regiment of the column this day. The 60th (five companies) crossed with the loss of one man. The 88th (Connaught Rangers) took so long a time to ford it, that when the 87th's grenadiers came to cross, the river presented a most formidable appearance. In short, the river rose so fast, from the dreadful rains of the preceeding evening, and that morning, that the men were above their middles in a floodied mountain river, in which the current was wonderfully rapid. One officer and fourteen privates were carried down by the stream, but were providentially saved by the exertions of the mounted officers. Two companies were unable to pass. Here the misfortunes of the Brigade commenced.

The whole of the men's bread, which was made of Indian corn, got wet and was destroyed. Several thousand rounds of ammunition were rendered unserviceable, without a possibility of replacing it. A number of firelocks, caps and shoes were lost. The business of crossing the river took the brigade four hours. The evening set in with a most dreadful fall of rain, which continued all night and the next three days and nights. On the first day we had three leagues, upwards of fourteen miles, to march, although we left Amarante at four in the morning. Our road lay over almost impassable mountains, made more so by the dreadful rain that swelled the mountain rivulets into rivers. The night turned out as dark as it was possible. The men were obliged to move in Indian files, and actually grope their way – no torches being provided, and the rain preventing lighted straw from being of service. As there was no road, many men lost the column, several fell into pits, excavated by the falling of the waters, numbers lay down in the river from fatigue and hunger, and the greater part of the Brigade lost their shoes. At length, after groping in the dark, totally unconscious whether we were right or wrong, from eight until nine o'clock, the brigade arrived at a straggling village. Some got shelter, others did not. I was fortunate in meeting an inhabitant with a light, and getting shelter for all of the regiment that were able to come up.

At five next morning we pursued our march, but without provisions, as we only received two day's bread, and one day's meat, the evening before we left Amarante, and the bread was either destroyed in the river, or by the rain. This day proved as wet as the two preceeding. At ten o'clock at night we reached a wretched little village on the mountains quite incapable of housing a Company.

Major Gough's letter makes clear the hunger, fatigue and exposure to the elements which were such a feature of these hard days for both sides. The British commanders were driven on by the very real prospect of catching Soult; and the French generals in turn were desperate to evade capture. It is likely that the private soldiers on both sides merely shared a need to keep putting one foot in front of the other. With Wellesley now moving east towards Salamondo, and Beresford nearing Chaves, Soult was really no better off than when he was at Penafiel, with Wellesley at Oporto and Beresford at Amarante. To make a final clean break he must again seek the safety of the mountains towards Montalegre on the Spanish border. But soon after setting out from Salamondo on the evening of 15 May, still in the rain, his vanguard came to an abrupt halt. In front of the five-mile column a bridge had had the cross-planking removed, and Portuguese peasants held the far end. Napier tells the story:

> In this extremity, Soult sent for Major Dulong, an officer justly reputed for one of the most daring in the French ranks. Addressing himself to this brave man, he said, 'I have chosen you from the whole army to seize the Ponte Nova, which has been cut by the enemy. Do you choose a hundred grenadiers and twenty-five horsemen; endeavour to surprise the guards, and secure the passage of the bridge. If you succeed, say so, but send no other report; your silence will suffice.' Thus exhorted, Dulong selected his men, and departed.
>
> Favoured by the storm, he reached the bridge unperceived of the Portuguese, killed the sentinel before any alarm was given, and then, followed by twelve grenadiers, began crawling along a narrow slip of masonary, which was the only part of the bridge undestroyed. The Cavado river was in full flood, and roaring in a deep channel; one of the grenadiers fell into the gulph, but the noise of the storm and the river was louder than his cry; Dulong, with the eleven, still creeping onwards, reached the other side, and falling briskly on the first posts of the peasants, killed or dispersed the whole. At that moment, the remainder of his men advanced close to the bridge; and some crossing, others mounting the heights, shouting and firing, scared the Portuguese supporting-posts, who imagined the whole army was upon them; and thus the passage was gallantly won.

At first light on 16 May, Soult's engineers set about making the bridge as sound as they could, but it was 8am before the long column could recommence its march. So rickety was the structure, however, and so many were Soult's men, that he posted a strong rearguard at Salamondo to cover what obviously would be a slow crossing. Wellesley's dragoons closed up at 1.30pm, and three hours later Sir Arthur had enough infantry and a couple of guns forward, to press an attack. The Brigade of Guards quickly turned the rearguard out and tumbled them back to the bridge. Sir Charles Oman takes up the story:

> The chase continued as far as the Ponte Nova, which the broken troops crossed in a struggling mass, thrusting each other over the edge (where the balustrades were wanting) till the torrent below was choked with dead men and horses. The British guns were brought up and played upon the weltering crowd with dreadful effect. But the night was already coming on, and the darkness hid from the pursuers the full effect of their own fire. They halted and encamped, having slain many and taken about fifty prisoners, of whom one was an officer. It was only at daybreak that they realised the terrors through which the French had passed.

The scene was perhaps even more vividly described by an eyewitness, Captain FitzClarence:

The rocky bed of the Cavado presented an extraordinary spectacle. Men and horses, sumpter animals and baggage, had been precipitated into the river, and literally choked its course. Here, with these fatal accompaniments of death and dismay, was disgorged the last of the plunder of Oporto. All kinds of valuable goods were left on the road, while above 300 horses, sunk in the water, and mules laden with baggage, fell into the hands of the grenadier and light companies of the Guards. These active-fingered gentry found that fishing for boxes and bodies out of the stream produced pieces of plate, and purses and belts full of gold money. Amid the scenes of death and desolation arose their shouts of the most noisy merriment.

Just as the Guards were assailing Soult's rearguard at Salamondo, the front of his column, led by Loison's troops, met a second serious blockade. Again it featured a ravine and a bridge (over the Misarella), and again the redoubtable Major Dulong was called into service for another forlorn hope. Napier explains:

> For the pass in which the troops were moving being cut in the side of a mountain, open on the left for several miles, at last came upon a torrent called the Misarella, which, breaking down a deep ravine, or rather gulph, was only to be crossed by a bridge, constructed with a single lofty arch, called the Saltador, or leaper; and so narrow that only three persons could pass abreast. Fortunately for the French, the Saltador was not cut but entrenched and defended by a few hundred Portuguese peasants, who occupied the rocks on the farther side; and here the good soldier Dulong again saved the army: for, when a first and second attempt had been repulsed with loss, he carried the entrenchments by a third effort; but, at the same instant, fell deeply wounded himself. The head of the column now poured over, and it was full time, for the British guns were thundering in the rear, and the Ponte Nova was choked with dead.

It was much to be regretted that this second bridge, like that at Ponte Nova, was but thinly held by militia, so two opportunities were missed in one afternoon to hold Soult's labouring column. The absence of Silveira's men from the line of the Cavado river made the difference. His orders from Beresford would have put him a couple of miles away from the crucial bridges that very morning; he actually appeared out of the mountains a day late on 17 May, by which time Soult had already reached the border town of Montalegre. Next morning Wellesley sent the Portuguese general and the 14th Light Dragoons after the French; but that day they progressed at last into the barren lands of Spain, running across countless rivers and ridges, towards Orense on 19 May. When it became clear, on that date, that Soult had broken clear, Silveira and the 14th returned to Montalegre.

Beresford's flanking operation, which had got to Chaves by midnight on 16 May, crossed the border to Monterrey, but on the 18th gave up the chase at Ginzo on the Orense road, when it became apparent that the French had been moving to their west, and had now slipped in front only hours before. With his men utterly done up – 'on their chinstraps', as the saying goes – Beresford returned across the border to Chaves.

Major Gough's letter to his father covers the final three days of the chase:

> We pursued our melancholy march at five next morning, the men nearly fainting with hunger. We, however, most fortunately at 12 that day fell in with some cars of bread belonging to a Portuguese Division. General Tilson immediately pressed it for the men, which, with some wine, enabled us to proceed, and we that night at 12 o'clock got to Chaves, the most northern frontier town in Portugal, after a forced march of three days – with only 12 hours halt – over almost impassable mountains, the men without a shoe to their feet, and some hundreds of the brigade fallen out with fatigue and hunger.
>
> The Officers Commanding regiments were ordered to assemble next morning at 10 o'clock at General Beresford's, when we were told that the enemy had fled from Oporto, and then were within some leagues of us, that it would be necessary for the Brigade to March at one o'clock. We, however, did not march until three – and even then the men's meat was uncooked from the lateness of the issue, and not a single pair of shoes could be got in town. We slept on the Spanish mountains that night. The next day, when within two miles of the village of Ginco in Spain, the advance came up with a party of the Enemy. We were again ordered to lead the attack, and although the men were but the minute before apparently incapable of marching a league, this news had the power of re-animating them, and we passed through the Portuguese as if the men had not gone a mile. The British were here again destined to be disappointed, as the enemy consisted mostly of Cavalry, and fresh. They retreated much faster than we could advance. Their exact amount could not be ascertained, but Talbot, who was within a few hundred yards of them, took them to be about 400. They joined Soult a league and a half to our left, and the whole preceded in their retreat, amounting to 9,000, out of 22,000 he brought in to Portugal but a short time before. Here the pursuit was given up as fruitless, we having taken 45 poor wretches…
>
> The Brigade was nearly annihilated by the fatigues on the road – and I was by far the most fortunate regiment. The 88th, out of 700 they joined us with, did not bring up 150… Part of the officers and almost all the men I brought up, had not a shoe to their feet, which were actually cut to the bone. We halted a day and returned by Chaves to Lumago, and from thence here. All our sick, with very few exceptions, we picked up on the road. But we have since suffered much from sickness. Nine officers and 47 men have been attacked by some fever in Lumago, and while in this town several have died from fatigue.

The commissary to the 14th Light Dragoons, that vivid diarist August Schaumann, describes the hardships of the march, the ruin left by the retreating French, and the vengeful cruelty of the Portuguese populace if riled sufficiently – what he describes as 'the peculiar vindictiveness of southern peoples':

> *At midday on 17 May* I passed a field where the French had bivouacked. All the furniture and even the crockery had been taken from the houses of a neighbouring village, and had been brought into the field. The beds and the mattresses lay in rows in the mud. The drawers from the various articles of furniture had been used as mangers. Wardrobes had been transformed into bedsteads and roofs for the huts; all the crockery and glass lay in fragments on the ground. The chairs, staircases and window frames had been used partly as fuel for the kitchen fires, and partly to feed huge bonfires which had been lighted when the French had withdrawn. The unfortunate inhabitants stood all around lamenting their plight. All the crosses and statues of the Saints on the road had been thrown from their pedestals, and the alms boxes in front of them broken open and plundered. All the altars and chapels had been ruined and polluted. In the churches even the graves had not been spared, and the sanctuaries had been rifled. Altar candlesticks, and arms and legs of apostles and saints, torn vestments, chalices, prayer books and the like, mixed up with straw and filth, lay all about them. In one chapel there were a number of French prisoners with an English guard over them. I saw one well-dressed Portuguese at the head of a band of peasants offering the English sergeant ten gold florins to give the prisoners up. The cruelties perpetrated at this period by the Portuguese hill-folk against the French soldiers who fell into their hands are indescribable. In addition to nailing them up alive on barn doors, they had also stripped many of them, emasculated them, and then place their amputated members in the victims' mouths – a ghastly sight!
>
> Towards evening I reached the bridge at Saltador... all the houses were chock full of men of the Coldstream Guards and the light cavalry, together with General Wellesley's staff. Here at last I reached the 14th Regiment, and reported myself to its commander. It was quite impossible to obtain either provisions or forage for the troops. All around there was nothing but hills and rocks, and every house for miles had been plundered by the French.
>
> *18 May, from Ruivas* All the streets in the village are full of troops, who with pale and famished faces are standing up to their knees in mud, waiting their turn to march out. I received a few bullocks for my Dragoons... The brutes were wild and intractable. What made them more particularly timid and unwilling to advance were the many naked and bloody corpses of French soldiers that were lying in the road, and the sight of broken bridges across roaring forest streams, which they had to cross. The hills seemed to be getting ever higher and bigger and the roads ever narrower and more impractical... I had walked thirty-five English miles that day... At Montalegre... it is raining incessantly here and I'm cold, tired and peevish.

Captain Hawker, 14th Light Dragoons, was himself at Montalegre that day, and he adds to the commissary's description:

Montalegre had been so despoiled, that the natives were nearly famished, and we had to trust entirely to the arrival of our own short stock of provisions. Nothing could be found here in the way either of meat, drink, or vegetables; save a few starved goats, bad water and dead cabbage-stalks.

And a final cameo from Captain Hawker, which paints the scenery of the road back from Montalegre:

20 May – Our regiment returned to Salamonde by a different route from that by which we had advanced. The road here winds round the great mountains, adhering to immense precipices; and is in many places so narrow, as barely to admit a mule with baggage. You are nearly the whole day in a chain of mountains, among woods, rocks, and water-falls: the distances that catch the eye between the heights, opposed to this varied foreground, present a charming landscape. Every thing has the most wild and romantic appearance; and, amidst the aweful roar of surrounding cascades, you may conceive yourself deserted by every living creature.

The passes, as every where else, were strewn with dead men; the majority of whom were in the most offensive state of putridity. The French had so many horses precipitated down the heights, that we concluded they must have passed them in the dark. We saw several lying at the bottom, apparently quite mangled by the fall.

Within three weeks of his letter of 24 April to Lord Castlereagh, Wellesley had created a flank force to block Victor; marched 200 miles north through rugged country with a brand new army, reorganizing it as he went; forced the passage of a great river 300 yards wide at its narrowest; captured Oporto; defeated Soult, and chased him a hundred miles, costing him nearly 6,000 soldiers together with his artillery and baggage abandoned; and then turned south to deal with Victor – surely a blitzkrieg operation to merit the envy of Rommel himself. It was opportunistic, bold and determined; above all, it spoke volumes for Arthur Wellesley's confidence in his own abilities, and his refusal to be impressed by the French. While Soult still creditably escaped with 20,000 men, they lacked cannon, wagons, money, food and all the stores necessary for an army's subsistence – whether spare boots, a brandy ration or the knapsacks on the men's backs. As Sir Arthur wrote home on 20 May: 'Of this I am certain, that Soult will be very little formidable to any body of troops for some time to come.'

The extent of Soult's embarrassment is indicated in Oman's unattributed quotation from one of his officers: 'When he arrived at Orense, the infantry had brought off their bayonets and their Eagles, the cavalry their horses and saddles – everything else had been left behind – the guns, the treasure, the sick.' One way and another, according to Oman's careful calculations, Soult retreated 5,700 men short of those he had advanced with, and 'thus it would seem that about one sixth of the 2nd Corps had been destroyed.'

Wellesley's achievements on the Duoro were the more impressive because his force of twenty-one battalions contained only five which had served at Vimiero and Corunna: the 2/9th (East Norfolk), 1/45th (Nottinghamshire), 1/29th (Worcestershire), 5/60th Rifles (Royal American), and 1/97th (Queen's Own Germans.) Of the other sixteen, ten were weak 2nd Battalions from the home establishment. (The present author's own 2/48th was one of them, from Ireland, and destined to fight at Talavera with a bayonet strength that morning of 567, compared to 807 for the 1st Battalion – a third fewer.) These small 2nd Battalions were new and unsettled; they had been hurriedly strengthened, to some degree, by drafts from the Militia, in rapid preparation for this unexpected foreign service. Only the previous year, given their reinforcing role, the reverse had been the case: they had been drained to bring their 1st Battalions up to full strength. Whatever their unpromising beginnings, the fire of experience was soon to begin tempering the steel. The 2/48th and its fellows had been blooded in small measure, and were now destined for a march of 150 miles ending at Talavera. They had collected the first Peninsular battle honour 'Duoro', sore feet, empty bellies and fresh evidence that their fathers seemed to be right: 'We just can't help beating the French.'

The fact remained, of course, that the French marshals had plenty more men, while there were never enough British troops for comfort. Man for man was one thing, but there are limits. Sir Arthur's fighting strength at Oporto was a mere 16,400 British and 2,000 Portuguese troops. Soult's, Victor's, Sebastiani's and Joseph's corps – never mind Ney's and Mortier's elsewhere in the Peninsula – comprised nearly 80,000. Of these, however, Soult's 20,000 were now temporarily embarrassed and out of the picture. Having set his sights next on Victor, Sir Arthur would necessarily have given thought to arranging alternative occupations for Sebastiani and Joseph, assuming the availability of General Cuesta's 35,000-man Army of Estremadura and General Venegas' 30,000-strong Army of La Mancha. Having delivered to his Portuguese allies, on 12 May, the political prize of a free Oporto, Wellesley could now turn south. He would have to be sharp about it: the great thing was not to let the French forgather.

*   *   *

The next phase opened rather abruptly, with an alarm call from down south, behind Wellesley. On 19 May a message rattled up to him at Montalegre, on the Spanish border sixty miles beyond Oporto. The news came from the substantial force he had left to block Marshal Victor, comprising a reinforced British brigade of four battalions, plus two cavalry regiments, and the equivalent of two Portuguese brigades: the whole around 12,000 men, under the command of General Mackenzie. He was down at Abrantes, only a few days' march from Lisbon, and sixty miles west of Alcantara, both towns being on the River Tagus. Alcantara sheltered a small outpost comprising a Portuguese battalion, an artillery battery and a cavalry squadron under Colonel Mayne. It was an important town: there the Tagus could be crossed reliably all year round via a great seven-arched Roman bridge. This massive structure, seven stories high and two football pitches long, provided a line of communication between the two halves of Estremadura; the next good bridge was seventy miles away to the east, at Almaraz.

News of Colonel Mayne's acquisition of this vital bridge had reached Marshal Victor on 11 May. He promptly sent Lapisse's division, on loan from the Madrid garrison, and a brigade of dragoons, and recaptured the bridge just three days later. Victor's rapid reaction indicated a lively suspicion that there was more to this Portuguese incursion, small as it was, than met the eye. Was it the advanced guard of a much larger force – Wellesley and the Portuguese? – looking to invade, or to play cat and mouse while the Spanish under Cuesta attacked him from the south? He was not to know for another month that Wellesley was actually 130 miles away to the north-west, setting about Soult at Oporto. But having satisfied himself that the Portuguese were no imminent threat, by sitting at Alcantara for three further days until 17 May, Marshal Victor then retired back beyond Caceres, between there and Merida. (Interestingly, Napier does in fact report a rumour which could have afforded Victor an excuse to abandon Alcantara – that Soult had retreated from Oporto; but it is unlikely that a messenger could have travelled over 200 miles in four days.)

Anyway, Colonel Mayne promptly retook the Alcantara bridge. Yet the message Wellesley had read on 19 May at Montalegre, sent by a somewhat alarmed Mackenzie (who at that stage had no great hopes for his Portuguese), rather indicated an opening gambit for a serious raid by Marshal Victor, towards Castel Branco, or down the Tagus to Villa Velha. Such a possibility threatened Wellesley's lines of communication, and Mackenzie's blocking position along the River Zezere, and would generally muddle up any embryonic plans to move south to join up with Cuesta's Spanish forces. So news of Victor's withdrawal from Alcantara was a relief to both Mackenzie and his commander-in-chief.

Victor, on the other hand, clearly felt defensive about his withdrawal and a need to justify the brevity of his foray. On 29 May he wrote to Marshal Jourdan, Joseph's chief of staff in Madrid, that he really had no option but to withdraw, keen and willing though he was to leave Lapisse at Alcantara, or indeed to probe forward into Portugal *pour inquieter les Anglais et degager le duc de Dalmatie* (Soult): but there just was not any food to be had. Over an area of sixty miles around Alcantara, the peasants had prudently disappeared up into the hills, taking their cattle and burying their corn – no doubt much as they had done when Trajan and his Romans came to build their great bridge in the first place. The same happened further south, thanks to old Cuesta, who had made a raid on Victor's southern outpost at Merida while his back was turned at Alcantara. The two German battalions from Leval's division at Merida saw off this optimistic attempt by Cuesta's detachment, but in the face of Victor's own advance on his return, Cuesta ravaged all the flat country before pulling back to the hills, taking with him the villagers from along the line of the Guadiana, cattle, stores and all.

Food had now become an urgent consideration for Marshal Victor. In early June we find him asking permission from King Joseph in Madrid to shift north over the Tagus: that is, to abandon the exhausted country between the Guadiana and the

Tagus, to give up Merida and Caceres in favour of the fertile and still well-stocked valleys of the Tietar and Alagon rivers, and the towns of Plasencia and Coria:

> *(24 May)* The troops are on half rations of bread: they can get little meat – often none at all. The results of starvation are making themselves felt in the most deplorable way. The men are going into hospital at the rate of several hundreds a day. ...
>
> *(29 May)* We have no flour to issue for a bread ration, so cannot bake biscuit. The whole population of this region has retired within Cuesta's lines, after destroying the ovens and the mills, and removing every scrap of food. It seems that the enemy is resolved to starve us out, and to leave a desert in front of us if we advance... Carefully estimating all my stores I find that I have barely enough to last for five days in hand. We are menaced with absolute famine, which we can only avoid by moving off, and there is no suitable cantonment to be found in the whole space between the Tagus and the Guadiana; the entire country is ruined.

To which blunt plea Marshal Jourdan responded somewhat inadequately, with a promise to send 300,000 rations of plain biscuit – and strong encouragement to Victor to move not east but west, take the Alcantara bridge again, threaten Portugal and thereby draw pressure away from Soult. But far from needing 'disengaging' as it pressed south from Oporto, what was left of Soult's 2nd Corps was licking its wounds up in northern Portugal at Lugo, 300 miles from Victor's 1st Corps. By the time Victor had retorted to Jourdan that the Portuguese had blown the Alcantara bridge anyway, the whole exchange was of purely historical interest; for on 10 June, King Joseph and Marshal Jourdan (and on the 11th, Marshal Victor) received the electrifying if belated news from Soult of his drubbing at Oporto a month before. They did not know that within hours of their hearing of this development, Wellesley was to write (to Villiers, Minister in Lisbon, on 11 June), 'The ball is now at my feet, and I hope I shall have strength enough to give it a good kick.'

Certainly he held the strategic initiative, with Victor starving and looking to redeploy; Soult in disarray; Sebastiani far south of Madrid, being taunted by the larger army of La Mancha; and, of the other French corps of Mortier, Junot, St Cyr and Ney, only the latter presenting any sort of proximate threat – and he was trying to control Galicia and the eastern Asturias. Napier gives the seven French corps in Spain, and their line-of-communication and garrison troops, a combined paper strength of 280,000 – ten times Wellesley's tiny British army; but the latter could take great consolation in the knowledge that infantry en masse could consistently cover only fifteen miles a day, day after day. Even this assumed that they and their horses could be fed, watered, and both kept well-shod – an unsafe assumption for planning purposes. Wellesley made his football remark the same day he was formally authorized, by London, to operate inside Spain if he thought fit, and so long as he left Portugal secure behind him. He was not the man to duck his duty just because his enemy outnumbered him 10:1 on paper.

As to strategy, we have seen how, on arrival at Lisbon, he stated his aims quite clearly: to drive out Soult, then turn on Victor. Thus the lengthy description in Oman of the pros and cons of a thrust to Salamanca, which would quite ignore Victor, seems a case of erecting a paper argument just to demolish it. Salamanca would have been a suicidal objective, since Soult, Ney and Victor would presumably have closed in behind Wellesley's much smaller force as he ground to a halt when faced by Mortier. This was never an option, and one suspects that Oman considers the case only because it was put forward by Napier.

Wellesley knew Victor to be located between Caceres and Merida – that is, between the Tagus and Guadiana rivers. He could therefore do either a left hook, or a right hook, or what a later generation would term the 'hey diddle diddle, straight up the middle' option. Left, that is, down the long and narrow valley of the Tagus via Coria and Plasencia, to take the bridge of boats at Almaraz, which Victor held by a single division only. He would thus threaten the French rear and cut Victor's northern communications with Madrid, while placing Victor between two fires, since Cuesta would operate from the south. However, he had to consider the danger that 1st Corps' 23,000 men could conceivably beat either Wellesley's 22,000 or Cuesta's 35,000 before the two allied armies could subsequently link up. A right hook, on the other hand, along the Guadiana from Badajoz, having met up with Cuesta's Spanish, would be a heavier and therefore a safer blow; but it might just push Victor back north-east towards Madrid. Unless he could bring Victor to battle at some point along that 150-mile line, Wellesley might find Victor joining with reinforcements rushed out from Madrid by Joseph and Jourdan. 'Straight up the middle' was not really a starter, the country being ill-served by roads east of Truxillo once an army got into the Sierra de Guadalupe foothills.

Within three days of turning south from Montalegre on 19 May, and with these thoughts in his head, Wellesley wrote to Cuesta with his suggestions for co-operating against Victor, and requesting Cuesta's own views. He informed the old Spanish general as a matter of courtesy that the lead elements of the British would reach the Mondego at Coimbra on 26 May, to concentrate near Abrantes on the Tagus in early June. Wellesley followed up his letter with one of his staff – Colonel Bourke – whose job it was to return with a private assessment of Cuesta's troop strength, capabilities and morale. Bourke was also to stress personally to Cuesta the need to give his broad view on whether the two armies should join together and operate from a single base, or from separate bases, or indeed not to combine physically at all but to share all intelligence and, of course, an agreed objective. Bourke was also to try to find out whether General Venegas' Army of La Mancha, then in the hills of the Sierra Morena north of Baylen, could be co-opted actively into the grand design.

Cuesta's views were obtained by Colonel Bourke in two tranches, dated 4 and 6 June, which he sent on post haste to Wellesley, who had reached Abrantes on the 8th, a few days' march ahead of his leading brigades. In these and subsequent letters from Cuesta, Wellesley was immediately to see, no doubt with sinking heart, the nature of the Spanish connection; for within five days he is complaining to Frere in Madrid of the 'obstinacy of this old gentleman... Throwing out of our hands the finest game any army's ever had.' For not only did Cuesta's considered strategic choices fail to impress, but Cuesta himself was clearly going to become an obstacle to efficient co-operation between the allies.

His first plan accepted Wellesley's proposed right hook via Badajoz, but ruined it with two outrageously impractical embellishments: that before the joint might of the British and Spanish armies should tackle Victor, two flanking columns should set forth on ambitiously massive marches to get behind Victor and cut off his retreat. A quick glance at the map demonstrates Cuesta's optimism (we must remember that at this stage Victor still lay between Merida and Caceres). Cuesta proposed a left flank column, based on Alcantara, going along north of the Tagus to capture the bridge at Almaraz – seven days' march at least; and simultaneously a right flank column to skirt south of Merida, crossing the Guadiana at La Serena, and then going north-east through the mountains of the Sierra de Guadeloupe, to threaten Talavera – a mere fortnight's march. Quite apart from Sebastiani's 4th Corps being ideally placed to frustrate such a right flank column, Victor would never sit obligingly in his cantounments while being surrounded in this grand fashion. Nor would King Joseph be inactive; he would move forward from Madrid, while Victor would move back, to the bridges at Almaraz and Arzobispo.

As Wellesley commented in his Despatch: 'At all events these two detachments on the two flanks appear to me to be too weak to produce any effect upon the movements of Victor… I think it would be nearly certain that the Marshal would be able to defend the passage of the Tagus with a part only of his force, while with the other part he would beat one or both of the detachments sent round his flank. Indeed, the detachment which should have been sent from La Serena toward Talavera, being between the corps of Victor and Sebastiani, could hardly escape.'

Cuesta's second proposal was equally over-hopeful: that the Spanish should attack Victor frontally while Wellesley operated against his northern flank, having crossed the Tagus at Alcantara (the bridge being made serviceable). Since Victor's flank lay a good four days' march from Alcantara, however, his outposts would warn him in ample time of the British approach, and again he need merely withdraw back over the Tagus at Almaraz. Wellesley's only intelligent counter-move then – placing himself once more also on the north bank of the river – would entail counter-marching laboriously back to Alcantara.

Cuesta's third proposal must have been received with some relief; it was in effect to agree to Wellesley's own proposed left hook, via the Tagus valley and Plasencia, to seize the bridges at Almaraz and Arzobispo, cutting off Victor's easiest withdrawal route. It is not clear what role Cuesta proposed for himself. But in his reply of 8 June, in accepting the 'Spanish' plan, Wellesley requested that Cuesta left Victor entirely to the British, and instead went east to join General Venegas' Army of La Mancha, to take on General Sebastiani's 4th Corps.

Supposing he had thus achieved a highly satisfactory allied solution, Wellesley was about to turn to the domestic problems of his brigades, as they continued to move down from the Oporto area to join him around Abrantes; but his peace of mind lasted all of five days. On 13 June came Cuesta's newest response, now rejecting the left hook he had himself proposed: it is not clear why, although Oman speaks of Cuesta's 'openly expressed dislike of being left to face Victor alone'. Whatever the reason, Cuesta now strongly urged Wellesley to adopt the joint right hook approach from Badajoz.

Sir Arthur was thus immediately faced with a dilemma. He himself had absolutely no expectation that Victor would go for the Spaniards: 'I entertain no apprehension that the French will attack General Cuesta; I am much more afraid that they are going away, and strengthening themselves upon the Tagus.' Yet this was the first real occasion for co-operation in the field with the Spanish, and there was an obvious pressure to concede and compromise, as a good ally should. Much against his own best judgement, Wellesley therefore wrote on 14 June to accept Cuesta's plea, undertaking in due course to march from Abrantes south-east to Badajoz. Fortunately, the very next day brought news which changed all plans.

Victor had apparently destroyed his convent base at Merida, and his artillery and baggage were en route north to Almaraz, followed during the next few days by all his half-starved 1st Corps. By 19 June, Victor was over the river and by the 26th he was repositioned along the line Almaraz–Arzobispo-Talavera, facing south. Victor's ready withdrawal to the eating grounds north of the Tagus was occasioned by the news, at last reaching King Joseph, of Soult's defeat on the Duoro, and by Joseph's natural wish to draw in his horns. Wellesley could now gratefully countermand his orders for a march on Badajoz and a pointless foray into southern Estremadura. Instead, he must rethink his next move, and again obtain Spanish agreement and co-operation. Since he could see by now that this would be neither easy nor quick, he used the breathing space at Abrantes to buckle down to his domestic duties. For as Napier notes, Sir Arthur's force by then was 'weak in every thing but spirit. The commissariat was without a sufficient means of transport; the soldiers nearly barefooted, and totally without pay; the military chest was empty, and the hospitals full.'

*   *   *

Not all these domestic duties posed problems, but the majority certainly raised difficulties enough to exercise both Sir Arthur's limited patience, and the undoubted skills as an administrator which he had acquired in India. It is likely that his primary concern was the shape he required his new army to adopt; all else was subsidiary to that shape – to the nature of the tool he wanted in his hand. Matters such as lax discipline on the march, or poor food, or lack of shoes, of course blunted the tool's cutting edge, in that he could achieve less with it. Indeed, one suspects that his irritation with plundering or straggling battalions arose precisely because, as he would see it, they were wilfully frustrating the full designs he knew were achievable by the army he was moulding.

Sir Arthur had gone after Soult with nine brigades of infantry and two of cavalry. Each brigade commander had just his own permanent brigade-major, with such other officers attached as Sir Arthur thought requisite: that is, from the Adjutant-General's or Quartermaster-General's departments. The attachments were for specific tasks or operations, after which these staff officers reverted to Headquarters. This old system was more than adequate in the days when a general commanding say, 20,000 troops could physically see his whole force drawn up on a field of battle and could cause it to manoeuvre by issuing orders via quite a small staff. However, as the French Revolutionary Wars had developed, a massive increase took place in the numbers of men, regiments and guns, and therefore of their administrative support. Two years earlier, in June 1807 at the battle of Heilsberg, Napoleon had 150,000 men under arms between Warsaw and the Baltic; four years later, at Leipzig in 1813, the opposing armies would field more than half a million together. More complex organizations were needed to allow the much greater delegation required. 'A corps of 25,000-30,000 can be left on its own', wrote Napoleon to Beauharnais in 1809. 'Well-handled, it can fight or alternatively avoid action, and manoeuvre according to circumstances without any harm coming to it, because an opponent cannot force it to accept an engagement but, if it chooses to do so, it can fight alone for a long time.' By mid-1809 the Emperor was routinely joining together two or more brigades into 'divisions', and two or more divisions into 'corps d'armées', each having its own headquarters, and each commander his own permanent staff. It was to the divisional concept that Wellesley now conformed.

He had already progressed to grouping brigades loosely together for the march on Oporto, with Generals Edward Paget and Sherbrooke assuming certain command functions over the brigades of Richard Stewart and Murray, and those of H. Campbell, A. Campbell and Sontag respectively, while the brigades of Hill and Cameron were under the charge of the former.

At Abrantes, the regiments limped into their allotted accomodation, or shifted for themselves. The 2/48th arrived on 7 June, with Hill's brigade. 'The troops were allowed to hut themselves in a neighbouring wood, and remained until 27 June', according to the regimental Digest of Service. The brigades were grouped into four divisions – 1st, 2nd, 3rd and 4th – each with permanent representatives from the Adjutant- and Quartermaster-General's branches. The six cavalry regiments were formalized into one heavy and two light brigades, as the Cavalry Division, under General Payne. The 2/48th, along with their Oporto comrades the 3rd and the 66th, remained in Tilson's brigade, and together with Stewart's brigade (in which the 1/48th would soon serve) they formed the 2nd Division under General Hill. It was Hill, therefore, who was to take the 4,000 men of the 2nd Division on to the field at Talavera a few weeks later; and his responsibilities including the food, clothing, ammunition, punishments and pay for his six battalions. In so far as he was merely a conduit for any of these items between Sir Arthur's HQ and those battalions, he was given Captain Alexander Fordyce, 81st (lately his own brigade-major), to act as his Deputy Assistant Adjutant-General; and Captain Robert Waller, 103rd, as his Deputy Assistant Quartermaster-General. Their loyalty lay with the new 2nd Division and they answered to General Hill; yet they reported also to General Charles Stewart and Colonel George Murray, respectively Sir Arthur's Adjutant- and Quartermaster-Generals. (Staff work was no soft option: Fordyce was to die at Talavera, while Waller was to loose his right arm two years later, at Albuera.)

The effect of the new divisional concept was to drag the British Army, not before time, into the new age of dispersed battlefields. Self-sufficient and powerful forces of all arms, with cavalry and artillery added as Sir Arthur required, could be detached for long periods on independent missions; the 1813 campaign in the Pyrenees probably saw the full if not always successful fruition of this new potential. It is noteworthy, however, that Wellesley was largely able – unlike Napoleon – to fight his battles by manoeuvring his divisions himself, not by delegating to subordinate and quasi-independent corps commanders: that would not have been in his nature. The furthest he went in that direction was the trust he placed in General Hill.

The adoption of the divisional organization, and the assimilation of his Portuguese troops within it, materially helped to shape the future Peninsular Field Army. Bar two regiments, as we shall see, his Portuguese troops were not to fight at Talavera; they went to Beresford to guard the Portuguese borders. However, five of their eighteen battalions had already been brigaded with his British battalions for the Oporto operation. The extra firepower was highly desirable, so long as it was reliable, while slotting them into the larger British line would no doubt assist morale, and encourage by example that convergence of standards so essential to an allied army. Wellesley had seen at Vimiero the rawness of the Portuguese cavalry (who turned tail rather promptly), and this had no doubt strengthened his belief in the importance of binding his ally in as snugly as possible.

A further pivotal measure by Wellington in the fashioning of his new army was the emphasis on the role of his light troops. Also at Vimiero, he had seen the value of the combination of a skirmishing line deployed forward, and his battalions temporarily held back on the reverse slope. He had put rifle companies of the 5/60th into his brigades for the Oporto march, and he now accordingly allocated five companies to the brigades of Cameron, Tilson, Kimmis and both Campbells, on a permanent basis. These light companies were additional to those domestic to each battalion. Hence, for example, Tilson's brigade at Talavera would deploy a total of about 200 men from the light companies of the 1/3rd, 2/48th, 2/66th plus rifle companies from the 5/60th – say 10 per cent of the brigade's bayonet strength of 1,891 shown on the 'morning state' for 25 July.

Wellesley's reallocation of the 60th's rifle companies meant that a French brigade of a similar strength of three battalions, put opposite a British brigade's line, would send out only three companies of *voltigeurs* to form a covering screen for its columns – an inferior skirmishing line. Given the superior range of the Baker rifle and the extra (fourth) British company, the *voltigeurs* could be contained; and the French columns would then have to contend with an intact British main line. The following year, Wellington (as he then was) incorporated whole Portuguese brigades into his divisions. With the addition of their light troops – the *cacadores* – an Anglo-Portuguese division of eleven battalions could field eighteen light companies, against eleven French. Sir Arthur's decision at Abrantes to chop up the 5/60th was therefore far-sighted, if scarcely welcomed at the time by the riflemen and their officers.

He was only too aware that of the 33,000 British troops on the peninsula ration strength, he could muster only 21,000 for the march into Spain. There were 8,000 in Lisbon or en route to join; but shamefully, there were 4,500 in the hospitals. Three weeks later, by the time the army reached Talavera, according to the morning state Wellesley had 20,641 present and fit for duty, with (on Oman's reckoning) a further 5,898 absent or non-effective on detachment in Portugal and Spain, of whom no less than 4,395 were still sick. That is, the sick represented some 17 pe cent of his army, or nearly one in every five men. Clearly the distressed state of so many men was attributable to marching fifteen miles a day for five weeks, to and from the mountains beyond Oporto, with just two rest days, in extremes of weather, while lacking proper regular food and replacement shoes, having out-marched the baggage animals. The soldiers were also two months in arrears of pay, so few could buy their own sustenance on the road even when opportunity offered. The inevitable result had been both malingering and plundering.

Some regiments had suffered more than others, as they would, too, from Wellesley's subsequent wrath when he determined to tighten what he regarded as slack discipline. He was especially angry with the depredations of the 2/87th and the 1/88th, who had had it hardest on the fifty-mile forced march chasing after Soult, under three days of non-stop rain and driving winds. The 87th and 88th were, of course, Irish, and moreover had been heavily reinforced with Irish Militia; widely held to be the worst-behaved troops in retreat or idleness, they were also the most keenly ferocious in advance and when in contact with the enemy.

Once they had turned south for Abrantes, after these gruelling experiences trying to come to grips with the French, the troops' behaviour deteriorated in all respects – straggling, looting, and forcing the Portuguese to provide food. Some 250 of the 2/87th fell out of the marching column. On 30 May Wellesley wrote to Secretary of State Castlereagh: 'The army behave terribly ill. They are a rabble who cannot bear success any more than Sir John Moore's Army could bear failure. I am endeavouring to tame them.' He issued orders that on marching days officers were to visit their soldiers twice after arrival at the next staging stop, and once before marching on next morning: they were to ensure that the men were in their appointed billets, conducting themselves regularly, and were to take any complaints from the landlords. On halting days, the men were to be so checked four times. A fortnight later, on 16 June, he wrote again of 'the accounts which I receive from all quarters of the disorders committed by, and the general irregularity of the 87th and 88th regiments… the number of men absent from these regiments in consequence of their late marches is scandalous.' Any more of it, and the regiments would be sent to garrison duty and reported to the King as unfit for service in the field. Wellesley sent provost staff to await the brigade at Castelo Branco, and required that on arrival 'the rolls to be called every hour, from sunrise to eight in the evening, all officers, as well as soldiers, to attend… an officer from each regiment may go back immediately the whole road by which the brigade has moved since 5 May [!], in search of the missing men.' That would be a popular job…

On 17 June we find Wellesley sounding off yet again to Castlereagh, in despairing, peevish language which showed how very angry he had become at the stream of misdemeanours being reported: 'the state of discipline… is a subject of serious concern… [It is] impossible to describe the irregularities and outrages committed… by the soldiers who have been left behind on the march, having been sick, or having straggled from their regiments, or who have been left in hospitals; yet there is not an outrage of any description which has not been committed on a people who have uniformly received us as friends.' Sir Arthur then ranted on about the inadequecies of the court martial system, the lack of a regular provost establishment, the lack of diligence in disciplinary matters shown by the subaltern officers, the lack of patronage within a C-in-C's gift to reward merit, and so forth; he finished his letter with the rather sad conclusion that 'we are an excellent army on parade, an excellent one to fight; but we are worse than an enemy in a country, and take my word for it that either defeat or success would dissolve us.' So uppermost in his mind, it seems, were two concerns: the effects on his plans of the inefficiencies of straggling, and the damage to his relationship with the Portuguese from looting and other outrages. He had seen the terrible retribution inflicted on French stragglers by the Portuguese peasantry, and there had been two or three early incidents of lone English soldiers suffering vengeance, doubtless with good cause following some imprudent arrogance on their part.

On 9 July, this time on the march into Spain, he wrote to Ambassador Villiers from Plasencia of 'the present acts of enmity committed by the people of Portugal on the troops, which I fear that the latter deserve but too well'; and he specifically referred to the question of a court martial for 'the artilleryman who has committed the murder at Cascaes... I shall most readily come into any measure proposed by Government to remedy the horrible abuses and hardships now existing, and occasioned entirely by the mode in which carts are taken for the service of the British army.' One can picture too easily a desperate scene in a crumbling little farmyard a mile or so into the hills off the main track south from Oporto, with a dozen sick and wounded soldiers – officerless, exhausted, starving – seeking cover from the vertical rain in a shed, limping and dragging one another inside to sink gratefully on to rotting hay and finding – a miracle! – a cart, still with its four wheels. Along comes a troop of 3-pounders, in fair order with a couple of spare horses. Picture a Portuguese farmer desperate to keep his family's one working cart, an aggressive artilleryman absolutely refusing to leave the poor bloody-bandaged infantry – and murder is all too predictable.

In soldiering it is always at the margins that such excesses happen, where – at the time, things being a bit extreme – they are never seen to be the least questionable. That is why God gave soldiers consciences, so that we think twice next time; but conscience speaks clearest on a full stomach. At the end of yet another march, fifteen miles of rain or sun, freezing mud or choking dust, flapping shoe-soles or blistered feet bound with straw, nightly bivouacs were not happy places when the rations were not ready, or non-existent, or at best half weight. No wonder, as Sergeant Cooper of the 2/7th tells us:

> At this period (the march to Abrantes) the English troops made sad work in Portugal by plundering the inhabitants. No sooner was the day's march ended than men turned out to steal pigs, poultry, wine etc. One evening, after halting, a wine store was broken open and much was carried off. The owner, finding this out, ran and brought an officer of the 53rd, who caught one of our Company, named Brown, in the act of handing out the wine in camp kettles. Seizing Brown by the collar, the officer shouted 'Come out you rascal and give me your name'. Brown came out, gave his name Brennan, then knocking the officer down, made his escape and was not found.

(Brennan, by the way, was a noted robber, active the previous year on the Dublin to Cork road when the 7th were stationed nearby, and thus an inspired spur-of-the moment choice of alias by Private Brown...)

The generally cavalier attitude towards the peasants was probably encapsulated in the incident related in his diary by Captain Hawker, 14th Light Dragoons:

> *22nd June 1809, near Thomar* Walked up the river, shaded by orchards, where the trees were breaking down with fruit, and everything around had the richest appearance. While we were in silent admiration contemplating the beauties of nature, a volley of dirt-clods was pelted at us by some Portuguese. What we had done to offend them I know not; but suppose, judging by themselves, they thought us thieves, and concluded we were planning operations to attack their orchard. Justice herself directed us to give them chase; and, after soundly thrashing those who were not then in wind for running away, we proceeded up the river.

It seems strange today that the 23-year-old captain thought it fitting, and not dishonourable, to punish Portuguese civilians for daring to protect their own property; but such armchair sniping is easy, 200 years later and far away from the harsh realities on the ground.

A major cause of general peevishness, from Wellesley down to the drummer boys, was that nobody had any money. Pay was by now two months in arrears and mounting. Wellesley had been horribly strapped for cash even before marching on Oporto, 'with the whole army about to proceed to the attack, with only £10,000, and with monstrous demands upon us.' After the attack he borrowed £13,000 in Portuguese silver from the grateful citizens, and tried to exchange bills on London for dollars in Cadiz. He sent £100,000 in Spanish gold coins (which could not circulate in Portugal) to be exchanged for more dollars. Wellesley simply could not get his hands on cash, the lack of which was to delay his march into Spain. While this was perhaps no bad thing, given the state of the regiments and of his commissariat, it gave away some of the tactical initiative to the French. Wellesley was not to know that the enemy were ignorant of his whereabouts and therefore were not in fact marching day and night to effect his downfall. Such uncertainty occasioned simply by lack of funds was a great aggravation; but his stern intent to pay his debts in Portugal before turning his back for Spain (and more debts) was typical, both of his sense of duty, and his pragmatic wish to keep all relationships with the locals as untroubled as possible.

On 30 May he wrote to Huskisson at the Treasury in London that: 'We have not a shilling or the chance of getting any. The money sent to Cadiz to be exchanged is not returned, and none can be procured at Lisbon for bills. In short we must have money from England, if we are to continue our operations in this country.' A fortnight later on 11 June he wrote to Villiers from Abrantes: 'I should begin immediately [to give the ball a good kick], but I cannot venture to stir without money. The army is two months in arrears, we are over head and ears in debt everywhere, and I cannot venture into Spain without paying what we owe, at least in this neighbourhood, and giving a little money to the troops.' Again, on 21 June, to Villiers: 'I cannot get supplies, or boats, or carts to move supplies from Lisbon without money.'

Wellesley knew full well that troops with no cash, particularly those sitting idle in bivouac while regaining their strength, will readily turn to other means of obtaining small comforts. The vicious circle of no cash = no move forward = greater boredom = more thievery = worse credit, just had to be broken. To Lord Castlereagh, he wrote the very next day: 'I hope that you will attend to my requisitions for money; not only am I in want, but the Portuguese government, to whom Mr Villiers says that we owe £125,000. I repeat, that we must have £200,000 a month, from England, and until I write you that I can do without it; in which sum I include £40,000 a month for the Portuguese government, to pay for twenty thousand men... Money must be sent to pay the Portuguese debt and our debts in Portugal... There are besides, debts of Sir John Moore's army still due in Spain, which I am called upon to pay.' By 25 June he had accumulated a modest £100,000 and, settling for that temporarily, he marched for Spain forty-eight hours later. The rest of the treasure convoy trailed in from Lisbon a few days later.

The army's lack of cash compounded its other shortages: of transport, rations, medical cover, reinforcements, even shoes. As each hot June day passed these shortages, too, enforced delay, while letters on high strategy were necessarily exchanged with General Cuesta. The lack of transport in particular bedevilled resupply across the border, and led inevitably to the enforced 'borrowing' of peasant carts of all kinds. Commissariat officers were generally young, raw and finding their feet (where they were not old, slow and on their backsides). Their frustrations are apparent from Schaumann's diary, often concerning the reliable employment of trains of local pack animals in the absence of sufficient bullock carts, an employment made the harder from the lack of cash to pay the drovers. There is one delightfully descriptive entry of a success in acquiring bullock carts – fifty, no less – the day after the capture of Oporto:

> Having reached Oporto, on the evening of 13 May... appointed commissary to the 14th and 20th Light Dragoons, which, however, had marched in pursuit of the enemy on the previous day... [I was] unable to load the rations for my two regiments, for I had no carts. I spent the whole day running up and down any number of extremely bad and hilly roads, in the sweltering heat, from the stores to the Commissary-General, then to the Regidor, and on to the Provedor and the Juiz. At last, at midday, the carts came, and then I had to draw salt fish, ship's biscuit, oats and rum, and see them all loaded. When at length I had completed every formality and got the carts across the river and on the march, it was five in the afternoon. I had had nothing to eat since seven o'clock, was saturated with perspiration, and was so tired after all that running about that I could hardly stand up. Mounted on a bad requisitioned mule, without any help, money, or office, and lacking even the means of taking the necessary writing materials and books with me, I was expected not only to overtake two cavalry regiments which had had three days start in pursuit of the flying foe, but also to satisfy all their wants and, in addition, to

cross the hills over most appalling roads, with fifty bullock carts loaded with provisions and forage.

That night Schaumann's mule, his muleteer and his guide dissappeared, so: 'I hired a man to carry my valise, and bearing my own small dispatch case with my writing materials myself, for it contained things of value, such as my instructions and my diary, I set off on foot for Penafiel.'

The long and arduous march from Lisbon to Oporto, the further trek via the stony mountain tracks of the Tras os Montes to Montalegre, the final leg of 150 miles back down to Abrantes – the whole something over 400 miles – saw the ruin of countless army shoes. Some contractors' practise was to glue the pieces together, with a minimum of sowing and with a layer of clay between the thin pieces of the sole: such travesties were the first to fail in the mud and on the rocks. The second pair carried as spare in the soldiers' knapsacks came, as like as not, from the same source, so the company cobbler would have been kept busy with running repairs. The 48th's Digest notes that 'the troops after a few days at Braga to recover from the fatigues of the harassing pursuit of the enemy, retraced their steps to Oporto. The 2/48th and the rest of Major General Hill's Brigade passed one night in Oporto and then proceeded to Coimbra... arriving by 26 May, when a supply of shoes, of which the men were much in want, was obtained'. On 31 May, Wellesley's staff requested a further 20,000 pairs to be sent urgently from England.

But it was perhaps in the matter of human reinforcements that Wellesley faced the greatest dilemma: to go into Spain as he was, or to wait for more troops to join the army? Three of the eight battalions just landed at Lisbon, or approaching the port, were the brigade of light troops under General Crauford (the 1/43rd and 1/52nd Light Infantry and 1/95th Rifles). These experienced men had been in Moore's army in the Galician hills, the 1/52nd and 1/95th fighting at Corunna and the 1/43rd coming out via Vigo. Requested by Wellesley in April, they sailed from England on 25 May, but contrary winds frustrated their complete arrival in Lisbon until early July. Wellesley, with his Portuguese debts paid off at last and some spare cash in hand, crossed the border into Spain near Zarza La Mayor, some 200 miles away, on the very day the final transports made landfall. He could wait no longer, but at least he knew that he had Crauford steaming up behind him. Stupendous efforts were indeed made to join, but in the end too late – just – for Talavera. Two batteries of horse artillery were also on the road, and would have made a material addition to Wellesley's three batteries, but it was not to be. One arrived with Crauford's brigade the day after the battle, the other much later.

Ahead of Crauford's 'light bobs', fortunately, were the 1/61st (South Gloster), who were able to join Wellesley at Abrantes before the army set off; and the 23rd Light Dragoons and 1/48th, who caught up ten days later at Plasencia. The 48th and 61st originated as Garrison battalions on the Rock of Gibraltar, and of course had to be replaced. Wellesley sent the 2/9th and 2/30th for that purpose, the former from Cameron's brigade, the latter from the Lisbon garrison; while the 23rd Light Dragoons from Sicily were replaced by two squadrons of the 20th Light Dragoons and one squadron of the 3rd Light Dragoons KGL, both belonging to Stapleton

Cotton's 1st Cavalry Brigade. Overall, therefore, Wellesley was really no better off for these changes, except for the extra bayonet strength the two fresh 1st Battalions brought with them. Against that must be set a loss of experience: the departing companies and squadrons had three months of active campaigning under their belts, but the newcomers nothing but a sea journey.

*   *   *

Napoleon once said, in conversation with John Jacques Pelet, 'We can decide nothing here, since events have long passed by the time we receive the first news... I cannot wage war 500 leagues away.' The general truth of such a sentiment is unarguable; but it did not prevent Napoleon himself, in June 1809, from trying to do just that. His despatch to his generals in Spain was sent on 12 June from Schonbrunn, three weeks before he crushed the Austrians at Wagram, and its contents would have a continuing effect on events in the Peninsula. It arrived with King Joseph on 1 July at El Moral in La Mancha (100 miles below Madrid), and with Marshal Soult at Zamora, up on the Duoro in Leon, the following day. It is probably best to consult Oman at this point, since Sir Charles provides a wonderfully concise summary of Napoleon's intervention. In reading it, there dawns upon us the realization that a document for eventual consumption in Spain, in early July, was necessarily written in Austria, based on intelligence about situations that had existed in Spain and Portugal back in mid-May. Oman's commentary provides an early insight into the game of blind man's bluff that had commenced, the players both spurred on by conflicting advice and orders, while yet reined in by nagging uncertainty bred of ignorance:

> On the French side, matters suffered a sudden change in the last days of June – the hand of the Emperor was stretched out from the banks of the Danube to alter the general dispositions of the army in Spain. On 12 June he had dictated at Schonbrunn a new plan of campaign, based on information which was already many weeks old when it reached him. At this date, the Emperor was barely aware that Soult was being pressed by Wellesley in Northern Portugal. He had no detailed knowledge of what was taking place in Galicia or the Asturias, and was profoundly ignorant of the intrigues at Oporto which afterwards roused his indignation. But he was convinced that the English army was the one hostile force in Spain which ought to engage the attention of his lieutenants. Acting on this belief he issued an order that the 2nd, 5th, and 6th Corps – those of Soult, Mortier, and Ney – were to be united into a single army, and to be told off to the task of evicting Wellesley from Portugal. They were to put aside for the present all such subsidiary enterprises as the subjection of Galicia and the Asturias, and to devote themselves solely to 'beating, hunting down, and casting into the sea the British army. If the three Corps join in good time the enemy ought to be crushed, and the Spanish war will come to an end. But the troops must be moved in masses and not march in small detachments... Putting aside all personal considerations, I give the

command of the united army to the Duke of Dalmatia [Soult], as the senior marshal. His three Corps ought to amount to something between 50,000 and 60,000 men.'

This dispatch… had been drawn up in view of events that were taking place about 15 May. It presupposed that the British army was still in Northern Portugal, in close touch with Soult, and that Victor was in Estremadura. As a matter of fact Soult was on this day leading his dilapidated corps down the Esla, at the end of his retreat from Galicia. Ney, furious at the way in which his colleague had deserted him, had descended to Astorga three days before. Mortier was at Valladolid, just about to march for Villa-Castin and Madrid, for the King had determined to draw him down to aid in the defence of the capital. Finally, Cuesta, instead of lying in the Sierra Morena, as he was when Napoleon drew up his orders, was now on the Tagus, while Wellesley was no longer in touch with Soult on the Douro, but preparing to fall upon Victor in New Castile. The whole situation was so changed that the commentary which the Emperor appended to his orders was hopelessly out of date – as was always bound to be the case so long as he persisted in endeavouring to direct the course of affairs in Spain from the suburbs of Vienna… It is clear that on 2 July Soult had no knowledge of Wellesley's movements, and thought that the British army was quite as likely to be aiming at Salamanca as at Madrid.

It says much for the future respect that the French would start to pay Wellesley's small British army that its presence in mid-1809 so quickly made itself felt – it certainly had a unifying effect on the individual French corps. Until then, Napoleon's marshals were pursuing their separate campaigns: St Cyr's 7th Corps in Catalonia, Suchet's 3rd versus Blake in Aragon, Victor's 1st versus Cuesta in Estremadura, Sebastiani's 4th Corps versus Venegas in La Mancha, Soult's and Mortier's 2nd and 5th Corps in northern Portugal and Ney's 6th in the Asturias. These six earlier campaigns had been quite disparate, unco-ordinated by Joseph and Jourdan (just as, indeed, were the Spanish counter-operations by the useless Junta in Seville). It was this fragmentation of effort that the Schonbrunn Decree sought to end; Napoleon had correctly judged the importance and danger of Wellesley's arrival on such a disunited and vulnerable scene. Soult's new single army of three corps was to put aside all else while it concentrated on destroying the British army. And if the unenthusiastic marshals would otherwise have been reluctant to eschew individual glory and start co-operating, Wellesley's strategic vision of combining with two Spanish armies to go for Joseph in Madrid, after seeing off Soult and Victor, would leave them little alternative. What was in store would certainly concentrate French minds, if too late to prevent Sir Arthur Wellesley becoming Viscount Wellington of Talavera by the end of this month.

For the French, Wellesley was a nearly unknown player, albeit with two irritating wins to his credit at Vimiero and Oporto. They may not have been privy to the British casualty list of 43 killed, 168 wounded and 17 missing at Oporto, but Soult could hardly hide his own staggering loss of nearly 6,000 men – surely a stinging revenge for his defeat of Sir John Moore. Just what this new English general was capable of, the marshals had yet to fathom. It is a compliment to the guerrillas' stranglehold on the French lines of communications that fully two months after Wellesley chased Soult out of Oporto, and one month since news of that event reached Joseph in Madrid, by early July no further word had come of subsequent British movements. On 2 July, Joseph wrote to his imperial brother: 'I am not in the least disquieted concerning the present condition of military affairs in this part of Spain.' A week later Joseph wrote again that Wellesley had 'not yet made any pronounced movement' – although he had in fact marched 150 miles south from Oporto to Abrantes, then east another 150 miles along the Tagus to Plasencia, and was then within a week's march – a mere 125 miles – of Madrid, and Joseph's complacent crown.

8

The Advance to Contact:
1–27 July 1809

THE French position in early July 1809 was that Napoleon's orders to Marshal Soult – to take overall command of the 2nd, 5th and 6th Corps, and kick the British out of Portugal – had arrived on 2 July, just as, unknown to Soult, Wellesley's headquarters was once again packing its bags. While Soult's own 2nd Corps would take some weeks to recover and re-equip itself after the retreat from Oporto, the Duke of Dalmatia nevertheless immediately exercised his new command (with some satisfaction, one may assume). He ordered Mortier and Ney to get their 5th and 6th Corps from Valladolid to Salamanca and from Astorga to Benavente, respectively – that is, to concentrate around 2nd Corps' flanks. With some 60,000 men in due course, such an army would surely prove sufficiently overwhelming to re-enter northern Portugal and crush the British.

The same day that Soult's messengers left, heavily escorted, to set in train this move to the south, Wellesley moved east into Spain, to join with General Cuesta's Army of Estremadura. Marshal Victor's 1st Corps had also just pulled east, to behind the Alberche river beyond Talavera, though not in reaction (Victor had no idea Wellesley was so close) but simply in his continual search for food. 'The position is desperate', he wrote to King Joseph on 25 June: 'the 1st Corps is on the eve of dissolution: the men are dropping down from mere starvation. I have nothing, absolutely nothing, to give them… I am forced to fall back on Talavera.'

Victor's army was about 22,000 strong – much the same as Wellesley's, at 23,000. Behind Victor was King Joseph, only sixty miles away to the north-east in Madrid, with (as the allies thought) another 12,000; also sixty miles from Madrid, but to the south, lay Sebastiani's 4th Corps, with (as they thought) another 10,000 men. So if they all came together the French could field some 44,000 men. Wellesley knew that Cuesta was just south of the Tagus with 35,000 infantry, and together they would thus be 58,000 strong, with a preponderance of 6:4 over the French. However, if Sebastiani could be kept from joining, the odds became 2:1; and fortunately, General Venegas's 23,000-strong army of La Mancha lay not far to the south of Sebastiani. He had already been taunting the Frenchman, and could do so again to keep him occupied.

But what were the true odds? Would the Spanish prove to be effective – skilled, manoeuvrable fighting forces? Wellesley had yet to meet them, and all he knew of them was hearsay, so it was important for him to get some 'feel' for the Spanish soldier and his officers. For while it would be tempting providence enough if he had to lead 23,000 redcoats on their own against the 34,000 bluecoats of Victor and Joseph, against 44,000 (if Sebastiani joined in) the odds would be prohibitive. (In fact Sebastiani had not 10,000 men but 17,000 – so it would be 23,000 against 51,000.) Since Wellesley would reach Plasencia by 8 July, and would then be only half a day's ride from the Tagus at Almaraz, he arranged to visit the Spanish near there on the 10th – necessarily to agree the joint plan of action, but also to judge their calibre.

The matter was the more urgent due to the arrival of new and mixed intelligence on the French locations, which was not all good: Soult was 150 miles away at Zamora, and Mortier a similar distance at Valladolid. The existence of these two further French corps within ten marches, even if one was still re-equipping, obviously raised anxieties for Wellesley's left flank; and the reports were reliable, since they came from letters captured with General Franceschi. More cheering was an intercepted copy of Victor's letter to Joseph of 25 July revealing the hunger suffered by 1st Corps. Another encouragement was the mention of Braganza as a possible objective for Soult, when rejuvenated, which would thereby take the French back into northern Portugal. But while this would keep them further away from Wellesley's eastwards thrust, there was no guarantee that Soult would not about-turn when he heard that Madrid was threatened – and Wellesley had every intention of threatening it.

So Sir Arthur had much to ponder as he rode south the forty miles to meet Cuesta. Their earlier exchanges of correspondence had not been encouraging, as he had told Castlereagh a fortnight earlier: 'My correspondence with General Cuesta is a very curious one, and proves him to be as obstinate as any gentleman at the head of an army ought to be.' Met by a Spanish dragoon escort sent out to do the honours, but who unfortunately managed to lose their way back, Wellesley and his staff arrived four hours late, in darkness. Sir Arthur's Adjutant-General and part-time leader of cavalry charges, Brigadier the Hon. Charles Stewart (later Lord Londonderry), has left us this wonderful description:

> Our arrival at the camp was announced by a general discharge of artillery, upon which an immense number of torches were made to blaze up, and we passed the entire Spanish line in review by their light. The effect produced by these arrangements was one of no ordinary character. The torches, held aloft at moderate intervals, threw a red and wavering light over the whole scene, permitting at the same time its minuter parts to be here and there cast into the shade, while the grim and swarthy images of the soldiers, their bright arms and dark uniforms, appeared peculiarly picturesque as often as the flashes fell upon them. Nor was Cuesta himself an object to be passed by without notice: the old man preceeded us, not so much sitting on his horse as held upon it by two pages, at the imminent risk of being overthrown whenever a cannon was discharged, or a torch flamed out with peculiar brightness. His physical debility was so observable as clearly to mark his unfitness for the situation he held. As to his mental powers, he gave us little opportunity of judging, inasmuch as he scarcely uttered five words during the continuance of our visit: but

his corporal infirmities were ever at absolute variance with all a general's duties.

In this way we passed by about 6,000 cavalry drawn up in rank entire, and not less than twenty battalions of infantry, each of 700 to 800 bayonets. They were all, without exception, remarkably fine men. Some indeed were very young – too young for service – particularly among the recruits who had lately joined. But to take them all in all, it would not have been easy to find a stouter or more hardy looking body of soldiers in any European service. Of their appointments it was not possible to speak in the same terms of commendation. There were battalions whose arms, accoutrements, and even clothing might be pronounced respectable: but in general they were deficient, particularly in shoes. It was easy to perceive, from the attitude in which they stood, and the manner in which they handled their arms, that little or no discipline prevailed among them: they could not but be regarded as raw levies. Speaking of them in the aggregate they were little better than bold peasantry, armed partially like soldiers, but completely unacquainted with a soldier's duty. This remark applied to the cavalry as much as to the infantry. Many of the horses were good, but the riders manifestly knew nothing of movement or of discipline: and they were on this account, as also on that of miserable equipment, quite unfit for service. The generals appeared to have been selected by one rule alone – that of seniority. They were almost all old men, and, except O'Donoju and Zayas, evidently incapable of bearing the fatigues or surmounting the difficulties of a campaign. It was not so with the colonels and battalion commanders, who appeared to be young and active, and some of whom were, we had reason to believe, learning to become skilful officers... Cuesta seemed particularly unwilling that any of his generals should hold any serious conversation with us. It is true that he presented them one by one to Sir Arthur, but no words were exchanged on the occasion, and each retired after he made his bow.

f we take Stewart's view to reflect that of Wellesley and his staff in general, then the pinion was that Cuesta's soldiers were mostly too raw and inexperienced, and his enior commanders too slow and set in their ways. That this was indeed his interretation was confirmed the next day, when Sir Arthur said to Sir George Murray, is Quartermaster-General: 'I'm sure I don't know what we are to do with these eople. Put them behind stone walls, and I dare say they would defend them, but to manoeuvre with such a rabble under fire, is impossible. I am afraid we shall find hem an encumbrance rather than otherwise.'

This was an amazingly confident statement. He did not exclaim, 'Oh Lord, Murray, they're so useless, I can't attempt Victor now – not at 3 to 2 against me, still ess 5 to 2 unless I can get that fellow Vinegar or whatever he's called to keep ebastiani out of it. Let's go home, and leave the damn Spaniards.' Two weeks later he stone walls on the outskirts of Talavera were indeed manned by Spanish efenders, not British; and since even that protection did not deter some from deserting at an early stage, Sir Arthur's reservations about the calibre of the Spanish army seem prudent.

He intended, of course, no slight on Spanish manhood as a warrior race: it was simply a fact that too many of Cuesta's battalions were under-trained, ill-officered and lacked battle experience. (Stewart's comment about the manner in which the Spanish handled their muskets is, in this context, entirely telling. A civilian, like a woman, will hold a firearm with no instinctive understanding of its centre of gravity; to the trained eye it looks quite wrong, and you know the weapon will be used with equal negligence.) The reformed Spanish army that King Carlos III passed to his son in 1788 had been far from negligible, although Spanish pride had resisted Prussian-style discipline; but during the 1790s it had suffered severely from the abuses of Godoy's corrupt regime. While starved of necessary resources, it was pestered with absurdly frequent changes to the uniform regulations that were typical of the frivolity of the court. It was largely officered by *hidalgos* who regarded military rank as the natural privilege of their birth, but for whom duty began and ended with physical courage on the battlefield; there was no culture of care for the efficiency and well-being of their men, and only a few artillery and engineer officers made any effort to master the latest advances in their profession. During the Peninsular War a vigorous and effective programme of reform would be pursued, but in 1809 it had yet to bear fruit.

For half the next day, Wellesley and Cuesta talked about what best to do – or rather, they each talked with Cuesta's chief of staff, the Irish-descended General O'Donoju, who then talked to the other, for Cuesta refused to speak French and Wellesley's Spanish was inadequate. This frustrating process at least gave Wellesley a chance to form a favourable impression of O'Donoju himself, if less so of his master whose contributions mainly comprised the single word 'No'. Writing two days later Sir Arthur said: 'I settled the plan of operations with General O'Donoju who appears to me to be a very able officer, and well calculated to fill his station. Ominously, however, he continued, 'It is impossible for me to say what plan General Cuesta entertains.'

Don Gregorio Garcia de la Cuesta was about to become a major pain in the neck for Sir Arthur. Before examining how they eventually agreed to set about the French we should therefore consider why Cuesta is described as obstinate, querulous, unreliable, impractical, proud, incompetent, whimsically perverse, decrepit, headstrong obtuse and touchy – to list some of the adjectives historians have hurled at this far old man over the years. It would appear nearer the mark simply to say 'suspicious' and 'jealous', since the commander of the army of Estremadura had good cause to be both, and to fear for his command appointment. While it was quite unjust of Cuesta to regard Sir Arthur's appearance on the Spanish scene as the cause of a threat against his position, he was nevertheless antagonistic and unco-operative towards the unsuspecting British general. At the same time, being a fiercely patriotic Spanish grandee, he loved nothing better than to kill Frenchmen – or rather, to dream of killing Frenchmen, since his military incompetence was of a high order. This had been fully demonstrated at Cabezon and at Medina de Rio Seco, and at Medelli four months earlier (he was still limping, when he could walk unaided at all, from the broken bones sustained when his own fleeing cavalry rode over him on the latter field).

Cuesta's attitude sprang from the realities of Spanish politics. As we have seen in Chapter 1, Spanish resistance to France was based on regional rather than centralized organization. Inevitably, therefore, the Central Junta in Seville, and the military, each comprised various struggling factions, and Cuesta was only one player in a complex game. The factions involved, among others, the supporters of Cuesta himself, of Venegas, of the Duke of Infantado, and of the Duke of Albuquerque; no love was lost between these groupings, and both Venegas and Albuquerque were at daggers drawn with Cuesta. Unfortunately for Sir Arthur, the British Minister in Seville, John Hookham Frere, was linked to Albuquerque through personal friendship, and quite improperly became embroiled in these domestic politics, with subsequent harmful effects on the progress of the British campaign. Frere and the Duke of Albuquerque shared a mutual admiration society, and the former did all he could to obtain advantage for the latter, including a search for an independent command in which Albuquerque could make his military name. Frere also vigorously pursued, semi-privately, the separate proposition that the various Spanish armies ideally required one single commander-in-chief – who should be Sir Arthur Wellesley.

Given Spain's entirely proper national pride, it was quite impossible that the Central Junta would stomach the appointment of a foreigner: Spain was not Portugal. She had not been invaded and defeated, but tricked into allowing partial French occupation; her head of state had not been forced to flee, but had been kidnapped; her army had not been disbanded, but had risen up spontaneously against the French; she had not been liberated by a foreign landing force, but was in the middle of a war in which the British were an ally, admittedly of huge financial generosity, but of only modest strength on the ground.

It is thus unsurprising that the 70-year-old Cuesta, the pride-soaked product of an extremely conservative culture, should regard the 40-year-old Wellesley as he would an upstart puppy contender for pack leadership – for the post of Generalissimo of all the Spanish armies. And this was as nothing to his reaction to Wellesley's first proposal: that the march eastwards should be screened by a left flank force of 10,000 Spanish, to be commanded by the Duke of Albuquerque. Even in Wellesley's relative innocence of Junta politics, it seems impossible that he could have orginated this suggestion unprompted; only Frere could have instigated a proposal so guaranteed to infuriate Cuesta, at such a time. It is thus understandable that Cuesta should view with suspicion any other proposal now made by Wellesley, and that he should respond with every possible show of independence. Moreover, as we shall see, while the joint plan of action was itself agreed on 11 July, Cuesta's seemingly irrational actions and inactions, at odds with that plan, would multiply over the days ahead. One imagines that his paranoia deepened as the days passed, and as his mind continued to dwell on what he saw as the machinations of his British allies as well as his Spanish rivals.

To consider now that plan of action: Cuesta's response to Wellesley's proposal for a left wing of 10,000 men was to suggest that, if Wellesley wanted a left flanking force so much, then they should be British troops. Since this would have consumed half the British army, a compromise was reached whereby Wellesley's small (1,500-strong) Portugese force under the experienced Sir Robert Wilson was to be reinforced by two Spanish battalions plus a squadron – say 3,500 men in all. Wilson was to move east from Plasencia, and along the north bank of the Tietar river, then turning south via Navamoveunde towards the French on the Alberche. He could thus provide both protection and early warning to the main body, from some twenty miles to its north.

This compromise ignored the small matter of defending two passes over the Sierra de Gata and the Sierra de Francia, at Perales and Banos. These could well be Soult's gateways south from the Salamanca region if, on hearing of the allies' threat to Madrid, he sought to cut their lines of communication. Both passes were held, but in minimum strength: 2,000 Spanish at the former and just 600 at the latter. Still, Wellesley supposed that for some time to come Soult could field only about 15,000 bayonets and no artillery. Nor had he any reason to doubt his latest intelligence that Ney was up in Galicia, at Lugo or Corunna; and that Mortier with only 7,000 men was heading for Avila, then possibly on to Madrid. Sir Arthur had not the least idea that a mere eighteen days after this planning meeting with Cuesta, and hours after his great battle at Talavera, three French corps totalling 50,000 men would be surging south over those very passes.

On the other, southern flank, Venegas' Army of La Mancha was to march north from its present positions around Santa Cruz de Mudela, forcing Sebastiani's 4th Corps back to the Tagus, while itself edging eastwards to cross the river either at Aranjuez or Fuenteduenas. It was thought that Sebastiani must then himself edge eastwards, to keep between Venegas and Madrid, and in so doing put the desired distance between himself and Victor at Talavera. Should Sebastiani nonetheless choose to join Victor, leaving Madrid open, then Venegas would gratefully march on the capital; its seizure and liberation must surely force King Joseph to counter-attack.

Either way, the allied plan assumed that they would not be fighting Victor, Joseph and Sebastiani on the same field. That this is precisely what was to happen, and that the assumption was overly optimistic, may safely be laid on the shoulders of Venegas alone. As we shall see, his inactivity, whether deliberate or merely incompetent, surely reflected the factional strains in the Spanish chain of command. And we shall also see how, at Talavera, Sebastiani's twenty-three extra battalions tested Wellesley very nearly to the limit.

As always when bodies of troops are to 'march divided but fight together', an arranged programme of progress was essential. Wellesley and (surprisingly) Cuesta stuck to theirs precisely: the British left Plasencia on 18 July, crossing the Tietar to Miajadas and Centinello and reaching Oropesa on the 20th, when they halted for one day. (The army now included the 1/48th, which arrived at Plasencia on 14 July to join the 2/48th in Hill's 2nd Division – the only regiment at Talavera to fight that day with both battalions.) Cuesta left Almaraz on 19 July, reaching La Calzada, just short of Oropesa, on the 20th. Both armies were now within one day's march of their enemy. Of course, by now Venegas would be occupying Sebastiani down in La Mancha – except that he was not.

Several days had to be allowed after the meeting of Wellesley and Cuesta, to get Venegas's timetable to him over the 150 miles of the Sierra de Guadalupe and the line of the Guadiana, and to give him time to prepare his army to march. The orders reached him on 15 July, and spelt out that he was to challenge Sebastiani in the Madridejos area on the 18th, the day Wellesley and Cuesta moved east. In the light of subsequent events, we may question whether Wellesley's use of time was really sensible. He did, after all, return to his army on 12 July, and thereupon issued his warning order to the divisions to be ready to move on the 18th; so he was prepared to sit on his hands for six clear days. Victor was four marches away; Sebastiani was five marches from Victor; and Joseph, with Madrid's small reserve, was three. The French did not know that the British were close – on 17 July Joseph's chief of staff Jourdan, in writing to Soult to agree the latter's plans to invade northern Portugal, showed that no intelligence had been received on any British advance; and that ignorance would continue for the next five days, until the 22nd. If the allied armies could have hit Victor on the Alberche on, say, the 18th, there was every chance that he could have been overrun before help could be summoned and could arrive. Otherwise, every day's delay increased the chance of the British presence being uncovered, and of the French reacting to it.

In the event, that is what happened. On 18 July Soult heard of Wellesley's move up the Tagus. He immediately sent General Foy to Madrid with proposals to cancel the push into Portugal, in favour of an immediate move south to cut Wellesley's supply routes. Foy arrived with the news on the 22nd; and Joseph promptly set out to join Victor with the Madrid reserve of some 5,000 men, leaving a similar force behind, and ordering Sebastiani to fall back on Toledo. So it is easy to argue that Sir Arthur should not have delayed.

Unfortunately – and Wellesley would have felt the constraint most keenly – he was hamstrung by his lack of transport and food, and was simply not able to crack straight on towards Victor. Before crossing the border he had trusted the Supreme Junta's warm assurances that everything he needed to fight the French, he would get. They even appointed a representative at the British headquarters with full authority to arrange local supplies. Sir Arthur therefore marched into Spain with little transport – the Portugese drivers were loathe to leave Portugal – and few provisions, expecting the host country to provide. Within the week (8 July) he was writing to Frere: 'We have not procured a cart or a mule for the service of the army... we really should not be worse off in an enemy's country, or indeed so ill, as we should there take by force what we should require.' The military chest and reserve ammunition were back at Abrantes, lacking wheels, and by 16 July things were so bad that he wrote threateningly to Cuesta's chief-of-staff that he would cease operations after the Alberche action if his wants were not addressed. He would 'begin no new operation til he had been supplied with the means of transport which the army requires.' After all, Wellesley was about to enter that wasteland between the Tagus and the Tietar which Victor had just stripped clean. On the 16th he also wrote to Frere: 'It is impossible to express the inconvenience and risk that we incur from the want of means of conveyance, which I cannot believe the country could not furnish, if there existed any inclination to furnish them.' These views are echoed in Commissary Schaumann's diary:

> On the 11th we diverged from the direct route, taking a zig-zag course, partly owing to lack of forage and provisions... the Junta in Seville gave us the most wonderful promises that vehicles, mules and provisions would be held in readiness for us. But of all these splendid supplies we have so far seen but little... we were obliged as far as possible to carry our provisions with us. We were seldom able to get corn, hay or straw for the horses regularly delivered by the Spanish authorities... often enough the ship's biscuit which we carried with us in bullock carts as a reserve had to supply all our needs. No trouble whatsoever was taken to supply us with transport or mules.

Clearly, for both lowly commissary and mighty commander-in-chief, a revealing light was beginning to shine on their allies. Perhaps Spanish promises should not have been so readily believed, given the many practical difficulties they obviously faced in gathering beasts of burden in a region that had already enjoyed the presence of the French. Perhaps the sanguine British, who otherwise might have chewed over the prospects more carefully, needed little Spanish over-optimism to fire them up. If the fault lay with Sir Arthur, it was not one he ever repeated. But it presented him now with a dilemma. If he set off immediately for Victor, unexpected and with superior numbers, his apparently good prospects would be diminished by the abysmal shortage of transport (to say nothing of the failure by Venegas to mount the planned diversion south of Madrid). If he waited for the latter to get on the move, and for more carts to arrive, he risked news of his presence reaching Madrid.

In the event, Wellesley got absolutely the worst of both worlds. He waited, yet the transport position did not materially improve; Madrid was apprised of his arrival; and Venegas proved useless, failing to hold Sebastiani in play. For the day before Cuesta's orders reached Venegas down at Mudela on 15 July, the latter had received slightly different orders from the Junta in Seville. These were, as Fortescue puts it, 'to draw the enemy's attention to his side, but without compromising himself.' Now that is a much more negative description of what had been decided, and it implied that Venegas could obey merely by demonstration – indeed, that any actual engagement with the French was to be avoided. Cuesta's orders for a fighting advance with phased daily objectives reflected more positively what was required and what had been agreed. By 16 July, therefore, having marched north a bare forty miles to the Guadiana, and located the French on the line Villarubia-Villarte-Herencia, Venegas stopped, held a council of war, and sent to the Junta for further instructions. The answer came three days later, on 19 July – the day when, according to Wellesley and Cuesta, he should have been entangled with Sebastiani thirty miles further north, around Madridejos. Fortescue says that the Junta's further orders were 'bidding Venegas continue his advance, since the armies on the Tagus were absolutely dependent upon his co-operation; but this he was to do only upon receiving certain intelligence of their progress, and after assuring himself that the enemy to his front had not been reinforced to a dangerous strength.'

To a commander who was at odds with Cuesta, with his own supporters in the Junta who would have had a hand in framing his orders, such half-hearted, mealy-mouthed instructions were a perfect excuse to do nothing. If there existed a conspiracy against Cuesta, here was apparent evidence. Venegas predictably pulled in such horns as he had sticking out, went back behind the Guadiana, and only ventured forward when, five days later, someone told him that Sebastiani's corps had quietly disappeared. Whether through antagonism towards Cuesta, innate timidity or deep military incompetence – and most likely a mixture of these – General Venegas had now caused Sir Arthur, a week later, to face 15,500 additional bayonets in twenty-three battalions, and some 1,200 extra sabres. Since Wellesley himself only had twenty-five British battalions in all, this abject failure by Venegas very severely altered the odds in Marshal Victor's favour.

To summarize the general position at first light on Friday 21 July: the armies of Wellesley and Cuesta were together halted around Oropesa, just one march from Victor, who was behind the Alberche just east of Talavera; King Joseph was in Madrid; and Sebastiani's 4th Corps was still at Madridejos, though only for one more day. Soult, still without artillery, was looking to move south to the area around Salamanca, having heard rumours of the British in the Tagus valley, and having sent Foy to King Joseph with his new plan (which would arrive next day); Mortier had been told to speed up his move to Salamanca, and Ney his march from Astorga to Zamora. It is important to add, of course, that in fact no one really knew where anyone else was located, nor their direction of movement. Just about all suppositions and assumptions were wrong, blinded by the usual fog of war, but two clear thrusts had commenced: 23,000 British, and their Spanish allies, were heading east against Victor's 22,000 Frenchmen; and 50,000 Frenchmen were marching south against the long British tail.

*   *   *

On the morning of Saturday 22 July the allies went to war, knowing from the previous day's patrolling that Victor's advanced cavalry vedettes were somewhere around Gamonal, nine miles west of Talavera. There, at mid-day, the Duke of Albuquerque and his six regiments of the 2nd Cavalry Division, acting as Cuesta's advance guard, came upon rather more than vedettes: drawn up on the plain outside Talavera were the six regiments of horse of General Latour-Maubourg's 1st Dragoon Division. They had dismounted to ease their horses and were plainly not in a hurry to be moved, being curious to see the extent of the opposition and the colour of their coats. There then ensued what Napier, given his contempt for most things Spanish, characteristically over-described as 'a display of ignorance, timidity, and absurdity, that has seldom been equalled in war; the past defeats of the Spanish army [were] rendered quite explicable'.

The prudent Albuquerque, refraining from the sort of instant violence that any British cavalry commander would unleash in a second, requested infantry reinforcements and guns. Cuesta sent forward the infantry division of General Zayas, who, as Napier put it, was then obliged by the French cavalry 'to display his whole line, consisting of 15,000 infantry and 3,000 cavalry'. Zayas then proceeded to skirmish for no less than four hours, according to the eyewitness Captain FitzClarence; but 'made no attempt to drive [the French] in but contented themselves with deploying into several long lines, making a very formidable appearance.' The skirmishing went on and on until – presumably unable to stand the boredom any longer – the 950 horsemen of the 23rd Light Dragoons and the 1st Light Dragoons KGL of Anson's cavalry brigade came up in warlike fashion. Thereupon the 3,300 French horse promptly disappeared round to the rear of Talavera. Long afterwards, Lord Munster commented of the Spanish version of skirmishing, 'It is my belief that they would have continued till now if we had not aided them.'

As Latour-Maubourg's division skirted the suburbs, two small columns of French infantry emerged and followed on – presumably the two battalions Victor had earlier left in Talavera town. Seeing an apparently soft target, Albuquerque sent one of his regiments to charge them down. So awful was the first attempt that Sir Charles Stewart, that renowned usurper of other people's cavalry, thrust himself to their head; but three times he failed to get the Spanish dragoons to follow him, writing later that: 'No men could have more carefully avoided coming to close quarters than did the Spaniards this day. The Spanish cavalrymen, every time they closed and came under fire, would stop and vere away.' His ADC George FitzClarence, who watched, wrote:

> Brigadier-General Charles Stewart, who happened to be on the spot [!], persuaded their officers to follow the French retreat along the fine Madrid road… the enemy were overtaken retiring in two small columns (together 4 or 500 men), and to the attack of one General Stewart led the Spanish cavalry. The result, as indeed all we saw on this day of our allies, was a proof of their total want, not only of discipline, but of courage. On this and two succeeding attempts, (to which the English General headed them), on receiving the enemy's fire, when the principal danger was past, they pulled up and fled in every direction… Cruelty and cowardice are ever combined, these same Spanish who had thus avoided closing with the unmaimed enemy, murdered in cold blood a few wounded and dying men their column left in the road when they retired, who were struck down by the artillery which was brought up after the cavalry's repulse.

By 2pm the French had completely retired behind the Alberche, and no doubt the report of British cavalry was very quickly passed to Victor, and on to Madrid, where it would confirm Foy's report of the British being on the Tagus. It is interesting to conjecture that during the fruitless four-hour Spanish skirmish, Wellesley would presumably have come up to watch, and gone away puzzled. The performance of the Spanish cavalry would have left the many British observers quite gloomy. Was this the measure of their ally – what had they let themselves in for? A flavour of the scorn is caught by August Schaumann, commissary to the 14th Light Dragoons, who out of curiosity had followed Anson's brigade:

> We posted ourselves not far from the gate [of Talavera], in order to watch the drama. All the balconies, windows and roofs were full of people, great jugs and buckets of cool water and wine were carried to the doors of the houses and held in readiness. Then came the horse artillery, followed by the blue Spanish dragoons, backed in their turn by the green dragoons, and they rushed into the place with such speed and rage that one saw and heard nothing but sparks and the snorting both of the horses and their riders. To judge from their expressions, they looked at that moment as if they would make mincemeat of the whole of the French army.
>
> The inhabitants greeted them with deafening yells of 'Viva Espanha! Viva Espanha!' the women waving handkerchiefs, were almost hysterical… It was with much laughter that we beheld this Spanish display of bravado, and galloped quickly behind them to see how they would continue to distinguish themselves. But oh, the pity of it! For hardly had they debouched from the town than the fatal guns of the French rearguard began to thunder forth again! Of course they halted. They were flabbergasted, and taking time to reform, they all calmly sat down at last, and before ten minutes had elapsed, left the English cavalry, which had gone round to the left of Talavera, the honour of continuing the pursuit. 'May God be merciful!' we exclaimed, riding back with much laughter.

At some point during the afternoon of 22 July, Sir Arthur would have reconnoitred the French line beyond the Alberche. He must have concluded that, the river being largely fordable and having mainly covered approaches to the near bank, Victor was vulnerable to a set-piece attack. Such intelligence as could be gleaned from the people of Talavera suggested that he had not been reinforced. Victor was being a very brave commander – or an arrogant one – to venture his 22,000 men behind a flimsy water obstacle, on a low line of hills, when faced by some 55,000. And while the Tagus satisfactorily closed off his left flank, it also barred escape to the south if he were to be successfully assaulted from the north. Wellesley would therefore immediately see the potential in outflanking Victor to the north-east, the direction from which the Alberche ran. To this end he brought up Sherbrooke's 1st Division to the left of Mackenzie's 3rd Division. It took until midnight to persuade Cuesta into a joint dawn assault, but it was agreed: the Spanish would attack over the unbroken bridge on the Madrid road and the nearby fords, with the British to their left.

Dawn at 3am came and went, without a murmur from the Spanish camps. The thirteen British battalions hidden among the olive groves and cork trees at the fords had made do with a cold breakfast. Lieutenant Charles Leslie of the 29th wrote:

> We were accordingly under arms before three o'clock in the morning, but had moved only a short distance when we were halted, and the men kept standing under arms. No one could tell the reason, but there we were kept for several

hours in a miserable state of suspense, all being hungry, and no one having anything to eat. No cooking could be done, as from our not having been dismissed we expected every moment to receive orders to proceed.

The sun rose behind the French positions, and still there was no Spanish movement. Eventually, Sir Arthur rode to the Madrid road, where he found General Cuesta in his bivouac nearly a mile from the bridge 'seated on the cushions taken out of his carriage, for he had driven to the outposts in a coach drawn by nine mules, the picture of mental and physical inability' (Lord Munster). At least he was awake, for as Napier tells us, 'Cuesta's staff were not aroused from slumber until 7 o'clock'; but it transpired that he had decided not to attack that day after all. Many and varied were the excuses he produced to Sir Arthur, right down to fearing the bridge might not bear his artillery, and anyway, was it not Sunday today? This last excuse became generally known, and the subject of much scornful mirth among the soldiery.

To Wellesley's great disgust and anger, it was agreed that the attack should go in only at dawn the next day, 24 July; yet, nothing daunted, Sir Arthur tried again to shift Cuesta in the afternoon, when he received information from the picquets that the French appeared to be thinning out. Cuesta was taken forward to observe, having been lifted on to a horse and held there by his aides; but seeing the French outposts, he declared that the enemy were obviously still in great strength, and he would not attack. 'Late in the afternoon,' says Leslie sourly, 'we were at last informed that the men might cook their dinners.'

By the next morning, naturally, Victor had gone, as indeed he should have done the minute he had seen Anson's British dragoons. That news in itself now seemed perversely to galvanize Cuesta into hyper-aggressive activity. He became furious when Wellesley reiterated the threat he had made the previous week, that he would not march further than the Alberche without the long-awaited delivery of carts and food. In response, the Spaniard announced that he would pursue Victor alone; of which idea Wellesley remarked to Frere the next day, 'In that case, Cuesta will get himself into a scrape… if the enemy discover that we are not with him, he will be beaten, or must return.' It was indeed curious that Cuesta should change his tune so quickly. It may not be irrelevant that at some point on 23 July he had received secret news: apparently the Junta had promised to promote Venegas to the chief command of all Spain's armies if he liberated Madrid. This would certainly explain Cuesta's anger that he could not get the British to do that for him.

As to the other curiosity – that Victor should sit so vulnerably all day on 24 July – Napier and Fortescue both raise the possibility of treachery within Cuesta's head-quarters, and the passing to Victor of the news of Cuesta's adamant refusal to disturb his army that day. The hispanophobe Napier even goes so far as to mention rumours that Cuesta himself was implicated. There is no plausible reason to suppose that he was; yet, if there was no treachery, how could Victor be so stupid? Since, in a matter of days, we shall again see him act with surprising lethargy, it may simply be that in Victor's case French arrogance took the form of a diminished sense of urgency.

He pulled back to the Guadarrama river, which runs down to join the Tagus some ten miles west of Toledo, and on the same day (25 July) Sebastiani's 4th Corps entered Toledo itself. King Joseph, who had been marching to join Victor at Talavera, now switched his Madrid reserve south, and also entered the concentration area west of Toledo. So two army corps were effectively together, with some 46,000 men and 90 guns (according to Oman's diligent researches, the figures were now Victor 23,000, the King 5,800 and Sebastiani 17,500.) Away in Leon, but also concentrating, Marshals Soult, Mortier and Ney were either at or marching towards Salamanca. Just five marches to the south lay Plasencia, and Wellesley's existing lines of supply back to Portugal. Sir Arthur was thus within sight of having put himself between five French corps totalling 96,000 men.

On 25 July, Cuesta gallantly chased after Victor's rearguard for thirty miles to Torrijos, only fifteen miles from Toledo. Two squadrons of the 1st Hussars KGL accompanied the Spaniards for a few miles, to Santa Olalla, to confirm that Victor had indeed taken the Toledo fork and not that to Madrid. 'On the morning of the 24th, it was my fortune to go with two squadrons of cavalry, in front of Cuesta's army, as far as St Olala; we had there a smart skirmish with the rearguard of the enemy just as they were quitting the town; and I was enabled to ascertain that the main body had fallen back to Torrejos, on the Toledo road.' The voice is that of a certain Charles Stewart, who had predictably put himself at the head of these squadrons, with what Fortescue describes as 'his usual busy restlessness.'

Cuesta's ardour to reach Madrid before Venegas cooled on hearing the combined strength of his foes. His horror, and subsequent willingness to back-pedal to Talavera, was matched by Victor's pleasure at finding no British on his tail, and his consequently equal willingness to attack the Spanish as soon as possible. At first light on 26 July the French accordingly marched west again to Torrijos, and routed Cuesta's rearguard, comprising General Zayas' infantry division and two regiments of cavalry. One of the latter was badly cut up, whereupon the infantry of the rearguard retreated in great disorder to Alcabon. Here, with relief, they found Albuquerque's cavalry, and Victor surprisingly pressed no further. A good deal out of breath, Cuesta's army made it to the Alberche under cover of Sherbrooke's and Mackenzie's divisions, which Wellesley had for this purpose sent across to the east bank. It would appear that quite a deal of blood would have flowed in the last mile or so before Alcabon, had Victor whipped on his dragoons before the foot-bound rearguard came up with Albuquerque. That he refrained from doing so is one of life's oddities (although we may recall that five years later, in February 1814, Napoleon relieved him of his command of 2nd Corps for dilatory behaviour).

When it became plain that the Spanish army intended to pass a needlessly dangerous night on the far bank of the river, Wellesley rode to Cuesta to urge him to cross over as soon as may be. He found Cuesta asleep, and his staff refused Sir Arthur access. Eventually, hours later and after initial refusals to move, Wellesley gained agreement to an early start on the 27th, though not without Cuesta bragging later that: 'He had first made the Englishman go down on his knees.' One assumes that was a metaphorical claim, since it is a posture one cannot readily imagine Sir Arthur adopting. It is likely that by now the old man was just one seething mass of frustration, mixed with physical pain and fatigue: frustration at not getting between Venegas and Madrid, at not having the British go with him, at finding the French too numerous anyway, at having his proud march out ruined by a tail-between-the-legs run back, and finally (a racing certainty), at having to endure the contemptuous looks of the redcoats as he came to safety through their lines.

His men filed west across the bridge and the fords during the morning of 27 July. Leslie of the 29th, who bivouacked right next to the Madrid road, tells us that: 'Before daybreak, symptoms of the Spanish being in retreat began to appear. Herds of cattle, pigs, and sheep, moving to the rear passed us, then followed ammunition wagons and baggage, and a few hours afterwards came the infantry, artillery and cavalry.' The Spanish went straight back to man their part of the defensive positions which Wellesley had already selected, in front of Talavera. Sherbrooke's division were next to fall back over the bridge and on to Talavera; Mackenzie's two brigades, and Anson's two regiments, used the fords and made their way through the olive and cork trees to a ruined house called Casa de Salinas, nearly a mile west of the Alberche and three miles in front of what was to become the Talavera battle line.

At Casa de Salinas events took place that were rather demeaning to the British – indeed, Napier makes no reference to them whatsoever. The affair reflected badly on all concerned, but the results could well have been immeasurably worse: not least, the loss of Wellesley himself. The trouble was partly the nature of the country between the Casa and the river, partly the pyromaniac tendencies of all retreating soldiers. The flat ground on the British side of the Alberche was covered with scrubby stands of cork and olive trees; the fields of fire were limited, and a clear view to the water's edge was only possible from quite close up. Any chain of piquets would need careful placing. But as Captain FitzClarence said, 'We were by no means such good soldiers in those days as succeeding campaigns made us, and sufficient precautions had not been taken to ascertain what was passing in the wood.'

Earlier, Mackenzie's soldiers had torched the long lines of huts built by the French when Victor stood on the low hills around Cazalegas, and on 27 July the wind was from the east. The smoke rolled down over and along the water. The Alberche ford was thus screened from the piquets of Mackenzie's left brigade; and General Lapisse was able quietly to infiltrate men into the woods to their front. As bad luck would have it, Sir Arthur and his staff were at that stage up one of the towers – about five stories high – on the roof of the Casa, with their horses and small escort below in the courtyard. Lapisse had the 16e Léger leading, and no less than twelve battalions following in columns. While Sir Arthur's three-foot telescope would be scanning forward to the river line, the 16e's *tirailleurs* were closing in to his left. Suddenly, musket fire rang out below, as the forward piquets of Donkin's and Mackenzie's brigades engaged the French at close range.

Many men in the ranks were asleep or preparing their bivouacs, packs off and arms piled, and the penetrating assault killed many before they could get straight. The 1,200 Irishmen of Donkin's 2/87th and 1/88th, and the 2/31st and 2/24th, were driven back; Wellesley descended the staircase of the tower with all due speed, leapt on his horse, and clattered out of the courtyard one way as Frenchmen entered the other, muskets blazing. He rallied the fleeing battalions a little way in rear, and the force retired in an undignified hurry out of the woods to the plain, where

Anson's horse assisted (though harried by two batteries of French horse artillery). We have an excellent description of this episode in the 1892 history of the 24th:

> The brigade halted in a very thick wood; the piquets were told off and ordered to pile arms. The 24th Regiment was at this time on the right of the brigade. It was observed that the other regiments of the brigade were piling arms and taking off their packs and accoutrements, the order having been passed along from the left. The 24th did the same. Shortly afterwards an order came to cut down wood and bushes, and it was generally understood that the brigade was to bivouac for the night. The officers collected in small groups near their companies to discuss the numerous and extraordinary reports in circulation relative to the situation of the army, it being well known that there was a French army of near 50,000 men on the same ground with the British… these facts created an extraordinary degree of excitement. The men dispersed among the trees, and were chopping off the boughs when the alarm sounded; but before the men could get on their packs and accoutrements the French light troops were in the wood. The piquets fortunately had not taken off their packs, and therefore had time to run to the front, and join some of the 60th [Rifles] who were keeping up a running fire and skirmishing with the advance troops of the enemy. The brigade retired.

Later that afternoon, when the shaken battalions of Donkin's and Mackenzie's brigades took up their positions on the Talavera feature, they did so with ninety-three men missing – taken by the French. This is a very substantial number of prisoners for them to have lost so haphazardly. It seems clear that, whether or nor the piquets had been told off, they had not actually deployed out front. It seems to have been thanks to the 5/60th that the affair did not turn out even worse, but the total losses were still significant. The 2/87th had 198 killed, wounded or taken (33 per cent of their strength), and the 2/31st, 119 (16 per cent); the total from the 3rd Division was 442 or 12 per cent. The 87th paid a particularly heavy price in officer casualties – one killed and ten wounded. Oman thinks that Lapisse lost no more than 100 men.

The affair around the Casa de Salinas was a classic case of being caught with the trousers down, and nearly led to Wellesley's capture. It is not known who was responsible for deciding where Mackenzie's outposts should be, but one imagines that Sir Arthur quickly found out, and that some wretched field officer was subsequently reduced to size.

9

A Bad Beginning:
Afternoon and Night,
27 July 1809

AROUND 4pm on Thursday 27 July, the Irish soldiers of Donkin's 2/87th and 1/88th continued to head west from the wooded Casa de Salinas on to the shimmering open plain. It was a three-mile march, a hot hour under the huge Spanish sun, right in their eyes and now well down to the horizon. They were on the route to be followed very soon by the French. Up ahead, they were thankful to see the red lines of their defensive positions, partly manned since the morning and still haloed with a dust cloud two miles long, thrown up by all the feet, hooves and wheels. But there was no dust over the dominating hill on their right, which was strangely empty.

Within the next day, 100,000 men of many nationalities, 17,000 horses and 140 guns of various calibres were to manoeuvre and suffer on this baked piece of land, of whom some 14,000 were to die or be maimed: 7,268 Frenchmen, 5,365 British (taking Oman's researches), and an unknown but probably modest number of Spaniards. Second only to Albuera two years later, it was to be the bloodiest battle in the whole Peninsular War.

The Irishmen in the rearguard crossed a flat plain studded with olive trees, woods, coppice and vineyard. Rough tracks fanned out across their route from the town away to their left; it was a walled town, eminently defensible, and populated in normal times by some 10,000 people. The map shows Talavera de la Reina crouched comfortably on a northern bend in the River Tagus, the centre of a web of roads and tracks, of which the most prominent was the main east-west route from Madrid towards Lisbon via Badajoz. The two capitals were otherwise only properly linked, but at greater length, via the great road through Salamanca, Cuidad Rodrigo and Coimbra. Talavera also boasted, of course, the bridge across the Tagus, some 500yd wide at this point. Built in a dog-leg series of forty-five arches, this structure was of prime military importance, sitting as it did in the centre of an eighty-mile stretch of the Tagus; with the bridges at Toledo and Arzobispo, to east and west respectively, it provided the sole access between New and Old Castile.

Into the town (and the Tagus) from the north ran the Portina, a stream fed, when there was rain, from the high east-west Sierra de Segurilla; these mountains filled the northern horizon, quickly climbing to 500ft above the town. Nearer than the Sierra, about a mile north of the town, two ridges stood up in the middle distance. On the west was the Cerro de Medellin, rising perhaps 250ft above the plain; the 150ft Cerro de Cascajal faced it on the east, and between the two the Portina ran in a narrow gorge.

Halfway between the town and the two Cerros, a hundred paces east of the Portina, was a low knoll perhaps 20ft high, the Pajar de Vergara. This knoll was the westernmost tip of a swell of slightly higher ground curving down from the Cascajal. The approaches to the Pajar were well concealed by olive trees, but these ceased about one hundred yards in front of it.

North of the knoll on both banks of the Portina the ever-rising land was covered by a mixture of growing wheat, barley and grass; southwards towards the town there were many walls and ditches around vineyards, olive groves, orchards and gardens, all rather enclosing the northern approaches to Talavera. Stretching away to the north, the largely waterless but tree-lined course of the Portina offered a shallow entrenchment or firing step to any defenders. Parallel to its front (east) ran an embanked track to the Pajar, and behind (west of) the Portina another embanked road led north to the Sierra, these banks providing natural protection.

At the Madrid gate on the east of the town was the Chapel, built on another knoll and adjacent to the town's Alameda or promenade and gardens, outside the old walls. More olive groves grew either side of the road to Madrid, right up to the bridge on the Alberche, another northern tributary of the Tagus about 3½ miles east.

The Cerro de Medellin was to be Wellesley's dominating feature. The eastern end fell abruptly into the Portina ravine, but was climbable – just. All other slopes were far gentler; a barley crop was growing shin-high overall, except on the very summit and in the ravine, where thyme and dry grass had taken over. The view from the top was extensive, and would give Wellesley a clear sight of the whole field of battle. The same could not quite be said of the Cerro de Cascajal opposite on the other side of the Portina, which was a 100ft lower.

Given Wellesley's available British strength, and his maturing doubts about the Spanish, he had chosen his ground well. Quite when he did this is not clear, but his army had passed over the Portina and through the town on Saturday 22 July, five days beforehand. He had prepared the abortive attack across the Alberche that day, and when it was cancelled he probably used the remainder of the 23rd for a first reconnaissance, with time enough to complete his plans as Cuesta disappeared off by himself on the 25th. Certainly, on the 26th he was well forward beyond the Alberche with Sherbrooke's and Mackenzie's divisions, to cover Cuesta's retreat; on the evening of that day he had agreed with Cuesta that the Spanish should hold the town and the surrounding enclosures for a mile to the north, with the British continuing the line to the Medellin, and we know that Spanish battalions started moving on to the Talavera line during the morning of the 27th. As to the valley between the Medellin and the Segurilla mountains – called throughout this text the 'north plain' – it was not specifically allocated; troops on the Medellin's northern slopes would of course be adjacent, to a limited extent.

Still, this was a Hobson's choice plan, there being no alternative fighting line in the area that embraced the town, as a centre of communications, and, more importantly, the Tagus bridge. The line of the Alberche was quite unsuitable. Yet

Hobson's or not, the position would serve the purpose well, and Wellesley would be glad to use it. In particular it solved the problem of his ally's limited skills to best advantage. Even given the inclusion of a walled town, just one mile of close country, with ready defensive positions, for 28,000 infantry in thirty-seven battalions (Oman's updated assessment for 27 July), was an exceedingly generous allocation of men to frontage. It would allow for double lines, and a substantial reserve, which on so narrow a front effectively formed a third and fourth line. The Spanish position was therefore as comfortable as Cuesta could hope: no manoeuvring required, no anxious weak points, and he could put his headquarters in a decent house in the town – a Spanish town defended by a Spanish army, where all the ladies would doubtless wave their handkerchiefs and cry 'Viva Cuesta!'

Presumably happy enough, the old man put his Vanguard and 1st Division (General Zayas) – no fewer than eleven battalions – to hold the eastern outskirts, and the knoll with the Chapel by the Madrid gate, where he also placed one gun battery. His 3rd and 4th Divisions (Portago's and Manglano's) held the ground running north on either side of the Portina, from the town up to the low hill of Pajar de Vergara, in a double line of thirteen battalions; and behind these sat the seven reserve battalions of Bassecourt's 5th Division, together with all the rest of the Spanish cavalry – ten regiments in all. The front or first line was the sunken track to the Pajar; the second was along the Portina, with three batteries. Such a deployment of manpower theoretically had the Spanish infantry almost shoulder to shoulder; few were not placed behind decent cover, and the depth of the defence – the sheer concentration of bodies – could not better have been designed by Wellesley for his allies' supportive role.

His own troops' deployment, however, posed a couple of problems: a longer frontage and far fewer battalions for the ground, and the responsibility for control of the commanding heights. Clearly his main decision was where to end his line: should he hold the north plain, between the Medellin and the Sierra? Surprisingly, perhaps, he thought not; whether the reason was shortage of bodies, or confidence that he could dominate the plain by fire, or reach it in timely fashion from the Medellin, remains a mystery. It is not as if he had an abundance of artillery to dominate the plain; but as the battle developed he would quite quickly adjust his thoughts about this flank. Whether the 23rd Light Dragoons in due course were to share them, we shall see.

The key was the Medellin. He knew that Victor knew it too – inevitably, having passed it frequently during his corps' recent travels. Wellesley would also recognize his two weak spots. Firstly, any troops he placed just south of the Medellin were in enfilade to cannon and telescopes on the front of the Cascajal, a most unpleasant prospect given a combination of professional gunnery (probably the prime French military skill) and a resolute simultaneous assault from the east. The second weakness, as we have implied, lay in the northern plain beyond the two Cerros providing a route for turning the British left flank. With these considerations well in mind, and based on the assumption that no harm could possibly come to the Spanish on his right, Wellesley issued his orders to his own divisional commanders.

His smallest division, of just five battalions (Alexander Campbell's 4th), was to be right of the line, connecting with the left hand Spanish battalions of General Portago's division at the Pajar. That knoll itself had been partly flattened to make a gun platform some 80 by 20yd with an unfinished breastwork or bank 3ft high to the front, on which were mounted Lawson's battery of (disappointingly light) 3-pounder cannon. Campbell's own brigade took the front line – 2/7th (Royal Fusiliers) and 2/53rd (Shropshire) – with Kemmis's behind, in rear of the Portina, with the 1/40th (Somersets), 97th (Queen's Own Germans), and the composite 2nd Battalion of Detachments. The 14th and 16th Light Dragoons of Cotton's brigade – a thousand sabres – were placed in support behind the Segurilla road.

Left (north) of Campbell's 4th Division the country opened out, with fewer enclosures, and ran flat before rising gradually to the Medellin. This central portion of the British line was to be given to Mackenzie's small 3rd Division of five battalions. Sherbrooke's large 1st Division of eight battalions was to hold the Medellin itself, with the Guards on the left above the north plain (the post of honour), Cameron in the centre, and the Germans on the right, next to Mackenzie. General Hill's 2nd Division was to be the second line on this crucial hillside.

This is Fortescue's interpretation of Wellesley's plan. Oman's interpretation was not quite the same; but in any event, things went badly astray on the ground and made the precise plan academic. For when Sherbrooke took the field, Mackenzie's division was absent from the line – it and Sir Arthur were forward at Casa de Salinas. For whatever motives, Sherbrooke thereupon decided that the four battalions he had to hand (his other four, of the KGL, were missing, having been misrouted past Talavera) should run along the line in Mackenzie's place. He put the 1/Coldstream Guards on the immediate left of Kemmis's left battalion; then the 1/3rd Guards, then Cameron's 1/61st (South Gloucestershire) and 2/83rd. He proposed to slot in Langwerth's 1st and 2nd KGL and Low's 5th and 7th KGL in due course as the missing Germans turned up – that is, on the other side of the 2/83rd, up the near slope of the Medellin overlooking the Portina ravine. The absence of the Germans is explained in Beamish's *History of the Legion*: 'The infantry brigades of the Legion, by some mistake of the staff-officer who was appointed to conduct them to their ground, had been led away an hour's march behind Talavera, where they were preparing to bivouac, when another order arrived, correcting the error, and requiring them to hurry forthwith to the left of the position.'

Also beginning to hurry, having heard the firing from the Casa de Salinas three miles away, were the 29th (Worcestershire), part of Richard Stewart's brigade in Hill's 2nd Division. They had been bivouacked for several days next to the Madrid road, a quarter of a mile outside the town walls, in the Alameda or promenade. 'Wounded men from our advanced guard began to come in… We ordered our dinner to be cooked in all haste, and lost no time in dispatching it. We then had our tent and baggage packed… shortly afterwards the drums beat to arms, the bugles sounded the alarm, and we got orders to move to the left' (Leslie). His fellow subaltern Andrew Leith Hay takes up the story: 'We moved left in front, the 29th being the senior regiment was in rear of the column, the 48th leading. In this formation we advanced about half a mile between the town of Talavera and the eminence then unoccupied, but which was destined to become the left and strongest part of the position. The brigade halted for a short time near to the division of Brigadier General Alexander Campbell, in rear of an unfinished Spanish redoubt' [the Pajar].

Leslie again: 'On getting clear of the enclosures and gaining the lower slope of the hill our brigade… was drawn up in rear of the front line. We could now see our advanced guard retiring across the plain, closely pursued by the enemy. A portion of the advanced guard moved directly towards us, and passed through our line, and proceeded to the different places in position.' Or as Leith Hay put it, 'Regiments of General Mackenzie's division, retiring, passed us diagonally, falling into the line.' Since Lieutenant Thomas Bunbury, of the 1/3rd in Tilson's brigade, said that 'When we were moving to the hill, the advance brigade of General Mackenzie crossed our line of march to the rear', we may take that as confirmation that Tilson's men led Stewart's on the move of Hill's division to the Medellin.

Mackenzie's division having thus returned from Casa de Salinas, Sir Arthur went immediately to the Spanish lines, where doubtless he and his staff would have had plenty to do. Mackenzie returned, as we have seen, to find Sherbrooke in his place – the first line – and so thought it best to deploy his own brigade in rear of the Guards, with Donkin's brigade on the left, behind Cameron's. At some later point, Donkin clearly must have become uneasy, seeing the Medellin above him completely bare, for he moved sideways higher up, above the ravine. Fortescue tells us that in Wellesley's continuing absence 'there appears to have been some uncertainty as to his wishes among the British generals', and that consequently General Hill, 'late in the evening', rode into Talavera to find Wellesley and clarify those wishes. But Hill himself makes no mention of a late evening visit: what he said in a memorandum of 1827 was: 'I recollect that on 27 July I got some dinner in my quarters in the town of Talavera about 4 o'clock. Immediately after I rode out, accompanied by Major Fordyce, towards the Alberche, in which direction we heard some firing. I returned to the bivouac of my division, I suppose about sunset, when I found it had moved to take up a position.'

With the sun setting, with his division not where he had left it some hours earlier before dinner, and with continuous firing coming across the plain, General Hill would have put his spurs to good use and rattled up the crowded track to the Pajar. This was about the time that Marshal Victor was pushing his infantry and horse artillery up to the Cascajal, with Lapisse's division closing towards the Portina in the centre, together with his field artillery.

*   *   *

Simultaneously with the opening of cannon fire from the Cascajal, French dragoons were sent to feel out the Spanish positions further south among the enclosures, and in the time-honoured fashion when facing raw troops, they did so by popping off their pistols – if at a 1,000yd range.

To this device for flushing out the nervous and making them show themselves, there can in all military history be no more remarkable reaction than was now displayed by the Spanish: it was what Leith Hay of the 29th described as 'a roll of musketry that illuminated the whole extent of the Spanish line. It was one discharge; of such a nature that I have never heard equalled.' The entire Spanish first line fired a rippling volley, some six battalions producing a smoke cloud one mile long; then the four northernmost battalions of Portago's division, from the Pajar downwards, raised a cry of 'Treachery!', threw aside their muskets, and 2,000 soldiers ran to the rear, some not stopping for twenty miles… They managed, however, to find time to plunder the British camp near the town, and to pick up some like-minded British malingerers. As the Spanish fired their amazing volley, Sir Arthur commented to Sir S. Whittingham, 'If they will but fire as well tomorrow, the day is ours; but as there seems to be nobody to fire at just now, I wish you would stop it.' Later, when the four battalions fled, he remarked with typically dry understatement, 'Only look at the ugly hole those fellows have left. I wish you would go to the second line and try to fill it up.'

Cuesta's cavalry were sent instantly to whip in the cowardly hordes, and most were in fact back in the lines quite soon; but hundreds were not on parade next morning, when Cuesta had twenty-five men executed. His pride would have suffered greatly from this episode, and initially he wished to 'decimate' the four battalions in the old Roman style – 200 men were chosen to die by lot before Sir Arthur prevailed upon him.

The four fleet-footed battalions were replaced easily enough from the Spanish reserve, and the whole event in that sense mattered little, except for the rumours spread to the rear, and the scornful retelling along the British lines. However, had the French understood what they had just seen, their plan of attack surely should have changed. (That is, if at that stage of the evening of the 27th any particular strategy had been thought through, which is extremely doubtful.) This clear public demonstration of Spanish skittishness might with advantage have been exploited – by a night attack, perhaps, or one at dawn – or by setting off a few fireworks?

Sir Rowland Hill passed through the Spanish lines a little while before their great volley, and, according to Leith Hay and Leslie, would have discovered Stewart's brigade spread out between the rear of Campbell near the Pajar and a hollow on the southern slopes of the Medellin. Oman states that 'Hill's division was already encamped upon its (the Medellin's) reverse slope… the two brigades were not lying on their destined battle-line, but had halted half a mile behind it'; while Fortescue says 'Hill parked… Tilson's brigade far back on the northern slope, and Stewart's as far back on the southern slope.'

That seems a little too cut and dried; Stewart was a good deal extended at this stage. Leslie makes plain that as night fell – and so too the French cannonade upon them – the 29th were ordered to lie down under it: that is, still where they had been when Mackenzie fell back through them. He talks of 'watching the shells from the moment they left the mouth of the howitzers, by the fuzes, burning like brilliant stars as they rose in the air, then rapidly descending right down upon us, or breaking over our heads. Many of us made narrow escapes.' Well, if the 29th had indeed been half a mile behind a battle line on or in front of the crest of the Medellin, itself a good half mile from the Cascajal, no French field howitzer would have got near them. Leslie writes, 'While this cannonade continued we were ordered to lie down... we lay on the ground... the night became very dark and gloomy. We continued in this way nearly an hour, when, in a moment, about 9 o'clock, there opened a tremendous fire on the top of the hill on our left.'

Lieutenant Edward Close, 1/48th, wrote in his diary that 'the 48th's 1st Battalion was placed this evening in reserve between the summits of two hills in a hollow.' Now as we have seen, according to Leith Hay, Stewart's brigade marched from their bivouac on the Madrid road 'left in front... the 48th leading', and then halted – that is, with the 29th, as rear in the column, behind the Pajar earthwork. Given that three battalions totalling 2,100 men, in a three-rank column, cover some 1,000 yards front to back, it is entirely feasible that the 29th were lying down under the howitzer fire behind Campbell, while the 48th were 1,000 yards ahead of them in Close's 'hollow'. It can be seen clearly on Fortescue's excellent map. Tilson's brigade, of course, would already be over the saddle, on the northern slope of the Medellin.

When General Hill caught up with his division, therefore, one supposes it was in that scenario well-known to all infanteers, where the front had arrived and was static, but the rear was still closing up. Hill's memorandum tells us that on reaching his division he 'found it deploying in line, and was shown by somebody where the right was to rest. I pointed out the hill on the line of direction we were to take up. I found, however, I had not sufficient troops to occupy the ground without leaving considerable intervals between the regiments.' Well, we don't know where his right of the line was decreed to be; but as General Hill wrote to his sister after the battle, 'As night was coming on, we did not expect any serious attack till the morning', perhaps the question of a precise deployment could await daylight.

*   *   *

The French infantry now on the Cascajal were from Ruffin's 1st Division of Victor's 1st Corps, and they had reached that far largely just as a matter of momentum after crossing the plain from the Alberche. Victor would have ridden well forward, and what would immediately bring his telescope into play – perhaps with some excitement – were the near-empty slopes opposite. He would see right down the line of the Portina, to the Pajar battery. There he would see Campbell's brigade, with Kemmis' behind; then, coming nearer, the Guards, with Mackenzie in rear; then Cameron's brigade; then – nothing, bar an isolated Donkin in front of him on the forward slope of the Medellin, but with nothing either side, and nothing on the summit. Hill's division would almost certainly be in the dead ground behind the south-eastern slopes of the Medellin. To Victor's astonished eyes it must have seemed that the vital ground was held by just three miserable British battalions.

With no more ado, Victor silenced his horse artillery (which rather gave away his intent), and warned Ruffin for an attack. Wishing to amaze, no doubt, as much as to avoid interference, he refrained from clearing this action with King Joseph.

At much the same time that Victor was giving his orders to Ruffin, the lost Germans of the KGL brigades appeared. According to Beamish, 'on Colonel Donkin's right, about eight in the evening, the two line brigades of the Legion were ordered to deploy', and were slotted in to the north of Cameron on the slopes of the Medellin. They were dog tired; and, believing themselves to be placed in the second line behind Hill – rather than in the first, in front of him – these sensible soldiers promptly rolled themselves up in their blankets and went to sleep. The 7th Line Battalion KGL were nearest Donkin, then southwards in order the 5th, the 2nd, and then the 1st next to Cameron.

So as the light begins to fail, we have the vital Medellin defended by four exhausted German battalions, fast asleep; and the 2/87th and 1/88th of Donkin's Irish brigade, who had suffered 22 per cent casualties that very afternoon at the Casa (262 out of 1,198 all ranks). Meanwhile, across the Portina ravine Ruffin's nine battalions are under orders to assault within the hour. We must ask, therefore, in the midst of such a dire muddle, where on earth was Sir Arthur Wellesley?

A commander earns his pay when anxious subordinates turn to ask him, 'What shall we do, Sir?'; and that question was surely being asked by his generals that evening. Rowland Hill, his senior subordinate, left his own command to try to find Wellesley and some answers. Yet no source accounts for Sir Arthur's whereabouts at this critical stage, save for two references: his return from the Casa with Mackenzie some time after 4pm, when he left to visit the Spanish; and his being behind Campbell's brigade at around 7pm, when the Spanish ran 'not one hundred yards from where I was standing'. This is the man with a ferocious reputation for attending to all details himself, for insisting on the closest control, and capable of fury if others flouted his arrangements or showed unwelcome initiative, however good their reasons. Yet he is nowhere to be seen for the six hours between 4pm and 10pm – while brigades seemingly choose their own positions; gaps are tolerated until a dangerously late stage; and there are misunderstandings at both divisional and brigade level as to who is in the first and who the second line.

That Sir Arthur was by now in effect commanding the Spanish army also, by dint of natural superiority, cannot be doubted, and nor can the time required for that extra burden. But it beggars belief that the Spaniards alone consumed his total energies that evening. His lengthy absence from his own line remains one of the mysteries of Talavera; because of it, and the apparent lack of any active co-ordinating officer from his staff, his battle-line was not in a fit state to repel a prod from enemies a good deal less dangerous than 5,200 Frenchmen in nine battalions.

Curiously, Sir Charles Oman makes small reference to the doubts that arise over locations, and by implication over Sir Arthur's grip on his generals. Indeed, there is no mention of the original layout as described by Fortescue, only of the final positions, as if they were what was intended all along. He concentrates on whether Hill alone was in error; but unfortunately Oman himself makes an important error, in placing the deployment of Hill's brigades with Tilson on the right or southern flank of the reverse slopes of the Medellin, and Stewart on the left or north. Fortescue quotes both Leslie and Leith-Hay of the 29th to the contrary; and this view is also confirmed by a single word used by Lieutenant Close, 1/48, of Stewart's brigade, when he wrote in his diary: 'It now began to get dark... [the enemy] directed his principal efforts against the hill we supported. We were put in motion to support the defence of the position, and advanced obliquely to our left...' That is, if Stewart's brigade had at that early stage been on the left or north flank, a left oblique move-ment would have taken them down the slope and away from the hilltop, which would be to their right; whereas left oblique is exactly proper for that objective, for a formation starting on the right or southern flank. Where the confusion enters, prob-ably, is that – as we shall see – the two brigades swapped flanks during the night. Thus Oman and Fortescue do actually finish up in agreement; but it is a little diffi-cult to follow Sir Charles's version of the last-light attack, knowing that he had Hill's two defending brigades transposed at the outset.

On one further point we must also take gentle issue with Oman: his belittling of this early attack by Marshal Victor, so soon after his advance guard reached the Cascajal. He writes that: 'the impetuous Victor took upon himself the responsibility of attacking the allies when only half the King's army had come upon the field… night attacks are proverbially hazardous and hard to conduct… Victor showed an excessive temerity in endeavouring to deliver such a blow.' One has to say in turn that Oman here shows rather an excessive timidity; and in any event, he was wrong to call the attempt on the Medellin a night attack. As we shall see, the summit was captured – however briefly – by two of Victor's battalions in enough daylight for General Hill, well back on the reverse slope, to see them, if not to identify them: 'I was with the 48th Regiment, in conversation with Colonel Donellan, when, it being nearly dark, I observed some men on the hill top fire a few shots at us.'

If a commander has time in fading light to get his troops accurately on to his objective, to capture his hill at last light, then he has the best of all worlds: his enemy's counter-attack must inevitably be mounted as a true night attack, which is indeed 'proverbially hazardous and hard to conduct'. By squeezing in a quick last-light assault, Victor saw the chance to snap up the vital high ground which his oppo-nent had apparently neglected. He was in every way right to make the attempt, and to do so without reference to King Joseph (who would probably have said no, or have taken so long to say yes that the light would have gone completely).

*   *   *

Marshal Victor's 1st Division under Ruffin had been instrumental in defeating the Spanish at Ucles six months before, and these same nine tough battalions – three each of the 9e Léger and the 24e and 96e Ligne – were now poised to cross the Portina.

The three regiments each shook out into battalion columns on the slopes of the Cascajal, one behind the other, thirty men wide – the 24e, 9e and 96e, from right to left. The flank regiments were to hook around the lower sides of the Medellin before ascending, and the 9e were to climb down the Cascajal and go straight ahead for the untended summit, crushing Donkin's two battalions en route. The light had not completely gone, but they had a decent smokescreen, with the wind still blowing from the east. Lieutenant Close, 1/48th, tells us that: 'The whole of the growing wheat in our front had become a dense mass of smoke from it having been set on fire, as we supposed, by the enemy to cover his advance. Obscured by this smoke he approached our line.'

The 9e descended easily enough the steep slope into the deep shadow at the bottom of the ravine, and then climbed 100yd of more gently rising ground to the track from Segurilla, at which point it is likely that they edged left, for the Medellin now rose sharply on their right. Instead of meeting Donkin's Irishmen at the top of the direct approach to the summit, they met the sleeping Germans on its south spur. Brigadier-General Low, while understanding himself to be behind Hill's outposts, had nevertheless sent out a party of his own light troops to position outposts, and these men got caught up by the 9e's leading column. The KGL's history states, from the journal of a Captain Stutzer:

> It was dark, and Captain von Ompteda of the 1st Light Battalion had been sent up the hill with a party of riflemen to plant outposts; the enemy's column fell upon part of this detachment consisting of skirmishers of the 1st Line Battalion under Lieutenant von Holle, and charging, obliged them to retire, and Lieutenant Holle was severely wounded. In retreating, the skirmishers received the fire of the 7th Line Battalion, which regiment and part of the 5th being thrown into confusion by the suddenness of the attack, were charged by the French column, and gave way; they were, however, rallied by Major Burger and adjutant Delius.

The French column thirty men wide, coming upon two lines of sleeping men – some sitting up, some few rising to their feet on hearing the too-late challenge of a dreaming sentry – made mayhem among the 7th KGL. Within five minutes nineteen men were killed, fifty wounded and seventy-seven were taken prisoner – 146 all ranks, out of 557. The remaining 411 Germans dispersed into the near-darkness, closing behind their neighbours of the 5th Battalion. Here the casualties were fewer, just forty killed and wounded, and only eleven taken; but Low's brigade front was undoubtedly broken to all intents and purposes. It would now have been absolutely the right moment for Ruffin's left hand regiment, the 96e, to arrive on the scene; fortunately, they had got stuck trying to cross the Portina, which they approached by chance down a very steep incline. Their attack finally amounted to no more than a bad-tempered exchange of fire with part of the 5th KGL, and with Brigadier-General Landwerth's 2nd KGL. The 96e Ligne did not press further forward.

Having driven the 7th KGL from their path and sent some eighty-eight prisoners back across the Portina, the 9e Léger made straight for the summit of the Medellin. Donkin's brigade, now level and to their right hand, showed no apparent interest in the firefight among their German neighbours, whom they would have seen arriving around 8pm. The Irish were 400yd away at most, and their inactivity is curious. Napier wrote that 'Colonel Donkin beat back the enemy in his front', but this must surely be an error, since the casualty return for the 9pm combat shows no losses at all attributed to any of Donkin's units.

The sound of the clash, which lasted but five minutes, did cause two British generals to take action, and their commander Sir Arthur at last to mount up and ride to the Medellin. Sherbrooke pulled Cameron's brigade out of the line, and was about to take it to clear the Medellin when he learned that Hill was ahead of him. Hill was with the 1/48th at the head of Stewart's brigade, in Close's hollow beneath the summit. The outbreak of firing had died down; he assumed that it had been a false alarm, or at worst a repulsed attack, but nonetheless gave orders to the 48th about going forward to support Low's brigade if required. Hill wrote in his memorandum:

> During this operation I recollect perfectly well that I was with the 48th Regiment, in conversation with Colonel Donellan, when, it being nearly dark, I observed some men on the hill top fire a few shots among us. Not having an idea that the enemy was so near, I said at the moment I was sure it was the Old Buffs [1/3rd, of Tilson's brigade], as usual making some blunder. I desired Donellan to get into line, and would ride up the hill and stop the firing. On reaching the hill top I found the mistake I had made. I immediately turned round to ride off, when [the French] fired and killed poor Fordyce, and shot my mare through the body. She did not fall, but carried me to the 29th Regiment which corps, by my orders, instantly charged the French, and drove them from the hill.

Also with Hill was Richard Stewart's brigade-major, Captain Daniel Gardiner (43rd), who died of his mortal wounds the next day. Hill's two ADCs, his 27-year-old brother Clement and a Captain Currie, both made good their escape.

Sir Rowland Hill's state of mind during that brief but violent episode might well be a little confused at the surprising turn of events, but the immediate implications were only too obvious: he must urgently get the French removed. He had Stewart form open column of companies – that is, each company in two lines forty or so men wide, the companies one behind the other, with enough space between them to allow the battalion to form line by oblique march. It is clear that in the darkness and hurry to respond to the threat, confusion briefly reigned. Stewart's brigade had climbed the slope of the Medellin in the order 1/48th, Detachments, and 1/29th; so the 48th should have led off for the summit. Somehow it was the Detachments who did so, followed by Hill leading the 29th, and the 48th became the rear rather than the leading battalion. Leslie of the 29th writes:

> As we were advancing up to the attack we came upon our next left regiment, the battalion of detachments, who appeared to have got into confusion, and we pushed our way through them to rush at the enemy. The gallant soldiers of the battalion seemed much vexed; they were bravely calling out, 'There is nobody to command us! Only tell us what to do, and we are ready to dare anything!' There was a fault somewhere.

These frustrated Detachments – formed out of the skeletons of six battalions left in Portugal by Moore six months before – had hit the better part of the two leading battalions of the 9e Léger. Each side engaged the other with musketry, but neither would charge; so with matters at a stand, General Hill took the 29th's companies straight through the Detachments, the leading company firing a point-blank volley and charging instantly with the bayonet. Following behind the 1/29th, the 1/48th came abreast of the Detachments, who mistook their nationality, and then they bumped a fresh party of French. Lieutenant Close:

> We were put in motion to support the defence of the position. Before we encountered the enemy, owing to the darkness of the night, the 2nd Battalion of Detachments, taking our left wing for the enemy, poured in two or three volleys, which was at last obstructed by Colonel Donellan riding in front of their line and telling them they were killing their own men. Little harm was, very fortunately, done [the 1/48th had only eight men wounded that night]… We advanced obliquely to our left, had scarcely formed line when a blaze of fire from a body of grenadiers, whose bayonets almost met ours, gave us the first information of the situation of the enemy. It was so dark we could hardly see, when the musketry proclaimed the firers. The firing however was soon terminated. The enemy called out with consternation 'Anglais, Anglais!', and down the hill they went.

Up ahead, the 29th's charge cleared the summit, as Leslie tells us:

> Our left [wing, in open column?] made a dashing charge, and after a short but desperate struggle drove the French off the summit of the position. We then wheeled into line, advanced obliquely to our left, and opened our fire on the French reserves which were pushing up in support of their discomforted comrades. This decided the affair; the enemy was completely overthrown and fled in confusion, leaving the ground strewed with their dead, dying, and wounded, among whom was the colonel of the 9th French Regiment, and quantities of arms and accoutrements. During this affair, when we formed into line, our right companies were some way down the slope of the hill. We could see the French column moving up across our front, their drums beating the charge, and we could hear their officers giving orders and encouraging their men, calling out, 'En avant, Francais! En avant, mes enfants!' But our well-directed volleys and cheers of victory stopped their progress, and their shattered columns returned in dismay. The wounded and the prisoners informed us that they were part of General Ruffin's division. The 29th Regiment took possession of the top of the hill, our Colours being planted on the summit.

Oman put the 9e Léger's casualties that night at 300, of whom sixty-five were taken prisoner, one of them their wounded commander, Colonel Meunier. The British loss was about the same, with a third captured, entirely it seemed from the sleeping KGL. So, taking the strength of one of Ruffin's battalions at say 600, that still left about 1,500 men of the 9e Léger leaving the Medellin in a hurry, and directly between them and the Cascajal were Donkin's brigade. He had some 1,200 men, including the 250 riflemen of his five companies from the 5/60th. In line he would have covered a front getting on for half a mile wide. Since such a distance would more than block the Frenchmen's path back across the main eastern slopes, we can only assume either that he was not in line (which in the circumstances is unlikely), or that the fleeing 9e took an indirect route. Knowing that their fellow 24e Ligne had not uttered a squeak to their north, on their separate flank march (during which they got lost and failed to enter the episode at all), the 9e may well have tended in that direction, to link up. But for the second time in an hour, it almost seems as if Donkin's brigade did not exist.

Unfortunately there are no extant accounts from Donkin's battalions. Major Hugh Gough, 2/87th, was severely wounded by a grazing cannon ball the next day, and not surprisingly left no record for 27 July; and William Grattan, the chronicler of the 88th, had not yet joined the Connaught Rangers. So we must remain, perhaps appropriately, confused as to some of the early details of that evening's work. Thanks to Lieutenants Leslie and Leith Hay of the 29th, and Close of the 48th, however, we at least have a fairly clear picture of events on the Medellin's summit.

*   *   *

With the French gone back, Wellesley was now free to arrange his defences for the morning, so far as that was practicable in the darkness. Hill would no doubt have given his opinion, already quoted, that: 'I found I had not sufficient troops to occupy the ground without leaving considerable intervals between the regiments.' In that situation a commander either takes out the insurance of a mobile reserve in depth, to deploy should any gap become threatened; or he 'puts it all in the shop window', in a comprehensive line with not a lot behind it. The latter was Wellesley's choice.

He placed the three brigades of Stewart, Tilson and Donkin in that order from north to south along the Medellin crest, with piquets a long way forward to the Portina. The KGL battalions were south again but further forward, on the track to Segurilla and overlapping, so that Donkin was partly in rear of Low. The reliable 29th retained their conquest of the summit, the place of honour on the left flank, then the Detachments, then the 1/48th, and then (a nice coincidence) their brothers in the 2/48th as left battalion of Tilson's brigade. Tilson was thus moved forward from behind, crossing to the right of Stewart, who the evening before had gone forward to the summit from their then right-hand location.

Wellesley's artillery was scanty and mostly of light calibre – the French had eighty guns, he and Cuesta thirty each. His own he deployed with Lawson's battery of 3-pounders on the Pajar, Elliott's with the Guards brigade, and Sillery's five 6-pounders as a central reserve with Cameron; Rettberg's KGL battery was on the Medellin, while Heyse's five 6-pounders were on the southern slope, to the right of Tilson's brigade. The cavalry were all in rear of the centre, Cotton near Kemmis, Anson and Fane further back.

With these dispositions duly made or confirmed, the British and Spanish armies now got their heads down for what was left of a hungry and unsettled night. The piquets above the Portina could hear 'Qui vive?' carried on the wind from the sentries opposite, as they challenged their visiting officers and NCOs not 300yc away. Around midnight, one of Sherbrooke's brigades fired a volley at a non-existen assaulting French column, to the detriment of their own piquets out front. Captain FitzClarence tells us of: 'The constant words "Stand Up!" being passed along the line… an individual soldier firing at some object to his front, which was taken up by the next, and so passed on… to the appearance being a running wildfire, down the front of one or more regiments, till stopped by the officers. In this, the troops unfortunately forgot their light infantry in front, and many brave officers and men fell a sacrifice to the fire of their comrades: amongst them was Colonel Ross of the Guards.'

Another casualty was Captain Charles Boothby of the Engineers, who was in front of Sherbrooke's line, to disperse what his divisional commander thought was a dangerous concentration of men (it turned out to be a large bush):

> We peered anxiously through the thick dusk… a volleying began from our left… I clapped spurs to my mule and pushed her to her utmost speed (thinking the firing could spread down the line) in which case we should be blown to pieces. But the blaze from the left came down with greater speed, and before I could reach the line I found myself galloping up to an uninterrupted sheet of fire. I was struck in the leg by a musket ball… I had to creep through the lines on my hands and knees.

(Poor Boothby had to have the leg cut off, but not for two days, when a surgeon could be spared to see him.)

The same event stuck in the memory of an anonymous sergeant of the 1/2nd (Coldstream) Guards. He too was on the receiving end: 'The left sections of the light infantry were not more than twenty-five yards from the muzzles of the firelocks, and I, who was one of them, seeing what was likely to happen, ordered the whole of my section to lay down on their faces, and thus probably preserved my life for that time.'

A little later much the same fevered imaginations were at work down south, and shots and sometimes volleys echoed back as the Spanish deterred the more determined French firewood gatherers – and, as the moon came up after 1am, faint dark shadows that might or might not be moving. At one point, according to FitzClarence, the Spanish actually discharged several cannons at 'a cow having got loose and cantered up to their line'. Some of the disturbances would be small parties from Ruffin's dispersed force, lost and going up the wrong hill; some would surely be reconnaissances for the morning. Most, however, emanated from the Cascajal, where the French were moving their guns up, with plentiful ammunition. Leslie writes effectively that:

> Looking towards the enemy in our front, we beheld a kind of illumination moving in advance in certain directions. This was caused, no doubt, by a number of flambeaux which they carried at the head of their reserves and artillery to enable them to find their various routes to their proper places in their position… We could also hear the noise of wheels and the cracking of whips as they brought up their guns to plant them against us.

And Leith Hay recalled that 'the rattling of gun carriages in our front bespoke preparations for renewed hostility at day break. It was evident from the sound that cannon were placing in position, at no great distance, and immediately opposite to the height we occupied.' There were no less than ten batteries to be positioned – four, totalling twenty-four guns, on the Cascajal, and six batteries with another thirty-six supporting Sebastiani on the open ground opposite the British centre. Captain FitzClarence wrote:

> The rest for the officers lying around Sir Arthur was hasty and broken, and interrupted by the uneasiness of the horses held at a distance, and the arrival of deserters… they generally informed us that we were to be attacked at day-light… Sir Arthur, occasionally asking the hour, showed he looked for day-light with as much anxiety as any of us.

It is probable that he slept as little as young Lieutenant Bunbury of the 1/3rd, up on the Medellin:

> We passed a very restless night amidst the dead and the groans of the wounded French, whose sufferings we could not alleviate. It was bitterly cold, and I was glad to avail myself of a greatcoat belonging to a poor fellow who no longer needed it. With this and the regimental colour wound around me, I tried to sleep. The men retained their muskets in their hands.

10
Morning of a Long Day: 5am–2pm, 28 July 1809

O N the morning of the 28th, Marshal Victor continued to disregard the nominal authority of King Joseph. He had attacked the Medellin the previous evening without even informing him; now he deployed his assault division right up on their morning start line, so that, once advanced, they were to be fully engaged immediately. His report to the King was more an ultimatum – that he would attack unless directly forbidden to do so – than a request for approval that allowed room for adjustment; and he backed it up with something not far short of blackmail.

The King of Spain was a diplomat, not a soldier; the 45-year-old Marshal Claude-Victor Perrin (*dit* Victor) had been a boy of 17 from the Vosges hills when he first enlisted to serve in the ranks of the artillery. He had come to the attention of his fellow-gunner Colonel Bonaparte in 1793 at the siege of Toulon, and was a divisional general four years later. Victor had distinguished himself in command of the French left at Marengo, going on to fight at Saalfeld, Jena, Pultusk, Graudenz, Friedland – which brought him his marshal's baton – at Espinosa, Cadiz, Somosierra, Ucles, Medellin and Alcabon. He had also served Napoleon as an ambassador, and as Governor of Prussia and of Berlin, and was rewarded with the Italian dukedom of Belluno in September 1808. Now he seems to have made a blatant threat to report any interference with his plans direct to the Emperor, in the most negative light. Joseph's chief of staff, Marshal Jourdan, wrote in his memoirs that:

> The Duke of Belluno reported to the King the result of his first attack, and warned him that he would resume it at first light. One should perhaps have ordered him to wait. But this marshal, having spent a long time in the vicinity of Talavera, should have had a perfect knowledge of the terrain; and he appeared so confident of success that the King left him free to act as he wished... He [Joseph] was aware that if he followed the advice of Marshal Jourdan the Duke of Belluno would not hesitate to write to the Emperor that 'one had cost him the opportunity for a brilliant victory over the English'.

Jean-Baptiste Jourdan was almost the same age as Victor and his background was similar. The son of a doctor from Limoges, he too had enlisted in the old royal army as a teenager, and had fought in the ranks of the expeditionary corps sent to aid the colonists in the American War of Independence. Like Victor, he had left the army briefly in the 1780s, taking up the trade of cloth merchant (Victor had been a grocer); and like Victor, he had risen rapidly in the National Guard during the French Revolution. He had been less successful as a general in the field, however; despite showing real talent as an administrator, he therefore lacked the moral as well as the formal authority to overrule Victor. His preferred course now was basically to do nothing other than wait for Marshal Soult to get across Wellesley's lines of communication – for word of that to reach the British, and preferably, to see Soult appear on the horizon. This passive approach was not unintelligent, but if it did not bear fruit it might be hard to justify to an angry Emperor.

Victor received the royal nod for his attack at first light, with the proviso – perhaps rather self-righteously cool – that Sebastiani's 4th Corps would not be allowed to enter the fray until the attack had succeeded. There was no co-ordinated plan beyond this: no diversionary effort on either flank, and no overall control. Holding back Sebastiani would obviously lessen the initial pressure on the British. What if Victor was not victorious on the Medellin – would Sebastiani reinforce failure? The King and Jourdan were not starting this action with much evidence of eagerness, or any real demonstration of the art of higher command.

Down on the ground, there was little rest for the French in the early hours of the morning. Placing 19,000 men just so, in the dark, in such a confined area – less than a square mile – was a task to make a staff officer blanch. There were the equivalent of eleven brigades of infantry – thirty-three battalions. To seize the Medellin, Victor again chose, from his own 1st Corps, Ruffin's nine-battalion 1st Division, presumably balancing their earlier rough handling by the 29th with their acquired knowledge of the ground – and a desire for revenge? They were to assault the north-east and east slopes; Ruffin understandably put his bruised 9e Léger out on the right for a quiet time, to attack round by the north plain between the hill and the Sierra. The 24e Ligne drew the short straw, to climb up the middle – never the task of choice – with the 96e on their left. These regiments were all now forward on the Portina, their *voltigeurs* already out in front.

Villatte's 3rd Division, with twelve battalions, was in rear on the top of the Cascajal, behind the gun line (twenty-four pieces according to Oman, thirty says Fortescue, while Leith Hay of the 29th counted twenty-two, and FitzClarence thirty). Whatever the exact number, it was a lot greater than Sir Arthur's six 6-pounders of von Rettberg's KGL Battery on the Medellin, and the six of von Heyse's in front of Langwerth's brigade on the southern slopes. Ruffin's guns were about twenty paces apart, stretching like a necklace for about a quarter of a mile around the forward slope of the Cascajal. They had been dragged there during the night, together with well over 100 rounds of ammunition for each piece – an enormous task in the dark for men and beasts. On the southern slopes of the Cascajal were 1,000 horse of Beaumont's 1st Corps cavalry – the 2e Hussards and 5e Chasseurs.

South of the Cascajal, Lapisse's 2nd Division would face the King's German Legion. Behind these twelve battalions waited the 1st Dragoon Division of Latour-Maubourg, comprising the 1e, 2e, 4e, 9e, 14e and 26e – some 3,300 riders.

On the left of Lapisse, Sebastiani's 4th Corps had artillery too – Fortescue says twelve guns with each of his three divisions. His twenty-five battalions of Frenchmen, Germans, Poles and Netherlanders, in his own division and those of Valence and Leval, were to be drawn up opposite Sherbrooke's Guards, Cameron's brigade, and the northernmost of the Spanish next to the Pajar. Behind him on the plain were his corps cavalry: Merlin's 1,200 sabres of the 10e and 26e Chasseurs, the Westphalian Light Horse and the Polish Vistula Lancers.

Opposite Cuesta's Spanish army not a single French foot soldier was deployed – just Milhaud's 2nd Dragoon Division, with some 2,300 men of the 5e, 12e, 16e, 20e and 21e and the 3rd Dutch Hussars. A couple of miles behind both 1st and 4th Corps sat King Joseph, with Godinot's reserve brigade of six battalions of the 12e Léger and 51e Ligne from Dessolle's Madrid division; his King's Guards, both foot and mounted; two squadrons of the 27e Chasseurs, and fourteen guns.

Sir John Fortescue, having studied Oman's research on relative strengths, and after making fair allowance for losses subsequent to the British morning state of 25 July and the French equivalent of 15 July, concludes that King Joseph commanded overall some 45,000 men and eighty guns, while Wellesley and Cuesta commanded 55,000 and sixty guns. However, with effectively all the French arranged solely against the British, and setting aside the cavalry, it is his unequivocal view that 30,000 French infantry were to attack 16,000 or 17,000 British infantry. We can, of course, put it more simply if we compare the basic fighting units to be involved initially on the Medellin: Marshal Victor had thirty-three battalions, Wellesley had a dozen (taking Tilson, Stewart, Donkin, Low and Langwerth as the brigades facing Ruffin's, Villatte's and Lapisse's divisions). Overall, French versus British, the line-up was sixty-two battalions to twenty-five.

All this we can state with hindsight. The British line, having seen the torches and heard the wheels on and around the Cascajal, would certainly know that they were 'for it' come first light; but only seeing is believing. Even the confirmation of the coming attack volunteered by the few French deserters who crossed in the night (actually, mainly Germans from Leval's division) would only increase the curiosity as to precisely what was opposite each man, and each battalion. Many eyes stared out across the Portina as the sky to the east hinted at the first thinning of the night. The moon had got up between 1 and 2am and, under its strengthening light, dark masses which men could not remember seeing the previous evening were just becoming visible – some of them, moving. Smoke continued to swirl across the hillside, for every blade of wheat or grass was bone dry after many days of 100° temperatures, hot winds and no rain; patches of ground continued to smoulder, despite the heavy dew.

From around 4am the Cascajal's summit and forward slope gradually showed themselves in the growing light. What had seemed to be three square black woods, side by side, not quite still in the easterly breeze, became solid human masses, sixty yards across and the same deep – some 5,000 men of Ruffin's three regiments. Behind and above them lay a line of guns; and behind those, on the very top of the hill, three more black squares – another 5,000 soldiers, of Villatte's command. To the right, on the plain at the foot of the Cascajal, another three black squares betrayed the presence of 5,000 more, under General Lapisse. Beaumont's 1,000 horsemen were becoming visible behind Villatte; and behind Lapisse, another 3,000, of Latour-Maubourg's six dragoon regiments. All this was merely Victor's 1st Corps.

Further to the right on the lightening plain, opposite the Guards and Campbell, stood Sebastiani's 4th Corps: on the left, four more huge columns, each of three battalions; and three columns to the right, the nine German battalions under General Leval, with Valence's two Polish battalions in rear. Behind the Polish infantry were Merlin's four light cavalry regiments; and far off to the right the redcoats could make out the six dragoon regiments facing the Spanish.

The light now fast improving, colour began to daub the crowded landscape. Such a vista from the Medellin would have occupied the excited brushes of many a subsequent battle artist: given the chance to be there that morning, Dighton, Caton Woodville, Detaille, Wollen, Lady Butler, Beadle – all would be shading their eyes from the low sun over the Sierra de Segurilla at half left, and trying to distinguish the identifying colours. French infantry wore black shakos, blue coats with red collars and cuffs, white waistcoats, lapels and breeches, with black again at the bottom – long gaiters reaching above the knee. The blue was well-faded, and the white well-dirtied, but no Englishman ever had to look twice to identify a Frenchman (nor did the enemy ever mistake a red coat, however faded). The massed divisions across the way were a uniform sea of blue above white, with black at top and bottom, and a handy aiming mark in the white crossbelts, which met conveniently in the centre of every Frenchman's chest. But the infantry were drab indeed alongside the cavalry. Beaumont's 2e Hussards were in brown jackets and pelisses, with sky-blue cuffs and gloriously impractical sky-blue breeches; his 5e Chasseurs were all in green with yellow cuffs. The dragoon regiments of Milhaud and Latour-Maybourg all wore green coats, with white waistcoats and breeches, and brass helmets with long black manes, but regimental facing colours on lapels, cuffs and plumes identified them to the educated eye – scarlet, crimson, orange, deep pink, yellow, white or green. In the words of Leslie of the 29th Foot:

> As the day began to break all eyes were strained to discern the disposition of the enemy. As things became more visible a very imposing sight presented itself to our view. The whole disposition of the enemy's force could be clearly distinguished. In the first place, immediately below us was formed a heavy solid column on the bank of the ravine, with reserves in its rear, with field batteries on both flanks, and the guns already pointed towards us, while light troops were thrown out as tirailleurs to cover their front and prepare the way for a grand attack, which was evidently to be directed against us on the hill. At some distance to the right were formed other masses in like manner. Others were also formed in front of our allies the Spanish. The columns of reserve, cavalry, spare artillery, and baggage extended a long way back in their rear. Our own lines presented an animated but not so formidable appearance, owing to the nature of our formation. Our front showed an extended line only two deep.

The sky was now lightening steadily; the night piquets withdrew, and the light troops went out. Stewart, Tilson, Donkin and Low together had ten battalion light companies, plus six rifle companies of the 5/60th – about 1,000 skirmishers to cover their front against Victor's initial 1st Corps assault. Sir Arthur rode up with his staff to the rear of the 29th, and then forward to await events amid a general solemn silence. Captain FitzClarence of the staff:

> Just before day-light, we quietly mounted our horses and rode slowly towards the height, where we arrived just as the light allowed us to see the opposite side of the ravine beneath us covered with black indistinct masses. Every instant rendered them more visible, and the first rays of the sun showed us Sebastiani's divisions opposite our centre, Victor's three divisions at our feet, with the reserve, guard, and cavalry extending backwards to the woods near the Alberche. Our eyes were, however, principally attracted by an immense solid column opposite but rather to the left of the hill. Its front was already covered with tirailleurs, ready to advance at the word… The gray of the morning was not broken in upon by a single shot by either side, and we had time to observe our position (which had not been completely occupied before dusk on the preceeding eve) and how the troops were posted.

According to Leslie of the 29th: 'Much about the same time we could plainly discern Joseph Bonaparte and a large suite of staff in his train, coming up at full gallop in rear of the French masses in our front.' Victor, no doubt happy to have his peers now present as audience, gave the nod, and from a central signal gun on the Cascajal a gush of smoke shot out to climb curling upwards, immediately followed by the crack as the sound carried aross the Portina. It was 5am, and according to Sergeant Cooper of the 2/7th the first gun fired 'just as the sun shot his first beams over the mountains on our left'. Captain FitzClarence again:

> A single cannon shot from the centre of the enemy's batteries was the signal for its advance [the 'immense column'], and for the opening of all their guns. A shower of balls instantly fell on all parts of our position, and the smoke (the wind being east, and the damp of the morning preventing its rising) was blowing across the ravine, and completely enveloped us in a dense fog… [The enemy column] consisted of a close column of battalions, of the same division of Ruffin which had attacked the night before.

*   *   *

The signal gun's example spread left and right around the Cascajal, two dozen more gusts of dirty white smoke belching forwards and linking up, followed down on the plain by the batteries with Sebastiani, firing half-right to bear on the red lines on the Medellin. The thundering became continuous as the first salvoes were followed by independent firing, and the ears of those in the line were assaulted by the slamming of the discharges, while their eyes followed the plumes of earth and stones cascading upwards where the roundshot tore into the hillside. While their infantry toiled down to the Portina, Victor's gunners concentrated every bearable piece on the foe above. Sir Arthur quickly ordered Hill to withdraw his men behind the crest and lie them down, and Donkin and Low to take what cover they could. Leith Hay:

> The 29th were ordered to lie down a short distance behind the brow of the hill, which the soldiers did with arms in their hands, ready to start up at a moment's warning… the regiment suffered little from the cannonade, although the enemy's practice appeared excellent, every shot either striking the ground immediately in front, or passing close over our heads.

And his fellow officer Leslie:

> A tremendous cannonade opened upon us on the hill, and on the regiment on the lower part of the slope to our right… which became so destructive that we were ordered to lie down on the ground. The shot flew thick and fast about us, but it went principally over us, the guns being too much elevated [or the balls ricocheting over the crest].

In the face of such heavy metal screeching across the Portina, Sir Arthur's counter-fire was thin, with only von Rettberg's KGL Battery of heavy 6-pounders on the Medellin able to bear directly on the French gun line; the other three batteries could not engage the far right of the French position. In a letter home written four days after the battle, Lieutenant-Colonel Sir George Bingham, 2/53rd, in Alexander Campbell's brigade, wrote: 'Some guns we had on the circular hill [the Medellin] commanded theirs and dismounted several of their guns, and there were frequent explosions of ammunition wagons, but they had so many guns in the field that they maintained the superiority of fire.' And as Captain FitzClarence commented, they were conscious of 'the inferiority of our calibres… all our guns, with the exception of one brigade of heavy, were miserably light six pounders, while the French returned our fire with eights and twelves.'

The gunsmoke was soaked up by the dew-laden morning air, and driven west on the breeze. It climbed the slopes, hugging the earth, and obscured each side from the other. However, French progress could be followed by the sound of musketry that had broken out down in the ravine. Borne on the wind came the deep repeating rythmns of their drums, and the shouts of command. As they lay waiting, the men of Tilson's and Stewart's brigades would feel their flints, and maybe tighten the screw a bit, for something to do. Many had loaded double balls. The musket fire crept up the slope. Leslie tells us that: 'General Hill, seeing the overwhelming force that was coming against us, gave orders that the light troops should be recalled, and the bugles sounded accordingly [the sound "Call in the Skirmishers" was three quick doubled notes rising to a long E]. The skirmishers were closing in and filing to the rear with all the regularity of field-day and parade exercise, which the General observing, called out, 'D***n their filing, let them come in anyhow.' For those who have forgotten their skirmishing drills, the following *Instruction for Skirmishers on*

Firing when Retreating will adequately explain the mild-mannered 'Daddy' Hill's unusual profanity:

> At the sound of the commence firing, followed by the signal to retreat, the first rank, which ever happens to be in front, begins to fire, then goes to the right-about, and marches twelve paces in the rear of the second rank, fronts and loads; when the Sergeant on the flank of the second rank sees that the first is formed and loaded, he steps two paces to the front and whistles, upon which the second rank fires, and faces to the right-about, and marches twelve paces in the rear of the first, fronts and loads. Thus, alternatively, each rank retires, supporting each other.

And raising the blood pressure of impatiently watching generals... Hill had no wish to inflict on 1,000 men that 'friendly fire' which the night before had hit the sapper Captain Boothby; but he knew his light troops were not now going to impede the French columns seriously, and he needed the ground in front clear for firing.

Of General Ruffin's three regimental columns, the 9e Léger on the right surprisingly played no part, moving into the unoccupied north plain between the Medellin and the mountains. Those of the 24e and 96e Ligne ascended the Medellin side by side, some 300yd apart – so as to allow space to deploy into line. Each column was a double company wide, perhaps fifty-five files across and twenty-seven or so ranks deep. As they climbed higher, their supporting cannon fire necessarily lifted and switched left to play on Donkin's and Lowe's brigades. That lifting signalled the moment to Sir Arthur and his generals. 'Our Brigadier-General, Richard Stewart, said, "Now, 29th! Now is your time!" We instantly sprang to our feet' (Leslie of the 29th). The line moved forward to gain the best field of fire, and found the French skirmishers falling back behind their columns; these were only 100 paces away, drums beating, swords waving – but crucially, not yet deploying into line. 'The summit, which had appeared deserted, now supported a regular line of infantry. Near the Colours of the 29th, stood Sir Arthur Wellesley, directing and animating the troops' (Leith Hay).

The 24e Ligne was seen to be heading for Stewart's Battalion of Detachments and the 1/48th. Some accounts say that von Rettberg's battery lay between the latter battalion (Stewart's right of the line) and the 2/48th (Tilson's left). The 96e Ligne, in that case, was heading for the gap that the junction would offer. At ninety paces 'We gave three tremendous cheers, and immediately opened our fire,' says Leslie – although the 29th were shooting obliquely to their right, into the side of the 24e Ligne's column, and at extreme range. Indeed, one doubts whether more than the 29th's right wing companies would be so engaged. Assuming some 270 muskets of theirs, plus the 530 and 792 respectively of the Detachments and the 1/48th, a volley of 1,600 balls could hammer across into the front and sides of the 24e Ligne – whose frontage, remember, was only about fifty-five men. The facing ranks were accordingly knocked over, and the column promptly stopped in its tracks. A firefight commenced during which, according to the regimental history, Lieutenant-Colonel

Donellan of the 1/48th had two horses shot from under him as he rode along his line encouraging and steadying his battalion. Seeing some men fall, and thinking the range was too great for his muskets, he said: 'Curse the fellows, those damned long guns of theirs can shoot at two miles off,' and immediately advanced the 48th to get nearer (at 45.4in, the barrel of the Charleville model 1777/1800 musket was nearly 10in longer than that of the British Short Land, New Land and India pattern models, giving slightly greater accurate range). The French tried to deploy into line and return the British volleys; but barely 150 muskets could they bring to bear from the column's new front three ranks, to answer the hailstorm from the 48th and the Detachments. How long this firefight lasted is uncertain. Although Jac Weller with his usual authority states categorically it was 'less than three minutes, long enough for British infantry to fire about ten volleys by platoons', the Donellan anecdote suggests rather longer. Some time after the assault developed General Hill was hit, and General Tilson took command of the division:

> About half an hour after the sun was up an immense column… moved on and attacked us… My horse was wounded early in the action. I got another from an officer. Shortly before the enemy gave up the conflict, I was struck by a musket-ball near my left ear and the back of my head. The blow was so violent that I was obliged to leave the field. I continued unwell the whole of the next day, and the next.

The 96e Ligne met a similar fate under the fire of the 2/48th and 1/3rd, with the added pressure of a flank attack on the left from Low's 5th KGL, sent across the slope by General Sherbrooke when he saw the limited extent of the current French assault. Beamish tells us:

> The German regiments in consequence of the guns having been brought up directly in their front, became much exposed to [the French cannon fire], and were ordered to throw back their left; this movement, which was performed with the greatest order and precision, but not without considerable loss from the constant discharges of grape, brought the retired flank of the brigades close under Captain Heise's Battery and the 5th Line battalion of the Legion which formed the left of the German brigades, was ordered to ascend the height, and the companies of riflemen became hotly engaged. The struggle was furious and obstinate. The inequalities of the ground not permitting the troops to retain their compact formation, separate contests of small bodies ensued. [That sentence is lifted almost word-for-word from Napier's description.] Major Wurmb gallantly leading on the German riflemen, was followed by Captain La Grehr bearing the regimental colour, at the head of the 5th battalion; the skirmishers fell upon the enemy's left flank, while the battalion attacked him in front, and furiously assailing one of the French columns with the bayonet and butt end of the musket, caused tremendous destruction around them. Near 400 of the 28th [sic – actually 96e] French regiment are stated to have fallen before the German battalion alone.

The British now charged both columns; Leslie of the 29th:

> No sooner said than done. In we went, a wall of stout hearts and bristling steel. The French did not fancy such close quarters. The moment we made the rush they began to waver, then went to the right about. The principal portion broke and fled, but some brave fellows occasionally faced about and gave us an irregular fire. We, however, kept dashing on, and drove them all headlong right before us down the hill into their own lines again. We kept following them up, firing, running, and cheering.

And Leith Hay:

> With one tremendous shout the right wing of the 29th, and the entire battalion of the 48th rushed like a torrent down, bayoneting and sweeping back the enemy to the brink of an insignificant muddy stream, nearly equidistant in the ravine which separated the two armies. In the pursuit all order was speedily lost. The men advanced in small parties, destroying those of the enemy who had not ensured their safety by flight. At this moment, when the whole valley was filled with troops, in all the confusion attending the eagerness of pursuit, a column of French infantry appeared close upon our right flank, facing towards the irregular mass. It became necessary to collect the pursuers, to form a front, and to charge these fresh assailants. This was, by great exertion, accomplished. Broken as we were, an irresistible impetus had been given, and the enemy's column followed the example of those who had mounted the hill at the pas de charge. So completely were these attacks repelled, that the British infantry were quietly collected in the ravine, and marched back to the height without being seriously assailed.

It is some 800 yards from the summit of the Medellin to the Portina. Much of that slope would seem to have been suitable for cavalry, for Charles Stewart (who else?) points out with much frustration:

> Had our cavalry been at this moment sufficiently forward in the plain and valley, they might have produced a terrible impression upon these fugitives; for the enemy retired in great confusion; and opportunities of making charges occurred such as could not have been by any possibility overlooked; but unfortunately, they were too far in the rear.

Stewart's ADC, Captain FitzClarence, supports his brigadier:

> The enemy fled in the utmost confusion and consternation… had the cavalry been present, the victory might have been completed at this early hour, but they had not come in from their bivouac.

If that was the real reason, it shows culpable lethargy on someone's part. It takes little imagination to picture the incorrigible Stewart's apoplexy at this missed chance for making charges.

For the French to be pursued such a distance, and then for their pursuers to be able to regroup in the ravine, without pressure, before returning, says much for the crushing injury inflicted on Ruffin. Oman carefully computes his loss at 1,300 killed and wounded – over a quarter of his division; and that excludes the 300 of the 9e Léger lost the previous evening. Unfortunately the British losses for this first action of the day cannot be separated out from the total losses for the whole day, unlike Ruffin's (whose division took no serious part in the subsequent engagements). However, one must question Oman's guestimate that of the 835 total losses known to have been recorded that day for General Hill's division, this first action accounted for 750. Oman himself states that of the total loss: 'much of it was suffered in the afternoon, when (though not attacked by infantry) his division was under a heavy shell fire'. Is it conceivable that the French imposed that order of casualties on the British in their abortive first-light assault up the hill?

Ruffin's casualties were all from the British muskets – ball or bayonet – since no cavalry were involved, and the British guns were engaged in counter-battery work across the ravine. Bearing in mind the time the French took to march up the Medellin, and the considerably shorter time required to run down it, Napier is probably correct to state that their loss of 1,300 men needed but a 'space of forty minutes'. Marshal Victor, who had not fought the British before, would now have to think what he was to say to King Joseph.

∗   ∗   ∗

In the muddy Portina brook, our eyewitness Charles Leslie of the 29th got hit: 'About 7 o'clock I received a ball in the side of my thigh, about three inches above the right knee.' Appropriately for our narrative, 'at length my friend, Andrew Leith Hay perceived me. He raised me up, and then, taking the musket out of the hand of Corporal Sharp of my Company, he directed him to conduct me out of action, and to find the surgeons... In quitting the field, I passed near Sir Arthur Wellesley, the Commander-in-Chief. He looked at me, seeing the blood streaming down my white trousers, but he said nothing.'

We must remember that from this point on Leslie is reporting at second-hand, as he reminds us: 'The following account of the continuation of the battle after I was wounded and obliged to quit the field' comes from 'the collected reports of various friends... The men from both armies were sent out to collect the wounded. They intermixed in the most friendly terms. Lieutenant Langton, of the 29th Regiment, gave to a French officer two crosses of the Legion of Honour which had belonged to officers killed far up the hill... The whole face of the hill was covered with the dead and dying.'

'During this cessation of hostilities', says Leslie's comrade Leith Hay, 'the troops of General Hill's division descended in parties to the stream in our front, for the purpose of procuring water, which was only obtained in small quantities, of a description that, under other circumstances, would have produced loathing; but the excess heat of the weather, added to exertion, occasioned a burning thirst.' That thirst also owed something to the saltpetre in the black powder; gunpowder is hygroscopic, and got on to the soldiers' lips every time they loaded their muskets, since they had to bite off the top of their paper cartridges.

The subsequent informal truce, which was to set an amicable precedent for others in following years, developed as the artillery duel gradually died away, and the French were seen to be lighting their cooking fires. 'From 9 o'clock the field of battle offered no appearance of hostility; the weather was intensely hot and the troops, on both sides, descended and mingled, without fear or suspicion, to quench their thirst at the little brook which divided the positions' (Napier). The dead, in the rising morning heat, soon demanded attention. Captain FitzClarence wrote: 'As the weather was dreadfully hot, and it was impossible to know how long we should occupy this ground, orders were given to bury the men who had fallen the night before and in the morning attack, lying around the hill interspersed with the living. The entrenching tools were thus employed, and it was curious to see the soldiers burying their fallen comrades, with the cannon shot falling around, and in the midst of them, leaving it probable that an individual might thus be employed digging his own grave!'

Burial parties were sent out; and since there were more than 1,000 French killed and wounded on the slopes of the Medellin, and some British on the other side of the Portina, there was much carting of bodies, dead and alive, by the bandsmen (their non-musical job in those days, as it still is) using either a plain blanket, or two muskets thrust through the sleeves of two greatcoats buttoned together, with four men to carry one. FitzClarence again:

> The dead of the enemy lay in vast numbers on the face of the hill, and had been tall, healthy, fine young men, with good countenances; and as proof of their courage, (the head of their column having reached within a few yards of the top of the hill before being arrested) the bodies lay close to our ranks. The face of the hill was furrowed out into deep ravines by the water rushing down its steep sides during the rains, and the dead and wounded of both nations lay heaped in them. We were occupied after this attack in carrying away our wounded in blankets, by four or five soldiers, and within a short time the number of unfortunate men assembled round our field hospital, a small house and enclosure behind our centre, barely out of cannon shot, proved our heavy loss.

Private Hewitt, a bandsman of the 1/48th, wrote in a letter to his wife (who, to her great frustration, was not at that time following the drum):

> During a long pause, the men of both armies met at a little stream which ran near the centre of the battle, and met together as friends, with one common desire, to satisfy a craving of nature, more urgent than the affairs of war. The British soldiers one side of the stream, and the French the other, filled their

cans without molestation of each other. Half our band went to the stream for water about ten o'clock, and each returned, bearing for his thirsty comrade under arms, the life-giving draught; many a poor wounded fellow did I that day receive a blessing from, when I held to his parched lips the anticipated cup.

Captain FitzClarence again:

The troops in the advance talked together, and the thirsty of both armies met at the bottom of the ravine and drank from the same stream. There was also a well at the foot of the hill to the left, where the same water was divided among the collected of both nations around its brink.

This unofficial armistice lasted two hours, with officers' agreement from both sides. This was ample time for all the discarded French knapsacks, and those whose owners no longer had breath to enjoy the contents, to be searched and their edible contents consumed. For it was quickly found that most contained bread, and often meat, and many a waterbottle held something stronger – comforts the British soldiers had long been missing. Half the army had been on half-rations since 24 July, and Beamish writes that the KGL 'since the 22nd had had no bread; a few ounces of raw wheat was the only subsistence issued to the army, and the Germans had more than once been obliged to seek nourishment from a sort of pea called corvanzen which they found in the fields.' As Leslie remarked, 'Our brave fellows had only their morsel of biscuit and a mouthful of rum or wine'; while Lieutenant John Carss, 2/53rd, wrote: 'It appeared the enemy was not so badly off for want of provisions as we were, for almost every man that we killed had bread about him.' Sergeant Cooper of the 2/7th recorded with heartfelt exactness that 'I had not tasted food for 43 hours... about 10am on the 29th we were served with 4 ounces of bread, which was for the next twenty-four hours. This might make six or eight decent mouthfuls.'

*   *   *

This quiet period allowed Sir Arthur to adjust his deployment. Having seen the 9e Léger move (albeit ineffectively) up the north valley that dawn, he could no longer risk having his left flank so exposed to another, more determined turning move-ment. That the French had twice tried and failed on one approach must guarantee that the next would be different. Yet he had no British infantry to spare, nor guns in reserve; and so he sent Fane's brigade of the 3rd Dragoon Guards and 4th Dragoons and Anson's brigade of the 23rd Light Dragoons and 1st Light Dragoons KGL around the western end of the Medellin to the western end of the north plain. From this area they could charge any body of foot intent on climbing the northern slope of the Medellin to take Hill in his left flank. Wellesley also moved two of von Rettberg's guns down a convenient spur, from which enfilade fire could be directed down the plain.

At a later stage, when Wellesley could see the likely shape of King Joseph's deployment for the next attack, he asked General Cuesta for assistance – and (perhaps surprisingly) got it. He was lent the reserve division of 5,000 men under Bassecourt, the six cavalry regiments and one horse battery of the Duke of Albuquerque, and a heavy battery of 12-pounders. Of the latter, four went into the redoubt at the Pajar, with Lawson's battery of little 3-pounders, and the other two went to the Medellin, near von Rettberg. Bassecourt's division took up a position on the lower slopes of the Sierra de Segurilla, on the same north-south line as the British troops over on the Medellin; and the Spanish cavalry, who moved in rather later, were drawn up behind Fane and Anson. In locating Bassecourt mainly on the far side of the northern plain Wellesley was leaving an inviting gap up the valley, precisely where a French turning movement would most appreciate one. By not simply continuing the British line immediately beyond the Medellin, he seems to have been laying a trap, to be closed by his heavy cavalry.

Around ten in the morning, Joseph and Jourdan went forward to the Cascajal for a conference with Victor, which lasted more than an hour. Marshal Jourdan left an account of it in his memoirs which, owing something to the wisdom of hindsight, unsurprisingly laid the burden of eventual defeat on the shoulders of his fellow marshal. It had been a mistake, he said, that the empty north plain had not figured in Victor's first two attacks, and particularly the dawn attack, when a decisive turning movement would have done the trick. Now was too late for that, for the British had at last understood their vulnerability: their cavalry, and Spanish infantry, was even then (he said, pointing) evident in the valley. He also feared that the Spanish army in front of Talavera could assail the King's left, in the event of a third but more general French reverse, and thus get between the King and his capital. Jourdan even raised the dread vision of a forced march over the mountains north to Avila, on tracks that could not take wheels. So, argued Jourdan, with Marshal Soult about to descend on Wellesley's rear, the safe thing to do was to sit tight here, or at most pull back to the Alberche, and then the British would be trapped.

Victor, having just watched Ruffin's division run back down the Medellin, was unable to contemplate such inactivity, the proposed scale of which offended even his own occasionally muted sense of urgency. It would not be honourable to retire now, without a proper try against a foe who had not yet been fully tested. The reason his earlier attacks failed was that no-one had supported him. If the whole French army attacked this time, then he would take the Medellin for sure, or *il faudrait renoncer à faire la guerre* – 'We might as well give up fighting wars!' This presumably insinuated a reminder of his threat to report any lack of aggressiveness to the Emperor.

In the face of this further implied threat, unlike that of the previous evening, the King could at least now point to Victor having failed twice; however, he clearly did not know what to do for the best, even asking Sebastiani for his views (which mirrored Jourdan's). At that critical moment came two letters, which widened Joseph's considerations by narrowing his options. The first was a despatch from General Valence, Governor of Toledo, informing him that troops of the Spanish general Venegas were approaching that city, while his advance guard was thought to be but two day's march from Madrid, nearing Aranjuez. The second was from

Marshal Soult, much regretting that he could not reach Plasencia before 3 August or perhaps even the 5th.

Toledo had only four Polish battalions between it and Madrid, so if the King wanted to keep his capital he must immediately send some 15,000 troops – say Sebastiani's corps – to the east. But he could not do that and wait for Soult at Talavera with his remaining 30,000, if Soult was still six to eight marches away from bringing pressure on Wellesley's distant rear, still less from actually appearing behind him – during that time the British and Spanish would assuredly walk all over Joseph and Victor. Since Joseph could not contemplate even a temporary loss of Madrid, with its base hospitals, reserve artillery and many storehouses (to say nothing of his throne and prestige), and since waiting passively for Soult without detaching Sebastiani would now entail just that consequence, Joseph decided to adopt Victor's plan. The aim must therefore be to beat the British that very afternoon, and then to do the same to Venegas on the 29th or 30th, outside Madrid.

Thus it is indeed ironic that General Venegas, criticized in earlier pages (and thoroughly, one supposes, at British headquarters a week earlier, for his suspicious inactivity) should now produce exactly the diversionary effect originally planned: not by keeping Sebastiani from joining Victor before the battle, but by ensuring by his late appearance at Toledo the hurried third and final bloody assault on Wellesley, which was to leave the latter victorious on the field.

The French plan of attack was for the Spaniards to be left alone again, except for Milhaud's strong dragoon division making suitably frightening noises. In the event that the Spanish thought to interfere, the division near the Pajar (Leval's) was to echelon its left backwards, to provide a flank. The main thrust of Leval's German regiments was to be against Campbell's division, the Pajar redoubt, and Cuesta's northernmost three or four battalions. Next to the north, Sebastiani's 8,000 strong division would go for the Guards, and most of Cameron's brigade; and Lapisse would challenge Cameron's left and the King' German Legion.   Victor's other two divisions would attempt the Medellin for the third time, Villatte by direct frontal attack and Ruffin via the north plain. Mindful of the latter's losses to date, Victor ordered the six battalions of Villatte's 27e Léger and 63e Ligne under Cassagne to support Ruffin's left on the plain itself, Ruffin being directed more into the foothills of the Sierra de Segurilla to oppose Bassecourt's deployment. The north plain was also allocated the four light horse regiments under Merlin, while Villatte was backed by Beaumont's two regiments, and Lapisse and Sebastiani in the centre by the six dragoon regiments of Latour-Maubourg. In reserve were to be King Joseph's Guards (the equivalent of three battalions), and the six battalions from the Madrid garrison.

Villatte received orders to stay put on the Cascajal until definite progress occurred elsewhere along the line. This decision was inevitable given the two earlier failures on the Medellin by the 9e Léger, and the agreement with Joseph for a concerted effort. Having got that promise, and having made his own, Victor was not going to cross the ravine again at half cock. But if the north plain turning movement might indeed provide an initial key (although a breakthrough by Sebastiani would do just as well), it is odd that it should be entrusted to Ruffin. His division had been reduced to 3,700 from the 5,200 of the previous day, and with more than a third of its officers out of action its willingness to fight robustly was surely questionable. And if Ruffin could not make headway through Bassecourt's division on the far side of the plain, in effect Victor's turning movement would comprise just the 27e and 63e regiments under Cassagne. Six battalions might well be inadequate to take the north slopes of the Medellin.

Both sides had made their deployments and all was still, except for the six regiments of Spanish horse under Albuquerque, still moving round behind Fane and Anson. Dust clouds thickened over the French: 'about twelve o'clock noon the enemy begun to get in motion again. Their reserve was seen closing up from the rear' (Leslie). The last watering parties scrambled up from the Portina; and some time before 2pm the French artillery opened up again, all along the line.

11
Five French Attacks:
Afternoon, 28 July 1809

U NDER fire from eighty French cannons, each of whose trained crews were
capable of loosing at least six rounds a minute and whose work was relatively
unhampered by the thirty light British and six Spanish guns, the red lines
suffering under this storm of iron awaited the advance of the French infantry impatiently. No relief was accorded the battalions on the Medellin, however, since the
French guns there would not need to lift their fire even when their columns did
move forward down the slopes of the Cascajal. Captain James Wilson, 1/48th,
describes the 'showers of shot, shell and grape [which] fell like hailstones about
them'. Nonetheless, 'never did men behave better... steady as a rock... not a man
flinching, dipping or quitting his ranks'. After a while, when it became plain that the
Medellin faced no early infantry threat and that the cannonade would therefore
continue, General Tilson moved Hill's division back behind the crest. Further south,
with no crest to shelter them, the line had no choice but to lie down and compose
themselves to endure it. Ensign John Aitchison, 1/3rd Guards, wrote:

> A tremendous cannonade – shots and shells were falling in every direction –
> but none of the enemy were to be seen – the men were all the while lying in
> the ranks, and except at the very spot where a shot or shell fell, there was not
> the least motion – I have seen men killed in the ranks by cannon shots – those
> immediately round the spot would remove the mutilated corpse to the rear,
> they would then lie down as if nothing had occurred and remain in the ranks,
> steady as before. That common men could be brought to face the greatest
> danger, there is a spirit which tells me it is possible, but I could not believe
> that they could be brought to remain without emotion, when attacked, not
> knowing from whence. Such, however, was the conduct of our men (I speak
> particularly of the [Guards] Brigade) on 28 July, and from this steadiness so
> few suffered as by remaining quiet the shots bounded over their heads.

In the second line behind the Guards, the 2/24th (Warwickshire) of Mackenzie's
brigade were also quick to hug the warm earth: the regimental history recorded that
'the men fell fast from shot and shell. The brigade was therefore ordered to lie down,
and then the roundshot did little damage, but the [explosive] shells annoyed the
men much'. Worst exposed were the Germans under Barons von Low and von
Langwerth, not much more than 500 paces from the French gunline and thus well
within the effective range even of canister shot. Among the KGL units there was

general relief when the thunder of the guns, the ripping apart of the drifting smoke, the explosions of shells, the spouts of cascading earth and stones, the humming and whirring of balls and ricochets gradually lessened, and they heard in the distance the French drums and trumpets, and the first crackling of the skirmishers' firefights.

The first clash of opposing infantry was at the Pajar, between the troops of Generals Leval and Alexander Campbell, at around 2.30pm, half an hour before the rest of the French engaged. It is said that Leval thereby displeased his King, who sought a simultaneous assault; however, Leval's routes for his columns lay through close country with ditches and enclosures, where control and visibility suffered, so, perhaps fearing to be late, he hurried on and arrived early. His troops were partly German, partly Dutch. It is not clear what column formations were used, but since eyewitnesses refer to named regiments it is probable that each of the five regiments advanced identifiably in a single column of the battalions of that regiment, each two companies wide: say, a sixty-man frontage and eighteen ranks deep. Their right hand unit was the Nassau Regiment, then reading to their left were the Netherlands, the Baden, the Hesse-Darmstadt and the Frankfurt. The Baden in the centre was effectively facing the ten guns of the Pajar redoubt. Each regiment had two battalions, except for the single Frankfurt unit.

They started forward well before the artillery lifted, of course, and under cover of this noise and in the close country were able to approach the British piquet line without discovery. Captain FitzClarence gives a possible reason: 'Trusting to the similarity of uniform, they advanced towards the 7th, 97th and 53rd crying out that they were Spaniards, and repeating the Spanish cry of "Viva los Inglesis!", though this did not deceive our officers, it did the men, who under this false impression, could not be brought to fire on them; this allowed their approaches to be quite close.' (The Spanish armies of 1809 wore a motley range of clothing, but many of their uniforms were indeed blue.) A converse opinion is given by one of the men, who in turn blamed an officer for the capture of some light infantrymen:

> One of these [the battalion columns], after threading its way among the trees and grape vines, came up directly in our front, and while deploying, called out 'Espanholas, Espanholas!' wishing us to believe they were Spaniards. Our captain thought they were Spanish, and ordered us not to fire. But they soon convinced us who they were by a rattling volley. We instantly retired upon our regiment.

So writes Sergeant John Cooper, who was out in front with the Light Company, 2/7th (Royal Fusiliers), together with his counterparts from the 2/53rd(Shropshire), 1/40th (Somersets) and the riflemen of the 5/60th, the 1/40th having been brought up into the first line from Colonel Kemmis' brigade in the second.

The redoubt on the Pajar hillock was eighty paces wide and had ten guns on it. A flat field ran sixty paces forward to a bank and ditch, and another forty paces forward again there was a second enclosure, with a thin wood beyond. The 2/7th were immediately adjacent to the guns, the 2/53rd next on their left, the 1/40th left again, and the 2/24th from Mackenzie's brigade left again, their neighbours being the Guards of Sherbrooke's division. We are fortunate to have three eyewitness accounts of Leval's attack, two from the 2/53rd and one from the 2/7th. The following passage is a compilation of extracts, in sequence of events: 'GB' is the 2/53rd's commanding officer, Lieutenant-Colonel Sir George Bingham; 'JC' is one of his officers, Lieutenant John Carss; and 'C' is Sergeant John Cooper of the 7th:

> (JC) We perceived three large columns of the enemy with twelve pieces of cannon coming down to attack us for the purpose of turning our right. Sir Arthur was on a hill in the centre of the line and saw every movement that took place; he sent down one of his aide-de-camps to say that this body of the enemy was moving down for the purpose of turning the right, and on our exertions depended the fate of the day, for if they turned either right or left our situation would be very bad. This body soon commenced their fire from the artillery in their centre. Their infantry kept advancing towards us in a thin wood.
>
> (GB) They drove in our light companies in front.
>
> (JC) We never fired a shot until they cleared the wood and got over a small bank which was about sixty yards from our line.
>
> (GB) Coming on the flank of the Fusiliers [they] drove them back; some of them penetrated nearly to the work in front (the embanked redoubt).
>
> (C) Our regiment... sprung up and met the enemy on the rising ground, but our men being all raw soldiers, staggered for a moment under such a rolling fire. Our colonel Sir William Myers seeing this, sprang from his horse and snatching one of the Colours, cried 'Come on, Fusiliers!' 'Twas enough. On rushed the Fusiliers and the 53rd regiment.
>
> (GB) They were immediately repulsed by a charge made by the Fusiliers, who had instantly rallied, aided by the second, right company of the 53rd, supported by the remaining seven companies of that Battalion.
>
> (JC) We gave them a volley, then rushed on them with the bayonet. They ran instantly when we charged, but before they could scale the bank again we killed nearly as many of them as our two regiments were composed of. During this charge their cannon had got close up to this bank which prevented the shot from hurting us, as they went over our heads. They were pulling down part of the bank to get the guns up to our right for the purpose of raking our line, but when we ran our charge to the bank we commenced a very brisk fire and almost killed every man at their guns in half an hour, which guns fell into our hands, and the firing ceased immediately.
>
> (C) They [the 7th and 53rd] delivered such a fire, that in a few minutes the enemy melted away, leaving six pieces of cannon behind, which they had not had time to discharge. The six pieces were immediately rendered unfit for use, as our balls were too large for their bore.
>
> (GB) In this charge, we passed at first the outermost of the two enclosures in front of the work, and in retreat of the enemy they left a brigade of ten guns and some tumbrels of musket ammunition. The brigade then lined the ditches of the enclosures, and thus formed a flanking fire on the column that

attacked our line more to the left [the 40th], by which means the Nassau regiment suffered severely.

Campbell's brigade had been augmented by the 2/24th, sent up on their left from Mackenzie in rear, between them and the Guards. The 24th's regimental history states: 'General Campbell's division was hard pressed by this tremendous attack. General Mackenzie's Brigade (or part of it) was ordered to support General Campbell's division, and the distance being short, the 24th was soon formed in line on the left of that division, and opened an independent fire on a French column, which was in the act of deploying into line. This column was so cut up that it soon retired.'

The canister shot scything forward from the muzzles of ten guns on the Pajar like giant shotgun blasts, at a range of only sixty paces to the bank in front, was quite unanswerable. No infantry in the world could go forward into such a blizzard of lead from guns emplaced every eight paces. The Baden regiment lost its commander, Colonel von Porbeck, and many soldiers, and, understandably, was the first to break. It may well be that Sergeant Cooper misremembered the point of Colonel Myers' seizing the Colour – not so much to rally his young and possibly shy soldiers, as to take advantage of the Baden's disorder caused by the canister. (We must recall that Cooper's book was published sixty years after the battle, whereas the accounts by 'GB' and 'JC' were in letters written only four and fourteen days later respectively.)

So the 2/53rd and 2/7th both went forward, seeing off the Baden and Netherlands Regiments, and capturing the six guns which they spiked and left for the time being. Across to their right they saw the Hesse-Darmstadt and Frankfurt regiments watching; these ceased their firefight with Portago's Spanish battalions, and also began to fall back. Campbell allowed his pursuing battalions little freedom to chase after the enemy into the close country ahead of their line, and prudently returned to the Pajar, if rather in advance of his first position. Lieutenant Carss of the 2/53rd: 'Sir Arthur sent down to General Alexander Campbell commanding our brigade to say we were the bravest fellows in the world, and he had not words to express how highly he was pleased with our conduct.'

Leval's losses were heavy, but not incapacitating. Oman puts them at 600 or 700 in the three-quarter hour action, which would be about 15 per cent of his force. British losses were minimal (*see* below); but Leval was not yet finished. Showing admirable determination, he reformed around the base in his rear provided by the two battalions of Valence's 4th Polish Regiment, and around 4pm set off again to take the Pajar feature from Campbell. Across to his right the action had by this time become general, with Sebastiani's 4th Corps fully engaged with Sherbrooke. Leval was conscious of the wider need to tie down the right of the British line, of course; but his second attack was not pressed with any great fervour – certainly not enough to defeat Campbell. Like Marshal Victor earlier in the day, General Leval by now was pondering the apparently inexplicable power in two thin red lines – something neither had ever seen before.

Leval's second attempt mirrored his first. Lieutenant Carss: 'The enemy sent down a much larger body of infantry to engage us again and to retake their cannon which we had got over the bank. When they got within forty yards of this bank, which we took for a breastwork, we let fly at them... they gave way and left the ground almost covered with their killed and wounded.' Sergeant Cooper: 'Here they come again' said many voices: 'so they did, but we were ready and gave them such a warm reception that they speedily went to the right-about. As in their first attack they now left behind several pieces of cannon, which we secured as before. After these two attacks and sharp repulses we were not troubled with their company any more.'

Brigadier Campbell had brought up the rest of his 4th Division into the line: the 97th and the 2nd Battalion of Detachments. Their musketry and the artillery were supplemented by a textbook cavalry charge – by the Spanish. Just as the Hessians and Frankfurters began to waver for the second time in the face of British volleys, General Henestrosa's Regimiento del Rey came rapidly upon their flank, and set about the Germans with their sabres, to good effect. Two squares being eventually formed, however, the Spanish horse were then checked. To top off this remarkable success, which both surprised and delighted the cynical British, while harrying the German infantry the Spanish horsemen came upon yet another four guns en route to the front. The gunners being swiftly despatched, the pieces were dragged to the Pajar. Oman calculates that altogether Leval lost seventeen guns this day; it indicates how desperate he was to counter the canister fire coming from the redoubt that he should tow so many pieces forward by hand, after their horses had been killed or wounded.

In these two attacks Leval's division lost a quarter of its strength – 1,007 all ranks – including two regimental colonels killed. Campbell's division lost just 236 all ranks, of whom only thirty-three were killed. The casualty return (reproduced as Appendix III at the end of this book) shows that the 2/53rd got off relatively lightly, but the 2/7th much less so. The curious item is the 'Missing' figure of one lieutenant and twenty-one men from the 97th. Since this battalion was in reserve during Leval's first assault, and since his second seems to have been a straightforward and speedy failure, it is hard to imagine how this understrength unit (totalling 502 in the morning state of 25 July) had any opportunity to mislay so many. Since the conduct of the 97th was singled out by Brigadier Campbell, together with that of the 7th and 53rd, and given special mention in his Talavera Despatch by Sir Arthur, no unworthy thoughts presumably need arise about any imagined reluctance of Germans to fight Germans. (The 97th had been raised as the Minorca Regiment in 1798, later being taken into the British line as the Queen's Own Germans; but by 1809 British recruiting had diluted its national character, and from the following year it would no longer be considered a foreign corps.) Wellesley's Despatch makes a point of congratulating Alexander Campbell on 'the manner in which this part of the position was defended'. He would have in mind the control exercised by Campbell over the duration of the charge following the retreat of the Germans and Dutch – control which was noticeably and nearly fatally absent in the case of his neighbour General Sherbrooke.

*　　*　　*

With the temperature well over 100°F and the sun right overhead, some 15,000 sweating soldiers in blue coats were lined up against 8,000 in red on either side of the stagnant trickle of the Portina. Sebastiani's force not only had its own twenty-four field guns, but the support of nearly the same again up on the Cascajal, which could bring enfilade fire down from his right flank. The thin British line facing him comprised, at the north, the four weakened King's German Legion battalions of Low and Langwerth's brigades, who the previous day had lost 262 men; then on their right, Cameron's brigade of the 1/61st and 2/83rd; and then Henry Campbell's brigade of the 1/2nd (Coldstream) and 1/3rd Guards. Beyond them, of course, around the Pajar, there already raged the battle between Leval and Alexander Campbell. Behind the Guards in second line was Major-General Mackenzie's brigade of the 2/31st and 1/45th. The 2/24th, as we have seen, had earlier been moved forward into the first line on the left of Alexander Campbell. His other brigade, the Irishmen commanded by Colonel Donkin, were up on the slope of the Medellin and partly in rear of Low.

Thus there was no infantry second line behind Langwerth or Cameron. The gap was filled to some degree by Cotton's two dragoon regiments; but the fact remained that across more than half a mile of front the British infantry line was only two men deep. Indeed, since (as we have seen) Alexander Campbell had deployed the reserve battalions of Colonel Kemmis' brigade into his front position adjacent to the Pajar in time for Leval's second assault, it would really be simpler to say that Sir Arthur had a second line only where Mackenzie's two battalions stood behind the Guards, and part of Donkin's brigade behind Low's northernmost Germans.

Up on the summit of the Medellin, Sir Arthur and his staff looked down at this emaciated line, and out across the Portina to the twelve advancing columns, drums beating, each of them a battalion of 500 or 600 fresh men. 'The staff at this time wore very long faces. The enemy's shot were flying in all directions' (Lieutenant Edward Close, 1/48th). Lifting their telescopes, they peered through the rising dust clouds to take in the sobering spectacle of yet another twelve columns behind the first; and behind them again, now scarcely visible, the menace of 7,000 horsemen, like vultures circling before the kill. 'To those who, elevated as we were, saw every movement, this was the most anxious moment of the whole battle. Heavy columns of French infantry seemed following in succession to press upon the weakest part of the line; nor did it appear... the centre could successfully resist this overwhelming force' (Leith Hay of the 29th). The French columns were spaced so that there was room to deploy into line. The first mass comprised four regiments each of three battalions, from their right to left Lapisse's 16e Léger and 45e Ligne, then Sebastiani's 28e and 58e Ligne. The second wave of columns, some 500 yards behind, comprised Lapisse's 8e and 54e Ligne, then Sebastiani's 32e and 75e Ligne – twenty-four columns in all.

They advanced from the vineyards and olive trees on to the open plain, led across the short-cropped arable by their skirmishers, who soon crossed the Portina. The French artillery lifted, to the delight of the patient British line. With Leval engaging Campbell on the left, the French now had all of thirty-three battalions in imminent action. The British light troops were easily forced back and, with the ground now clear, the batteries in front of Cameron and Langwerth at last opened with round-shot, explosive shell, and finally with canister as the range shortened. Lieutenant-General Sherbrooke had ordered musket fire to be reserved to fifty paces, and to be followed immediately by the charge.

The French made no attempt to deploy into line, but arrogantly kept on coming, to beat of drum. These were veterans of the Grande Armée who had served in the campaigns of 1805–07, and who were therefore justifiably self-confident; the battle honours of Ulm, Austerlitz, Jena, Friedland, Eylau and Wagram were embroidered on most of their Eagle banners, and three had also fought at Essling. Yet only two of the nine regiments had battalions who had fought the British before, at Vimiero: the 2/32e had been in Charlot's brigade before Vimiero Hill, and the 3/58e had been with Solignac's on the eastern ridge. One has to comment that two out of thirty-three battalions with prior experience of the red line was an inadequate basis for any radical rethinking of tactics. While the penny may have dropped for a few, for the many what awaited them on the Portina line was to come as a rude shock.

There were some 6,000 muskets trained on these French columns, and all could bear at once. Only their front three ranks, however, could return the compliment, say 1,100 weapons, and those unsteady as the chests of the men who held them heaved from the exertion of a sweltering march. With some 7,000 of their muskets masked in the middle of the crowded columns and effectively unusable, it was no contest despite the huge French advantage in mere numbers. General Chambray's account written in 1824 is vividly clear:

> The French charged with shouldered arms as was their custom. When they arrived at short range, and the English line remained motionless, some hesitation was seen in the march. The officers and NCOs shouted at the soldiers, 'Forward – march – don't fire'. Some even cried, 'They're surrendering'. The forward movement was therefore resumed; but it was not until extremely close range of the English line that the latter started a two-rank fire which carried destruction into the heart of the French line, stopped its movement, and produced some disorder. While the officers shouted to the soldiers 'Forward – Don't open fire' (although firing set in nevertheless), the English suddenly stopped their own fire and charged with the bayonet. Everything was favourable to them; orderliness, impetus, and the resolution to fight with the bayonet. Among the French, on the other hand, there was no longer impetus, but disorder and the surprise caused by the enemy's unexpected resolve: flight was inevitable.

We have already seen how General Mackenzie had moved the 2/24th to assist Alexander Campbell; with great prescience he now moved them left again, according to their regimental history sending a staff officer with 'orders for the battalion to support the Guards. The battalion was faced to the left, and moved off in as quick a run as the men were capable of. It did not move over the same ground, but ran along in the direction of the front line. The left hand had only just come upon the right of the brigade of Guards when the latter charged the enemy, and the 24th instantly took up the ground vacated by the Coldstreamers.'

For the Guards had disobeyed Sherbrooke's orders, choosing to charge without the preliminary volley: 'On their approaching within two hundred yards we were ordered to advance without firing a shot and afterwards to charge, this we did as became British officers' (Ensign John Aitchison, in a letter three days later). And, several weeks later: 'In the centre where at last the enemy made his grand push, we charged when he was within 100 yards, and our fire was reserved until they were flying.' The anonymous sergeant of the Coldstream wrote, 'Instead of waiting to receive them, our centre advanced upon them with a cheer, which struck them with a panic, they faced about, and received two volleys whilst retiring in confusion.'

This characteristic rejection of the norm by Household troops, and their typical substitution of what they saw as a higher standard of behaviour ('You may need to fire a volley at the French first, but we don't'), persuaded the 58e Ligne not to stop and argue. Neither did their neighbours, as the 61st, the 83rd and the four Legion battalions all opened fire and then surged forward. The front three ranks of the other French columns (the 58e not being fired upon by the Guards) were down in the corn, staggering back or still, and chaos also prevailed down the sides of these columns. Attempts here and there to deploy into line failed, for they were left too late, and the men shrank from leaving their columns with the charging British so clearly serious behind their bayonets. Captain FitzClarence writes: 'When the enemy came within about fifty yards of the Guards, they advanced to meet them, but on attempting to close the enemy by a charge, [the French] broke and fled.' So to the right-about the nine headless French battalions went, even those three opposite the Guards who were still intact, withdrawing as quick as may be towards the supporting twelve battalions in the second wave, through whose ranks a quarter-mile in rear they showed every sign of wishing to pass.

Brigadier Cameron halted the 1/61st and 2/83rd just beyond the Portina, so the 28e Ligne opposite them were able to fall back without too much harassment; the Guards and Germans, however, did not halt at all. On they scampered, 200, 300, 400, 500 yards, shooting and bayoneting, looting the discarded knapsacks for food – and at every yard they were becoming smaller groups and mere individuals, no longer a line: more than 4,000 redcoats spaced out, and out of control. As Leith Hay comments, 'Who has ever seen an unbroken line preserved in following up a successful bayonet charge?' Captain FitzClarence again: 'The flying enemy led [the Guards] on till they opened a battery on their flank, which occasioned so heavy a loss, that the ranks could not be formed after the disorder of the pursuit and, on being ordered to resume their ground, produced confusion.' Viewed from behind French gunsights on the Cascajal to the north, those hundreds of yards of arable land presented – once the moving colour had mainly changed from blue to red – a target for canister and short-fused shell. Viewed from the south, from the saddles of the dragoon regiments of General Latour-Maubourg, the scattered guardsmen presented an equally tempting target for heavy swords – and one which two of his regiments could not resist.

Thus gradually, as the British impetus evaporated in the face of the fresh French troops, the tide turned. The survivors of the 16e Léger, 45e, 28e and 58e Ligne reformed once they reached the protection of the second wave of columns. All the Cascajal guns which could do so switched targets left and took the Legion and Guards battalions in flank; the French dragoons played merry hell with the Guards, and back they came, harried and hustled. Lapisse and Sebastiani were quick to see the two huge gaps that had opened in the British line. Cameron's brigade having remained on the Portina, a wide empty space had also opened in the centre, between the Germans and the Guards, and into this the French 32e now poured, unopposed.

As Beamish writes rather sourly in his *History of the Legion*: 'The Guards had inconsiderately quitted the line and passed beyond the German brigade... the French swarmed in the centre of the position.' The Legion battalions had even got part way up the Cascajal, and 155 of the German soldiers would stay on it, cut off, try as they might try to regain the Portina. Beamish: 'The fire of the second line opening upon them, and being also exposed to a murderous discharge of grape, the Legion Brigade was ordered to retire, and it fell back with little disorder [!], leaving General von Langwerth among the slain.' Captain FitzClarence again: 'The enemy instantly rallied and followed [the Guards] and were so confident of victory, that their officers were heard to exclaim "*Alons, mes enfants, ils sont tout nos prisonniers.*"' So hard did the French press on British heels that Cameron's 1/61st and 2/83rd were swept up in the movement, back once more over the stream. Of the Germans, Major Edward Cocks of the 16th Light Dragoons reported that: 'the whole of their infantry ran fairly away. Poor Langwerth seized the Colours and, planting them, called to the men to form. He was killed in attempting to rally them. Colonel Derenham was equally unsuccessful. He got 40 or 50 round the Colours but the instant he went to collect others these set up [set off].'

In those ghastly twenty minutes the 1st Line Battalion KGL lost 291 men; the 2nd, 387 (half its strength) including twenty-four taken; the 5th more than 255, with over 100 taken; and the 7th got off with a loss of only 110, half of whom were captured. The total Legion losses were 1,043, including 39 of its 107 fighting officers. Brigadier-General Langwerth was killed, and his brigade's bayonet strength was halved from 1,300 to just 650; Low's 5th and 7th Battalions were reduced to 600 between them. The casualty rate for the Legion overall was 46 per cent – almost every second man, and a terrible price to pay for their over-keeness.

It was a frightful change of fortune, and Sir Arthur was faced with sudden disaster in the northern part of his centre. The German Legion was effectively broken, with more than a third of its officers gone. In his centre, Cameron's prudent pursuit saw him propelled back with fewer losses, but by the end of the action his brigade would be down to two-thirds of its starting numbers; while to the south, the routed Guards lost over 600 men – a casualty rate of 31 per cent: 'We faced about, retired to the ravine, slower and in better order than we advanced. Here we made a stand and did considerable execution' (Ensign Aitchison). Which sounds well enough, but not for long, for they were then pushed back again. The 2/24th having been appointed the firm base for the Coldstream, according to their history they 'wheeled back by companies, to allow the retreating Coldstreamers to pass through, and then formed line'.

This was the potential tipping point in the day: something like 20,000 French were coming after 2,800 very shaken British. If they could penetrate either the Guards or the KGL, there was space to turn sideways and roll up the remainder; and behind the second wave of 8,000 men there were also the now reforming 5,000 or so survivors of the first wave. And 7,000 sabres were waiting to exploit on to the plain behind the Portina. It really should have been all over bar the shouting.

From the Medellin, Sir Arthur had watched the initial assault develop, their repulse, the advance of his line, Cameron's control, but the obvious lack of any on his flanks. The further the Legion and the Guards rushed forward beyond any sensible limit, the clearer he saw the outcome. It is certain – and here we have evidence of his supreme military competence – that Wellesley at the earliest stage gave one of the two orders that were to save the day. In his Talavera Despatch he reported that 'as soon as I observed the advance of the Guards' he had ordered the 1/48th 'from its position on the heights... and it was formed on the plain, and advanced upon the enemy.'

Actually, it is improbable that he would shift his strongest battalion from the summit of his vital ground without grave necessity; that need would not have been established merely by the advance of a brigade from its fighting line, but rather by that advance becoming more and more excessive. How Sir Arthur must have cursed their enthusiasm, while he waited to decide if the 48th must go down. However, send the 48th he did, and in remarkably good time, for they had to cover all of 900 paces. The battalion, says their Lieutenant Close, were on 'the top of the hill... in open column at quarter distance'. A letter to the *Star* a month later states that 'Sir Arthur called to one of his staff "Where is the 48th? Send the 48th to bring them out"'; but according to both Leith Hay and Leslie of the 29th (the 48th's neighbours on the summit, and surely here sucking sour grapes), in the first instance he 'directed the 29th to go down; and the regiment was in the act of moving, when, considering probably its weakness in numbers, he ordered the 48th to proceed' instead, all 700-plus bayonets.

The other vital decision had already been made, by Major-General Mackenzie, in the second line with his brigade of the 2/31st and 1/45th. He had watched to his front his fellow brigade commander Henry Campbell set off into the smoke with his two battalions of Guards, and had already sent to the 24th – earlier ordered to assist Alexander Campbell – now to get next to the Coldstream. To his half-right he was also watching Campbell's battle with Leval's Germans. This was in full swing around the Pajar, and Mackenzie was therefore concerned that should Leval make progress, then, with the Guards absent and only the 2/24th as substitute, Campbell's battalions would have an open flank. To close that, he now advanced the rest of his brigade to the line the Guards had quit. This decision was crucial to what was to follow.

Mackenzie was to die in the next few minutes. After the battle, since no report was sent from his brigade to Sir Arthur, the Talavera Despatch omitted any fair mention of the role his brigade played. Sir Charles Oman set the record straight for posterity, but it is sad that Mackenzie's 24th, 31st and 45th were not lauded at the time, except by those who were present and saw what they had done.

* * *

The various scenarios of the battle becoming intermingled in time, it is probably sensible at this point to try to summarize the position. There are five concurrent actions; from Sir Arthur's right of the line to his left, they are: (1) Leval being harassed backwards, after the awesome musketry of Alexander Campbell's six battalions (including Mackenzie's 24th), by the Spanish del Rey cavalry regiment; (2) Mackenzie moving forward on Campbell's left, into the gap left by the Guards; (3) the 1/48th doubling down the Medellin into the gap somewhere behind the Germans; (4) Stewart, Tilson and Donkin – and Wellesley himself – under continuing French shellfire behind the crest; and (5) the first stirrings of a new and potentially terminal threat – some fifteen French battalions edging forward on the north plain. Each of these actions was, for Sir Arthur, a moving ball in the air, to be juggled in relation to the others, all five spinning now and not to be dropped. For he was totally committed, with no reserves, no infantry second line whatsoever.

When the Guards over-pursued the 58e Ligne, they did so at a slight tangent to the north of east, veering left, like the Germans, towards the Cascajal; as Cameron did not go so far forwards, there was space on their left side. This slightly crab-like movement is shown quite clearly on the Talavera battle map in the 48th's *Regimental Digest of Service*, drawn by an officer of the 1st Battalion in 1816. This movement explains, as we shall see, what has hitherto been an historian's conflict of opinion concerning the 48th's contribution to the day. The anonymous Coldstream sergeant gives us confirmation, and a possible reason: 'our Brigade advanced in order to preserve the line entire, and *bringing up our right* threatened to cut off the retreat of their flying columns.'

So we have Mackenzie's two battalions coming up to join his 2/24th between (on his right) Alexander Campbell, and (on his left) Cameron's 83rd and 61st, which are about to be swept backwards. Mackenzie's battalions were from right to left the 2/24th, the 1/45th in his centre and the 2/31st next to Cameron. Disordered guardsmen fell back through their ranks, reforming in rear as best they could. Their 'spirit and appearance of good humour and determination after having lost in twenty minutes five hundred men', says Captain FitzClarence, 'was shown by their giving a loud hurrah as they took up their ground.' Major-General Cotton trotted forward his brigade of the 14th and 16th Light Dragoons, some 1,000 sabres, to cover the gap between Mackenzie's right flank and Alexander Campbell's left. 'After making our way through a grove of olives in some confusion, we gained the open ground, and had to form under an incessant fire of artillery and musketry; the small shot literally pouring in like a shower of hail' (Captain Hawker). One squadron, at least, went to support the 1/48th. Oman notes (without being specific) that: 'contemporary accounts by officers of the 2/24th speak of the Coldstream passing through them to re-form: the Scots Fusiliers (3rd Guards) therefore must have had the 2/31st and 1/45th behind them'. That is confirmed by the 48th's map, where the Coldstream are shown behind and to the right of the 3rd Guards.

Sebastiani's 32e and 75e Ligne of course had their tails up, and they pressed on with vigour and confidence. They had seen redcoats approaching them, but breaking up under shot, shell and cavalry attack into shapeless groups, hesitating on meeting the fresh French infantry, and turning to flee – just like the Austrians, Prussians, Russians and all the others. The French columns stepped out to beat of drum with all their old bombast. Mackenzie's three battalions numbered some 2,200 bayonets and the three battalion columns of the 75e Ligne had very much the same, but the substantially re-formed 58e were behind them in strength. We have no accounts of this clash of line versus column, but Oman avers it lasted twenty minutes. Such a firefight does not challenge in length and bloody annihilation that at Albuera two years later; but in theory it allowed some sixty volleys to be fired, and must have entailed much mutual destruction. It also stood evidence for Mackenzie's grim determination that none should pass.

The hovering 14th and 16th Light Dragoons ensured the safety of Mackenzie's flanks, until such time as the re-formed Guards could come up into line; and Captain Hawker of the 14th is a lone voice in mentioning two Spanish infantry battalions 'under General Whittingham, who came forward to support the Guards'. Otherwise, Mackenzie was on his own. It is curious, given the relative strengths, that the action continued so long; and curious also that the British appeared shy to charge. It may be that with the earlier experiences of the Guards so fresh in mind, some caution welled up. And it may well be that for once the French columns deployed into line, to allow a musket-versus-musket shoot-out on equal terms. We do not know; but we can be sure that bodies piled up on both sides.

Oman states that the Light Dragoons charged the 75e Ligne and cut down 150 men, but Hawker does not mention this, nor Cocks, whereas the French Colonel Desprez says that these were actually Spanish horsemen. We know that the Regimiento del Rey had earlier been active against Leval, no distance away. Since at this stage of the war the dress of Spanish soldiers was extremely varied and in a number of colours, misidentification was not unusual; in this case – since both the British light dragoons and the Regimiento del Rey wore dark blue jackets with basically red facings – it would have been plausible, despite the difference in headgear.

The butcher's bill among the British infantry was frightful – one man in every three. 'The gallant General Mackenzie, the man who did more than anyone towards our victory, is killed,' wrote Captain Cocks. Fifteen of his officers and over 600 men fell killed or wounded, and over half belonged to the 2/24th on the right. Their history states that after the Coldstream retreated through them, and they checked the advancing French, 'the fire of round shot, grape and musketry had in a short space of half an hour almost annihilated the battalion, and when the Coldstream returned to their former ground, the 24th had only one rank to show front, and even in that there were long gaps.'

But with General Mackenzie's death, we can for the moment pause our narrative of his action on the right centre. We must look also at that action concurrent on the left centre, fought by the 1/48th.

*   *   *

Descending the hill at the double, it took the 1/48th five minutes or more to get behind the position which Langwerth had held, to the left of where the 2/83rd had been. The distance was some 900 paces – nine football pitches end to end – which can be marched in ten minutes, and double-marched in half that, at what we would call today a jogging pace. They got there just as the over-enthusiastic German advance was driven back to the Portina with Lapisse's 8e and 54e Ligne hard on its heels. 'Two columns were advancing with rapid stride, following the broken troops,' wrote Lieutenant Close of the 1/48th. His anonymous brother officer, already quoted, recalled: 'We came on double-quick and formed in rear by companies, and through the intervals in our line the broken ranks of the Guards retreated.' Captain James Wilson, also 1/48th: 'Our regiment immediately advanced alone in the most gallant manner and prevented the French columns crossing the ravine.' Napier – who was not a witness – describes how the 48th 'wheeling back by companies... let [the Guards] pass through the intervals, and then regaining its proud and beautiful line, marched against the right of the pursuing columns'. The 2/83rd had clearly not yet sorted themselves out to the right, nor the Germans to their left. Lieutenant Close again:

> We fired a volley and ported arms. We advanced, and fired another volley... for a considerable time we had the fight entirely to ourselves, not a single regiment was near us. A very destructive fire was opened on us at this time from their guns. All the shot and shell was directed at us. A squadron of Dragoons came to our aid at this juncture. They were no sooner perceived than all the artillery was levelled at them, and they were obliged to retire from the shower; but, before they did so, our men fell fast from the shot directed at them... When Ensign Vander Meulen was wounded, I went to take the colour from the Sergeant who held it. When I arrived at the centre a shell fell. We lay down till it had burst. My head was between the legs of a soldier, and a soldier was on my right and left side close against me. The shell burst; the man whose legs my head was protected by had half his head carried off; the other two were dreadfully mangled: the body of one was laid bare from his loins to his breast, and both the legs of the other were carried off near the knee. We were ordered to shorten our front by doubling our right wing in front of our left... the aspect of things at this period was somewhat disheartening. The right wing suffered very much, nearly half the Grenadier Company were hors de combat.

Captain James Wilson, commanding that Grenadier Company, wrote:

> I lost a great number of my Grenadiers. I went into action with sixty men and three subalterns and came out with ten... I was constantly in front of my Grenadiers, encouraging them to be firm and steady, and they were so indeed. I would not allow them to stoop when a shot or shell came and one man said there was no use in ducking, when immediately a shell burst among the

Company and I asked who it was blown up. They said Mitchell, the man who had just spoken.

Close again: 'Colonel Donellan having been wounded when we were on the point of advancing the first time, Major Middlemore took the command.' It is said that when he was struck (he died four days later) the colonel sent for his senior major and, seated erect in the saddle, took off his old tricorne hat, bowed and said 'Major Middlemore, you will have the honour of leading the 48th to the charge.'

So it would seem that the 1/48th, having put themselves across the front of the French and stopped Lapisse's infantry, were then subjected more to artillery fire from the Cascajal on their left than to musketry from their front. For the French gunners to do that, there must have been no blue-coated infantry too close to the front of the 48th; and the presence of British dragoons was a deterrent. At some point after the artillery chased the squadron away and the cannon fire slackened, the French infantry advanced again. Then came Major Middlemore's moment of glory, for as Close writes: 'under his command our charges were made. They would not stand our charge... the French eventually retreated close under their guns.' In the words of his anonymous brother officer: 'As the enemy came on the men gave a loud huzza; an Irish regiment to the right [the 2/83rd] answered it with a thrilling cheer. It was taken up from regiment to regiment and passed along the whole British line. The leading files of the French halted, turned, and fled back and never made another effort.'

Here we have a reference to the 83rd in the line again, to the right of the 48th, which clearly positions the 48th in Langwerth's old KGL position. Historians have always been confused over this point, since there are various accounts (as we have seen) of the Guards retreating through the 48th – as, indeed, Wellesley implies in his Talavera Despatch – but none specifically of the Germans doing the same, which is curious. Equally, however, we know that guardsmen retreated through Mackenzie, a good half mile to the south. Historians have sought an either-or solution. But the 48th's battle map, showing the Guards angled left shoulder forward when chasing the 58e Ligne, strongly suggests that both are possible. That is, that having brought their right shoulder up, the Guards rather drifted across the battlefield, so that some of their companies would find their quickest route back via the 48th, and others via Mackenzie's battalions.

As to the King's German Legion, one suspects that Beamish felt able to downplay their disastrous retreat, since he took Napier as his guide in all things – thus, if Napier says that the 48th saved the Guards, while the Germans were merely 'sorely pressed', then evidently the Germans must not have needed saving... In fact, of course, their terrible losses suggest otherwise.

It is clear that Lapisse's second wave battalions did not press against the 48th too enthusiastically. Artillery played the greater role; yet even so, the 48th's 168 casualties (and some of those would have been suffered in the morning) were not excessive, if all six of Lapisse's second wave battalions – say 3,000 men – were determined to walk over them. Mackenzie's brigade lost four times the number to Sebastiani, from only three times the strength of the 48th. The 14th and 16th Light Dragoons between them lost only twenty-nine men during the entire battle, so the squadron that Lieutenant Close reports as assisting the 48th, and which brought such unwelcome artillery fire on their heads, can have suffered hardly at all. Captain Cocks of the 16th makes no mention of heavy gunfire against his troopers, although Captain Hawker of the 14th disagrees.

The French themselves wrote that a mortal wound to Lapisse was the last straw, before his division withdrew; others, that the retrograde movement by Sebastiani, hastened by the cavalry charge against his flank (Spanish or otherwise), was the catalyst for the general retirement. Needless to say, such was the utterly exhausted state of the British line that no pursuit was considered. The day's hazards had so far been fended off, on the right by Mackenzie's brigade, and on the left by the 1/48th. Had either given way, Sebastiani or Lapisse would surely have penetrated and, with no second line to check them, 7,000 cavalry must have cut into the British rear. Sir Arthur's own cavalry were by then, as we shall see, mostly deployed on the other side of the Medellin.

*   *   *

On the Medellin itself, it had been an afternoon of waiting under cannon fire, endlessly listening for the shell you would not hear; the battalions of Stewart, Tilson and Donkin had had no attack to repulse since the dawn attempt by Ruffin. That had been a long time ago now, with not much to think about in the meantime except your stomach: 'Dear Mother, we was in want of Victuals all the time for the two days as They could get nothing to us in that Part of the Country as the French Armies had eaten all up. Dear Mother on the third day they served us many ounces of unground Wheat to each Man...' (Private William Coles, Light Company, 2/48th). Back behind the crest, as the hours passed, the casualty numbers slowly crept up. Knowing the redcoats were there, but just out of sight, infuriated the French gunners – rather as, in earlier centuries, their forebears had had to watch British archers raising their two arrow fingers and jeering. To counter Wellesley's tactical device, therefore, the French came up with their own: the under-charged or ricochet shot.

While an airburst shell was a delight to see, and (if they could cut the fuses really accurately) entirely appropriate against a human target just out of sight, you could not beat a slowly rolling roundshot – rather like ten-pin bowling without being able to see the skittles – and certainly better than hammering away with a full charge only to see your shot bounce a couple of times, way beyond the red lines. Thomas Bunbury of the 1/3rd, in Tilson's brigade: 'We suffered greatly from the fire of the enemy's artillery. Our regiment lay rather under the crest of the hill, concealed from observation but, suspecting we were there, the French plied us with ricochet shot, fired with so small a charge of powder, that we could see the shot rolling along like a cricket ball, and the stranger might imagine that its progress could be stopped at pleasure.' Which, of course, was not the case however slowly the ball rolled, given the kinetic energy involved: many are the instances where men lost a leg by thoughtlessly or naively putting out a foot, to trap the roundshot as if it were a football. Bunbury of the Buffs continues:

> Our poor Colonel was spinning a yarn, seated within a circle of officers who were listening to him, when one of these shots struck outside the circle and bounding over the heads of those seated with their backs to it, struck the Colonel and carried away the lower part of his face. I had seen the ball coming, and had time with two or three others to get out of the way. Although nearly spent, the shot then struck the flank of the Light Company, and tumbled the men down like a pack of cards. Some of them were killed and several much hurt. The Colonel died the following day.

Captain FitzClarence, who as the Adjutant-General's ADC spent much of the day on the Medellin, had reason to remark that: 'The French had the most exact range of the height, and threw shot and shell upon it with terrible precision... Their fuses, however, often burst too quickly, exploding the shells high in the air and forming little clouds of smoke.' Which actually sounds like the right thing to do, and good gunnery; but with no Major Shrapnel on their side, such accuracy was probably under-rewarded – the simple fragmentation of a spherical shell case did far less slaughter than a load of musket balls packed round the bursting charge.

The casualty figures for the eight battalions on the Medellin cover both the dawn attack by Ruffin and the present shelling, and so cannot be separated. They are: Stewart's brigade, 503 all ranks; Tilson's, 336; and Donkin's, 145. The latter brigade's 88th, according to Grattan (though he was not present), did not fire a musket shot all afternoon. Since the Connaught Rangers were scarcely involved in the morning action either, it would seem that their eighty-five casualties must all have fallen to the French artillery. They and the 87th were more exposed than the battalions of Stewart and Tilson; but it is reasonable to suggest that of the 984 total casualties of all the battalions on the Medellin, perhaps half were from shot, ricochet shot and shell.

The afternoon cannonade was a great nuisance for Sir Arthur and his staff, necessarily on the summit to view the whole field, their heads and telescopes turning routinely from left to right, right to left, for hour after hour. For we must reiterate that the actions we have had to record here separately in fact occurred concurrently, all along the line (except for that sparked by Leval's arrival at the Pajar half an hour early). It has been argued that this was not so; however, we have Sir Arthur's Talavera Despatch (reproduced in Appendix VI), where he uses the phrase 'at the same time' to link the attacks on the Pajar by Leval, the attacks on the centre by Lapisse and Sebastiani, and the advance upon the north plain by Ruffin, and thus the ill-fated charge by the 23rd Dragoons. The latter action we now examine – as it were, from a saddle high on the Medellin, our attention torn between the a titanic infantry conflict to the right, and an unfolding cavalry disaster to the left.

*   *   *

At the foot of the Medellin's north slope, next to a dried-up ravine that in winter fed the rains across the north plain to the Portina, stood a small farmhouse called Valdefuentes. It was overlooked by half of Rettberg's battery of 6-pounders, and the two Spanish 12-pounders borrowed from Cuesta. It was also overlooked by Stewart's infantry brigade up on the Medellin; and more importantly, by the thousand horsemen of Anson's light cavalry – the 23rd Light Dragoons and the 1st Hussars, KGL – a few hundred yards in rear. Behind them, in turn, lay the same number of heavy dragoons (the 3rd and 4th Dragoons) under General Fane; behind them again, yet another 3,000 horse commanded by the Duke of Albuquerque. Over on the other side of the flat valley and opposite the farm, a whole division of Spanish infantry under Bassecourt held the near slopes of the towering Sierra de Segurilla.

Across this north plain, from the farm up to the Sierra, stood 7,000 French infantrymen, and 1,200 horse including a regiment of Polish lancers. Their approach march had been hesitant, since Generals Ruffin and Villatte had no great keenness for what they saw. If they turned left to climb the northern slopes of the Medellin, the allied cavalry would swoop down on their right flank; if they continued further down the plain they would surely come under fire from Hill's men on the Medellin, as well as from his cannon. They were lined up with Villatte's 27e Ligne next to the farmhouse, then Ruffin's 96e, then his 24e to the north but rather in rear, and finally his 9e Léger up on the slopes opposite Bassecourt's Spanish. The four French regiments each had three battalions; and Villatte's 63e Ligne was held in reserve next to the Cascajal.

Leith Hay, a spectator on the Medellin, commented: 'Their light troops skirmished closely and seriously… the right of the French army had a very imposing appearance… a serious effort was every moment to be expected. Sir Arthur crossed with rapid step from the right of the 29th to the part of the hill looking directly down upon General Anson's brigade of cavalry, which mounted on the instant' (orders by telepathy, it seems). Various accounts suggest that Wellesley did not turn his attention to the situation on the north plain until Lapisse's and Sebastiani's attacks on the centre were over; Ruffin and Villatte's hesitancy were therefore a godsend. It is likely that the noisy crescendo of artillery and musketry associated with the culminating climax of the battle to the south of the Medellin was the spur necessary to galvanize Ruffin and Villate to its north.

Off their columns marched, crossing the track from Talavera town north to Segurilla. Ahead of them the dried plain started to show a rising dust cloud as the British cavalry tightened girths, mounted up, dressed lines and closed files. The dust and the blue jackets of Anson's men seen through French telescopes were immediately enough to halt the columns, and regimental squares were formed, for the first time in the Peninsula. The 27e Ligne was some 1,500 strong, so – formed four rank deep – their square would be nearly a hundred yards long on each side. Those of the 24e and 96e were somewhat smaller.

The 23rd Light Dragoons – handsome in blue jackets with crimson facings, and bearskin crests topping their leather helmets – comprised four squadrons in two lines. The right hand squadron was commanded by Captain William Drake, with Captain James Allen on his left. Out front was their Colonel Seymour, and well ahead of him, on a grey, was the cavalry division's Assistant Adjutant-General, Colonel Sir John Elley of the Life Guards, sent by General Anson to set the two regiments on the right line. On the left and slightly to the rear of the 23rd were another 450 sabres of Anson's 1st Hussars KGL, their blue jackets set off by yellow-braided pelisses and scarlet busby bags. The brigade's front covered some 300yd, with each trooper's knees the regulation six inches from those of his flanker's.

When the order 'Draw swords!' was anticipated, each man's left hand shortened the curb rein and took a firm contact with the horse's mouth. Reaching over to his left to grasp the curved sabre, his right hand threaded through the sling loop on the hilt; when the order came, he drew the blade and rested it on his right shoulder. On 'Walk march!' the troopers jiggled their spurs – needlessly, since no troop horse was ever going to let itself be left behind, and each knew its place in the line. Dressing, dressing, keep your dressing by the centre, don't touch, look in and keep the line, walk, damn you – wait for it… Then 'Trot!', and some fool bounded forward and others followed, the line straggling and bending as those behind sought to catch up and those suddenly in advance sought to slow. The line steadied and regained its dressing. A cheer started up on the hill to the right, taken up by all the redcoats of General Stewart's brigade, and 'the encouraging shout', in Beamish's phrase 'met with a corresponding answer from the fearless horsemen who gallantly advanced upon the bayonets, the 23rd taking the large square that was in front of that regiment, while the Hussars moved upon the two smaller squares on the left.'

The cheering fired the spirit at just the right moment, for French cannon now sent shot and shell from the Cascajal; the trot extended, and the line naturally veered away from the explosions and their source, on the right of Captain Drake's squadron. 'After the first order to trot, no further word of command was made known to the squadron officers, but as soon as the leading squadrons of the 23rd came within range of the French artillery, the horses crowded to the left and began to canter. The Hussars were now galled by the enemy's riflemen [sic] from the mountain, and several from the serre-file [that is, packed ranks] of this regiment were killed and wounded.' The trot was now a general canter, the sabres at the 'Carry', and the order 'Gallop!' was overdue as the range to the French squares closed rapidly. The final command 'Charge!', when the sabres came down to the 'Engage', would signal acceleration to that shattering speed essential to disintegrate and smash over anything standing in the way. No square has ever been broken at the trot.

But it was not to be. Hidden in the valley's long grass, 100yd or so in front of the squares, lay a dried-up watercourse, or what Beamish (stealing from Napier) calls a hollow cleft: 'in front of the Hussars… it was from six to eight feet deep and from twelve to eighteen feet in breadth; while widening in front of the 23rd, it was more shallow.' Beamish's eyewitness von Decken makes a point of stressing that the cleft presented itself… just when the pace had been increased and the charge had commenced.' It is said that Colonel Elley's horse, presumably a quality mount, cleared the obstacle, whereupon he endeavoured to halt, turn and wave a warning. The 1st Hussars on the left, being slightly in rear of the 23rd, may well have seen this; but of course, at a fast canter the impetuous charge was unstoppable at such minimal notice. Whereas a lone horse may swerve away to avoid a sudden hazard, and its rider may stay on board so long as he anticipates the turn (and the present author speaks with much experience to the contrary), troop horses cannot swerve, being jammed together. A ditch of such dimensions in the hunting field is too wide to cat-jump from the halt. It needs impetus (which the 23rd had), but also a visual measuring of the take-off stride and the height required for clearance of the far side (which the 23rd lacked).

As the ditch appeared out of nowhere, some horses nearly stopped on the brink, tipping their riders over the top; some jumped neatly into the gully and then could not get out; some rammed into the far face, horse and man both head first; loose horses ran in all directions, and so too dismounted troopers, those without broken limbs and necks. And then the second line was upon the scene, madly hauling on the reins and adding to the utter chaos, amidst whirling dust clouds and – to cap it all – volleys from the square of the 27e Ligne.

Leith Hay observed: 'The enemy, formed in squares, opened his tremendous fire. Horses rolled on the earth; others were seen flying back dragging their unhorsed riders with them; the German Hussars coolly reined up; the line of the 23rd was broken.' Captain FitzClarence, who surprisingly discounted the very existence of the ravine, put it all down to the French musketry: 'On arriving within firing distance, [they] received a well-directed volley. It stopped them in their career – while the country was instantly covered with horses galloping back without riders, and men struggling to the rear without horses.' One can imagine the delighted surprise of the French at seeing the 23rd suddenly disappear into the ground – or is it possible that they knew the old watercourse was there?

The 23rd could scarcely be blamed, when within musket shot of the enemy square, for moving at best speed preparatory to the final charge; but at speed no massed body of horse could cope with such an obstacle. Fortescue makes a fair point, that patches of rushes among grass always indicate the presence of watercourses of some sort, and that the 'instinct of caution' should have been triggered. But caution, rightly, was not a word known to many cavalry officers, and we may dispute his verdict that this was a 'mad exploit'.

The charge had lost all momentum; many of the second line were still trying to find a way through the loose horses, and an easy crossing point. The French volleys were ripping across the 100yd gap. Colonel Seymour, helped by Major Ponsonby, and Colonel Arentschildt of the 1st Hussars, shouted and waved and brought some order to the jumbled horses, and turned a new line to face the squares once again. The KGL Hussars put in the spurs and rode into a volley from the 24e Ligne. Beamish again: 'The Hussars... rear squadrons crossing the ravine more cautiously on seeing the fate of the front... few of them arrived at the bayonets... no impression was made upon the square.' The 23rd's left division failed likewise against the 27e, repulsed through lack of momentum and close range musketry.

The 1st Hussars and half the 23rd retired back across the watercourse; but Captains Drake and Allen, together with Colonel Elley on his grey, who were more to the right, skirted between the 27e's square and the farmhouse. On breaking through this gap, and the inevitable volley from the square's side ranks, they were confronted by Merlin's 10e and 26e Chasseurs, with the Polish Vistula Lancers and the Westphalian Light Horse behind – a mere 1,200 riders. Nothing daunted, Elley, Drake and Allen (it is unclear if Colonel Seymour had got this far) charged on, leading what Elley reckoned were 160 troopers. A somewhat understated sentence was written in 1829 by Major Ponsonby: 'the right squadron under Captain Drake, having an easier passage of the ravine, and no French column immediately in front, passed through the intervals, and caused much confusion.' Colonel Elley gives a rather clearer summary of the episode in a letter to his sister: 'The charge of the cavalry was led by your humble servant, at the head of two squadrons of the 23rd Light Dragoons, and so desperate was the undertaking, out of the two squadrons, consisting of about 160 men, all were either killed or wounded, with the exception of myself and six or seven dragoons.'

As the 23rd, by now at a decent speed, careered past the 27e Ligne's square (and in the process bundled over General Villatte and his brigadier, Cassagne, but without stopping to capture them), the French 10e Chasseurs adroitly moved to one side at the last moment. Their brigadier, Strolz, then closed them behind the British squadrons, who were by then confronting his second line, the Westphalians. So Elley and his followers, with some 160 troopers, were surrounded by 1,000 sabres, with the inevitable result: after a gallant and very bloody struggle, three officers, seven sergeants and ninety-eight rank and file were taken after fighting bravely until overwhelmed. Lieutenants John King and William Power were killed; Captains Drake and Allen were both wounded and taken, so too was Lieutenant Francis Anderson. Colonel Elley escaped unharmed; with him were Captain Lord William Russell (later ADC to Wellington) with a 'slight wound' – a deep cut to the shoulder. Captains Thomas Howard and James Franklin, severely wounded, and Cornet James Dodwell, slightly, are also listed on the casualty return (our Appendix IV), but their squadrons are not known. The total casualties for the 23rd Light Dragoons were seventy horses killed, twenty-five wounded and 129 taken; two officers and forty-seven men killed, four and forty-six wounded, and three and 105 taken: a total of 224 horses and 207 men, out of 459 shown as fit for duty on the morning state of 25 July (the nearest we can get) – that is, half the regiment gone, one way or the other.

When Wellesley launched the two regiments he would not seriously have expected Anson to overrun and break the French columns. In the main, cavalry were loosed at already broken infantry, fleeing and unformed (like the 20th at Vimiero). When formed, a line or column challenged by cavalry merely redeployed into square, and cavalry alone cannot break squares. (Not when they are formed by stout troops on a fine day, that is, although who is to say what might happen if the infantry lacks stomach or dry powder – Ruffin's 9e Léger, perhaps; but they had sensibly been put out of the way for this assault.) While Sir Arthur may have been encouraged to chance his cavalry's arm by apparent French shyness in the valley, what must have been in his mind was the ability of cavalry to force an enemy to form square – for squares normally remain static, and do not unform while still threatened. Sir Arthur's heart must have sunk when he saw Elley and the two squadrons disappear into the green mass of French and Westphalian cavalry, and not reappear; yet his purpose was achieved.

The French were now free to continue their advance on the Medellin; but they did not. Two things stopped them, of which the first was undoubtedly the 23rd Light Dragoons, who had demonstrated Sir Arthur's intent, while their telescopes showed the French generals that there were plenty more where they came from. Captain FitzClarence: 'Though this desperate charge cost the 23rd two-thirds of its men and horses, it had the effect of astounding the enemy who, seeing not only the 1st Germans and the 3rd and 4th Dragoons prepared for a similar act, but the Spanish cavalry moving into the valley in support, and their efforts unsuccessful elsewhere... gave up all further idea of penetrating in that quarter.' The second cause of their reluctance was, as FitzClarence implies, that they had by then heard of Lapisse's and Sebastiani's failure to breach the British centre. So, as Major Ponsonby says: 'the delay caused by the charge prevented the masses of infantry, which were in readiness on the French right flank, from joining the general attack on our line.' The 23rd had bought time.

Remarkably similar sentiments were expressed by the 29th Foot's Charles Leslie, who wrote in his journal that: 'this desperate charge and brave conduct in our dragoons so astonished the enemy, that seeing our other corps of light cavalry also formed ready to advance in the similar manner, they brought their columns to a stand, and no further attempts were made to gain possession of the hill.'

*   *   *

The furious frustration of Marshal Victor may be imagined: three times his efforts against the Medellin had failed, and the damnable British were still there. He urged Joseph to commit his reserves – the 5,000 men of Desolle's brigade and his own Guards, and Villatte's two unused brigades on the Cascajal – for yet a fourth attempt. The King needed time to ponder, and in the meantime had the reserve moved forward. Perhaps Victor was right, and one final push would break the resolve of the British; perhaps Soult was nearer than the last intelligence suggested. But what of the Spanish? The whole battle had been between himself and Wellesley what if Cuesta's 25,000 Spanish troops were actually close to exerting themselves at last?

Exactly on cue came a report from General Milhaud's 2nd Dragoon Division, to the effect that the Spanish in front of him, whom he had watched throughout a long, boring day, were at last showing signs of forward movement among the parched olive groves. King Joseph had already heard of one active Spanish regiment of cavalry – del Rey, which had sallied forth on the British right flank next to the Pajar; their useful charge was a precedent to bear in mind, given this new report. The hazard was that if he agreed to Victor's demand for yet another assault, using up his final reserve, then the Spanish, after hours of supine inactivity, could hurl themselves at his left flank. Whatever he thought of Cuesta's qualities as a general, the sheer number of his troops would surely be decisive in such a situation; despite the limitations of their officers and training, Joseph was well aware that Spanish troops were capable of extraordinary courage in unsophisticated frontal assaults. Milhaud's and Latour-Mauberg's 5,000 horsemen alone would not be sufficient to stop a general attack. Far better, advised Marshal Jourdan, to deny Victor and get back behind the Alberche; and his king agreed.

One does not envy Colonel Desprez, bearing such unwelcome orders to Victor on the back slope of the Cascajal; indeed, imagination is inadequate to picture the marshal's reaction. Victor, one of the heroes of Marengo, veteran of twelve major battles since he became a general, was being denied a fourth attempt to capture this little hill in Spain. Not surprisingly, he refused to join in the general withdrawal; he sat where he was on the Cascajal (and was to remain there until well past midnight, when cold reality overcame his pride).

Jourdan and Joseph were certainly right to be prudent at that late hour in the day. It was now twenty-four hours since their army had closed on Wellesley's line, and last light would soon be coming down again. Their army was exhausted, more than decimated, and bereft of ideas. The wounded and dead lay thick over the two-mile field: 13,000 or thereabouts, of whom over half were French – Oman's figures are 761 dead, 6,301 wounded and 206 missing. The casualty reports coming in to Joseph's headquarters weighed heavily on his decisions, and across the Portina, those being reported to Wellesley ensured that there was to be no question of pursuit. There the wounded lay thickest before the Germans, the Guards, the 24th, and on the north plain.

Fresh suffering was now to afflict those unable to move. Captain FitzClarence: 'The ripe corn and dry grass took fire from the cartridges and wadding, and hundreds of acres were rapidly consumed, involving in their conflagration the more seriously wounded and helpless, adding a new and horrid character to the misery of war.' William Lawrence of the 40th was similarly appalled: 'A very dreadful occurrence happened after the battle, for the long dry grass in which many of the wounded were lying caught fire, and many were scorched to death before assistance could be brought to convey them to hospital in Talavera.' The 24th's history: 'Some of the men who were severely wounded while the battalion was moving in double-quick time, from the left of General Cameron's division to the right of the Guards, were burnt to death by the flames from the long dry grass, set on fire by the shells. The men who went out to save their unfortunate comrades were forced back with their clothes burnt, and their pouches blown up on their backs.' In front of the Guards, 'lines of running fire half a mile in length were frequent and fatal to many a soldier, some by their pouches blowing up in passing the fire… thus perished many' (the anonymous Coldstream sergeant).

So the urgent work of moving the wounded began, as the cruel lines of flame flickered and smoked over the field; but soon daylight faded, and little could be achieved by torchlight. Since the French 1st Corps remained with Victor on the Cascajal, and Sebastiani's 4th were not pulled back very far from the field, it was unclear to Wellesley what Joseph proposed for the morning. Ironically, it was Victor, rousing himself from his mood of furious denial, who spurred the stalled French into activity, having heard and believed a report that the British were making a quiet move around his right flank. When he finally left the field at around 3am, denuding the Cascajal of troops, he condescended to let Joseph know his decision; thereupon Sebastiani, observing the movement to the rear, conformed on it. With both his corps underway, King Joseph himself crossed the Alberche, his whole army halting at dawn around Cazalegas. The battle of Talavera was now over, in the immediate fighting sense. For the battalions it was to continue, however, in succouring the wounded, disposing of the bodies, getting food to the famished soldiers – and for their commander-in-chief, in avoiding being caught by 50,000 fresh French soldiers coming up behind.

Before moving to these aspects of the story, and while the fighting is clear in the mind, there are comments to be made on certain aspects of this, the first large battle between Napoleon's generals and Sir Arthur Wellesley.

12
Assessments and Aftermath

IT is not difficult to see how close Wellesley came to losing this battle, for he made two mistakes. From the first – his disregard for the north plain – he was spared by the arrogance of the French; from the second – his reliance upon an inadequate staff – he was saved by the commonsense of his generals. A third he adroitly avoided – that of giving any active role to the Spanish, or indeed of relying upon them in any way (and nor would he in the future, until serious reforms had improved the reliability of their units). Of course the French, with their numerical superiority (disregarding Cuesta's army) and much stronger cavalry and artillery, should in any event have walked all over the pint-sized British force. They even enjoyed an enormous stroke of luck at the outset, at the Casa de Salinas on 27 July, where Lapisse's coup against Donkin's inattentive Irish battalions kept Wellesley with his rearguard, when he should have been back on his Talavera line organizing the defence.

As a result, there was confusion as to his plan for defending the Medellin. The Guards were not where they should have been (on the Medellin); the vital hill was not held by a double line, and those that were there (Hill's battalions and the Germans) wrongly thought that they were the second of those lines. We have remarked the lack of Sir Arthur's presence on the Medellin before and after darkness fell; we have seen the staff (perhaps Sherbrooke's) misdirect Low's brigade; we have seen Hill's division moved from bivouac apparently without his knowledge; and we have seen Mackenzie and Donkin forced to shift for themselves in the fading light – and thank heavens they did. It is not hard to suspect both that Sir Arthur's staff were on a steep learning curve at this early stage in the campaign, and also that he himself was taking too much on his own shoulders. The confusions of last light on 27 July were shameful. They very nearly let Ruffin take the vital ground, and had his 24e and 96e Ligne pressed on like the 9e Léger, he would have done. Victor would have pulled off a magnificent feat of audacity, entirely justifying that arrogance at which we British routinely sneer.

The key to Talavera was the north plain. Since Wellesley chose not to put troops there at the outset, an approach to the Medellin by this route was as valid an option as the direct one across the Portina chosen by Victor. Jourdan's hindsight suggestion was quite proper: that the dawn attack should have concentrated on a combination from both east and north. At the very least a noisy demonstration in the valley before first light would have ensured that Wellesley thinned his defence, to cover the eventuality. The greater mistake, of course, was Joseph's, for not exploiting

Wellesley's omission; but the fact remains that he was presented by Sir Arthur with a partly open back door. Even half a dozen regiments of cavalry, bursting out from behind the hill feature on to the southern plain in rear of the Spanish, would surely have opened a front door to Sebastiani. The potential for a great British disaster then needs no explanation – nor the political damage it would have done at home, and indeed throughout Europe.

Fortunately for the allies, there seemed to be little team coherence among the French commanders, and too much individual manoeuvring. Victor's repetitious attempts against the front of the Medellin drew Wellesley's attention to the uncovered flank; and Joseph's deliberate lack of support doomed the second of these attacks, at dawn on 28 July. Of course, Sir Arthur would be perfectly aware of the position on his left; but he obviously took the decision, on the 27th, that he could not extend himself further to include it in his plan. He took a chance, and got away with it. That dawn opportunity was what Victor missed – or rather Joseph, as overall commander.

Sir Arthur's absence during the early evening may well have been forced upon him. The Spanish panic shortly thereafter included, apparently, Cuesta's driver and escort, for the mule-drawn coach (presumably with the immobilized general aboard) is recorded by both Napier and FitzClarence as being seen among the fleeing rabble. Sir John Fortescue is in no doubt that 'on the evening of 27 July, the Spanish army was for a time without a commander.' That would not necessarily have put Wellesley in the Spanish driving seat, since we have gained the impression that he thought highly of General O'Donohu, Cuesta's chief of staff. But given Wellesley's natural powers of dominance, it seems certain that he stepped immediately into the breach, which offered him a marvellous chance to get his right flank disposed to his liking. The thought lingers, nonetheless, that this possible reason for his absence from his own line still looks a bit thin, in terms of proper priorities.

It is all very well for him to say in his battle Memorandum (*see* Appendix VI) that '… the left of the position in the first line, I had intended this part for the Guards; but I was unfortunately out, employed in bringing in General Mackenzie's advanced-guard, when the troops took their ground'. But when he and the advanced-guard came back, according to the 29th Foot's diarists, Hill's division was then only part way up the Medellin and not fully deployed. Yet Sir Arthur did not look to his own defences and compliance with his orders, but, it seems, busied himself instead with the Spanish; and was apparently still with them around 7pm when the great panic occured. One would think that an hour later his attention might have been caught by the belated arrival of the four missing battalions of tired Germans (around 8pm, according to Beamish); yet they were allowed to go to sleep under the impression that they were in the second line. And it is odd that Sir Arthur resisted that natural inclination of all field commanders as light fades: to have a last look around. So by any reckoning, his lengthy absence is a mystery, not least because it seems out of character.

On the broader view of his generalship, Sir Arthur Wellesley displayed all the cool competence we later come to expect from him, year in, year out. As at Vimiero, his use of ground was superlative – in rejecting the Alberche in favour of the Medellin, in allocating the Spanish in a way best suited to their capabilities, and in providing reverse slope protection for more than a third of his brigades. His use of cavalry to assist hard-pressed battalions whose flanks were open to enemy horse; his redeployment of Anson and Fane's dragoons to the north plain in good time, and his employment of them there; his amazing diplomatic success in persuading Cuesta to lend Bassecourt and Albuquerque for that same flank; his prescience in dispatching the 1/48th, and his constant visits (or sending of ADCs) down to the battalions with immediate commendations for their good conduct – all these were the marks of a skillful and forward-thinking commander.

His worst moments certainly included that which was to colour all future dealings with his Spanish allies: the panic flight of four completely unthreatened Spanish battalions 'not one hundred yards from where I was standing'. Despite the laconic tone of his reported comments, the timing of this incident was unfortunate for his composure. He would by then have been conscious that Victor was developing an imminent attack on the Medellin. Just when he needed to get to the left end of his line, the Spanish on the right were demonstrating their lack of reliability in the most dramatic fashion. Would the French swoop on the huge gap in the Spanish line before it could be plugged? Should he bring British cavalry down – or an infantry brigade in reserve – and which one? Where, anyway, was Cuesta?

Another of his worst moments must have been when he heard the sound of musketry at last light on his vital ground, when Ruffin's 9e Léger climbed the Medellin. Uncertainty over the extent of the French penetration, and the difficulty of controlling the counter-attack in fading light, must have caused him serious concern – darkness is a great multiplier of uncertainty.

Worst of all, however, must have been the sight, on the afternoon of the 28th, of the King's German Legion and Guards battalions careering uncontrollably onwards after Sebastiani's and Lapisse's retreating first wave. He could see what they could not: the second French wave. From his command post high on the Medellin, the central three-quarter-mile section of his line would then have looked sickeningly bare, apart from Cameron's two battalions. He watched Mackenzie go forward with the 2/31st and 1/45th to join his 2/24th, and plug one gap; he then sent for the 1/48th to plug the other. They did not let him down; but it could easily have gone disastrously wrong. It is no wonder that later, on one of his morale-boosting visits, he stopped by the 48th and said (according to Lieutenant Close), 'Forty-eighth, you are like a wall!'

The power of the volley, line against column, worked again, as it had done at Vimiero; but probably superior to that power was that of the bayonet. For it seems quite clear, given the earlier eyewitness accounts from Vimiero, that the battalions at Talavera were similarly imbued with a belief in Birmingham steel. Only four of Sir Arthur's battalions fought at both battles (1/29th, 1/40th, 1/45th and 97th), but at Talavera the other twenty showed identical skills in that department. The heart of infantry doctrine was to await in silence the near approach of the enemy until the last possible moment – or until he started to deploy into line; then to fire one or two devastating volleys and immediately, before the enemy could recover, rush in with lowered bayonets. It was, after all, the safest tactic: compare the 11 per cent casualties among Alexander Campbell's men, who volleyed and charged Leval away from the Pajar, with the 45 per cent among the 2/24th, further left, who had to stand and slog it out while the Guards regrouped. No wonder the British private soldier preferred cold steel (the sight of which commonly caused the French not only to run, but also to discard knapsacks, with their gratifying contents). Something of the attraction of a charge is caught in this piece by Sergeant James Anton, 42nd (not at Talavera):

> No movement in the field is made with greater confidence of success than that of the charge; it affords little time for thinking, while it creates a fearless excitement, and tends to give a fresh impulse to the blood of the advancing soldier, rouses his courage, strengthens every nerve, and drowns every fear of danger or of death; thus emboldened amidst shouts that anticipate victory, he rushes on and mingles with the fleeing foe.

One distinguishes, of course, between a bayonet charge and a bayonet fight. The latter were rare, the former invariably being sufficient to bundle the French away, and certainly no fighting with the bayonet was reported to have occurred at Talavera.

As at Vimiero, time and again we find the attacking columns not deploying into line, or leaving the attempt too late. Thus the full French musket power could not be unleashed, and their columns were vulnerable to the wrap-around line. Once they were stopped in their tracks – and with three ranks of corpses or writhing wounded at their feet, that was not difficult – they were then literally on the back foot when the charge came. The British had the momentum, the aggression, the cool intent; and that appeared to astonish the French.

If the steel of bayonets was not crossed, that of sabres certainly was. Like the 20th Light Dragoons at Vimiero, the 23rd in the north plain just did not know when to stop. We should recall that only seven months earlier, at Sahagun, Villada, Mayorga and Benavente, Sir John Moore's cavalry regiments had established a clear moral superiority over their opposite numbers. It seems the 23rd wished to add to the army's camp-fire stories. Yet there is a thin line between superiority and over-confidence, and that line was to be crossed repeatedly in the coming years.

One final aspect of the fighting which is worthy of comment is the extent of the casualties. We have already noted that where the fighting comprised straightforward volley and charge, with the French not standing to dispute the ground, the butcher's bill was lightest: at the Pajar, Kemmis's brigade lost only 7 per cent of its 25 July strength, and Alexander Campbell's brigade 11 per cent. On the other flank, on the Medellin, the losses were slightly greater, with Donkin's battalions averaging 15 per cent, Tilson's 19 per cent and Stewart's 28 per cent (which included the 48th's battle on 28 July alone. Despite the shelter of the crest, we must recall that this end of the line was under the heaviest artillery fire. Down on the plain, the Guards and their rescuers from Mackenzie's lost about a third – 31 per cent and 34 per cent respectively; and of the latter the 2/24th were hit hardest, losing 45 per cent. Cameron's battalions averaged 44 per cent with the 2/83rd losing 53 per cent. Then we come to the Germans. Over the two days, the four battalions' casualties averaged 51 per cent (1st KGL 50 per cent, 2nd KGL 58 per cent, 5th KGL 50 per cent, and 7th KGL 46 per cent). Langwerth's brigade was thus down by 54 per cent. A rough calculation shows that over that central half-mile section of the British line, for every 300 of Langwerth's, Cameron's and the Guards' men who stood at the start of the battle, 132 would be knocked over by the end of it. As Captain FitzClarence wrote, 'The gaps in our lines now forcibly showed themselves, by the regiments not covering one third of their former ground.'

Sir Arthur's Talavera Despatch of 29 July details a total casualty list of 5,423: 857 killed, 3,913 wounded and 653 missing (together with 441 horses).

All these cold figures numb the imagination; by way of human contrast, in Appendices II and IV, are the names of the officer casualties, together with their regiments, by the usual categories. A glance through the list of thirty-nine German names makes one ponder; so, too, the deaths of Generals Mackenzie and Langwerth, and the wounding of Generals Hill, Alexander Campbell and Henry Campbell. The commanding officers of the Coldstream Guards, 1/48th, and 2/83rd were killed, and those of the 3rd Guards, 1/3rd, 2/24th, 2nd Line Bn KGL, and 1/45th were returned wounded, along with four ADCs and various staff officers. When those 238 names began to appear in the *London Gazette*, the scale of Sir Arthur's battle was made real. For those still upright on the field on the evening of 28 July, it was already real enough.

* * *

As darkness fell once more on Friday 28 July, and in the absence of further French aggression, a start was made on getting the wounded in. Stothert of the Guards wrote: 'A dim and cheerless moon threw a faint lustre over the surrounding objects after the close of day. Small parties were sent out to bring in the wounded; the enemy was engaged in a similar manner, and had made large fires along the whole front of his extensive line.'

Three days later the queueing wounded were still having smashed arms and legs cut off, and on the field the exhausted troops continued to bury and burn corpses. It went on and on, and there was neither the time nor the manpower to do it properly. The 24th's history tells us that 'the wounded were collected and sent off towards the town of Talavera. There were not fifty men left with the Colours when the fatigue parties were sent off'. About 1,600 corpses lay out under the hot summer skies, and more than 10,000 wounded – to say nothing of the thousand horses killed and maimed. (The French, of course, took their walking wounded with them.) We have several eyewitness accounts of the aftermath of the fight: a sergeant in the Fusiliers, another in the Coldstream, a company commander in the Rifles (who arrived next morning), and a cavalry commissary. All contribute to a picture that needs no explaining, and which, when viewed as a whole, provides dramatic insight into the so-called fruits of victory. We start with Sergeant John Cooper, 2/7th (Royal Fusiliers):

> About 11pm all was still. Not a voice was heard, but the cry of agony and distress from the wounded and dying. Both armies rested on the same ground

they had occupied the previous night except our brigade, which had advanced about 200 yards.

Long before daylight next morning, we were startled by drums being beaten in the enemy's lines. Of course we expected another brush, but when morning dawned no enemy was to be seen. It was ascertained that they had in their retreat crossed a branch of the Tagus and carried away 70 or 80 carts laden with their wounded. Surely the French did not fight well in this battle, when it is considered that they threw nearly the whole force of about 50,000 upon our small army of 19,000. They had been well supplied with provisions previously. We had been half starved. They had dined on the field of battle, and liquor had been served out to them before they attacked us. This was proved by what was found in the possession of the dead. On the contrary, nothing was served out to us from 2 or 3pm on the 27th, until about 10am on the 29th.

The British in this engagement lost nearly 5,000 and the enemy by their own account about 9,000. The morning after the battle, the Light Brigade consisting of the 43rd, 52nd, and 95th Regiments, joined us on the bloody field, having made a forced march of 60 miles in 24 hours. We received them with loud cheers though they arrived too late.

The first work to be done, was to remove nine or ten thousand English and French wounded into Talavera; and to bury four or five thousand dead bodies. What a task for 16 or 17,000 hungry worn out men to undertake! 'Twas impossible! We had but few tools, and the ground was hard and rocky, therefore the dead were either thrown into the dry beds of winter torrents, &c., and scantily covered with earth; or, together with dead horses, gathered into heaps and burned. The smell was intolerable. As for the wounded, they perished in great numbers while lying in the blazing sun, in want of water, dressing and shelter.

The excitement of battle being over, we all severely felt stomach complaints. I had not tasted food for 43 hours. This was not Wellington's fault, for previous to the battle much flour had been collected, and made into bread by bakers belonging to the army; but during the battle, the Spaniards had broken open our stores and left very little for us. In the heat of the fight, many of these boasting Spaniards deserted, and spread the news that the English were defeated.

Next we have the words of the anonymous sergeant of the Coldstream:

This was a dismal night, great numbers of wounded on both sides lying on the field, their cries & groans were most piercingly grievous however at daylight all the assistance that could be, was given & parties were sent out from every Corps to collect them & bury the dead. This was a part of service by no means pleasant; mangled Carcases & broken limbs, was a Spectacle truly shocking & notwithstanding the utmost tenderness was used, the removal of the wounded occasioned the most piercing shrieks – It was my lot to go with a Corporal of the company to the general Hospital in Talavera, & I beheld what I never wish to see again – the road (about a mile) leading to the town was literally covered with the wounded, & wounded men dying whilst being carried there. Every street in the town was filled with them & absolutely impassible for no place had been prepared for their reception, & the Spaniards would not admit them into their houses, not even the Officers who had been billeted on them previous to the Action, without the interference of the Alcalde. They seemed to look upon us with a sort of admiration mingled with horror for it was incomprehensible to them how a handful of Men could beat off... the hitherto victorious legions of Buonaparte... we remained on the ground until 3 August when the air became extremely offensive, & notwith-standing that parties of Spanish Peasantry had been daily employed in burying the Enemy's dead it was scarce completed when we broke up for Oropisa & latterly the smell became so offensive that the dead bodies were collected in heaps & laid on piles of faggots which being set fire to were thus consumed!

The Light Brigade came on the scene too late to fight, after much hard marching, with the light of the new day (the 29th); but they were in time to provide a screen on the Alberche, and to help with the fatigues. Captain George Simmons, 1/95th:

It was early in the morning of 29 July, and our bugles had struck up merrily as we crossed the field of battle. The scene, however, was appalling, especially to us young soldiers who, having taken no part in an encounter as yet, had here missed the interest which blunts the feelings of the men engaged. We 'raw ones' had scarcely seen the enemy, and could recognize no comrades among the fallen, although the experience of one engagement would effectively break the ice.

The field of action occupied an extensive valley, situated between two ranges of hills, on which the British and French armies were posted. It was strewn with the wreck of recent battle. The dead and dying, thousands of them, conquerors and conquered, lay in little heaps, interspersed with dismounted guns, and shattered ammunition wagons. Broken horse trap-pings, blood-stained shakos, and other torn paraphernalia of military pomp and distinction, completed the battle scene.

The long grass, which had taken fire during the action, was still burning, and added dreadfully to the sufferings of the wounded and dying of both armies. Their cries for assistance were horrifying, and hundreds, exerting the last remnant of their strength, were seen crawling to places of safety.

In the midst of this I saw, for the first time, our immortal chief, Sir Arthur Wellesley. I also beheld that deformed-looking lump of pride, ignorance and treachery, General Cuesta. He was the most murderous-looking old man I ever saw.

The horrid sights were beyond anything I could have imagined. Thousands dead and dying in every direction, horses, men, French and English in whole lines, who had cut each other down, and, I'm sorry to say, the Spaniards butchering wounded Frenchmen at every opportunity, and stripping them naked, which gave admission to the attacks of myriads of pernicious flies, and the threat of a burning sun. You may be sure everything was done on our part, and the commanding officer's, to put a stop to such horrid brutality and give assistance, but the ground was covered for at least five miles with the dead and dying.

The last eyewitness – characteristically robust, cheerful and ebullient – is our old friend Lieutenant Augustus Schaumann of the KGL, Deputy Assistant Commissary-General to whoever needed food and forage, whose pen entertains and reveals in equal measure:

> At dawn on 29 July we heard some troops marching along quite close to us. It was Crauford's division which, coming up from Lisbon, had covered twelve Spanish leagues in twenty-four hours, in order to be able to take part in the battle. They went forward as outposts. As soon as we heard that the enemy had retreated to Saint Olalla in the night, with the object of covering Madrid, we rode back to the town again. But, heavens! What did our quarters look like! They had been plundered by the Spanish soldiers themselves. All our boxes and cases had been burst open, and their contents strewn over the ground, robbed, broken or hacked to pieces; our beds had been cut open and the feathers and horsehair had been shaken out and stolen, and our bookcase lay in the middle of the room with the shelves piled on top of it. We waded knee-deep in feathers and plunder of every description, while all about the floor lay broken crockery, pots, books and written records. It was only with great pains that we were able to find a saucepan in which to prepare our usual breakfast of thin chocolate and water and ship's biscuits. We made a fire out of an armchair, a few histories of the saints bound in pigskin, and a number of crusty old legal authorities.
>
> After we had refreshed ourselves in this way, we hurried off to find our regiments. The battlefield presented a shocking spectacle. Corpses lay thickly all about for many miles around, particularly on the hill which our troops had so bravely defended. Here indeed, their dead were so plentiful that it looked as if several battalions were merely sleeping there. Our own men could be distinguished by their red coats, and fifty paces off could be seen the blue and grey uniforms of the enemy. Altogether 5,000 English and about 8,000 French had perished. A number of French wounded who had been left behind cried plaintively to us for help, and begged us to move them away so that the Spaniards could not cut their throats...
>
> Every trace of vegetation, and all trees and houses in this area had been burnt, and the ground was all singed black. At six o'clock on the previous evening the dry grass and shrubs had caught fire, and most of the badly wounded men who had not been able to move from the spot had been singed or roasted alive. In addition to all this devastation, there was also the burning sunshine, which greatly aggravated the trials of the combatants. Not a trace of shade or of coolness, or of water was to be found over the whole length and breadth of this wilderness, except under the olive trees on the Alberche and

the Tagus. The rest of the country round Talavera was desolate, naked and devoid of trees. Many a man wounded on the 27th had died of hunger and thirst. Amid the thousands of warriors there were also dead and wounded horses, weapons of all kinds, broken carts, ammunition wagons, chests, harness, shakos, light dragoon helmets, grenadier busbies, shreds of clothing, ammunition pouches, scattered all over the ground. In a barn not far from the hollow cleft above mentioned, I found the men of the 23rd Dragoons who had fallen – all young and fine-looking fellows – lying dead in three rows. They had been carried thither for burial.

We found our regiment on the Alberche, where they were camping out under the trees and foraging amid half-ruined cornfields. Our sentries were posted on both sides of the river. I took the squadron quartermaster with me, in order to send along all the bread, meat and wine I had been able to collect. In the town the troubles of the commissariat began afresh. We had to find food and there was nothing there. At last a few belated convoys, which had been left behind, began to appear in the town, and we were able to begin our deliveries. For three days I had subsisted only on water, chocolate, biscuit, and a little wine. I felt completely exhausted, and almost dried up with the heat. Both face and my lips were blistered and smarting. At night, in our plundered quarters, we had to sleep on the bare ground.

On 30 July we were busy on our legs the whole day, and only at midnight were we able to take a little soup and meat. But this late supper did not disturb us; for, in spite of it, we slept like logs on the bare ground. Early next morning each of us returned to duty. Towards midday I stood at the entrance of the town and saw the wounded, both friend and foe, being brought in on bullock carts. It was a distressing sight. Many who had been taken prisoner had escaped in the night; among them two officers of the 23rd Dragoons, Captain Drake and Lieutenant Anderson. These men, who had cut their way into the centre of a French squadron and had been seized by the enemy, had found their way back, and could not tell us enough about the ill-treatment they had received at the hands of the enemy.

While on an errand in the town I passed a convent where the wounded were having their limbs amputated and dressed. Never shall I forget the heartrending cries which could be heard coming from the windows in the front of this building; while from one of the windows the amputated arms and legs were being flung out upon a small square below. In front of the door lay the wounded, who had been deposited there as fast as they arrived, awaiting their turn. Many of them were already dead. The total losses in dead, wounded and prisoners were 5,367 English and 3,000 Spanish. The French lost 12,000 men and numbers of guns and ammunition wagons. They had had whole brigades annihilated. According to information given by one of the captured officers, they had marched up to the Alberche on 22 July with 47,000 men commanded by Generals Victor, Jourdain and Sebastiani, with Joseph Bonaparte as Commander-in-Chief. On the afternoon of 30 July Victor is said to have complained bitterly that he had been left in the lurch by Soult, who should have marched from Plasencia to strike us in the rear. The

French generals, Merlot (?) and Lapisse, and a great number of their officers had fallen. The French had, moreover, declared that during the battle they had not regarded our allies, the Spaniards, as dangerous; they had not once been properly aware either of the latter's position or their strength; for they knew that when once we had been beaten, the Spaniards would take to their heels. In ourselves, however, they had encountered soldiers of the right kind. And I have no hesitation in believing them. King Joseph is said to have ridden away from the battlefield in a very miserable and depressed mood.

On the morning of 31 July I once again rode round the scene of the battle. Two battalions were still busy gathering the dead into heaps, and with the view of preventing pestilential smells and of saving time, partly burning and partly burying them. Here and there, however, one could see arms and legs appearing above the soil. Many corpses, both of men and horses, had been burnt brown by the sun, and, swollen to an immense size, filled the suffocatingly bad air with the most poisonous stench. In the afternoon various auctions were held in the bivouacs. At the auction held of the belongings of Colonel Gordon, who had been killed by a howitzer, I bought, for a mere song, his extremely fine dark blue overalls with two rows of buttons. And I wore them a very long time.

The town is full of tumult. Eight to ten thousand wounded of all nations occupy all the churches, convents and houses. They are all shouting for help, but the doctors cannot be found. The inhabitants have fled. But what seems almost incredible is that, according to all accounts, this evening the English army, owing to lack of transport and provisions, is not going to push forward, but is going to retreat.

For all Sir Arthur's efforts and hopes, the rumour of retreat was true. Bad news had arrived, which left him no option: the army will retire, about turn.

*   *   *

Four days after the battle Sir Arthur followed up his Despatch with a letter to Lord Castlereagh, in which he wrote: 'The extreme fatigue of the troops, the want of provisions, and the number of wounded to be taken care of, have prevented me from moving from my position.' On that evening of 1 August, however, he received news which finally extinguished any plan to chase Joseph to Madrid.

Hitherto he had had only rumours of the approach of Marshal Soult. It had been on his mind throughout the march from Plasencia, since that would be the destination of any French force crossing the mountains from the north. He had arranged with the Spanish for a blocking position to be placed at the Pass of Banos. The news that evening was that Soult had reached Bejar, near Banos, three days earlier – on the 29th – and that the blocking force was under threat. Plasencia, just two marches from Bejar, was of course Wellesley's half-way house to Portugal, an important staging post where several hundred wounded and sick had been left, along with a stores depot, the base for the commissariat. The French would by now have captured it, and were sitting astride his route home. This news altered everything.

Next morning Wellesley conferred urgently with Cuesta. The Spanish general proposed in all seriousness that the British army be divided, to support both him at Talavera, in case Joseph returned, and Bassecourt, whose division Cuesta had earlier sent west to reinforce his token force at Banos. Rejecting any idea of splitting his force, Sir Arthur gained agreement that the British should march west to attack Soult (who was believed to number only some 15,000) and that Cuesta would look after the thousands of wounded in Talavera's hospitals. To Marshal Beresford, Wellesley wrote: 'The movement of Soult has deranged my plans and I am obliged to return to drive him out.'

Early on the morning of 3 August he set off west with 18,000 men. Fortunately, just as he was about to put his head into a noose, he was overtaken at Oropesa by a messenger from Cuesta. The old man had had the wit to send on captured intelligence of the utmost importance: that the French in front of the British comprised not 15,000 but three times that – some 45,000 men of the corps of Marshals Soult, Ney and Mortier combined. The British cavalry's advance guard had already bumped their opposite numbers twenty miles ahead, at Navalmoral, and Sir Arthur had no option now but to halt. This further news was really bad, for his troops were weak with hunger, so too the horses. He could not take on the army that was now gathering to his front. If he did and it went wrong, with Soult already in front of the Tagus bridge at Almaraz, he could be trapped by Victor if he came up behind. Then Cuesta appeared, with his whole army, saying exactly that: that Victor was expected at Talavera later on 4 August. Thus the bridge at Arzobispo, just half a march south of where they were at Oropesa, was their one and only escape route.

Sir Arthur determined – what choice had he? – to head for his alternative line back to Portugal, to the south of the Tagus via Truxillo, Merida and Badajoz, and accordingly sent on the Light Brigade to seize the great bridge at Almaraz, to keep the French on the other side of the water. There was a usable ford near the Arzobispo bridge that would ease the traffic crossing to the south.

Victor did not in fact reach Talavera until the 6th, and it seems clear that Cuesta had lost not a minute in moving reassuringly close to the British. He was understandably concerned at being trapped north of the Tagus with no bridge – that at Talavera itself indeed led westwards, but on a very poor road, passage of which would have required Cuesta to abandon his transport (including, presumably, his own precious coach). So he had to reach Oropesa and use the Arzobispo bridge himself, before Soult could get there.

Thus the British wounded in Talavera were abandoned. Forty or fifty wagons and carts were all that Colonel Mackinnon, in charge of the evacuation, could scrape together, and these were a drop in the ocean. Those who could walk, walked: 'The road to Oropesa was covered with our poor limping bloodless soldiers. On crutches or sticks, with blankets thrown over them, they hobbled woefully along. For the moment panic terror lent them a force inconsistent with their debility and their fresh wounds. Some died by the road, others, unable to get further than Oropesa, afterwards fell into the hands of the enemy' (Captain Charles Boothby, RE, now missing a leg). Of the 4,000 or so wounded in the hospitals, 1,500 could not be moved even if the transport had been available, and these were left for the French. Some 500 died on the march or were captured en route; and 2,000 made it to

Truxillo. It is well recorded that the French behaved humanely to the wounded, and accepted their unwelcome responsibilities with good grace.

Among those who eventually got to Truxillo was Captain Peter Hawker, 14th Light Dragoons, who wrote in his journal:

> My man ran in, to say the French were close to the town, and that every one who was able to stir was making the best of his way to the rear. I had but a short time to take my choice of falling into the hands of the enemy a perfect cripple, or moving at the risk of dying on the road. Preferring freedom to captivity, under any circumstances, I soon decided to attempt a retreat – was then taken out of bed, and carried down stairs; and, with pillows fixed to the saddle, was just able to support myself on a horse – my man leading him at a slow walk, under a broiling sun, towards Oropesa… whither there was little difficulty in finding my way, the road being soon crowded with wounded men… Faint with the heat of the day, I was obliged to be placed in a caleche; and the road being one of the roughest that ever wheels travelled, I was in torture the whole way. The hipbone, which a rifle-ball had gone through and shattered, and the muscles of my back, where it was then lodged, were bumped with the greatest violence against the hard sides of the carriage.

Hawker travelled with his broken hip for six days to reach Truxillo, via the small matter of the Guadaloupe Mountains.

A further conference took place between Sir Arthur and Cuesta at Oropesa; predictably the unpredictable Spaniard now proposed another Talavera, defying Soult on the north side of the Tagus. With Victor somewhere behind Cuesta, Wellesley refused this disastrous invitation, and that evening crossed the bridge at Arzobispo. Cuesta followed on the night of 5 August, having drawn nearly 50,000 men of all three French corps upon himself, with a breath-taking mixture of carelessness and aggression.

By 6 August the Light Brigade and Donkin's had marched rapidly west to seize the bridge at Almaraz, with the rest of the starving British toiling in their wake. Cuesta still held the bridge at Arzobispo and the nearby ford, but the latter only with cavalry. During the Spanish siesta next afternoon, Soult sent twelve regiments of horse across the ford, taking both crossings, routing 6,000 Spanish, and retaking fourteen of the guns lost at Talavera.

And that, effectively, was the last offensive action of the Talavera campaign; when Cuesta had closed up again on Wellesley, who had taken an extremely strong defensive position in the mountains south of Almaraz, Soult declined to disturb them. He had examined various options to chase Sir Arthur back into Portugal, but was overruled by his king. Joseph feared that if Soult disappeared into the west, the combined forces of Wellesley, Cuesta and Venegas might magically pop up before Madrid. In any event, he had 12,000 sick and wounded of his own in Madrid's hospitals, and was every bit as worn out as the British. Finally, Napoleon himself intervened to order a cessation of all operations until the hot season was over. So Joseph told Soult not to march on Portugal, but to regroup and rest, and wait for cooler weather. To make sure Soult could not get ideas above his station, one of his three corps – Ney's – was ordered away, back north beyond Salamanca, where Kellerman was under pressure from the Spanish generals Romana and Del Parque. Soult thereupon adopted a defensive posture north of the Tagus, and Wellesley was able to rest his troops while waiting to see what the French intended. Once it emerged that Portugal was safe, he moved down towards Merida and Badajoz, and began to draw supplies from Portugal.

In early October he visited Lisbon, to think quietly about a secret concept – the Lines of Torres Vedras. But that, and the preceeding great battle of Busaco, is another story.

* * *

Back home, the concurrent woes of the Walcheren expedition were triumphantly set off by the arrival in London of news of the victory of Talavera. The nation craved for a soldier to mirror the naval genius of the late Lord Nelson, and Assaye, Rolica, Vimiero, Oporto and now Talavera gave them a name – which, in regal gratitude, was promptly changed from plain Sir Arthur to Baron Duoro of Wellesley, Viscount Wellington of Talavera, and accompanied by £2,000 a year. The red mail coaches carried the news across the land, 'horses, men and carriages dressed in laurels and flowers, oak-leaves and ribbons… young and old understand the language of our victorious symbols, and rolling volleys of sympathizing cheers ran along with us, behind us, before us' (De Quincey). The Tower guns crashed out and church bells pealed; but not for long.

Since Madrid was the next name anticipated on all lips, great was the subsequent disappointment and puzzlement when, within days, came news of the retreat towards the Portugese border. Political and professional enemies of the Wellesleys were quick to apply words like rash, adventurous and vainglorious to Sir Arthur's judgment in putting the precious British army into a cunning Gallic trap.

Further, the dishonour of the 1,500 wounded abandoned in Talavera was, however unfairly, an obvious reproach; the people recalled how Soult's own humiliating escape from Oporto had been measured in what he had had to abandon, as much as by his conventional losses. The butcher's bill for Talavera had been shocking, but discounted by victory; the nation found the fate of the wounded harder to stomach.

It is quite true that Wellesley made a huge error in venturing so deeply into Spain with such uncertain support, and we may agree that he was lucky to get away with it. His own more cautious attitude to future peninsula operations indicates that he knew it too, particularly with regard to co-operation with the Spanish, and to his logistics. Both contributed to the real reason he could not stay and fight the various assembled French marshals: his army was literally starving to death. That the French were in the same predicament got him off the hook, but did not ease his chagrin at being unable to take advantage of their limitations. The charge against Wellesley appears quite plain. It was that he had led 18,000 British troops into a foodless plain, with a virtually impassable river on one flank, mountains on the other, 40,000 enemy in front and 50,000 adjacent to his open flank. Put it like that, and a child would have drawn back from such a prospect – Balaclava, writ early and large.

But this is all hindsight. Firstly the 50,000 Frenchmen on his flank: at the time the plan was laid, there was no indication that the force could be other than Soult's corps alone – not more than 12,000 or 15,000 men at most, and gunless. Nor were they on the flank; they were way to the north. Secondly, half the 40,000 enemy in front of him were going to be pre-occupied many marches distant by the Army of La Mancha (Venegas vs Sebastiani). Thirdly, the other half left in front of Madrid were to be hit not by 18,000 British but by 53,000 British and Spanish – that is, 35,000 effective Spanish, living up to their endless boasting. Remember Sir Arthur had seen them once, by torchlight only, and while his military suspicions were instantly aroused, the die by then was cast.

And how close this plan to march on Madrid actually came to success. On the Alberche, on 23 July, it was a racing certainty. On that day, Victor had placed his 22,000 men behind a minor and fordable water obstacle, on a low line of hills, with the mighty Tagus barring any escape to the south. Joseph's small reserve was two marches away, Sebastiani was embroiled by Venegas five marches away, and Soult was not in the game at all – over the mountains in Leon. So Victor must inevitably be beaten that morning, flattened by the allied force of 53,000, and his remnants then pursued by 10,000 cavalry. They could run either to Joseph or Sebastiani, as they chose, for it would matter little: the latter was fighting far south of Madrid, the former positioned in front of it, but weakly. Madrid was there for Sir Arthur's taking; and the loss of their royal headquarters and staffs, storehouses, gun parks, transport reserves, hospitals, fodder and food would have been both a tremendous blow to French morale – doubtless driving the Emperor apoplectic – and crippling to their immediate actions, as well as a corresponding boost to the allies. The capital could not have been held indefinitely, of course; but linking up with Venegas from the south would have produced a total force of 73,000 men – a daunting Grand Army, with alternative lines of communications to Portugal and England via Badajoz and Cadiz.

That all this was soon to drift into the realms of the might-have-been does not invalidate the position on 23 July, and we cannot castigate Wellesley for trying. He brilliantly drove Soult from north Portugal, buying time and clearing his flank, with a declared aim to combine with Spain's armies of Estremadura and La Mancha for a march on Madrid. Victor would stand in his way, of course; the area north of the Tagus was already denuded of supplies, of course; Soult might indeed eventually descend on his rear, of course. But war, as Wolfe said, is an option of difficulties, after all. That Venegas would not engage Sebastiani after all, and that Cuesta would not fight on the 23rd, and that his army would prove incapable of the simplest manoeuvres, and that the Spanish authorities would not deliver on their promises for transport and food – this whole combination of disappointments was just plain unlikely. Yet these things happened; if they had not, Sir Arthur would have become Viscount Wellington of the Alberche – or even of Madrid.

Instead, he was forced on to his back foot by the ebullient Victor, rampaging after the hapless Spaniards, and obliged to put together an encounter defensive battle at Talavera as best he could. It is certainly true in the broadest sense that the entire campaign was effectively a draw, the British failing to liberate Madrid, and the French failing to destroy the British. Yet the balance in his soldiers' minds, if not in their hearts, was Wellesley's. Not just because the French had had to abandon Galicia, the Asturias and northern Portugal to cope with him, and failing; but because in the process, on the actual fields of battle, their fortune had been read.

As we have seen at Rolica, Vimiero, Corunna, Oporto and Talavera, assorted English, Scottish, Welsh, Irish and German regiments had come together with surprising commonality of tactics, leadership, and the greatest handiness with volley and bayonet. Together they built the view that they could beat the French; man for man, they thought, they were the better soldiers. The spirit of the line infantry was epitomized by the 1/29th, who went up the ravine at Rolica after their mad Colonel Lake; who repelled Brennier on the Ventosa heights at Vimiero; who bundled Ruffin's 9e Léger off the darkening Medellin (and who were indignant the next afternoon when Old Nosey instead chose the larger 1/48th to save the day). The accounts by their Lieutenants Leslie and Leith Hay, like those of Close of the 48th and all the others we have read, show little concern for their own skins, but much for duty, honour and the regiment. Of these, perhaps the strongest sense is of doing the right thing in the face of adversity, and going on doing it longer than the other side. Belief in this robust superiority saw them through the trials of hunger, of endless long marches, of lying for hours under shell and shot, of standing silently shoulder to shoulder while the noisy masses drummed up the slopes, of closing the files to the centre over their mates' bodies, of going forward with the bayonet with no guarantee that the French would turn and run.

The amazing thing about Talavera was that our soldiers came to the field with all these qualities to hand. That is, that they were somehow innate, since few could have brought them from earlier experiences elsewhere. As Napier wrote, and he should know: '… the greater part [of these truly formidable soldiers] were raw men, so lately drafted from the militia regiments that many of them still bore the number of their former regiment on their accoutrements.' If this was what raw inexperience could do, heaven help the French in later campaigns. For while Sir Arthur would necessarily have much to do over the coming months in putting right the more glaring recent mistakes – dozy piquetting, lack of transport, poor staff work, insufficient artillery, provision of fodder and food, the cavalry's penchant for death or glory – he need have no qualms about his men's fighting abilities.

To this day, the scroll 'Talavera' is the pre-eminent battle honour embroidered on the Colours of the 2nd Battalion The Royal Anglian Regiment, out of the 141 awarded over the years to its predecessor the 48th (Northamptonshire) Regiment, both of whose battalions fought that day side by side on the Medellin. Also to this day, 27/28 July each year, wherever the battalion happens to be, continues to be celebrated and remembered. Dinners, balls, sports and general festivities have been the order of the day for 195 years, throughout the world. Of course, there have been the occasional rude interruptions by whoever were our current foes: French, Americans, Australian bushrangers, Russians, various Afghan, Indian and Arab tribes, Maoris, Zulus, Boers, Germans, Italians, Japanese, Koreans, Chinese, Iraqis, and other less serious people. These celebrations – and all British regiments have their equivalents – are to recall for today's young men what their forebears did, and how they conducted themselves; and long may such annual celebrations continue.

Appendix I

Return of Killed, Wounded, and Missing, of the Army under the command of Lieutenant-general Sir Arthur Wellesley, K.B. in action with the French Army, commanded by Joseph Buonaparte in person, in front of the town of Talavera de la Reyna, on the 27th July, 1809.

Killed

Regiments	General Staff	Colonels	Lieut. Colonels	Majors	Captains	Lieutenants	Ensigns	Staff	Qr. Mrs. or Cty.	Serjeants	Drummers	Rank and File	Horses
14th Light Dragoons												2	9
1st Do. Do. K. G. L.													7
Royal British Artillery			1										
Do. Engineers													
1st Bn. Coldstm. Guards												1	
2nd Bn. 24th Regt.					1							10	
1st Bn. 29th Do.												22	
2nd Bn. 31st Do.												4	
1st Bn. 45th Do.													
1st Bn. 48th Do.												3	
2nd Do.												3	
5th Do. 60th Do.												26	
1st Do. 61st Do.						2	1					7	
2nd Do. 87th Do.						1						13	
1st Do. 88th Do.				1								2	
1st Bn. Detachments										1		4	
1st Line Bn. K. G. L.													
1st and 2nd Lt. Bn. Do.												6	
2nd Lt. Battn. Do.													
5th Do. Do.										1		19	
7th Do. Do.													
General Staff	1												
Total	1		1	1	1	3	1			2		122	16

Wounded

Regiments	General Staff	Colonels	Lieut. Colonels	Majors	Captains	Lieutenants	Ensigns	Staff	Qr. Mrs. or Cty.	Serjeants	Drummers	Rank and File	Horses
14th Light Dragoons						1						1	2
1st Do. Do. K. G. L.						1						1	6
Royal British Artillery												2	
Do. Engineers								1					
1st Bn. Coldstm. Guards												6	
2nd Bn. 24th Regt.					1		2			3		42	
1st Bn. 29th Do.												85	
2nd Bn. 31st Do.												13	
1st Bn. 45th Do.												8	
1st Bn. 48th Do.												3	
2nd Do.												4	
5th Do. 60th Do.			1		1	5	3			3		3	
1st Do. 61st Do.			1		2							124	
2nd Do. 87th Do.				1	2	3				2		23	
1st Do. 88th Do.												38	
1st Bn. Detachments						1				2		7	
1st Line Bn. K. G. L.					1	1						23	
1st and 2nd Lt. Bn. Do.												8	
2nd Lt. Battn. Do.										2		32	
5th Do. Do.								1		5		43	
7th Do. Do.													
General Staff													
Total			1	1	6	9	5	2		17		165	6

Missing

Regiments	General Staff	Colonels	Lieut. Colonels	Majors	Captains	Lieutenants	Ensigns	Staff	Qr. Mrs. or Cty.	Serjeants	Drummers	Rank and File	Horses
14th Light Dragoons													2
1st Do. Do. K. G. L.												1	
1st Bn. Coldstm. Guards												5	
2nd Bn. 24th Regt.						1						1	
1st Bn. 29th Do.												2	
2nd Bn. 31st Do.												7	
5th Do. 60th Do.												18	
1st Do. 61st Do.					2	1						33	
2nd Do. 87th Do.											1	30	
1st Do. 88th Do.										1		13	
1st Bn. Detachments												5	
1st and 2nd Lt. Bn. Do.												11	
7th Do. Do.											1	76	
Total					2	2				1	2	202	2

Total

Regiments	General Staff	Colonels	Lieut. Colonels	Majors	Captains	Lieutenants	Ensigns	Staff	Qr. Mrs. or Cty.	Serjeants	Drummers	Rank and File	Horses
14th Light Dragoons						1							11
1st Do. Do. K. G. L.						1							13
Royal British Artillery			1									2	
Do. Engineers								1					
1st Bn. Coldstm. Guards					1							12	
2nd Bn. 24th Regt.					2		2			3		53	
1st Bn. 29th Do.												109	
2nd Bn. 31st Do.												24	
1st Bn. 45th Do.												8	
1st Bn. 48th Do.					1							3	
2nd Do.												25	
5th Do. 60th Do.			1		2	5	4			3		6	
1st Do. 61st Do.					2	2				2		183	
2nd Do. 87th Do.				1	1					2	1	62	
1st Do. 88th Do.												64	
1st Bn. Detachments						1				4		9	
1st Line Bn. K. G. L.					1	1							
1st and 2nd Lt. Bn. Do.												49	
2nd Lt. Battn. Do.										2		3	
5th Do. Do.								1		2	2	49	
7th Do. Do.										5		138	
General Staff	1												
Total	1		2	1	9	13	6	2		20	3	789	24

Appendix II

Names of Officers Killed, Wounded, and Missing, Talavera de la Reyna, 27th July, 1809.

Killed.

Rank and Names.	Regiments.
Capt. Fordyce, D. A. A. G.	81st Regiment.
Lieut. Col. Ross	Coldstream Guards
Capt. Lodge	31st Regt. 2d Bn.
Lieut. Graydon	88th Do. 1st Do.
M'Carthy	Do. Do.
M'Dougall	91st Regt.
Ensign La Serre	87th Do. 2d Do.

Wounded.

Rank and Names.	Regiments.	Remarks.
Lieut. Hembruck	1st Lt. Dns. K. G. L.	Severely
Capt. Boothby	Royal Engineers.	Do.
Capt. and Adjt. Bryan	1st Bn. Coldstr. Gds.	Do.
Lieut. Popham	29th Reg.	Do.
Capt. Coleman	31st Do. 2d Bn.	Do.
Lieut. George Beamish	Do.	Slightly
Ensign Gamble	Do.	Do.
Soden	45th Do. 1st Bn.	Severely
Lieut. Col. Guard	60th Do. 5th Do.	Do.
Capt. Woolf	61st Do. 1st Do.	Do.
Major Coghlan	87th Do. 2d Do.	Do.
Capt. M'Crea	Do.	Slightly
Souersall	Do.	Do.
Lieut. Kavenagh	Do.	Severely
Barnall	Do.	Do.
Kingston	Do.	Do.
Johnson	Do.	Do.
Carrol	Do.	Slightly
Ensign Moore	Do.	Severely
Knox	Do.	Do.
Butler	Do.	Slightly
Capt. During	Rifle Corps, K. G. L.	Severely
Lieut. Holle	Do.	Do.
Adjt. Deliris	7th Line Bn. K. G. L.	

Missing.

Rank and Names.	Regiments.
Capt. Poole	1st Bn. Detachts. 52d Regiment
Walsh	91st Regiment
Lieut. Cameron	79th Do.

Appendix III

Return of Killed, Wounded, and Missing, of the Army under the command of Lieutenant-general Sir Arthur Wellesley, K. B. in action with the French Army, commanded by Joseph Buonaparte in person, at Talavera de la Reyna, on the 28th July, 1809.

Regiments	Killed R&F	Wounded R&F	Missing R&F	Total R&F	Total Horses
General Staff					
3rd Dragoon Guards	3	7	1	2	14
4th Dragoons	8	6		10	13
14th Light Dragoons	6	5		9	37
16th Do. Do.	44	43	96	13	25
23rd Do. Do.	7	29	2	183	224
1st Dn. Do. K. G. L.	2	25		31	64
Royal British Artillery				28	40
Do. German Do.				30	
Do. Engineers					
Do. Staff Corps					
Coldstream Guards, 1st Bn.	33	239		272	
3rd Do. 1st Do.	45	249		295	
3rd Regt. Foot, 1st Do.	25	102		134	
7th Do. 2nd Do.	6	51	1	58	
24th Do. 2nd Do.	42	255	21	318	
29th Do. 1st Do.	25	98		125	
31st Do. 2nd Do.	20	97		122	
40th Do. 1st Do.	7	47		55	
45th Do. 1st Do.	9	130	10	149	
48th Do. 1st Do.	22	132		155	
48th Do. 2nd Do.	11	50	1	61	
53rd Do. 2nd Do.	6	29	10	36	
60th Do. 5th Do.	6	24	10	40	
61st Do. 1st Do.	42	183	16	241	
66th Do. 2nd Do.	15	93	28	108	
83rd Do. 2nd Do.	37	189	5	254	
87th Do. 2nd Do.	8	40		53	
88th Do. 1st Do.	11	69		80	
97th Do. 1st Do.	6	25	21	52	
1st Battalion Detachments	26	159		186	
2nd Do. Do.	7	13		21	
1st Line Batt. K. G. L.	36	227		264	
1st and 2nd Light Bn. K. G. L.		34	24	40	
2nd Line Bn. K. G. L.	57	271	100	352	
5th Do. Do.	25	109		234	
7th Do. Do.	15	28	49	92	

Names of Officers Killed, Wounded, and Missing, Talavera de la Reyna, 28th July, 1809.

Killed

Rank and Names.	Regiments.
Major Gen. M'Kenzie	
Br. Gen. Langworth	
Captain Beckett (Bde. Mx.)	Coldstream Guards
Gardner Do.	43rd Foot
Lieut. King	23rd Lt. Dragoons
Power	British Artillery
Wyatt	Do.
Ensign Parker	Coldstream Guards
Captain Walker	1st Bn. 3rd Guards
Buchanan	Do.
Dalrymple	Do.
Ensign Ram	Do.
Adjutant Irby	Do.
Lieutenant Beaufoy	2nd Do. 7th Foot
Major F. Orpen	61st Do. 1st Bn.
Captain H. James	Do.
Lieutenant Hemus	Do.
Lieut. Col. Gordon	83rd Do. 2nd Bn.
Lieutenant Dahman	Do.
Montgomery	Do.
Hood	Do.
Captain Blake	88th Do. 1st Do.
Worsabe	1st Line Bn. K.G.L.
Lieut. Hy. Hodenburg	Do.
Evert	5th Line Bn. K.G.L.
Dachenhausen	Do.
Hemelman	Do.

Wounded

Rank and Names.	Regiments.	Remarks.
Major General Hill	13th Lt. Dns. D. A. Q. N. G.	Slightly
Brigr. Gen. A. Campbell	Brigade Major	Do.
H. Campbell	A. D. Camps to Lieut. Gen.	Severely not dangerous
Capt. Whittingham	Sir A. Wellesley	Slightly
Blair 91st Regiment	A. D. C. to B. G. Langworth	Severely
Bouverie Cold. Gds.	Do. to Lt. Gl. Sherbrooke	Slightly
Burgh 92nd Regt.	3rd Dn. Guards.	Severely
Zerisen 1st Le. Bn.	14th Lt. Dragoons	Slightly
Craig (Sicilian Rt.)		Severely
Captain Brice	Do.	Slightly
Colonel Hawker	Do.	Severely
Captain Chapman	Do.	Do.
Hawker	Do.	Do.
Lieutenant Ellis	Do.	Slightly
Wainman		Do.
Smith		Do.
Bence		Do.
Capt. Howard	16th Do. Do.	Severely
Frankland	23rd Do. Do.	Do.
Lord W. Russell		Slightly
Cornet Dodwell		Do.
Lieutenant Poten	1st Do. K. G. L.	Severely
Cornet Tueto	Do.	Slightly
Lieut. Colonel Framingham	Royal British Artillery	Do.
Captain Taylor	Do.	Do.
Baynes	Do.	Do.
Lieutenant Stanway	Royal Engineers	Do.
Captain Todd	Royal Staff Corps	Do.
Lieutenant Shanahan		Severely
Lieut. Col. Stibbert		Do.
Sir W. Sheridan	Do.	Do.
Captain Millman	Do.	Do.
Christie	Do.	Slightly
Collier		Do.
Wood	Do.	Severely
Jenkinson		Do. not dangerous
Ensign Sandilands	1st Bn. 3rd Guards	Slightly
Lieut. Col. Gordon	Do.	Do.
Major Fotheringham	Do.	Do.
Captain Giels	Do.	Do.
Ensign Aitchison	Do.	Do.
Towers	Do.	Do.
Scott	Do.	Severely
Lieut. Col. Muter	3rd Foot or Buffs	Severely
Major Drummond (Bt. Lt. Col.)	Do.	Slightly

Wounded

Rank and Names.	Regiments.	Remarks.
Lieutenant Kirwan	7th Foot 2nd Bn.	Severely
Muter	Do.	Do.
Adjutant Page	Do.	Slightly
Lieut. Col. Drummond	24th Do. 2nd Do.	Severely
Major Popham	Do.	Do.
Captain Collis	Do.	Do.
Evans	Do.	Do.
Lieutenant Vardy	Do.	Slightly
Ensign Grant	Do.	Severely
Skeene	Do.	Do.
Johnson	Do.	Do.
Jessamin	Do.	Do.
Adjutant Topp	Do.	Slightly
Captain Gauntlett	29th Regiment	Severely
Newbold	Do.	Slightly
Lieutenant Stannus	Do.	Severely
Leslie	Do.	Do.
Stanhope	Do.	Do.
Nicholson	Do.	Slightly
Captain Nichols	31st Do. 2nd Do.	Severely
Lieutenant Girdlestone	Do.	Slightly
A. Beamish	Do.	Severely
Captain Colquhoun	40th Do. 1st Do.	Slightly
Major Gwynn	45th Do. Do.	Do.
Lieutenant Cole	Do.	Do.
Lieut. Col. Donelan	48th Do. Do.	Do.
Major Marston	Do.	Do.
Captain Wood	48th Do. Do.	Slightly
French	Do.	Do.
Lieutenant Drought	Do.	Do.
Page	Do.	Severely
Cheslyn	Do.	Do.
Gill	Do.	Do.
Cuthbertson	Do.	Slightly
Ensign Vandermeulen	Do.	Do.
Lieutenant Johnson	48th Do. 2nd Do.	Severely
Ensign Renny	Do.	Slightly
Major Kingscote	53rd Do. 2nd Do.	Severely
Captain Stowell	Do.	Slightly
Garliffe B. Major	Do.	Do.
Andrew	Do.	Do.
Lieutenant Zuhlke	60th Do. 5th Do.	Do.
Ritter	Do.	Do.
Mitchell	Do.	Severely
Ensign Altenstein	Do.	Do.
Captain Furnace	61st Do. 1st Do.	Slightly
Laing	Do.	Do.

Appendix IV (continued)

Wounded.		
Rank and Names.	**Regiments.**	**Remarks.**
Captain Goodman	61st Regiment 1st Bn.	Slightly
Hartley	Do.	Do.
Lieutenant McLean	Do.	Do.
Trench	Do.	Do.
Collins	Do.	Severely
Givin	Do.	Slightly
Ensign Brackenbury	Do.	Severely
Adjutant Drew	Do.	Slightly
Captain Kelly	66th Do. 2nd Do.	Severely
Stewart	Do.	Do.
Adams Bt. Lt. Col.	Do.	Do.
Lieutenant Morris	Do.	Do.
Dudgeon	Do.	Do.
Humbly	Do.	Do.
Steele	Do.	Do.
Shewbridge	Do.	Do.
Morgan	Do.	Do.
Ensign Cotter	Do.	Slightly
McCarthy	Do.	Do.
Captain Summerfield	83rd Do. 2nd Do.	Leg amputated
Reynolds	Do.	Severely
Lieutenant Nicholson	Do.	Slightly
Baldwyn	Do.	Severely
Johnson	Do.	Slightly
Abell	Do.	Severely
Pyne	Do.	Do.
Ensign Boggie	Do.	Slightly
Carey	Do.	Do.
Lettoller	Do.	Do.
Adjutant Brahm	Do.	Severely
Major Gough	87th Do. 2nd Do.	Slightly
Lieutenant Rogers	Do.	Do.
Ensign Pepper	Do.	Severely
Captain Brown	98th Do. 1st Do.	Do.
Lieutenant Whittle	Do.	Do.
Ensign Whitelaw	Do.	Do.
Major Ross	38th Regiment	Do.
Captain McPherson	35th Do.	Slightly
Bradby	28th Do.	Do.
Chancellor	38th Do.	Severely
Lieutenant Gilbert	28th Do.	Do.
McBeth	42nd Do.	Slightly
Fullerton	38th Do.	Do.
Munroe	42nd Do.	Do.
Brown	43rd Do.	Do.

(Bracket against the last group: **1st Battalion Detachments**)

Wounded.		
Rank and Names.	**Regiments.**	**Remarks.**
Major Bodecker	1st Line Bn. K. G. L.	Severely
Captain Marshall	Do.	Do.
Captain Saffe	1st Line Bn. K. G. L.	Slightly
Petersdorff	Do.	Do.
Lieutenant Goeben Senior	Do.	Severely
Em. Hodenberg	Do.	Do.
Fk. Hodenberg	Do.	Do.
Saffe	Do.	Slightly
Schlutter Senior	Do.	Do.
Ensign Allen	2nd Line Bn. K. G. L.	Severely
Lieutenant Colonel Brauns	Do.	Slightly
Major Belleville	Do.	Severely
Captain Breyman	Do.	Slightly
Heldrill	Do.	Severely
Sharnhoust	Do.	Do.
Lieutenant Buerman	Do.	Do.
Wenckstern	Do.	Do.
Wessell	Do.	Do.
Wick	Do.	Do.
Holle	Do.	Do.
Ensign Tinch	5th Line Bn. K. G. L.	Slightly
Schniat	Do.	Severely
Billeb	Do.	Do.
Blumenhagen	Do.	Do.
Captain Hamelberg	Do.	Do.
Gerber	Do.	Slightly
Lieutenant Linsingen	Do.	Severely
During	Do.	Do.
Ensign Brandes	Do.	Slightly
Koller	Do.	Do.
Major Berger	7th Line Bn. K. G. L.	Slightly
Lieutenant Volger	Do.	Do.
Freytag	Do.	Severely
Ensign Offen	23rd Lt. Dragoons	⎫
Captain Allen	Do.	⎬ Wounded and Missing
Drake	Do.	⎭
Lieutenant Anderson	45th Foot 1st Bn.	⎫
Captain Leckey B. Major	48th Do. 2nd Do.	⎬
Ensign Reeves	97th Do. Do.	⎭ Missing
Lieutenant Shipley		

Appendix V

Recapitulation of Killed, Wounded, and Missing, on the 27th and 28th July, 1809.

Dates.	Killed.													Wounded.													Missing.													Total.												
	General Staff.	Colonels.	Lt. Colonels.	Majors.	Captains.	Lieutenants.	Ensigns.	Staff.	Qr. Mrs. of Cav.	Serjeants.	Drummers.	Rank and File.	Horses.	General Staff.	Colonels.	Lt. Colonels.	Majors.	Captains.	Lieutenants.	Ensigns.	Staff.	Qr. Mrs. of Cav.	Serjeants.	Drummers.	Rank and File.	Horses.	General Staff.	Colonels.	Lt. Colonels.	Majors.	Captains.	Lieutenants.	Ensigns.	Staff.	Qr. Mrs. of Cav.	Serjeants.	Drummers.	Rank and File.	Horses.	General Staff.	Colonels.	Lt. Colonels.	Majors.	Captains.	Lieutenants.	Ensigns.	Staff.	Qr. Mrs. of Cav.	Serjeants.	Drummers.	Rank and File.	Horses.
27th July, 1809.	1	..	1	..	1	3	1	..	..	2	..	122	16	..	..	1	1	6	9	5	2	..	17	1	465	6	..	..	..	..	2	1	..	..	..	1	2	202	2	1	..	2	1	9	13	6	2	..	20	3	789	24
28th Do. Do.	4	..	1	1	6	12	2	1	..	26	4	613	195	9	..	9	11	47	62	29	4	..	148	15	3072	65	..	..	..	..	3	2	1	..	..	14	7	418	157	13	..	10	12	56	76	32	5	..	188	26	4103	417
Total Loss	5	..	2	1	7	15	3	1	..	28	4	735	211	9	..	10	12	53	71	34	6	..	165	16	3537	71	..	..	..	..	5	3	1	..	..	15	9	620	159	14	..	12	13	65	89	38	7	..	208	29	4892	441

RETURN OF ORDNANCE, &c. TAKEN.

- 4 Eight-pounders
- 4 Six Do.
- 1 Four Do.
- 1 Six-inch howitzer
- 2 Tumbrils, complete with ammunition

⎫ Taken by Br. Gl. Campbell's Brigade.

- 6 Pieces of ordnance, ⎱ left by the enemy, and found in the wood.
- 1 Six-inch howitzer, ⎰
- 1 Standard taken, and 1 destroyed by the 29th Regiment.
- 3 Do. taken by the King's German Legion.

Appendix VI

Despatch to Viscount Castlereagh from Talavera de la Reyna, July 29th 1809, following the Action of the Army under the Command of Lieutenant-General the Hon. Sir Arthur Wellesley, KB, with the French Army commanded by King Joseph Buonaparte in Person, on July 27th and 28th, 1809.

GENERAL Cuesta followed the enemy's march with his army from the Alberche, on the morning of the 24th, as far as Sta Olalla, and pushed forward his advanced guard as far as Torrijos. For the reasons stated to your lordship in my despatch of the 24th, I moved only two divisions of infantry and a brigade of cavalry across the Alberche to Cazalegas, under the command of Lieutenant-General Sherbrooke, with a view to keep up the communication between General Cuesta and me, and with Sir Robert Wilson's corps at Escalona.

It appears that General Venegas had not carried into execution that part of the plan of operations which related to his corps, and that he was still at Daymiel, in La Mancha; and the enemy, in the course of the 24th, 25th, and 26th, collected all his forces in this part of Spain, between Torrijos and Toledo, leaving but a small corps of 2,000 men in that place.

This united army thus consisted of the corps of Marshal Victor, of that of General Sebastiani, and of 7,000 or 8,000 men, the guards of Joseph Buonaparte, and the garrison of Madrid; and it was commanded by Joseph Buonaparte, aided by Marshals Jourdan and Victor, and by General Sebastiani.

On the 26th General Cuesta's advanced guard was attacked near Torrijos and obliged to fall back; and the General retired with his army on that day to the left bank of the Alberche, General Sherbrooke continuing at Cazalegas, and the enemy at Sta Olalla.

It was then obvious that the enemy intended to try the result of a general action, for which the best position appeared to be in the neighbourhood of Talavera, and General Cuesta having consented to take up this position on the morning of the 27th, I ordered General Sherbrooke to retire with his corps to its station in the line, leaving General Mackenzie with a division of infantry and a brigade of cavalry as an advanced post in the wood, on the right of the Alberche, which covered our left flank.

The position taken up by the troops at Talavera extended rather more than two miles: the ground was open on the left, where the British army was stationed, and it was commanded by a height, on which was placed *en echelon*, as the second line, a division of infantry under the orders of Major-General Hill.

There was a valley between the height and a range of mountains still further on the left, which valley was not at first occupied, as it was commanded by the height before mentioned; and the range of mountains appeared too distant to have any influence on the expected action.

The right, consisting of Spanish troops, extended immediately in front of the town of Talavera, down to the Tagus. This part of the ground was covered by olive trees, and much intersected by banks and ditches. The highroad leading from the bridge over the Alberche was defended by a heavy battery in front of a church, which was occupied by Spanish infantry.

All the avenues of the town were defended in a similar manner. The town was occupied, and the remainder of the Spanish infantry was formed in two lines behind the banks on the road which led from the town and the right to the left of our position.

In the centre, between the two armies, there was a commanding spot of ground, on which we had commenced to construct a redoubt, with some open ground in its rear. Brigadier-General Alexander Campbell was posted at this spot with a division of infantry, supported in his rear by General Cotton's brigade of dragoons and some Spanish cavalry.

At about two o'clock on the 27th the enemy appeared in strength on the left bank of the Alberche, and manifested an intention to attack General Mackenzie's division. The attack was made before they could be withdrawn; but the troops, consisting of General Mackenzie's and Colonel Donkin's brigades, and General Anson's brigade of cavalry, and supported by General Payne with the other four regiments of cavalry in the plain between Talavera and the wood, withdrew in good order, but with some loss, particularly by the 2nd Battalion 87th Regiment and the 2nd Battalion 31st Regiment in the wood.

Upon this occasion the steadiness and discipline of the 45th Regiment and the 5th Battalion 60th Regiment were conspicuous, and I had particular reason for being satisfied with the manner in which Major-General Mackenzie withdrew this advanced-guard.

As the day advanced, the enemy appeared in larger numbers on the right of the Alberche, and it was obvious that he was advancing to a general attack upon the combined armies. General Mackenzie continued to fall back gradually upon the left of the position of the combined armies, where he was placed in the second line in the rear of the Guards, Colonel Donkin being placed in the same situation farther upon the left, in the rear of the King's German Legion.

The enemy immediately commenced his attack, in the dusk of the evening, by a cannonade upon the left of our position, and by an attempt with his cavalry to overthrow the Spanish infantry, posted, as I have before stated, on the right. This attempt entirely failed.

Early in the night he pushed a division along the valley on the left of the height occupied by General Hill, of which he gained a momentary possession; but Major-General Hill attacked it immediately with the bayonet, and regained it. This attack was repeated in the night, but failed; and again, at daylight on the morning of the 28th, by two divisions of infantry, and was repulsed by Major-General Hill.

Major-General Hill has reported to me, in a particular manner, the conduct of the 29th Regiment, and of the 1st Battalion 48th Regiment, in these different affairs, as well as that of Major-General Tilson and Brigadier-General R. Stewart.

We lost many brave officers and soldiers in the defence of this important point in our position; among others, I cannot avoid mentioning Brigade-Major Fordyce and Brigade-Major Gardner, and Major-General Hill himself was wounded but, I am happy to say, but slightly.

The defeat of this attempt was followed about noon by a general attack with the enemy's whole force upon the whole of that part of the position occupied by the British army.

In consequence of the repeated attempts upon the height upon our left, by the valley, I had placed two brigades of British cavalry in that valley, supported in the rear by the Duque de Albuquerque's division of Spanish cavalry.

The enemy then placed light infantry in the range of mountains on the left of the valley, which were opposed by a division of Spanish infantry, under Lieutenant-General Bassecourt.

The general attack began by the march of several columns of infantry into the valley, with a view to attack the height occupied by Major-General Hill. These columns were immediately charged by the 1st German Hussars and 23rd Light Dragoons, under Brigadier-General Anson, directed by Lieutenant-General Payne, and supported by Brigadier-General Fane's brigade of heavy cavalry; and although the 23rd Dragoons suffered considerable loss, the charge had the effect of preventing the execution of that part of the enemy's plan.

At the same time he directed an attack upon Brigadier-General Alexander Campbell's position in the centre of the combined armies, and on the right of the British. This attack was most successfully repulsed by Brigadier-General Campbell, supported by the King's regiment of Spanish cavalry and two battalions of Spanish infantry, and Brigadier-General Campbell took the enemy's cannon.

The Brigadier-General mentions particularly the conduct of the 97th, the 2nd Battalion 7th, and of the 2nd Battalion of the 53rd Regiment; and I was highly satisfied with the manner in which this part of the position was defended.

An attack was also made at the same time upon Lieutenant-General Sherbrooke's division, which was in the left and centre of the first line of the British army. This attack was most gallantly repulsed by a charge with bayonets by the whole division; but the brigade of Guards, which were on the right, having advanced too far, they were exposed on their left flank to the fire of the enemy's batteries, and of their retiring columns, and the division was obliged to retire towards the original position under cover of the second line of General Cotton's brigade of cavalry, which I moved from the centre, and of the 1st Battalion 48th Regiment. I had moved this last regiment from its position on the heights as soon as I observed the advance of the Guards, and it was formed in the plain, and advanced upon the enemy, and covered the formation of Lieutenant-General Sherbrooke's division.

Shortly after the repulse of this general attack, in which, apparently, all the enemy's troops were employed, he commenced his retreat across the Alberche which was conducted in the most regular order, and was effected during the night, leaving in our hands twenty pieces of cannon, ammunition, tumbrels, and some prisoners.

Your Lordships will observe, by the enclosed return, the great loss which we have sustained of valuable officers and soldiers in this long and hard-fought action with more than double our numbers. That of the enemy has been much greater. I have been informed that entire brigades of infantry have been destroyed; and, indeed, the battalions which retreated were much reduced in numbers.

I have particularly to lament the loss of Major-General Mackenzie, who had distinguished himself on the 27th, and of Brigadier-General Langwerth, of the King's German Legion, and of Brigade-Major Beckett of the Guards.

Your lordship will observe that the attacks of the enemy were principally, if not entirely, directed against the British troops. The Spanish Commander-in-Chief, his officers and troops, manifested every disposition to render us assistance, and those of them who were engaged did their duty; but the ground which they occupied was so important, and its front at the same time so difficult, that I did not think it proper to urge them to make any movement on the left of the enemy while he was engaged with us.

I have reason to be satisfied with the conduct of all the officers and troops. I am much indebted to Lieutenant-General Sherbrooke for the assistance I received from him, and for the manner in which he led on his division to the charge with bayonets; to Lieutenant-General Payne and the cavalry, particulary Brigadier-General Anson's brigade; to Major-Generals Hill and Tilson, Brigadier-Generals Alexander Campbell, Richard Stewart, and Cameron, and to the divisions and brigades of infantry under their command respectively, particularly to the 29th Regiment, commanded by Colonel White; to the 1st Battalion 48th, commanded by Colonel Donellan, afterwards, when that officer was wounded, by Major Middlemore; to the 2nd Battalion 7th, commanded by Lieutenant-Colonel Sir W. Myers; to the 2nd Battalion 53rd, commanded by Lieutenant-Colonel Bingham; to the 97th, commanded by Colonel Lyon; to the 1st Battalion of detachments, commanded by Lieutenant-Colonel Bunbury; to the 2nd Battalion 31st, commanded by Major Watson; the 45th, commanded by Lieutenant-Colonel Guard; and to the 5th Battalion 60th, commanded by Major Davy.

The advance of the brigade of Guards was most gallantly conducted by Brigadier-General H. Campbell; and, when necessary, that brigade retired and formed again in the best order.

The artillery, under Brigadier-General Howorth, was also throughout these days of the greatest service; and I had every reason to be satisfied with the assistance I received from the Chief Engineer, Lieutenant-Colonel Fletcher; the Adjutant General, Brigadier-General the Hon C. Stewart; the Quartermaster-General, Colonel Murray; and officers of those departments respectively; and from Lieutenant-Colonel Bathurst and the officers of my personal staff.

I also received much assistance from Colonel O'Lalor, of the Spanish service, and from Brigadier-General Whittingham, who was wounded in bringing up the two Spanish battalions to the assistance of Brigadier-General Alexander Campbell.

Memorandum upon the Battle of Talavera

The position was well calculated for the troops which were to occupy it. The ground in front of the British army was open, that in front of the Spanish army covered with olive-trees, intersected by roads, ditches, etc. The Spanish infantry was posted behind the bank of the road leading from Talavera to the left of the position.

The German Legion were on the left of the position in the first line. I had intended this part for the Guards; but I was unfortunately out, employed in bringing in General Mackenzie's advanced-guard, when the troops took up their ground. The 5th and 7th Battalions of the legion did not stand their ground on the evening, and in the beginning of the night of the 27th, which was the cause of the momentary loss of the height in the second line.

General Sherbrooke moved his division, which was the left of the first line, to support General Hill's attack, in order to regain the height; and it was difficult to resume in the night the exact position which had been first marked out; and in fact, on account of these circumstances, we had not that precise position till after the enemy's attack upon the height at daylight in the morning had been repulsed.

The advance of the Guards to the extent to which it was carried was nearly fatal to us, and the battle was certainly saved by the advance, position, and steady conduct of the 48th Regiment, upon which General Sherbrooke's division formed again.

The ground in front of the Spanish troops would not have been unfavourable to an attack upon the enemy's flank, while they were engaged with us, as there were broad roads leading from Talavera and different points of their position, in a direct line to the front, as well as diagonally to the left. But the Spanish troops are not in a state of discipline to attempt a manoeuvre in olive groves, etc., and if they had got into confusion all would have been lost.

Arthur Wellesley

Sources and Further Reading

Eyewitness sources quoted

Anon., Officer of No. 5 Company the 29th, in Clarke, Francis (1812)

Anon., Officer of 1/45th, in *Star* newspaper (1 November 1808)

Anon., Officer of 1/48th, in *The Naval & Military Sketchbook* (1844)

Anon., Subaltern of the 36th, *Diary*, etc. (1808)

Anon., 'Soldier of the 71st' (1819)

Anon., Sergeant of 1/2nd (Coldstream) Guards

Anon., Trooper of 15th Hussars, *Jottings from my Sabretache* (1847)

Regimental History of the 24th (1892)

Regimental Digest of Service of the 48th

Regimental History of the 48th (1934)

Aitchison, Ensign John, 1/3rd Guards, *Letters*

Anstruther, Brig Robert, *Journal*, etc.

Anton, Sgt James, 42nd, *Retrospect* (1842)

Bingham, Lt Col Sir George, *Letters*

Boothby, Capt Charles, RE, *A Prisoner of the French* (1898)

Bunbury, Thomas, *Reminiscences of a Veteran* (1861)

Carss, Lt John, 2/53rd, *Letters*

Chambray, Gen G. de, *De l'Infanterie* (1824)

Close, Lt Edward, 1/48th, *Journal*

Cocks, Maj Edward, 16th Light Dragoons, *Letter* of 11 Sept 1809

Coles, Pte W., 2/48th, *Letter* of 1 Dec 1809

Cox, Lt John, 2/95th, *Journal*

Cooper, Sgt J. S., *Rough Notes*, etc. (1869)

Decken, Lt Col von der, 1st Hussars KGL, in Beamish

D'Urban, Maj Gen Sir B., *The Peninsula Journal* (1930)

Elley, Col Sir John, *Letter* to his sister

FitzClarence, Lt George, 10th Hussars, *The Campaign of 1808*

Foy, Gen Maximilien, *Histoire de la Guerre de la Peninsule* (1827)

Gordon, Capt Alexander, *A Cavalry Officer*, etc. (1847)

Gough, Lord, *Letter* to his father (1809)

Gurwood, Lt Col W., *The Despatches of FM the Duke*, etc. (1837)

Hale, Sgt James, *Journal*, etc. (1826)

Harris, Rifleman B., *Recollections etc* (1848)

Hawker, Capt Peter, *Journal*, etc. (1810)

Hay, Lt Andrew Leith, 1/29th, *A Narrative of the Peninsular War*

Hewitt, Pte Thomas, 1/48th, *Letter* of 29 July 1809

Hill, Gen Sir Rowland, *Memorandum* (1827)

Jourdan, Marshal, *Memoires*

Landmann, Col G., *Recollections*, etc.

Landsheit, Sgt Norbert, *The Hussar* (1844)

Lawrence, Sgt W., *Autobiography* (1901)

Leach, Jonathan, *Rough Sketches*, etc. (1831)

Leslie, Charles, *Military Journal*, etc. (1887)

Linsingen, Col von, KGL, in Beamish

Londonderry, Lord (Charles Stewart), *Narrative of the Peninsular War*, Vol. 1 (1829)

Morley, Sgt Stephen, *Memoirs of a Sergeant of the 5th* (1842)

Napier, Maj Charles, *Life of,* etc. by W. Napier (1857)

Neale, Surgeon Adam, *Letters from Portugal,* etc. (1809)

Patterson, Capt John, *The Adventures of,* etc. (1837)

Ponsonby, Maj Frederick, 23rd Dragoons, *Letter* to W. Napier (1829)

Ross-Lewin, Maj H., *With the 32nd in the Peninsula* (1904)

Schaumann, August, *On the Road with Wellington* (1827)

Stothert, Lt William, 3rd Guards, *Journal of the Campaign 1809* (1812)

Stutzer, Capt, KGL, *Journal*

Thiebault, Baron, *Memoires*, etc. (1896)

Torrens, Lt Col Henry, *Evidence to the Cintra Inquiry* (1809)

Victor, Marshal, *Despatches*

Walker, Lt Col G., *Memorandum* (1812)

Warre, Capt W., *Letters from the Peninsula* (1909)

Way, Maj Gregory, *Letter* to his father in 29th's archives

Wellesley, Sir Arthur, *Letters*, etc. (various)

Wilson, Capt James, 1/48th, *Reminiscences* (1831)

Further Reading

With a few exceptions, the five dozen eyewitness accounts listed in Appendix VII are available in the Reading Room of the National Army Museum in Chelsea, London. Anything published after mid-1840, however, should be read in the knowledge that the author would have had at his elbow William Napier's magnificent six-volume *History of the War in the Peninsula*, for the next sixty years the pre-eminent general history, which naturally inspired many veterans' memoirs. It also provided a ready-made solution for veterans with memory loss concerning any particular event, and Napier's words were accordingly well borrowed.

However, with no disrespect to Napier, Sir Charles Oman's seven-volume *History of the Peninsular War*, first published between 1902 and 1930, must remain the academic bible of ultimate reference. Volume I covers Rolica, Vimiero and Corunna, Volume II the Oporto and Talavera campaigns. Oman's immense source research and battlefield investigations produced a massive definitive work which surely – warts and all – will never now be superseded by a single author. His nearest rival is his contemporary Sir John Fortescue, whose thirteen-volume *History of the British Army* devotes seven volumes to the Peninsula – Volume VI for Rolica, Vimiero and Corunna, Volume VII for Oporto and Talavera. We have used his excellent maps as the basis for those in this book.

So Napier, Oman and Fortescue are the undisputed general historians, to whom an under-rated Charles Stewart, Lord Londonderry, perhaps should be added. His two-volume work *A Narrative of the Peninsular War from 1808 to 1813* came out in 1829, the same year as Napier's Talavera volume. As Wellesley's Adjutant-General, Stewart was well placed to write with that same authority he seems frequently to have exercised at the head of other people's passing cavalry. He gives us the invaluable bonus, common to all good adjutants, of detailed lists of parade states, casualty returns, and so on. Five of the earlier Appendices in this book come straight from his *Narrative*.

An excellent book on Rolica and Vimiero is Michael Glover's *Britannia Sickens* (Leo Cooper, 1970); and for Sir John Moore's campaign I recommend Christopher Hibbert's *Corunna* (Batsford, 1961), notwithstanding the blatant if occasional paraphrasing of Napier. Oporto and Talavera have no specific works devoted to them, but much relevant detail can entertainingly be consumed in August Schaumann's *On the Road with Wellington*, not published until 1924. This diary stands ahead of all others; Schaumann recounts a commissary's trials and tribulations with rewarding factual description, but above all with that same huge enjoyment in the actual storytelling seen in some of the Rifles' memoirs. He is superb on the woes of Corunna, and on the chase after Soult from Oporto; while his word-picture of Spanish cavalry clattering into Talavera town, 'with such speed and rage... sparks and snorting from man and beast' for the benefit of the watching ladies, is as enchanting as his later descriptions of the casualty-strewn field are deeply affecting.

Captain Peter Hawker's *Journal of a Regimental Officer* (1810) also covers the aftermath, particularly his painful eighteen-day journey back to Lisbon with a shattered hip bone and a ball in his back; but it is otherwise intensely disappointing. How could any man stand at the head of his squadron for all those hours at Talavera, and play a part in Sherbrooke's desperate sturggle, and write so little afterwards?

George Landmann's *Recollections*, if taken with the pinch of salt necessary for a publication as late as 1854, give a useful roaming sapper's view of Rolica and Vimiero. He has a habit of placing himself in the centre of the action perhaps suspiciously often, but much can be forgiven in return for some of his descriptions: how the 50th Foot set about two battalions of the 86e Ligne on Fane's hill in front of Vimiero, and how the wounded were murdered and robbed in the woods after Rolica.

For a wider interest in Wellington's army in the Peninsula, it is hardly necessary to mention such masterpieces as Oman's *Wellington's Army*, S.G.P. Ward's *Wellington's Headquarters*, or Anthony Brett-James' *Life in Wellington's Army*, or almost anything in the past twenty years or so carrying the bylines Fletcher, Griffiths, Hayhornthwaite or Muir – all respected peninsula scholars of deep knowledge and experience. Nor should we forget to nod vigorous appreciation towards Bernard Cornwell, whose televised novels about Richard Sharpe and his riflemen have added an entertaining but properly researched visual dimension to the story of the Peninsula campaigns. May these programmes be repeated at regular intervals, so that new generations of Peninsula-lovers can be hooked...

Index